QUEEN ELIZABETH II AND THE AFRICANS

QUEEN ELIZABETH II AND THE AFRICANS

Narrating Decolonization, Postwar Commonwealth, and Africa's Development, 1947 – 2022

RAPHAEL CHIJIOKE NJOKU

LEUVEN UNIVERSITY PRESS

This book will be made open access within three years of publication thanks to Path to Open, a program developed in partnership between JSTOR, the American Council of Learned Societies (ACLS), University of Michigan Press, and The University of North Carolina Press to bring about equitable access and impact for the entire scholarly community, including authors, researchers, libraries, and university presses around the world. Learn more at https://about.jstor.org/path-to-open/

© 2024 Leuven University Press / Presses Universitaires de Louvain/ Universitaire Pers Leuven
Minderbroedersstraat 4, B-3000 Leuven / Louvain (Belgium)

All rights reserved. Except in those cases expressly determined by law, no part of this publication may be multiplied, saved in an automated data file or made public in any way whatsoever without the express prior written consent of the publishers.

ISBN 978 94 6270 434 3
eISBN 978 94 6166 580 5 (ePDF)
eISBN 978 94 6166 581 2 (ePUB)
https://doi.org/10.11116/9789461665805
D/2024/1869/29
NUR: 686, 697
Cover design: Daniel Benneworth-Gray
Front cover illustration: Queen Elizabeth II Applauds Chiefs Tamale in Ghana 16 November 1961. Smith Archive / Alamy Stock Photo. Image ID:2GC47AD. https://www.alamy.com/queen-elizabeth-ii-applauds-chiefs-tamale-in-ghana-16-november-1961-image437728661.html
Typesetting: Crius Group

To
Holy Mother Mary

CONTENTS

Preface	9
Abbreviations	13
Introduction	15
Chapter 1—The House of Windsor: African Subjects and the Princess-Queen	33
Chapter 2—Deconstructing the 1947 Cape Town Speech: Decolonization Rhetoric and the Commonwealth	51
Chapter 3—The Cold War: African "Radicals" and Her Royal Stateliness, 1953–1961	73
Chapter 4—Her Majesty's Africa Tour-De-Force: Feasting with the Obedient, the Noble, and the Nonconformist, 1961–1989	97
Chapter 5—Majestic Milestones: The Commonwealth and Africa's Development	121
Chapter 6—King Charles III and Africa's Commonwealth Future	149
Conclusion	163
Notes	177
Bibliography	235
Index	261

PREFACE

This book has been many years coming. While I was growing up in the 1970s and 1980s in a Nigerian village, my late aunt, Catherine Anosike, often spoke with candor about the Queen of England, the Princess of Wales, and the Duke of Edinburgh. She had immortalized the British royal family by her daughter's name, "Anne," and would not hesitate to tell those who tangled with her that she "will not yield an inch to anyone except Queen Elizabeth II." Aunt Catherine had no formal education, so I was always astonished listening to her endless, prideful royal lectures. Later, when I summoned the courage to inquire how she got her extraordinary expertise in British royal history, her face radiated with life: "Who does not know about the great queen? She brought dignity to all of us [women]. The White man does not tolerate nonsense! When they were here, women gained respect. They brought education, electricity, radio, television, shoes, and Christianity."

High reverence for Her Majesty, chiefly in my aunt's generation, remains among ordinary Africans. I was interested in the history of the British African empire primarily because of the constellations of culture Elizabeth's monarchy spurred on the continent, but the blackout of the Crown in my high school and college history curricula lowered my curiosity. There is more to the calculated omission or oversight. It highlights the contrasting views of the African public about Her Majesty—the nationalists, the first-generation postcolonial educated elite, the unlettered older masses, whose voices are unheard, versus the much younger and educated generation.

Though many Africans revered Queen Elizabeth II, her passing reignited difficult conversations on the repercussion of the British Empire, whose officers in Africa perpetrated orgies of cruelty in the name of the Crown. The anticolonial nationalists had nursed a sense of betrayal concerning what they perceived as Elizabeth's lack of openness and outright commitment to the decolonization struggles. The younger generation that did not directly witness the colonial world but now lives with its legacies of political crisis and economic poverty understandably lament that the Crown did not stop the colonial degradation or express regret for the oppression their forebears endured in the name of the Crown. Indeed, there is no more painful time to remember one's stolen inheritance than in a period of penury. From Cairo to Cape Town, African youth are straddled with the worst conditions of bleakness and anxiety. Some have demanded that the British government return treasures, including rare diamonds (the Crown jewels) the empire carted away from Zimbabwe, South Africa, Sierra Leone, Kenya, Ghana, and Nigeria. Alice Mugo, a Nairobi-based Kenyan lawyer, contends that when one looks at the monarchy from the glamorous and celebratory viewpoint, there is also the ugly side that cannot be ignored.

The Queen admitted in 1992 that while she had lived through some of the most significant challenges of her reign in that year, she never expected to be free from criticism from admirers and opponents alike. Criticism, she argued, "is good for people and institutions that are part of public life." But Elizabeth also pleaded that scrutiny is more effective "with a touch of gentleness, good humor, and understanding."

This book speaks to the challenges and triumphs in Her Majesty's seventy-five years of engagement with Africa. As a historian, I have taken a more unbiased and judicious view in examining Elizabeth's African records than some contemporary commentators would. If I sometimes appear more sympathetic to the Queen, it is because I am conscious of how patriarchy and colonialism reinforced each other as systems of domination, exploitation, and control. The anger and frustration nursed by the Africans today is righteous indignation against a long history of European violence and robbery. With a scholarly inquiry, it is easier to see Elizabeth's genuine intents, advocacy, and immense contributions to the continent's growth. Her African story should be fully documented; it cannot be consigned to the ugly pits of colonial history. Africa had no more passionate believer than the queen. Her overall African vision through the Commonwealth leadership positively impacted the continent more than any other European visitor.

Contemporary African problems must be addressed now in mutual partnership with the Europeans. In the Commonwealth, Elizabeth bequeathed a global framework through which this partnership could be harnessed in the twenty-first century. In the later chapters of this book, I have stressed that the light of the Commonwealth spirit Her Majesty ignited must not be smothered. I reiterate to those who arrive at the middle of a story to observe some caution or risk excavating a dismembered corpse. I empathize with the Africans' anger and frustration. Emotionally charged narratives are not tools of historical methods or academic debates. An account constructed from a studied distance (without prejudice), soothed with patience and insightful interpretations of evidence, often lends an extra dimension to judgment, giving it a leavening of moderation, compassion, and wisdom, even to the less striking views.

While all mistakes and errors of interpretation are solely mine, I owe immense gratitude to the many who have helped me complete this study. I am heavily indebted to Dr. Mirjam Truwant, the acquisitions editor at Leuven University Press, and the entire Editorial Board who supported this work. I greatly appreciate Mrs. Grace W. Kiragu, the senior librarian in the Division of Library and Information Services at the University of Nairobi, and her colleague, Hamington A. Aluvisia, for their assistance with rare books and newspaper materials. Similar gratitude goes to Hassoum Ceesay, the archivist in Banjul, and his counterpart, Millicent Aryee, the head of the archives in Teshie, Ghana, and the National Archives, London. Rachael Johnston, Exko Ramey, Mylee Primm, and her dad, David Primm, were generous in lending logistics and creative support. I thank Professors Chima J. Korieh, Tim Stapleton, Philp Zachernuk, Joseph Bangura, Apollos Nwauwa, Ogechi Anyanwu, Bonny Ibhawoh, Arunima Datta, Kristine Hunt, Stephen Shapiro, Dimeji Togunde, my colleagues in the Department of History at Idaho State University, Pastor (Dr.) Eric Branham, and friends from the Igbo Studies Association for graciously reading earlier drafts of this manuscript and providing constructive lines of revisions. I am also indebted to Drs. Rebecca Hayes and Craig Miller, who constantly reminded me to complete this work.

I must thank the ISU Research Office, the College of Arts and Letters, the Department of History, and the Department of Global Studies and Languages for funding my research.

Raphael Chijioke Njoku
Pocatello, Idaho, April 2024

ABBREVIATIONS

AAAR	African Academy of Arts and Research
ACP	Africa, the Caribbean, and the Pacific
ANC	African National Congress
ASA	African Students Association
ATS	Auxiliary Territorial Service
AU	African Union
BBC	British Broadcasting Service
BUS	Bantu United Society
CAAP	Commonwealth African Assistance Program
CBF	Commonwealth Business Forum
CEIC	Commonwealth Enterprise and Investment Council
CFTC	Commonwealth Fund for Technical Cooperation
CHOGM	Commonwealth Heads of Government Meeting
CIA	Central Intelligence Agency
CO	Colonial Office
CPA	Commonwealth Parliamentary Association
CRO	Commonwealth Relations Office
CSC	Commonwealth Scholarship Commission
CSO	Commonwealth Secretary's Office
DFID	Department of International Development
EC	European Commission
EU	European Union
FDI	Foreign Direct Investment
FOCAC	Forum on China-Africa Cooperation
GDP	Gross Domestic Product
ICT	Information Communication Technology
IMF	International Monetary Fund
INC	Indian National Congress
KBE	Knight of the British Empire

KCMG	Knight Commander of the Most Distinguished of St. Michael and St. George
KLFA	Kenyan Land and Freedom Army (aka Mau Mau)
KN	Kebra Nagast
KY	Kabaka Yekka
LDRRP	Lusaka Declaration on Racism and Racial Prejudice
MBE	Member of the British Empire
MOU	Memorandum of Understanding
MP	Member of Parliament
MTWA	Ministry of Tourism, Wildlife, and Antiquities
NAC	Nyasaland African Affairs Congress
NGO	Non-Governmental Organization
NP	Nationalists Party
NPC	Northern People's Congress
OAU	Organization of African Unity
OBE	Order of the British Empire
OBOR	One-Belt-One-Road
OIF	*Organization Internationale de la Francophonie*
PSFTSL	Professional Standards Framework for Teachers and School Leaders
QCM	Queen's Coronation Medal
QEPNCAA	Quality Education Provision to Nomadic Communities for Africa and Asia
RAAC	Rhodesia Air Askari Corps
RAR	Rhodesia African Rifles
RWAFF	Royal West African Frontier Force
SLCF	School Leaders Capability Framework
UDI	Unliteral Declaration of Independence
UPC	Uganda People's Congress
USSR	Union of Soviet Socialist Republics
UTB	Uganda Tourism Board
WAAF	Women's Auxiliary Air Force
WASU	West African Students Union
WRNS	Women's Royal Navy Service
WTO	World Trade Organization
ZANU	Zimbabwean African National Union

INTRODUCTION

This book examines Her Majesty Queen Elizabeth II's role in the trajectories of African decolonization and the postcolonial state's quest for genuine political and economic growth since 1947. The study inserts Elizabeth at the center of the independence agitations in Anglophone Africa, teasing out the monarch's dilemma of satisfying conservative ideals while slowly pushing for social reforms, racial equality, and support for development in Africa. It goes beyond the empire's end in the second half of the twentieth century, locating Elizabeth in a full context with a primary interest in her records relating to Africa's transition to independence from the postwar period to the first two decades of the twenty-first century.

The account harnesses the African interests in the Queen's postwar Commonwealth leadership as fate entrusted her with the dissolution of the British Empire.[1] With British policymakers asserting that "self-government meant self-government within the Commonwealth," the Queen occupied a central position in her subjects' quest to untie colonial bonds.[2] The study argues that to gratify the British lawmakers in her complex and marginal place under the British Parliamentary system with conservative versus reformist agitators, Elizabeth came short of the expectations of African nationalists with her silence and inactions during the African decolonization crises. But in the end, she built an inclusive and unified organization where the Africans could play a vital role and appropriate political and economic autarky.

The postwar colonial reforms were driven by a revival of the rights-based ideology articulated in John Rawls's *A Theory of Justice*.[3] Like Rawls, egalitarians and libertarians such as Robert Nozick and Friedrich Hayek argue that government should uphold fundamental civil liberties, including political and economic rights. Regardless of their minor philosophical variances in what rights individuals and groups have, rights-oriented advocates concur that the principles of justice should be universal and sacrosanct.[4] This pivotal ideology, central to the liberalism of Immanuel Kant, Rawls, and others, upholds the ultimate claim that the right takes precedence over the good.[5]

Her Majesty's sensitization to the liberal reforms in the African colonies, first touted in a 1947 birthday speech in South Africa, was constrained by the exertions of pragmatic conservatism—the belief that preserving traditions, prescriptive rights, and customs is the path to thoughtful changes. This utilitarian doctrine in ethics aligns with the legal philosophy of H. L. A Hart and J. S. Mills. While Hart separates fairness (implying justice) from morality (notions of right and wrong), Mills sees justice as an obstacle to utility, contending that actions should be taken based on consequences.[6] The conformist view of the monarchists with imperialist nostalgia often mired the imperatives of African independence and welfare. The disparate conservative and liberal positions on Africa's needs within the British Establishment in the Cold War world order explain the Crown's inability to hasten the African program, especially before the 1980s.

This book is essential because Queen Elizabeth II's reign and the African continent were connected in profound ways that scholars still need to account for fully. Ignoring this history engendered a pattern of bitterness among Africans in which the Queen is portrayed as unresponsive to the people's plight—specifically in the 1950s through the 1970s when decolonization took on violent and unpredictable dimensions.[7] Five years before her monarchy began, Princess Elizabeth and a renascent Africa crossed paths during the royals' 1947 visit to South Africa. The journey coinciding with her twenty-first birthday was marked in Cape Town by Elizabeth's mission announcement and future leadership principles and goals. In a subsequent coincidence with implicit idioms and motifs, Elizabeth experienced her rites of passage from princess to monarch in Kenya, where she received the news of her ascension in 1952. Given the role she would play in decolonization, these events tied together the continent and Her Majesty in ways that must be emphasized. Elizabeth's earliest two trips to Africa gave her first-hand education on the African colonial situation. The knowledge shaped her original outlook on decolonization and the Commonwealth's part in the African subjects' struggle for self-determination.

But Her Majesty's African agenda unfolded slowly and sometimes stalled because she was an invested tool in the hands of the British Establishment, who called the decolonization play. The Crown was never the all-powerful sovereign the Colonial Office and British colonial servants on the ground had made the Africans believe. Reexamining decolonization through the Elizabeth prism allows for a deeper insight into the "official mind" in the game of subterfuge converging on the invention of Elizabethan monarchy and the retooling of the Commonwealth under the Crown as Whitehall moved to regulate and manage the end of the Empire on terms favorable to the UK.

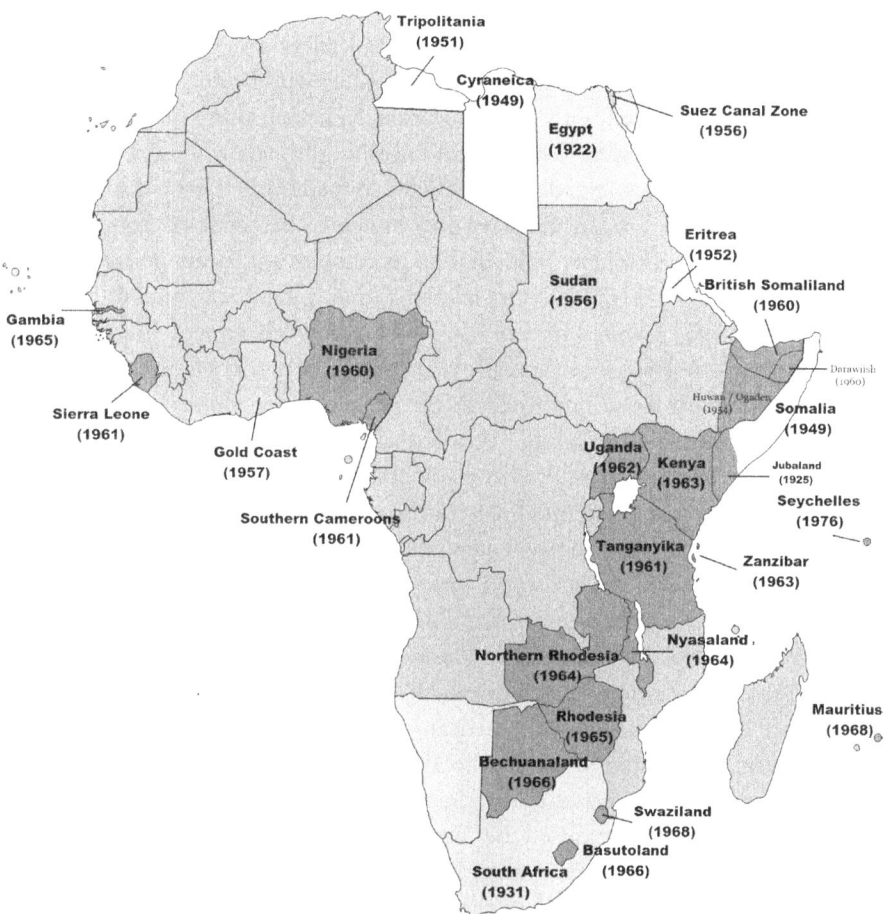

Figure 0.1: Map of British Decolonization in Africa (Brown, Judith (1998) *The Oxford History of the British Empire: Volume IV: The Twentieth Century*, Oxford University Press, p. 348)

Contrary to Getachew's *Worldmaking after Empire* and Gilly's inciting "The Case for Colonialism"—studies that attacked the principle of self-determination and ridiculed the African nationalists and postcolonial elites—the manner of the UK's retreat from Africa was a sober reconsideration of colonial wrongs.[8] In the exit scheme, the British political elite groomed and used Elizabeth as the antidote for African nationalist agitation. The Queen's role in the end-of-empire process was notable by her readiness to forgo some monarchical prerogatives, suppress her convictions, and strictly follow the government playbook, including risky royal trips to decolonization hotspots in Kenya, Uganda, Nigeria, and

Ghana.[9] Her interventions barred some African leaders from turning a different direction when communism was winning new allies worldwide.[10]

Elizabeth engaged with decolonization, believing that serving the UK would lead to harnessing her African mission through a Commonwealth rebranded as voluntary developmental cooperation. First floated on December 11, 1931, as an inclusive and humane alternative to empire, the Commonwealth was sold by Whitehall to its colonies as a forum where shared values and goals would guide future relations among member nations under the Crown. In a 1967 Cabinet memo, Mr. Herbert Bowden, secretary of state for Commonwealth affairs, reiterated the point that "The modern Commonwealth was a triumphant technique to cover the process of decolonization, turning 'Empire' into 'Commonwealth.'" Bowden added that the transmutation enabled the UK to extricate itself "from colonial responsibilities with honor and psychologically cushioned the shock for the people of Britain in adjusting to a new era (though it may also have encouraged some illusions)."[11] In other words, the Commonwealth project was a *cover*, a face-saving escape strategy from imperialism's albatross that mortified the UK after the war.

Bowden's passing reference to *illusion* in the empire devolution *scheme* is central to understanding Queen Elizabeth's entire African record and the lows and highs of emotion held by the Africans toward her reign. The grand misrepresentation project started during the 1947 royal African tour when Princess Elizabeth unveiled what her monarchy would portend for her father's restive colonial subjects. She promised the "imperial family" a deviation from the violent imperialism's past and to work for a prosperous and peaceful future for all races.[12] The proclamation launched the heir to the throne at the center of the UK's search for postwar global influence and respect. As this book details, Elizabeth was not just the human face Whitehall implanted on the ugly ruins of imperialism but also the scapegoat for the crisis that engulfed a dying colonialism. She was the political Establishment's baby with hypnotic power, the periapt that entrapped the African nationalists in utter delusion while the withering empire transitioned from disorder to more orderly and open relations. Trapped at the crossroads between the prewar and postwar world order, Elizabeth embodied the creativity of a nation seeking a dignified end-of-empire process through the Commonwealth scheme.

By revisiting Elizabeth's tours of Africa in the 1950s and 1960s, one sees how the diplomatic forays amplified her popularity among the Africans and tempered growing nationalist resentment toward the UK. Nothing epitomized that success better than the royal visit to the disputed Gibraltar peninsula in 1954. With Spain shifting blame for Gibraltar's woes to the UK and offering immediate independence as a sop for peace, the inhabitants asserted their loyalty to the British Crown. "When it comes to allegiance to Britain, we Gibraltarians are terribly Victorian… . You wouldn't get away with a derogatory remark about the Queen here."[13]

Similar declarations of fidelity to the new Queen in the 1950s and 1960s were common among the African masses. Central to the discourse is the contrasting or misconceived views of the Queen held by the educated African elite. While the political elite expected Elizabeth to intercede on their side in every crisis and otherwise blamed her for African misfortunes, the ordinary people were enthralled by the cultural symbols the Queen represented and her feelings for the less privileged, including women. In this duality, Her Majesty worked to steer the UK from the alchemy of colonial prejudice and might-is-right conduct in Africa to the quietude of a postwar Commonwealth family. Her trials and triumphs in this tricky project are some of the allegories of decolonization and postcolonial changes this book tells in detail.

Studies on decolonization, the Commonwealth, and Queen Elizabeth II are never in short supply, but they have yet to systematically center the monarch as a looking glass to the more nuanced process that brought about the postcolonial African state. Decolonization studies routinely focus on the careers of colonial officers, administrators, African nationalists, and peasants. A few examples of works on privileged colonial officials are Colin Baker's biography of Sir Glyn Jones, Malawi's governor (later governor-general), and Clyde Sanger's study of Malcolm MacDonald (aka "troubleshooter"), Kenya's last governor-general. While Baker gave an expedient account of Malawi's sudden shift from loyalty under the Crown to republican status under the Commonwealth, Sanger completely ignored Elizabeth and the republican imperative. Likewise, although Sanger covered Kenya, Rhodesia, South Africa, and Nigeria from a comparative perspective, the study ignored Her Majesty's role.[14] The silence reflects a common trend in similar studies such as John Johnson's edited volume *Colony to Nation* and Harry Mitchell's *Remote Corners: A Sierra Leone Memoir*.[15] While the contributors to Johnson's anthology focused on British administrators in Kenya from 1940 to 1963, Mitchell's memoir was a self-absorbing story of a colonial official who accepted his West African posting as a second career choice compared to, as Ashley Jackson put it, "the horrors of a career selling ladies' underwear in the employ of Marks and Spencer" in London.[16]

Other studies, including Sarah Stockwell's *The British End of the British Empire*, emphasize Western perspectives on the sociopolitical tides of decolonization. Stockwell's outside-in approach explored the impact of empire dissolution on the metropole. The cross-sectoral examination of institutional building in the period, including the colonial development grants, remains an influential contribution extending her previous edited work, *The British Empire: Themes and Perspectives*.[17] However, Denise Judd's *Empire: The British Imperial Experience from 1765 to the Present*, which highlighted the significant events that fashioned the British Empire, and Ronald Hyam's *Britain's Declining Empire*, which placed high politics at the center stage of the process of the Empire's desolation, there are the littlest mentions of the African agency in the movement for self-determination under Elizabeth's reign.[18]

The profusion of postwar Commonwealth studies in the 1960s through the 1990s has often treated the association's history as autonomous from Africa's quest for freedom under the Crown. For example, in a detailed and engaging study of the British monarch's place in the Commonwealth, Vernon Bogdanor rarely considered the crucial topic of the sovereign's part in African decolonization. Even more audacious is Bogdanor's questioning of the continued relevance of the monarchy in a democracy. He proposed that a radical reform of the British institution was in order because it had outlived its usefulness.[19] Bogdanor ignored the dualism of conservatism and change that trapped the UK and the Crown under Elizabeth II. The present study reveals that Elizabeth had wanted to support development and democracy in Africa, but the bounds of her constitutional prerogatives would not allow her to override the decisions of elected politicians under whom her office and activities revolved. This assertion requires some clarification in light of Kwasi Kwarteng's *Ghosts of Empire*, which denounced associating "notions of democracy" with the imperial administrators.[20] The roots of Elizabeth's advocacy for the colonized go back to 1947 but acquired life under the aegis of the Commonwealth, especially in the 1980s. The idea, implied in Bogdanor's *The Monarchy and the Constitution*, that the Queen was a hindrance to innovation ignored the reality that she was a tool in the hands of Whitehall and therefore could not overstep her confines of authority or pursue a different part.

A year after Bogdanor's work, Ben Pimlott's *The Queen: A Biography of Elizabeth II* gave good coverage of African affairs, although focused only on Southern Rhodesia and South Africa.[21] The present study locates Elizabeth in the middle of the decolonization drama, underlining the challenges of conservative approaches to colonial freedom and Africa's developmental needs. While Philip Ziegler of the *Daily Telegraph* had praised Pimlott's book, predicting that it would remain unsurpassable "for many years," it is critical to recall that Buckingham Palace commissioned the study, which makes it a partisan project.

Anecdotal assertions have moored the corpus of biographical works on Queen Elizabeth, including Robert Lacey's *The Crown*, which focused on Winston Churchill's influence in making a young monarch from 1947 to 1955 but was mute on the orchestrated and phony claims of monarchical power in the entire colonial/decolonization scheme.[22] Like Pimlott and Lacey, Andrew Marr's *The Real Elizabeth* is "an intimate" account of the Queen's life history. Although it is a compelling addition to the monarchy's biographical literature, the book remains an extension of the allegory of illusions and mythmaking, a retrospective description of the sovereign's challenges and successes from a third party.[23]

In 1998, American historian Walter Arnstein lamented that the "New Elizabethan Monarchy" as a field of study remains consigned to tabloids such as *People*, *National Inquirer*, and *Us Weekly*. Arnstein notes that experts' tendency to ignore the Crown has left it susceptible to frequent misrepresentations.[24] In 2009, royal historian David Cannadine echoed a similar sentiment, urging for studies that would include chronological, biographical, thematic, analytical, and anecdotal cues.[25] Cannadine's appeal is yet to resonate with many. Ronald Hyam's *Understanding the British Empire* treated a broad range of topics, including King George VI, Winston Churchill, sexuality, empire and sexual opportunities, concubinage, and colonial service. However, like Piers Brendon's *The Decline and Fall of the British Empire*, published the same year, Hyam excluded Elizabeth from the historical equation.[26]

Eventually, Philip Murphy, a historian of the Commonwealth, came up with *Monarchy and the End of Empire*.[27] Although devoted to the political processes that ended the UK's African colonies in the 1960s through the 1970s, Murphy's study is pivotal for neatly tying, with broad strokes, the House of Windsor, Whitehall, and the postwar Commonwealth in a storied fashion. It did not touch on the complex partnership between the Crown and the British Establishment—specifically the misleading use of the "Her Majesty" legend to represent or justify elected politicians' political decisions. The current study goes beyond the empire's end from the mid-twentieth century. It follows the African concerns to place Elizabeth's entire African engagements in a full context and beyond the 1960s, following the trail of disappointments and triumphs from decolonization to the post-Brexit, post-COVID-19 world order.

It is crucial to consider why African historians have shied away from documenting Elizabeth's place in the emergence of the postcolonial state. Instead, African scholars dwell on Elizabeth's ancestors, like King George VI, and other sundries associated with colonial rule. For example, African historian Chima J. Korieh devoted his recent work, *Nigeria and World War II*, exclusively to the

African subjects' robust support of King George VI during the war. Like Hyam and Brendon, Korieh's book is a must-read, though it did not mention Queen Elizabeth once.[28]

Elizabeth, who served as a driver and mechanic with Second Subaltern's rank during the Second World War, symbolized unity and Englishness for the UK and its ex-colonies in what Edward Owens recognized as "the popular memory of the home front."[29] This study shows why Elizabeth was one of the most secret and indeed misunderstood creations of the British Establishment. Her family background and circumstances caught her between the old and more conservative Victorian ideals and the new and more liberal aspirations of the postwar order conceived on soft power and shared values. She shouldered the complicated tasks the British leaders assigned her—the burdens of remaking the UK's global image, which often conflicted with the dual mission of preserving respect for the monarchical institution at home and abroad. The unique story of Elizabeth is not her longevity or the luxury her position provided. Instead, it was her unflinching obedience to the British State and the confidence that her Commonwealth project would help redeem the ills of colonial degradations.

Elizabeth followed the British mission to the letter, despite Whitehall's 1952 passing of the fourth bill authorizing an alteration of royal titles. The lawmakers coordinated a dynamic described by Philip Murphy as "pragmatic fatalism."[30] The policy gave the new African states the liberty to discard loyalty under the Crown to republican status under the Commonwealth.[31] Mr. Gordon Walker (MP) explained it better by stating that the Afrikaners in South Africa did not share the same feelings toward the Queen as British stock in the country. "One danger of trying to impose the doctrine of indivisibility of the Crown was that it was thought to be an attempt to impose upon other Commonwealth peoples a feeling which was appropriate only to those of British stock."[32] The consequence of the 1952 bill, as this book explains, was a rift between the African nationalists and Her Majesty. However, ordinary people preferred the young Queen in their hearts.

The Dove and the Hawks

At the war's end, the republican alternative endorsed by the United States became the UK's master plan to promote an amicable foreign policy that would reassure its remaining colonies of a future of multiculturalism and freedom implied by the Allied Powers.[33] The Colonial Development Bill of June 25, 1947, which set aside £100 million for the colonies, typified the UK Parliament's urgent steps to ward off communist intrusion in Africa by sponsoring economic advancement and voluntary and equal engagement under the Commonwealth.[34] Viscount Hall (MP) explained the bill as an immediate "need for improved machinery for developing Colonial resources." He reminded everyone that the previous Colonial Development Welfare Act did not do enough for the continent's economic welfare. Hall added that there was a need for an apparatus enabling the UK to "undertake individual productive projects likely to increase the wealth of the Colonies themselves and to stimulate the supply of products of which this country and the world at a large stand in need."[35]

The postwar economic development policy marked a significant shift from the colonial approach based on resource extraction and mercantilism. Historical sources show that Parliament passed the first Colonial Development Fund program in 1929.[36] Subsequent bills, from 1930 through 1940, followed.[37] However, Lord Geoffrey Lloyd, the secretary of state for the colonies, noted in 1940 that the underlying principle for colonial assistance "has all along been that each Colony should get along as best it could on its own resources." Accordingly, the policy clarified that the UK's grants-in-aid were given only when it was proven that "the Colony could not pay its way without it."[38]

As the ghost of the prewar welfare policy fleetingly haunted the postwar development plans, the UK dragged its feet with decolonization on the rationale that it was "entirely delusory" to grant self-government without "economic prosperity." Filled with apprehension, the colonies grew suspicious of the imperial intents.[39] Mr. Creech Jones, the secretary of state for the colonies, stated the obvious in his address to the House of Commons on July 29, 1947: "In the aftermath of the war, all colonial territories have been anxious that their affairs should receive the close attention of the British Government."[40] As the African adage goes, if a snail cannot run, it must crawl with modesty. In light of the increasing demands from its colonies, Elizabeth stepped in as a moderating figure in a new world order marked by a rebellious and nationalist ethos.

Flanked by characters like Sir Winston Churchill as mentors in the early years, Elizabeth stood as a rudder for policies scripted by the senior guards—the pivots of colonization. For example, on the eve of the royals' departure for the postwar South Africa tour, Churchill designated General Louis Botha and General Jan Christian Smuts—individuals known for opposing racial equality—as "the greatest friends of progress and civilization throughout the world."[41] Considering the influences of these two on racial divisions in the region, Churchill's comment was significantly insidious. Indeed, Prime Minister

Jan Smuts rejected King George VI's intention to decorate African veterans of the Second World War during the 1947 visit. Smuts's bigoted choice contrasted with Elizabeth's vision of respect and shared values in the postwar order.

During the South African royal tour, the Africans' plight in the region caught Princess Elizabeth's attention, prompting her promise to fight for freedom and unity and practice the virtues of consultation and cooperation. The avowals reverberated loud and clear across the world. "If we all go forward together with an unwavering faith, a high courage, and a quiet heart, we shall be able to make of this ancient Commonwealth, which we all love so dearly, an even grander thing—more free, more prosperous, more happy and a more powerful influence for good in the world—than it has been in the greatest days of our forefathers."[42] In reflecting on her career in 2015, the Queen believed she had fully accomplished the compelling dream that may have come across as wishful in 1947.[43] Many Africans think otherwise.

Queen Elizabeth II and the Africans reveals that the road to the Queen's implementation of the African policies was rough, especially in the first two decades of her ascension. Political hardliners and unapologetic imperialists occupying power positions in Africa and the UK surrounded the young and inexperienced monarch. These officials continued to advance their self-interests and colonial ideologies under the guise of British national interests. Illustrative of the fact are the records of J. E. W. Flood, a middle-level administrator at the Colonial Office; Clive Salter, a judge and an opponent of decolonization, who presided over the Special Emergency Assize Courts in colonial Kenya; Governor Andrew Cohen, who deported the Kabaka of Buganda in 1953, and David Hunt, the British high commissioner in Lagos, Nigeria.[44] While Flood's opinions on everything related to Africa shed light on how personal whims negated administrative imperatives under colonial rule, Salter's fiery judicial pronouncements were not as edifying to Her Majesty's reputation as he thought. Likewise, Cohen's quirky decision to exile the Kabaka forever altered Uganda's political history, giving birth to General Idi Amin's rise in 1971. Meanwhile, David Hunt's hatred for Colonel Emeka Ojukwu, the ex-Biafra leader, was central to the controversial British policy toward the Nigeria-Biafra civil war.[45] Understanding how the various decolonization crises turned Queen Elizabeth into a villain in the eyes of the African nationalists and postcolonial leaders is central to this study.

Caught in between persistent colonial paternalism and African nationalist rebellions, Elizabeth sometimes found herself in the middle of divisive policies such as those related to the Mau Mau uprising (1952–1960), the

Central African Federation/Nyasaland Emergency (1953–1953), the exile of Uganda's Kabaka Mutesa II (1953–1954), the Suez Canal crisis (1956–1957), the Rhodesian Unilateral Declaration of Independence (UDI) of 1965, and the Nigeria-Biafra civil war (1967–1970).[46] Yet, amid these conflicts that negatively impacted the educated African elite's perception of the Crown, Elizabeth continued to plod through the ideology of a brighter future for the ex-British colonies under the Commonwealth.

Too Little History: "The Royal Branding Mix" and Privileged Sources

The question remains as to why few scholars have shown interest in Queen Elizabeth II's role in shaping modern Africa. Cannadine notes that Elizabeth's story has "too little history, a surfeit of mythmaking and a dearth of scholarly skepticism."[47] This study speaks to some myths and clichés in the Elizabethan story. The problem of accessing sources for the historian, especially scholars outside the UK, is underlined. The secrecy tradition associated with the House of Windsor, the British Establishment's underground agenda in the institution, and the British press's duty to protect the sovereign lower the African student's incentive to research the subject.[48]

The stakeholders' investment in the monarchy, the Queen's silence on all controversial issues related to Africa, the Church of England's stake in the monarchy, and the shielding press culture cohere in what John Balmer identified as "the branding credentials of the Crown." The dynamic instrumentation of five elements (royal, regal, relevant, responsive, and respected) is central to a Crown Whitehall managed as a corporate entity: "The Royal Branding Mix."[49] Given the public relations image management culture, this study adopts a robust discourse analysis approach by interrogating the Crown's public image of Buckingham Palace presented to the world. The Parliamentary Debates, Foreign Office Records, Colonial Office Records, Commonwealth Relations Office Records, Dominions Office Records, the *British Documents on the End of Empire* in several volumes, and the numerous biographical studies of Elizabeth and other members of the royal kinship and their close associates contain a trove of information on Her Majesty's African affairs.[50] Additional sources of information for this study came from colonial servants' biographies, private correspondences with individuals, archived newspapers, material artifacts in arts, music, fashions, personal correspondences, and the British Pathé multimedia and newsreel resources, especially since the passing of the Queen.

In looking at these sources in Europe and Africa, caution has been exercised following the increasing concerns of scholars like Antoinette Burton, Nicholas Dirks, Barbara Harlow, and Arunima Datta. These critics remind us that colonial archives are emblematic of an opacity through which the prudent see colonialism's alterations and imbalances—characterized by silences, the virtual preventability of truth, obscurity of facts, crime scene cover-ups, planting of intellectual land mines, and misleading whispering galleries.[51]

Elizabeth—the African Queen?

Queen Elizabeth II and the Africans shows that Her Majesty's decolonization mission bonded with Africa's future in dynamic ways beyond the 1947 South Africa tour to the Kenya trip in 1952. Many news and print outlets have retold both trips, but none has carefully teased the implicit significance and idioms. Cape Town stands in the sands of history as Elizabeth's most important speech—unfailing service to empire and country, a commitment to work with everyone worldwide.[52] The dialogue on freedom and a family of mankind free from bondage delivered on African soil tied the continent to the Queen's mission. It also provides the parameters to evaluate her African records for good or bad.

During the Kenya visit in 1952, Elizabeth experienced what is depicted here as a vital rite of passage—an encounter that transformed the young princess into a conscientious sovereign.[53] On February 6, 1952, she received the news of her accession to the throne, which introduced another layer of ties with Africa—the history of starting her reign as Queen of Kenya before her inauguration in the United Kingdom on June 2, 1953.[54] The *Mombasa Times* of February 7, 1952, reported that constitutionally, Elizabeth went "through a ceremony of acceptance of the Crown while in Kenya."[55] A memo signed by Chief Secretary C. H. Thornley on February 8, 1952, confirms, "Her Majesty Queen Elizabeth II [was] proclaimed with all formality at Nairobi."[56]

In Kenya, two days before George VI's death, the royals received the £2,000 Royal Lodge wedding gift from the colony. The structure, now known as Sagana State Lodge, was commissioned by Governor (Sir) Philip Mitchell on February 4, 1952, with over one hundred community leaders as witnesses. The next day, the royals entered further into the forest to an iconic game-viewing lodge called the Treetops because it was erected into the branches of an old fig tree.[57] In the eyes of the Africans, the Royal Lodge handover event indigenized the royals as Kikuyu because the dwelling was located on Kikuyu's ancestral

Figure 0.2: Treetops Hotel Plaque – Njeri, Kenya, where the royals stayed in 1952. (Photograph by Mickerigg (2005), public domain)

lands near Mt. Kenya (Kere-Nyaga)—a holy place, a source of life, believed to be the abode of God Almighty.[58]

To the outsider, the Kikuyu mythology has no connection with Her Majesty's career. In the African agency approach, what matters is not what the outsider thinks but how the indigenes perceive their world. It is imperative for a society that strives on legends and mythologies to appreciate the psychology of action and the surrounding intersubjective relations.[59] The Africans had entertained the belief that a home for the Queen in their midst would arouse positive energy in the Crown and British politicians to shelter them from further colonial assaults.

The royal dwelling in Kenya's holy lands may offer an opportunity to grasp Jürgen Habermas's communicative action theory but, more importantly, provide an understanding of why the Mau Mau activists were deeply disappointed in Her Majesty's elusive and distanced posture during their plights. The paradigm projects how actors coordinate their choices based on "consensual norms."[60] The model adopts the Aristotelian notions of *technē* and *praxis* to illuminate the distinctive critical social theory.[61] Habermas reinforced his philosophical anthropology in *Knowledge and Human Interests*, an engaging framework for an interdisciplinary social theory.[62] It provided an essential critique of the positivist philosophy of science and historicist hermeneutics. In the poststructuralist theorem, the royals' interests in Kenya tied them to Kikuyu's natural history and sociocultural life's imperatives—including freedom from colonial subjugations.[63]

"The She-Elephant": Motifs of Elizabeth's Ascension in Africa

It was not a happenstance in 1995 when school kids in Durban, South Africa, welcomed Queen Elizabeth II to the country with chants of "Zulus, be happy! The she-elephant is among us."[64] Princess Elizabeth's transformation into Queen in Kenya came after a night watching thirty elephants at the grounds of the Sagana State Lodge. The phenomenon, described by a local as "visiting ancestors of the land," needs extra illumination.[65] In indigenous African society, elephants symbolize stability, unity, wisdom, loyalty, sensitivity, peace, intelligence, determination, reliability, and precious memory. In some measures, at least since the end of the Cold War in 1989, these attributes resonate with Elizabeth's personality, Commonwealth leadership records, and environmental conservation and biodiversity advocacy.[66]

Jim Corbett, Elizabeth's safari bodyguard, captured the substance of the 1952 event: "For the first time in the history of the world, a young girl climbed into a tree one day a princess and, after having what she described as her most thrilling experience, she climbed down from the tree next day a Queen."[67] The occasion was the end of a carefree life for the princess. As experts remind us, rites of passage help the participant "obtain wisdom about the self, and connect the spiritual and material realms of being."[68] In Kenya, Elizabeth gained a better knowledge of self and embraced the transcendent and material parts. Dona Richards adds that a rite of passage in Africa "involves the attempt to strengthen our *force vitale* or life force."[69] The humble condition of the Sagana Lodge is a metaphor for the old order's passing and the new order's dawn—a new beginning the Africans had hoped for, of freedom from oppression and equality in the comity of nations.[70]

In mourning with the bereaved, the Africans reinforced the transcendent bonds between the continent and the new monarch—the expectation that Elizabeth's reign would bring freedom and justice to the colonial subjects. In

Kenya, Vice-Admiral C. E. Lambs, the Royal Yacht flag officer, informed a *Mombasa Times* reporter that the royal visit's entire plan has "to be recast" because of King George's death. The *Gothic*, the H.M.S. *Kenya*, and other vessels flew their flags at half-mast, and a children's party organized for the event was canceled.[71]

All the evening performances at the three Kampala cinemas in Uganda were canceled.[72] On February 9, 1952, the *Uganda Herald* vividly depicted the pains of a princess away from London. It reported that Elizabeth was still in her holiday attire, comprising a "light pink frock, white halo hat, and white accessories," when she emerged from the Dakota aircraft *Sagana*, arriving at the Entebbe Airport from Kenya on her journey home.[73]

Inclement weather, marked by heavy lightning and the rising wind, whirled dust devils gusting at fifty knots per hour across the runway, delayed the Royal Argonaut *Atlanta* waiting to take the royals back to the UK. Ochieng Mbalazi, a Ugandan, noted that "the panorama was as if African gods were mourning King George VI's demise and at the same time announcing an extraordinary leader's ascension."[74] The *Ugandan Herald* reported that Governor Andrew Cohen, dressed in black, met with the royals before the flight left for London through Libya's Royal El Adem Airbase (now Gamal Abdul Nasser Airbase).[75] The next day, the newspaper carried Cohen's message about the King's demise "to the great sorrow of the Royal Family and all His Majesty's subjects." Cohen conveyed to Her Majesty the colony's "profound grief and deep sympathy at the death of His Majesty, her father."[76] How these profusions of emotions and expectations translated to expected freedom or lack of it is central in the Elizabethan story.

Chapter Layout

Imposing a strict chronological order on this study was tricky because of the spread of the events and their fluidity chain. Chapter 1, "The House of Windsor: African Subjects and the Princess-Queen," provides an ample opportunity to test and expand on John Balmer's paradigmatic view of the British Crown as a corporate brand whose actions and inactions are scripted by the Establishment and all it entails. It examines the influence of the royal family culture and education and the royal stakeholders and mentors in shaping Elizabeth's personality and career, especially her relationship with Africa.

Chapter 2, "Deconstructing the 1947 Cape Town Speech: Decolonization Rhetoric and the Commonwealth," offers a dynamic template for gauging Elizabeth's initial stand on Africa's independence and postcolonial welfare from a hermeneutic standpoint concerning the continent's place in the postwar world order and the Commonwealth's future as a multicultural association of free peoples. It shows a web of the high and composite political game in which the initial intentions of a twenty-one-year-old princess staggered when they encountered the Liberal versus Conservative agendas within Whitehall.

Chapter 3, "The Cold War: African 'Radicals' and Her Royal Stateliness, 1953–1961," is an excursion through the complex politics of the East–West rivalry and its impact on Her Majesty's decolonization and Commonwealth journey. The implications of the American-British alliance on the illusions of monarchy and the self-determination movement were significant. For Elizabeth, it was challenging to navigate through the Anglo-American friendship without losing sight of her plans for emerging new nations. British and American policymakers took advantage of the young monarch, turning her into a good-luck charm for keeping suspected African radicals and potential communists within the Western ideological camp. Whitehall orchestrated royal tours to Africa, crucial in erecting a contemporary global UK. As the trips to Uganda, Nigeria, Ghana, and Sierra Leone turned out, Elizabeth's charisma served to stave off these countries' potential crises. The royal trips' efficacy and popularity encouraged further exploration with diverse purposes, challenges, and outcomes.

Chapter 4, "Her Majesty's Africa Tour-De-Force: Feasting with the Obedient, the Noble, and the Non-Conformist, 1961–1989," details Whitehall's stratagem of expanding royal visits as an instrument of connecting friendships with African governments and citizenry. This plan succeeded when dealing with moderate and polite African leaders; it proved a disaster with non-conformists like Uganda's Idi Amin.

Chapter 5, "Majestic Milestones: The Commonwealth and Africa's Development," recounts the association's African accomplishments under the Crown. Despite the turns and twists of decolonization and Whitehall's efforts to sabotage it, the post–Cold War Commonwealth has helped strengthen Africa's quest for sociopolitical autonomy more than many have yet to fully acknowledge. Elizabeth never abandoned the group's ideals but continued to push for growth in education, peace missions, human rights protection, women's empowerment, sports, environmental conservation, poverty reduction, and more. In addition, Elizabeth inspired new tropes of culture in arts, music, dance, and fashion, refined English as a second language, and transformed leadership ideals. Any account of Elizabeth without her Commonwealth records is flawed.

Chapter 6, "King Charles III and Africa's Commonwealth Future," surveys the organization's future after Elizabeth. For continued unity and strength in the post-Brexit, post-Covid-pandemic, and post–Ukraine-Russia conflict world order, the Commonwealth must find a way to reenact a "rediscovery of Africa" in the twenty-first century.

The conclusion speaks to some of the perceptions about the Queen held by Africans by illuminating the complex and multifaceted idioms of monarchy and the British Empire traditions, the African decolonization drive, and the postwar Commonwealth mission. Elizabeth's African engagements were shaped by the complex constraints and demands of British conservative and liberal politics in changing world order. These constrictions make sense from the prism of the royal corporate branding mix and the stakeholders' dialectics.

CHAPTER 1

THE HOUSE OF WINDSOR: AFRICAN SUBJECTS AND THE PRINCESS-QUEEN

Shortly after Queen Elizabeth II passed in 2022, the royal stakeholders' move to celebrate her political bequest under the British Empire's dissolution scheme met an instant pushback. The ghosts of the brutal responses to the postwar African nationalist movements deadened what one opponent called "the mythmaking machine."[1] The critics recalled that Elizabeth was often aloof to the subject people's plights in moments of decolonization raptures. In Nyasaland, for instance, bitterness lingers as to the Queen's silence to the protests starting with the Federation of Rhodesia and the Nyasaland proclamation in 1953. Memories of the deaths of many Africans consequent to the declaration of a state of emergency on March 3, 1959, left unanswered questions on the monarch's intentions for Africa and the overall character and purpose of her reign.[2]

The primary target is to offer insight into the grand invention of Elizabeth—how a peculiar leadership training structured her measured approach to Africa's needs. The postulation is that the interplay of kinship, imperial traditions, and postwar imperatives of freedom and peace brokered by Whitehall imposed a dualism in which Elizabeth was trapped, hindering a wholesale liberal agenda. Three reinforcing dynamics are inherent in this process, which explains the Crown's struggles to break from the old order to advocate for the Africans without bias. These are Windsor's influence on her upbringing, the competing postwar ideology and social discourse, and the British Establishment's investment in the Crown as a corporate institution. These forces shaped what is shown here as the push and pull of conservatism and liberalism in Elizabeth's African records.

In scrutinizing the royal family that nurtured Elizabeth, Luise White's *The Comforts of Home*, which focused on socioeconomic and gender relations in colonial Kenya, reminds contemporary historians to look at class and kin interaction because "kinship permeates a vast majority of the relationships we tend to think of as anonymous, furtive, and sordid."³ The family plays a central role in childhood socialization, self-concept formation, personality development, career choices, and compliance with the established norms or rebellion with the counterculture.⁴ In concert with Windsor, the royal stakeholders systematically raised Elizabeth to protect the Crown for national unity, pride, and all it demands. Ensuring the princess retained sight of the national mandate was fundamental to British national interest in an era of rapid flux.

Postwar discourses on the incompatibility of the moral demands of freedom with imperialist practices formulated along conservative/liberal lines revived the eighteenth-century works of Montesquieu's *De l'Esprit des Lois* (1748). Four decades before the French Revolution of 1789, Montesquieu's excursion into constitutional diversity led many to see the notion of a universally natural right as a chimera. The Frenchman dismissed the idea of an ideal society by propagating the belief that a durable constitution must be predicated on society's circumstances and needs.⁵ Like other opponents of modernist thoughts, Edmund Burke argued that respecting social conventions, prescriptive rights, and customs was the path to thoughtful reforms instead of a sweeping or sudden change in Western Europe.⁶

In British politics, the conservative philosophy was central to the monarchists—the custodians of Windsor's ideals of domesticity and social conventions of marriage, support for military power, and imperial holdings. The right to safeguard the Crown's core principles in Elizabeth's psyche was divergent from the more open postwar sentiments empathetic to the pains of the colonized and oppressed.⁷

As management professionals underline, corporate brands embody an informal agreement or covenant between an organization and its brand community.⁸ For an institution that served as a tool for colonial acquisitions, the royal brand Elizabeth inherited in 1952 is covenanted with everything British at a deeper level than meets the eye. Analogous to corporate business management, the unwritten contract between the Crown and Britons (brand community) is intricate. For example, the Rotary Club's slogan is "Service Above Self," and Google operates on "Do the Right Thing." Similarly, royal stakeholders run the Crown on British "National Identity, Unity, Pride, Stability, and Continuity."⁹ These mantras are inviolable for all the investors in the monarchy—the government, Church of England, citizens, businesses, and consumers—and transcend everything else.

John Balmer has distilled the branding character of the Crown to illuminate its mysteries and secrecies, its backers' expectations, value systems, taboos, and its innermost workings. He concludes that the institution is run as a corporate brand because everything coheres with its public image. Understanding this simple but consequential fact illuminates the secret to Her Majesty's confusing, distanced, and often elusive responses to Africa during crises.[10]

Balmer explicates that his "Royal Branding Mix" model implicates the instrumentation of five elements: royal, regal, relevant, responsive, and respected. He equates the royal and regal characters to the brand's identity with an explicit organizational focus. Elizabeth's actions and inactions, pronouncements and silences, and engagement and retreats were deliberate and measured to boost the royal and regal image of the Crown's brand. The relevant, responsive, and respected expectations mirror a public (stakeholder) emphasis.[11] The Crown exists primarily to serve the needs or concerns of Britons before those of Africans or others.

To further illustrate, Nyasaland in the 1950s was more than a flashpoint in the inherent ideological wrestling match between British conservatives and liberals in the postwar era. It also represented one among other crises during which the royal stakeholders insisted that the Crown retreat to insulate her from potential vulnerability. Although some liberals supported the Colonial Office's Emergency policies for a different reason, friends in the Labour Party, such as James Griffiths, lobbied for the Nyasaland delegation of 1953 to London to receive an audience at Buckingham Palace. But Oliver Lyttelton, the Conservative colonial secretary, frustrated the efforts. The right-wingers had announced that it was "impossible" for the African chiefs to see the Queen because they came without an official invitation. However, the main reason that aligns with the branding identity matrix was to avoid "compromising" the new and inexperienced Queen.[12] In other words, encouraging Elizabeth to parley with the visiting African chiefs at this point in history would undermine the royal and regal image of the Crown's brand.

Her Imperial Family and the Africans

For a nation that amassed immense wealth and global influence through *nkamanya*—an Igbo concept for blatant, undisguised, and unapologetic dispossession of others—the culture of crime scene cover-ups and planting misleading narratives began with Queen Alexandrina Victoria. In a documentary on Victoria, the British Broadcasting Corporation (BBC) credited her with rescuing the Crown's reputation from her royal uncles' misdeeds. From 1837 to 1901, Victoria reconnected with the people through civic duties and set the antecedents of royal authority and cultural trends on which the tenure and aura of succeeding monarchs, including Elizabeth II, rested. While this assertion may be true, the BBC did not fully explain the context of Victoria's popularity among the Brits. Although the Republican Commonwealth of England scaled down the Crown's power in the seventeenth century, Victoria garnered tremendous influence as a symbol of British identity by aligning her interests and values with Whitehall's policies and goals during her reign.[13]

After Victoria, the serving monarchs retained the titular power to open the House of Lords and House of Commons (Parliament). The Crown signs off Parliament Acts before they become laws and can dissolve the legislature when necessary. The monarchy appoints the prime minister after general elections and chooses political party leaders. However, when the political landscape becomes partisan and raucous, the Crown retreats from the infighting until the elected politicians restore order.[14] As this study highlights, the monarchical prerogatives, in theory, created a silo of illusion/opacity of power and influence that the African nationalists erroneously ascribed to Queen Elizabeth II. The misunderstanding explains why the Africans misjudged Elizabeth's disinclination to override elected politicians or command immediate answers to Africa's pressing nationalist questions.

The Africans saw the Crown as the oldest secular institution in England and, as Cahal Milmo noted, "a unifying figurehead gifted by history and surrounded by ritual."[15] However, what eluded the Africans' imagination was Walter Bagehot's 1867 conclusion that the monarch embodies a constitutional "mystery" since its most important duties are covert: "It is commonly hidden like a mystery and sometimes paraded like a pageant, but in neither case is it contentious. The nation is divided into parties, but the Crown is of no party. Its apparent separation from [the] business is that which removes it both from enmities and from desecration."[16] For Elizabeth to succeed, she must comply with the elected politicians' directives, safeguard the Crown's mystery (which she often demonstrated through silence), and focus on national unity by partnering with all the stakeholders. This expectation required her to distance herself from controversies and combine the affection of conflicting parties—the conservatives who stood for piecemeal changes and the liberals who advocated for immediate colonial reforms.

The uncodified British constitution, defined by custom, statutes, usage, and precedents, allowed the Crown to sway the subjects even in the most challenging times. In retrospect, Frank Hardie argued in *The Political Influence of Queen Victoria, 1861–1901*, that she partook in her ministers' political affairs far beyond the realms of neutral exercise of limited influence. During Victoria's tenure, Britain was governed by younger prime ministers, Lord Salisbury (r. 1885–1892, and 1895–1902) and Lord Rosebery (r.1894–1895), who looked up to her for direction.

Victoria's sixty-three-year reign enthroned a culture where respect for age became a norm in the monarchy-Parliament interrelationship. As this study reveals, in the early period of her reign, Queen Elizabeth's young age limited the degree to which she could push her personal convictions (such as overriding Oliver Lyttleton over the Nyasaland delegation imbroglio) through the more senior politicians like Sir Winston Churchill. With age, Elizabeth became the most experienced political figure in modern Britain. Hardie reminds us that "long experience and accurate memory made Victoria's political interventions increasingly decisive as the years passed."[17] High-ranking ministers and other individuals and groups indulged in royal functions to gain recognition and patronage.[18] Concerning Elizabeth, there is still a lot to learn about how she leveraged the degree of respect her age commanded in the latter period of her reign to push through her African mission or lack thereof.

The truth is that Victoria, "the Warrior Queen," endorsed Whitehall's colonial foreign policies for her successors to emulate or amend. She supported Britain's international relations with an ideology of imperialism, masculinity, and country-first policy goals.[19] This legacy would impact Elizabeth's reign in peculiar ways that mirror a history of misrepresentation in African-Anglo relations. In their aggressive territorial acquisition and wealth extraction worldwide, notably in Africa, the British colonial servants routinely invoked "Her Majesty" in branding the wars of conquests, skewed treaties of protection, racially biased judicial administrations, and deposition and exile of African sovereigns.

In the late nineteenth century, when Britain was planning for the Boer War (1899–1902) in South Africa, Prime Minister Salisbury, eleven years younger than the Queen, took pains to inform Victoria about the army's poor state. "We have no army capable of meeting even a second-class Continental power."[20] She rebuked the government for being "too timid." "They do not take my advice or the advice of experts about the Army, and civilians *cannot* understand military strategies."[21] That Britain proceeded with the war despite Salisbury's concerns is a pointer to the Empress's imperial foreign policy voice.

Other acts of intimidation that permanently altered lives and cultural landmarks in Africa followed similar chains of command. Before the 1900 Anglo-Ganda Agreement, the Buganda monarchy Kabaka Mwanga II Mukasa resisted the British colonial presence. In 1888, Her Majesty's agent, Frederick

Lugard, deposed and exiled Mukasa.[22] The Buganda monarch returned home in 1889 after promising not to fight the Crown's authority in the region. More than five decades later, Queen Elizabeth II found herself in a similar situation requiring her to defend the country-first policy by approving Governor Andrew Cohen's banishment of Kabaka Mutesa II of Buganda. During the exile of 1953–1955, a Ganda-educated elite peddled the rumor in London that Mutesa I (r. 1856–1884), Mwanga II's father, had proposed marriage to Queen Victoria, whom he had sent a letter in 1876 requesting "May your Queen be a mother to me, and may I become her son."[23]

While the idea of an African monarch seeking an intimate relationship with the Queen of Great Britain in the nineteenth century is laughable, the underlying cause and import of such rumors are apparent. In indigenous African society, marriage was a diplomacy tool, friendship connection, and power relation. The crushing force of imperialism left Africans believing the British Crown was the de facto global figure. The Kabaka wanted to tap into her authority through marriage or fictional mother-son relations. Similar idealism from Uganda linked Queen Elizabeth II with exiled Kabaka Mutesa II in the 1950s and General Idi Amin in the 1970s.

Victoria routinely supported military confrontations with African sovereigns. On November 11, 1895, colonial officer Arthur Neville Chamberlain, who later served as prime minister of Britain (r. 1937–1940), secured Victoria's support to launch "necessary military measures" against the Kumasi Kingdom in West Africa "in consequence of the failure of the King to observe his treaty engagements."[24] In February 1897, Admiral Harry Rawson led British forces in Lagos, Nigeria, on the bloody Benin Expedition with the Crown's consent.[25]

One of the few exceptions where an African king was treated with dignity was in 1898 when the Crown sent a recorded message to Emperor Menelik and Empress Itege Taitu of Ethiopia. The August 8, 1898, dispatch read: "I, Victoria, Queen of England, hope your Majesty is in good health. I thank you for the kind reception which you have given to my Envoys, Mr. Rodd, and Mr. Harrington. I wish your Majesty and the Empress Taitou all prosperity and success, and I hope that the friendship between our two Empires will constantly increase."[26] Lieutenant Colonel J. L. Harrington reported from Ethiopia that Victoria's message "was received with a ceremony by the [Ethiopian] King, and after it was delivered, an artillery salute was fired, the King standing to show his respect for the honour paid him."[27] The sovereigns' exchanges are significant because of the respectful tone. Later, it inspired the celebrated relationship between Emperor Haile Selassie and Queen Elizabeth II in the postwar era.[28]

In 1902, when King Edward II succeeded Queen Victoria on the throne, the unrest created by European imperialism was still unfolding in Africa. However, some calm returned in Uganda, where the British had a memorandum of understanding with local collaborators. The Kabaka of Buganda sent his ministers, Apolo Kagwa and Vizier Ham Mukasa, to King Edward VII's coronation in England in 1902.[29] Otherwise, African kings and queens were routinely humiliated throughout the scramble and colonization when they objected to colonial control.

A strong belief in racial differences, which informed Europe's relationship with the African colonial subjects, ensured that the succeeding monarchs continued to project British power overseas. By implication, unwavering support for the army and empire remained one of Elizabeth's inherited principles. How she applied this tradition to Africa in the restive decolonization period is central to understanding Elizabeth's African ties.

Another observable value Elizabeth got from the House of Windsor is domesticity and reverence for patriarchal authority. Victoria did little to enthrone gender equality in her time. Her pronouncements, family life, and actions often contradicted the initial pledge to "steadily protect the rights and promote to the utmost of my Power the happiness and welfare of all Classes of my Subjects."[30] One could read her career in different directions, including a survivalist mentality in the nineteenth-century British patriarchal society. By presenting herself as the country's mother, Victoria reinforced separate spheres for the sexes and prioritized the rules of behavior and women's subservience to male authority. In contrast with feminine virtues of beauty and kindness, masculine ideals of strength and courage dominated the bonds of marriage, love, romance, and family life. Indeed, these ideals have been the defining attributes of Queen Elizabeth II's personal life and survival credo.

Kathryn Hughes, an authority on Victorian Age culture, recalls that women required a special education to prepare them for a role as "Angel in the House." Like those less privileged families, middle-class women attracted husbands through their domestic abilities. The middle-class girls took training in "accomplishments," which was about some skills expected of a woman.[31] In Jane Austen's *Pride and Prejudice*, we learn that the skills required of an accomplished young woman preceded Victoria's reign: "A woman must have a thorough knowledge of music, singing, drawing, dancing, and the modern languages, ... she must possess something in her air and manner of walking, the tone of her voice, her address and expressions."[32] These ideals were reinforced in Victoria's time as part of the Windsor culture in which Elizabeth was raised.

The sociopolitical legacies lingered in British life and its dependencies long after Victoria. Colonial officials under Edward VII (1901–1910), George V (1910–1936), Edward VIII (1936), and George VI (1936–1952) extended the culture to the colonies. The conservative dressing manners for women embodied by Elizabeth spread to Africa through the colonial administrators, Christian missionaries, colonial schools, and later the newspapers and cinema. Michael Echeruo's *In Victorian Lagos* details the "strongly felt and keenly cherished passion of the native Lagosian of the period to have a local version of what they considered to be established civilized habits."[33]

Religion is another instrument of the royal branding that shaped Elizabeth's innate conservative personality and could hinder all-out liberal policies. The bonds between the Church of England and the monarchy ensured that most Victorian Age cultural tropes were interpreted from the prism of morality. The Church is theoretically under the Crown, with specific bonds of ecclesiastical voice reserved for the clergy. The Crown's position as the symbol of political unity and the guardian of the spiritual realm has endured today in the British system.[34] Altogether, Victoria's conformist legacies, treasured among the Windsors, could hinder wholesale changes even in the most reformist-minded. With this understanding of the Victorian background to the culture of the twentieth-century monarchy, it is time to trace Elizabeth's experience from the interwar years to the end of the Second World War.

Childhood, Abdication Trauma, and Queenship Preparation

The sociopolitical milieu into which Princess Elizabeth Alexandra Mary Windsor was born on April 21, 1926, was a mixture of male control, royalist reverence, and imperialist pride. The interwar years were marked by uncertainty and tension as the Europeans prepared for the 1939 sequel. Being the first child of Prince Albert (later King George VI) and Duchess Elizabeth Bowes-Lyon, Elizabeth was not in the direct line to the throne. If her uncle, Edward, had married fittingly and had children, Elizabeth would not have been the Crown's inheritor.[35] However, accidents and luck operate in history, notably when love and emotions cross paths with established royal norms.

Elizabeth's life changed forever in December 1936, when King Edward VIII abdicated the throne to be free to marry a divorced American socialite, Mrs. Wallis Warfield Simpson.[36] An American native of Maryland, Mrs. Simpson had arrived in England five years earlier with her then second husband, Ernest

Simpson, an American-born British shipbroker. The negative fallout from the Simpson affair reinforced the royal family/stakeholders' resolve to protect the monarchy's traditions against future threats. King Edward's plan was denounced by the royal stakeholders—the Church of England and the Parliament—as a rebellion against British pride.[37] The Archbishop of Canterbury, William C. G. Lang, echoed Prime Minister Stanley Baldwin's demand that Edward hand off Mrs. Simpson or leave the throne.[38]

Weighing in on the matter, *The Times* took the side of the Church, emphasizing that Edward was "the most visible embodiment of the monarchical principle, and any personal default of his gives a shock to the principle, which is mischievous and even dangerous."[39] The *Daily Mail* countered, "Abdication is out of the question because its possibility of mischief is endless. The effects on the empire would be calamitous."[40] The *Daily Express* concurred with the *Daily Mail*, arguing, "No government can stand in the King's way if he is resolved to walk that way. Let the King give his decision to the people."[41] Edward tested the resolve of the monarchy's image brand and failed to overcome its strength.

On December 10, 1936, King Edward informed the House of Commons of his resignation. "I, Edward VIII, of Great Britain, Ireland, and the British Dominions beyond the Seas, King, Emperor of India, do hereby declare My irrevocable determination to renounce the Throne for Myself and for My descendants, and My desire that effect should be given to this Instrument of Abdication immediately."[42] Edward pleaded to his critics for an understanding in a December 11, 1936, radio address: "You must believe me when I tell you that I have found it impossible to carry the heavy burden of responsibility and to discharge my duties as king as I would wish to do without the help and support of the woman I love."[43] Edward later said, "I always told those idiots not to put me in a golden frame."[44]

The abdication trauma lingered in the British spirit to demonstrate how a nonconformist royal marriage could undermine Windsor's honor and survival and the entire British pride—the emotional soul of the royal corporate brand. The British monarchy was the exception among its German and Russian cousins that collapsed following the First World War.[45] The King also gained respect in the African colonies despite the colonial situation—a social capital that constituted the basis for the Africans' expression of goodwill toward Elizabeth.

Nonetheless, the Africans decried the subordination and racial segregation imposed by the minority White elite in Africa. On the South African minefields, where the colonists treated Africans as second-class citizens, the aggrieved workers showed frustration by applauding news about German forces' advancement.[46] Elsewhere, Africans exhibited bitterness toward the alien rule through open rebellions against conscription, especially when recruiters approached them with force and threats. British Nyasaland (Malawi) witnessed this reaction earlier than in West Africa. By 1915, far-reaching labor recruitment had started amid demoralizing German counterattacks led by General von Lettow-Vorbeck. Pastor John Chilembwe, the zealous apostle of Ethiopianism, used the pulpit to attack the British war policy, offering his life as a ransom for the much-desired African freedom.[47]

Most Africans supported the Allied war efforts with material and human contributions. London tasked the West African Students' Union (WASU) and colonial governors to support the war effort with propaganda.[48] While the colonial press depicted the Germans as devils—destroying churches and slaying babies with bayonets, the Africans perceived the war as a struggle for freedom. In this context, freedom implied a kind of compensation for material donations and labor enlistments.[49]

Africans came out of the First World War believing King George V had saved them from German savagery. It became incumbent on the royal house to validate this ascribed savior's reputation. In response, Edward, Prince of Wales, launched a three-month tour of West Africa and the Union of South Africa in 1925 as part of the unified action to stop the spread of communism by impressing people worldwide with Britain's prestige and its sociopolitical institutions. The royal's presence in The Gambia, Sierra Leone, and Nigeria was greeted by an outpouring of "enthusiastic loyalty," exemplified by passionate durbars, parades, dances, church services, eulogies of the advances credited to missionaries, mission schools, and colonial administrators.[50]

The West African royal rebranding tour was less politically challenging than the delicate South African trip, which was planned to strengthen the imperial tie with the dominion by effecting a reconciliation between the Whites of British and Dutch (otherwise Afrikaners) origins.[51] The marginalized and oppressed South African communists and Indians reminded the Africans that the royals and the Whites were "largely responsible" for their exploitation. They argued that showing allegiance to the prince was "foolish" while several wounded natives shot by the police were "lying in the Bloemfontein hospitals."[52]

In retrospect, Edward explained in his 1951 memoir that he wanted to be "more responsive to the changed circumstances of his time."[53] But the crux of the matter was that his goals should have aligned with the stakeholders' expectations of the Crown. As King, he served as a custodian of religious ideals and as supreme governor of the Church of England. In a post–First World War society in which many had questioned the place of religion in their lives, the Church hoped that Edward would help resuscitate a popular trust in faith. The King's marriage to a divorcée and abdication did not align with the moral expectations established by the corporate royal stakeholders.

In a psycho-biographical interpretation of Edward's action, Linda Rosenzweig concluded that the renunciation was Edward's desperate route to secure "possession of a mother figure whom he was able to please, and so he triumphed symbolically over his father." She diagnosed Edward's problems as an "unresolved oedipal anxiety, which governed his relations with women and eventually dictated his choice of a wife." Rosenzweig asserted that this "psychological defect caused him to give away an empire and to renounce the unique way of life to which he had been born."[54]

Rosenzweig's reading of Edward is open to debate. First, he did not willfully give up the throne; the Establishment pressured him into abdication because his choices were detrimental to the royal and regal image of the Crown's brand. Two, Rosenzweig's dismissal of Windsor's arranged marriage culture's influence on the King is inconsiderate. In perspective, Elizabeth Bowes-Lyon's marriage to Albert (Elizabeth's father) was by measured arrangement.[55] The government and palace's calculated decision aimed "to dilute the German element in the family and bring it closer to the people." Inner sources argue that part of the reason Albert found his wife unique was "her background as part of a loving, happy family so different from his own."[56]

In response to the 1936 crisis, Mary of Teck refused to exhort her son, Edward. Instead, she depicted Albert's ascension as "ignominious capitulation to the wiles of his ambitious wife." Mary resolved to "never, ever forgive" her brother-in-law (David Bowes-Lyon) and "that woman" (Wallis Simpson) for rupturing the family and pushing an unprepared Bertie (Albert) into a job that killed him in 1952.[57] Here, the Queen Mother associated leadership preparation with a flourishing monarchy and protection of family honor. In other words, the traditional royal branded values will guide the family in raising Elizabeth for the Crown.

The Formative Years

One of the ultimate beneficiaries of the 1936 event was Princess Elizabeth, who emerged as the presumptive heir when her father, King George VI, ascended the throne. Underlining the lessons emerging from the royal family's marital snafu is vital. How did it affect Princess Elizabeth's worldview, especially concerning her marriage? What were the implications for her education, leadership preparation, and devotion to the Crown and its traditions? Edward's behaviors jolted the monarchists, who became mindful that leadership preparation demands absolute duty, loyalty to the institution's honor and ideals, and adherence to marriage expectations. Courage and strength were observed as part of Elizabeth's natural qualities. "She had adored her grandfather and was one of the only people in the country who seemed to be unafraid of him." Lang, the Archbishop of Canterbury, was impressed when he observed "Elizabeth leading the king by the beard as if he were a horse."[58]

Royal stakeholders carefully tailored Princess Elizabeth's education for the leadership emotions cannot betray. In the Victorian Age sense of domesticity and all it entailed, the royals conceived a home education instead of formalized schooling to prepare her for the high office she would assume. Elizabeth's training began under the supervision of her mother, Duchess Bowes-Lyon, and Clare Cooper Knight, a strict disciplinarian who started as a royal nanny.[59]

Like other British children, Elizabeth and her sister Margaret spent most of the day apart from their parents during the Second World War because Germany bombed civilian targets. Like her parents, the princess remained in Britain despite advice to the contrary. "The children won't go without me; I won't leave the king. And the king will never leave."[60] Buckingham Palace suffered nine direct strikes during the German Blitz from September 1940 to May 1941.[61] By declining to flee, the official biographer, William Shawcross, recorded the "King and Queen came to embody the national spirit."[62]

Princess Elizabeth carried the mantle of national spirit after her parents. At fourteen, in October 1940, she shored up morale by speaking to war refugees over the radio. During a "Children's Hour" program on the BBC in October 1940, the princess asked her fellow kids to persevere and steady the war course: "Thousands of you in this country have had to leave your homes and be separated from your fathers and mothers. My sister Margaret-Rose and I feel so much for you, as we know from experience what it means to be away from those we love most.... We would like to thank the kind people who have welcomed you to their homes in the country."[63] The gesture mirrors the monarchy's long tradition of supporting the army.[64] In 1943, Elizabeth served as the 3rd Grenadier Guards' guest at Hawick and visited the Italian battlefields in 1944 as a counsellor of state to Allied forces.[65]

At seventeen, the princess studied constitutional history with Henry Marten, who later became the vice-provost of Eton College. Elizabeth took it seriously to know more about European and American history. Her reading list included G. M. Trevelyan's *History of England*, David Saville Muzzey's *The American Adventure: A History of the United States*, William Russell's *The History of Modern Europe*, Walter Bagehot's *The English Constitution*, and Edward Hyde (Earl of Clarendon)'s *The History of the Rebellion*. While the Archbishop of Canterbury, W. C. G. Lang, provided spiritual lessons, Canon Crawley of St. George's Chapel, Windsor, tutored Elizabeth in biblical history. Elizabeth attained fluency in French and German.[66]

Knowledge of Africa was not considered necessary for educating a future monarch supervising the dissolution of British African dominions. European armchair historians and visitors like David Livingstone, the Scottish missionary doctor, had dispersed the falsehood that the continent had no history and no civilization, branding the inhabitants "weak and cowardly."[67] Unless someone was inclined to know more about primitive cultures, as Winwood Reade's *Savage Africa* suggests, there was no inducement to include African history and culture in the royal curriculum.[68]

As nineteenth-century American politician P. T. Barnum noted, literature is one of humanity's "most interesting and significant expressions." However, "books are thickly peppered with Humbug."[69] Besides its importance in developing critical thinking skills, literature expands our horizons and projects the learner into the past to better understand the present and the cultures and beliefs. Young Elizabeth's interests in English literature were focused on Shakespeare and *The Canterbury Tales*, as well as books by Coleridge, Keats, Browning, Tennyson, Scott, Dickens, Austen, Trollope, Stevenson, and Conan Doyle's *The White Company* and *Sherlock Holmes*.

In 1943, Wilson Harris of *The Atlantic* published a remarkable story on Princess Elizabeth to ascertain her readiness for the monarchy. The narrative starts with the admission that the war had hindered the princess from receiving the benefit of foreign travel education. However, Harris noted that Elizabeth was "far more fortunate in her parentage and early surroundings."[70] Compared with Queen Victoria, strong support for the army was a vital part of her life. Elizabeth loved "the Army and its tradition—in particular, naturally, of the Grenadier Guards, of which she is Colonel."[71]

In February 1945, the princess joined the Women's Auxiliary Territorial Service (ATS). The Company, established four years earlier, prepared women for service in one of the two auxiliary areas: the Women's Royal Naval Service (WRNS) or the Women's Auxiliary Air Force (WAAF). Elizabeth received driver and mechanic training with the rank of second subaltern. She was subsequently promoted to a junior commander's position, the equivalent of captain.[72]

Experiential Learning in Africa

Elizabeth and her sister Margaret accompanied their parents to Southern Africa two years after the war. It was her first foreign travel, which became quite educational for the princess.[73] Douglas Williams, who accompanied the royals, reported they spent sixty-five days from February 17 to April 24, 1947, covering Cape Town in South Africa to the Union of Rhodesia (Zimbabwe and Zambia).[74]

Three central issues made the 1947 royal tour significant. First, it happened on the eve of the independence and the partition of the Indian subcontinent into Hindu India and Muslim Pakistan. Second, the trip occurred a year before the segregationist Nationalist Party came to power in South Africa. Both events are central to Africa's future because India's freedom from colonial subjugation inspired fierce nationalist agitations in the African colonies. The rise of the White nationalists in South Africa was an affront and a flashpoint to Africa's dreams of independence.

Third, and more crucial, Elizabeth met with Africans during the trip. She observed the people's respect for the royals, sacrifices, pains under oppression, and future hopes. The princess also witnessed anger against the royal family's presence by right-wing Afrikaners, Indians, and Black political bodies like the African National Congress (ANC). Hilary Sapire observes that while postwar African politics was viewed as "radicalized" and "anti-colonial," Africans' involvement "with the royal tour indicates that professed faith in the British monarchy as the embodiment and guardian of the rights and liberties of all peoples living under the crown."[75] It is critical to further qualify "African loyalism" as an expectation of reward with political rights for their immense contributions to the Allied victory. The question then was less about whether the royal family appreciated the Africans enough to translate their sacrifices into freedom but more about when Whitehall would be willing to make this happen. Briefly revisiting Africans' involvement in the Second World War is central to understanding their postwar hopes, expectations, frustrations, and anger.

The Second World War, Royals' Visit, and African Response

Unlike the First World War, which saw Africans' limited role, the Second World War provided African Americans and Africans openings to fight racial injustice on multiple fronts. The conflict exposed an ugly, racist inclination in the US system and the European colonial dominions. Like in the First War, the colonial state depicted the conflict as a battle against German racism and totalitarian control. The Atlantic Charter circulated the belief that the war was waged for self-determination and the subjugated peoples' right to choose the government they aspired to live in.

The Charter corroborates Joanne Toor and H. G. Picknell's postulation that for propaganda to be efficient, it should have a "universality of appeal and generosity, which can serve to remove undue suspicion from the minds of the propaganda consumers."[76] Wilson's steadfastness in favor of people's right to choose the form of government that meets their needs held a Universalist aura for the Africans, who welcomed the Charter as an inevitable end of colonial rule.

The colonial powers, who held a different understanding of the Atlantic Charter, initially proposed keeping Africans out of the conflict. What transpired in Rhodesia represents a pertinent illustration of the European mind and the imperative of African support in the war. Tim Stapleton reminds us that in Southern Rhodesia (Zimbabwe), the British officials assured their African subjects that only Whites would partake in military combat. They asked the Africans to contribute "to the war effort by remaining loyal and producing for the home economy."[77]

In a sudden turn of events, Charles Bullock, Bulawayo's chief native commissioner, claimed that some Africans had volunteered for military service. This claim was validated with a statement on September 20, 1939, credited to Mr. Makhgato, the Bantu United Society's head, that the members "shall stand for the British Empire."[78] Other Africans also wrote to the newspaper, asking the colonial officials to create an African regiment for the war.[79] There are speculations that the Africans wanted to use wartime service to earn citizenship rights from the colonial state, although many Africans genuinely expressed loyalty to the besieged British Empire. While Italy's imperial interests in the war severely threatened British interests in East and North Africa, it was also a real danger to Ethiopia in 1935–1936. African volunteers fought to preserve the British Empire and protect Africa from Axis aggression.

In 1940, Rhodesian officials commenced recruiting African soldiers for the new Rhodesian African Rifles (RAR). The infantry battalion under White officers arrived in East Africa after the fighting was over. In Burma, they engaged the Japanese until 1945. Additionally, colonial officials created the Rhodesian Air Askari Corps (RAAC), comprising African soldiers protecting Allied pilots' training facilities. From 1940 to 1945, the RAR conscripted 3,947 Africans for the war.[80] This number represents 28 percent of the 14,302 Africans in Southern Rhodesia who offered to fight in defense of the King and the British Empire.[81]

David Johnson observes that British wartime propaganda in Africa emphasized loyalty to the King, protecting justice and freedom.[82] The message, repeated by media and cinema, appealed to many because it came with a promise. In her study of Rhodesian soldiers' role in the Second World War, Ashley Jackson disputed the consensus among scholars that the colonial state pressured Africans to enlist in the military service, arguing that the enlistment's motivations were rather complicated.[83] In his study of Zimbabwe, Peter McLaughlin argued that many Africans joined the war out of loyalty to the colonial regime.[84] A middle-ground argument balancing the material motivation and the call of duty to the British Empire is ideal.[85]

Africans in other regions of the continent exhibited similar responses to the war. A striking example was the faculty, staff, and pupils of the Qua Iboe Mission Institute in Uyo, Nigeria. Soon after Britain declared war against Germany, the school authorities sent a letter of support to the King. They criticized the Germans and wished they "be brought to their knees in the shortest possible time."[86]

The nationalist newspapers vigorously promoted anti-German sentiments. For example, the *Gold Coast Times* of March 13, 1939, depicted Great Britain as the "great protector of small nations" standing up to evil Germany.[87] The *West African Pilot*, owned by Nnamdi Azikiwe, offered the Allies unwavering support for the war. An editorial of September 4, 1939, stressed that Britain and France were "shedding their blood in order that the ideals of liberty, democracy and peace might strive in the world."[88] In February 1942, the newspaper declared it "the duty of every citizen of [Nigeria], as it is of every liberty-loving soul in every part of the world, to bear the greatest sacrifice ungrudgingly." It called on the African "to contribute his maximum in every way possible, little or great, to bring the success of the Allied forces nearer."[89] The *Nigerian Daily Times* added that the war was a struggle "Against Habits of the Jungle" and "A Stand for Fair and Free Negotiation."[90]

The preceding offers the historical context in which the Africans responded to the 1947 royal visit with their concerns and expectations. They saw the royals as partners in the struggle against racial enmity and believed that Allied victory equaled Africa's triumph over colonial oppression, fascism, Nazism, and racism. Elizabeth noted all these cues and spoke to them in her Cape Town speech when she called for the country and empire to work together to save themselves after the war: "I am sure that you will see our difficulties, in the light that I see them, as a great opportunity for you and me. Most of you have read in the history books the proud saying of William Pitt that England had saved herself by her exertions and would save Europe by her example. But in our time, we may say that the British Empire has saved the world first and has now to save itself after the battle is won."[91] In this context, Africa's nationalist agitations became a fight for peaceful decolonization rather than a conflict within the withering Empire.

Princess Elizabeth Weds Philip Mountbatten

On November 20, 1947, six months after the royal visit to South Africa, Elizabeth married Philip Mountbatten. The great-great-grandson of Queen Victoria and the son of Prince Andrew of Greece was five years older than the bride. As Hughes reminds us, in the Victorian Age culture, "Girls usually married in their early to mid-20s. Typically, the groom would be five years older." This tradition reinforced "the natural hierarchy between the sexes and made sound financial sense. A young man needed to show that he earned enough money to support a wife and any future children before the girl's father would give his permission. Some unfortunate couples were obliged to endure an engagement lasting a decade before they could afford to marry."[92] The prenuptial expectations adhered to by Elizabeth also mirror several African cultures, including the Igbo, Efik, Ibibio, and Yoruba, thus indicating the cultural affinity among human societies across time and space.

The couple's first child, Prince Charles, arrived in 1948, and Princess Anne followed in 1950.[93] By the 1950s, Africa's newspapers, radio, cinema, and television had come of age to facilitate the royal branding mix. While a handful of the literate and semiliterate could read and afford ownership of radio and television, they habitually shared with the less privileged stories of the White man's society and imperial politics. Through these avenues, the new Queen's popularity rose in the colonies.

One must recognize the critical significance of Elizabeth's marriage. She needed a man beside her to manage the onerous burdens of kinship, royalty, empire, national leadership, and culture. Elizabeth was targeted by patriarchal chauvinists, and her marriage to Philip worried an ultraconservative group and allies in power positions within and outside the royal family.[94] Uncovered documents reveal a last-ditch palace conspiracy to bar Elizabeth from the throne before her father died in 1952. Led by King George VI's brother-in-law David Bowes-Lyon, Lord Eldon, the Marquess of Salisbury, and Lord Stanley, the plan was to tell Britons that Elizabeth was too young to reign and bring back the former King Edward VIII as regent.[95] The conspiracy failed, and Elizabeth became the Queen at age twenty-five on February 6, 1952, during an official trip to Kenya with her husband, when her father died.[96]

African royal guests to the Queen's ceremonial investiture on June 2, 1953, included Buganda's Kabaka Mutesa II, Chief Kawinga of Nyasaland; Sultan Khalifa bin Harubn of Zanzibar, Oba Adesoji Aderemi of Nigeria, Moshoeshoe II of Lesotho, Kgari Sechela of Bechuanaland, Amha Selassie, the Crown Prince of Ethiopia, and the prime minister of the Union of South Africa, Daniël Françoise Malan.[97] The event's splendor on radio and television left a lasting impression on the global audience, notably the British African Empire.

Contextualizing Queen Elizabeth's personality in her social milieu illuminates the family and imperial politics that impacted her career. These influences permit us to develop a robust discursive approach to identifying how she moved within the African history we study. The complexities of postwar realities, including the Cold War, decolonization movements, and the counterculture struggles in the United States and Europe, allow for an appreciation of the situations that fashioned Her Majesty's ideas and priorities. Elizabeth's actions and thoughts—whether geared to protect the monarchy or promote Africa's freedom—are original rather than copies of her forebears. The critical fact is that the Queen was an invention of the royal brand stakeholders: Whitehall, the Church of England, and elected politicians.

The 1947 African trip was part of the royal branding project the British stakeholders approved for Elizabeth as the future monarch. Setting foot on African soil was life changing for a princess whose educational curriculum had nothing on the continent. The tour defined her long-term relationship with the Africans. The 1952 Kenya tour's symbolism was her transformation from a princess into the sovereign. The speech in Cape Town ultimately announced her presence on the decolonization train under the Commonwealth scheme.

CHAPTER 2

DECONSTRUCTING THE 1947 CAPE TOWN SPEECH: DECOLONIZATION RHETORIC AND THE COMMONWEALTH

> I declare before you all that my whole life, whether it be long or short, shall be devoted to your service and the service of our great imperial family to which we all belong.[1]
>
> —Princess Elizabeth, 1947

On April 21, 1947, almost two years after the Second World War, Princess Elizabeth celebrated her twenty-first birthday in Cape Town, South Africa. The occasion was one of the highlights of a three-month royal family tour of the dominions of Southern Rhodesia, Swaziland, Basutoland (Lesotho), and the Bechuanaland (Botswana).[2] Invited by Governor-General Brand van Zyl and Prime Minister Jan Christian Smuts, King George VI came to open the Union of South Africa's Parliament as its constitutional head, thank the veterans of the Second World War, shore up respect for the Western ideals embodied in the monarchical institution, and bring "the territories closer to the Empire."[3] The visit was planned with all the royal pomp and pageantry to help the King recuperate from the war's traumas.[4]

Despite the festive atmosphere, the presumptive heir had much on her mind. Neither the birthday gift of diamonds (for a necklace) from the South African government nor her royal wedding to Philip Mountbatten (later Duke of Edinburgh), planned for November 20, 1947, provided Elizabeth relief from the ominous and complex political issues she had to confront at her young age.[5] It is noteworthy that while Sir Winston Churchill, MP Clement Davis, and other supporters of imperialism endorsed the trip, the anticolonial advocates in the Parliament, such as MP William Gallacher, spoke out against it because of the heightened political situation in the Southern African region. "I want to draw attention to the fact that the conditions of the negroes in South Africa are even worse than the conditions of the negroes in the South American States, and that the South African Government are proposing, in defiance of the United Nations, to take South-West Africa into the Union. We stand by the United Nations."[6]

Although Elizabeth was yet to succeed to the Crown, the air in which she delivered her speech was pregnant with expectations, and the entire world was listening. For instance, in June 1946, Nyasaland's Dr. Hastings Banda had bitterly complained to Colonial Secretary Arthur Creech Jones about the extent of White minority oppression in his native land: "As a country or a state, Nyasaland is, chiefly, the 2,000,000 Africans and not the 2,000 Europeans."[7] Similar complaints about colonial oppression across the continent ensured that the speech, converging on the colonies' future under the Commonwealth of Nations patronage, propelled Elizabeth into the decolonization limelight. She used the platform to unveil plans to reposition the organization for future needs. Elizabeth's announcement of total commitment to the "imperial family" indicated that the British Empire's postwar challenges would occupy the early years of her reign. The thought of bearing this onerous task was a cause for anxiety. "I am sure you will see our difficulties in the light that I see them," said the princess.[8]

In context, the push for colonial reforms and the idea of cooperation among the various British dominions began long before Elizabeth. Understanding the dynamics that gave rise to the speech, starting with a brief history of the Commonwealth, is crucial. The first steps to the organization's founding commenced in 1911 with the summit of "the dominions within the British Empire."[9] The gathering focused on military cooperation among Australia, New Zealand, South Africa, India, Ireland, Newfoundland, and Canada. Subsequent follow-up meetings, known as the Imperial Conferences, culminated in the historic decisions of November 1926 and October 1930.[10]

In 1926, the United Kingdom and its territories approved a memorandum of understanding; otherwise, the Belfour Declaration recognized the members as "Autonomous communities within the British Empire equal in status."[11] It declared that a member should not be subordinate to another in any aspect of their domestic or external affairs, though joined "by a common allegiance to the Crown, and freely associated as members of the British Commonwealth of Nations."[12] In December 1931, the British lawmakers passed the Statute of Westminster, reiterating the terms of the Balfour Declaration, including a common fidelity to the British Crown.[13] This resolution that recognized the independence of Canada, South Africa, Australia, and New Zealand ended the UK's power to veto the dominions' legislation. This was the basis for further negotiations about British dominions' legal positions everywhere.[14]

The pertinent point is that the Cape Town speech was Whitehall's strategic response to various unfolding events marking imperialism's ending—a public launch of a future face of the royal brand as the clamor in the postwar world order demanded. Acknowledging this fact requires a more robust reevaluation of the extant studies on decolonization. The decolonization train crossed a threshold after India's independence in 1947 and subsequent Commonwealth membership as a republic without the encumbrance of allegiance to the Crown. Hitherto, membership in the old Commonwealth was exclusive to the former dominions under White settlers' control with fidelity to the sovereign. The 1949 Commonwealth prime ministers' meeting created the London Declaration that allowed "republics and other countries [to] be part of the Commonwealth."[15]

Point of No Return: Empire and the Decolonization Rhetoric

In his thought-provoking essay on "Planned Decolonization," John Flint emphatically argued that the movement originated *not as pressure* from nationalists but as "an entirely British inspiration for colonial reforms." According to Flint, when the world passed through the gore of the Second World War devoid of "the moral and physical bases of the prewar imperialism," the end became apparent to Britain.[16] Contrary to Flint, decolonization was not merely Britain's gift of "inspiration." Instead, the relationship between Britain and its African colonies in the postwar era was like a bull rider who has lost control of the animal. The evidence of documents on the end of the empire reveals that the impetus for empire dissolution came from many changes in attitude, thought, and awareness from the late 1930s. These issues, including the Cold War problems, became more intractable in the international arena after the war, thus requiring that Whitehall readjust the entire colonial ideological underpinnings with an Elizabethan Commonwealth royal brand.[17]

The catalysts of the reforms visible in the metropole and the colonies were increasing socioeconomic differences and a rapid spread of Western education. The lust for freedom engendered by the war meshed with the consequences of the practices of fascism, racism, Nazism, communism, and liberal democracy. The demands for self-determination were a promissory note from the Allied Powers that the anticolonial agitators were determined to cash soon after the war. The forces behind the agitations ensured that reneging on the wartime promise of freedom would be tumultuous. John D. Hargreaves adds that Britain's anxiety about jeopardizing its special relationship with the United States by clinging to "the residues" of its colonial holdings in Africa—particularly Nyasaland, Rhodesia, and Kenya—were flashpoints and, therefore, a cause for decolonization.[18] In fact, John Darwin makes the case more explicit in contending that British policymakers were uneasy with the "constraints" existing on the African continent compared to US and Cold War pressures.[19]

The colonial powers, especially Britain and France, misjudged the nature of the nationalist struggles and the complications of negotiating statehood, ethnicity, and patriotism under the leadership of new cadres of postwar African agents and inexperienced European colonial officials. Along this line, Flint was correct in pointing out that the social thought underlying decolonization preparation "was deeply in error as the entire edifice was based on the concept of detribalization and the assumption that a class formation was inevitably replacing colonial ethnicity in Africa."[20]

Carefully examined, the eve of the Second World War marked the point of no return to colonialism as a battery of developments converging on moral and logistic hiccups came into play. In his authoritative work, *The Turning Point in Africa: British Colonial Policy 1938–1948*, Robert Pearce examined the central theme among policymakers when the Colonial Office began to formulate and execute policies to return power to the colonized people.[21] Pearce identified 1938 to 1948 as a remarkable colonial policy shift. In this period, Britain realized the unsustainable racial and paternalist assumptions that underlined the belief in the limitless time for reforms in the colonies. By the late 1940s, it started to push for a commitment to steady social, economic, and political progress toward self-government. The political dimension of this policy of "nation building" rested on the twin pillars of modern local government structures (replacing the Native Authorities of indirect rule) and the transformation of legislative and executive councils into a central government structure on the Westminster model. The vital ingredients for realizing both goals resided in the hands "of the African intelligentsia and the ditching of the chiefs."[22]

Flint and Pearce agree that the interwar years were a watershed in British policy change. However, Whitehall's investment in Elizabeth's Commonwealth scheme and the pressure brought by the African intelligentsia were conspicuously missing from the accounts. In *Facing Mouth Kenya*, published in 1938, Kenya's nationalist Jomo Kenyatta declared that his peers had a duty to lead the continent forward.[23] The crux of the book on complete freedom from the

Figure 2.1: Hastings Banda of Malawi and Jomo Kenyatta of Kenya. (National Archives Malawi, August 2014, used under Creative Commons Attribution-Share Alike 4.0 International license)

shackles of colonial rule questioned how a group could attain a "higher level" of advancement and still be "denied the most elementary human rights of self-expression, freedom of speech, the right to form social organizations to improve their condition, and above all, the right to move freely in their own country." Kenyatta claimed that the colonizers had usurped his Gikuyu people's rights and failed to promote a higher intellectual, moral, and economic level by reducing the African "to a state of serfdom; his spirit of manhood has been killed, and he has been subjected to the most inferior position."[24]

In several letters and speeches between 1938 and 1939, Kenyatta used the Kamba rebellion and the general situation of colonial politics in Kenya to reinforce his stand on decolonization. The Kamba crisis, provoked by an ill-advised destocking policy, represents a common practice of capitalist exploitation and alien interference in indigenous people's lives. Recognizing that the ordinary people—cattle farmers—who led the uprising were disinclined to colonial politics and urban lifestyles, Robert Tignor concluded that the government's adamant policy regarding the indigenous cattle-rearing economy and polity galvanized the people to fight for their survival.[25] The conflict exposed the propaganda of overstock, a pretense on which the colonial rulers tapped the British-owned monopolist Liebig's meat canning firm to exploit Kamba's livestock produce and disrupt the traditional ways of life in which every other thing cohered.[26]

Kenyatta called for immediate colonial reforms in a speech to the Manchester Fabian Society on October 28, 1938. His commentaries prompted an exchange of letters between William Temple (the archbishop of York) and Malcolm John MacDonald (the colonial secretary) concerning possible censoring. In response to his boldness and articulation of the events, a Colonial Office agent recorded in the minutes that "Mr. Kenyatta is becoming very mischievous."[27]

Kenyatta and his cohorts in Britain continued criticizing opponents of decolonization and social change in the Colonial Office. However, some colonial officials joined ranks with the Fabian Colonial Society, the Aboriginal Protection Society, and other London-based groups in advocating for expanding colonial education and economic reforms in the African territories. The demands of these groups and individuals prompted Lord Hailey's *African Survey*.[28]

In 1939, following Hailey's report, Colonial Secretary Malcolm John MacDonald and Sir H. Grattan Bushe (the Colonial Office's legal counsel) proclaimed that the indirect rule system was obsolete. The duo admitted to the increasing numbers of the African-educated elite as rightful inheritors of the postcolonial state.[29] Sir Arthur James Dawe, the assistant undersecretary for the colonies, corroborated with a comment that based on the fast pace of change, the doctrinaire adherents of the indirect rule principle may be already living in self-denial.[30] Repeatedly, MacDonald informed the Commons Committee that African society was undergoing rapid change, with more African doctors and nurses, school teachers, agricultural officers, civil servants, lawyers, and leaders in all areas of life.[31] The general point is that a new cohort of African nationalists like Kenyatta became more prominent in the late 1930s through the 1950s. Their anticolonial advocacy gathered momentum during the Second World War, anticipating urgent and compulsory changes.

Articulating the increase of nationalist rhetoric in *Britain and Axis Aims in Africa* published in 1942, Kingsley O. Mbadiwe (aka K.O.) noted that it would be critical for Britain to launch a viable plan for colonial reforms immediately after the war.[32] Mbadiwe could have also been speaking about the war's worrisome development in Africa. For example, the situation got worse instead of improving in Kenya. In 1942, the Kamba, Kikuyu, Meru, and Embu ethnic groups swore to fight for colonial freedom. Except for Egypt, no former British colony regained its independence throughout the Second World War. Early in 1931, the Union of South Africa and its League of Nations–mandated territory,

South West Africa, effectively gained independence from Britain as part of the Statute of Westminster.[33] In 1936, the existing colonies of Italian Somaliland, Eritrea, and the newly occupied Abyssinia (Ethiopia) merged to form Italian East Africa. In 1941, Eritrea and Ethiopia came under British control after Italy was expelled from the region. In 1943, Britain added Tripolitania and Cyrenaica (Libya) to its power after imperial troops ousted the territories' Italian and German forces. In 1945, the Union of South Africa declined to yield its mandate to the United Nations. It took over South West Africa (later Namibia) as its province against Africans' loud protests led by Ethiopia and Liberia.[34]

These broader developments explained Mbadiwe's mixed bag of moderate views and selected colonial order criticisms. On the positive side, Mbadiwe expressed his appreciation of the British Empire and colonial protection in Africa. He saw no power on earth to shake the confidence of the West Africans in Great Britain—in a direct reference to the alternative of a potential Nazi world order if Hitler emerged victorious over the Allies.[35] During a later visit to Britain, Mbadiwe commented, "The history of England is the story of man's courage, adventure, fortitude, faith, and confidence. I have come to discover that, in many ways, we are similar. My country shares with your country your love for tradition, ceremonials, rich color protocol, and pageantry. The only difference is in the degree."[36] For these flattering views of imperial Britain, E. A. Ayandele, the combative Nigerian historian, saw Mbadiwe's generation of the educated elite as "deluded hybrids" and "collaborators."[37]

Ayandele's appraisal of Mbadiwe brushed aside the attack on Britain's colonial development policies. In comparing the indigenous government system with the British indirect rule system in Nigeria, Mbadiwe corroborated Kenyatta's view that the "Indirect Rule is a failure. It can never be a system of government. It trains rulers in evil practices and stirs hate among the various classes of people under its rule ... a futile system fostering corruption, divided alliance, and confusion."[38] Mbadiwe disparaged colonial policies alongside its economics of trusteeship.

In line with the nationalist rhetoric, Mbadiwe noted that Africa had been poorly portrayed on many cultural, political, and economic issues, concurring with Kenyatta and others that its contact with Europe had robbed the Africans "of their old ways of life. And nothing better has been offered to replace them."[39] He sought to rescue Africa's voice and remedy its image by projecting the continent's rich cultural heritage to America. Together with other African students in the United States, Mbadiwe founded the African Students Association in 1941 for "the crusade to publicize Africa's conditions," and articulate its aspirations for freedom.[40] The association's mouthpiece, *The African Interpreter*, was a powerful voice for Africa's freedom from colonial rule. In December 1943, Mbadiwe, with Mbonu Ojike, founded the African Academy of Arts and Research in New York. The academy broadened the sphere of the struggle for freedom and created awareness of what liberty and freedom could bring to Africa.

After the war, the African intelligentsia pressed on with their reproach of imperialism. Speaking for the Nyasaland African Affairs Congress in 1946, Hastings Banda requested that Colonial Secretary Creech Jones accept that "the time has now arrived when Africans should have direct representation in the Legislative Council." He described it as "grossly unfair" that all the council's members were Europeans.[41] Instead of responding to Banda's complaint in good faith, the Nyasaland colonial officials moved to create the context of the Central African Federation. Toward this end, it conspired to force Banda to relocate his residence to Accra, Ghana, on August 15, 1953, "so [that] Nyasaland may be spared his mischiefs."[42] In *Path to Nigerian Freedom*, published in 1947, Nigeria's Obafemi Awolowo reignited the nationalist flame by demanding rapid action toward independence.[43] Princess Elizabeth addressed her father's subjects in 1947 in this international climate.

Within British politics, the period's critical lessons were somehow lost to Prime Minister Churchill, who attempted to leverage the Allied victory to secure an electoral advantage for his Conservative Party. Churchill's wartime popularity had misled him to call for an early election in 1945. The result of the vote left no one in doubt: "Of all Churchill's colossal misjudgments, that was probably the most egregious." The voters rejected wartime austerity and prewar economic depression. Three years before the war ended, Britons had made to believe that the good days would return "in the bright dawn of victory."[44] The contrasting choices were glaring. Churchill represented the past violent world order; Clement Atlee, who defeated Churchill at the polls, was the future of peace and goodwill the British hoped for.

The Cape Town Episode

Elizabeth's insertion into the decolonization discourse was part of the general developments in the interwar years. Building on the provisions of the Statute of Westminster agreement and the politics of freedom from colonial rule, the Cape Town speech of 1947 offered the liberals among the British policymakers an auspicious opportunity to redefine the goals and directions of the Commonwealth in light of the widening scope of new sovereign states emerging in Asia and Africa. Cape Town was Elizabeth's matriculation into imperial politics and the public testing of the dynamic instrumentation of all the Royal Branding Mix—royal, regal, relevant, responsive, and respected. In Africa in 1947, the scheduled independence of India (August 14, 1947), Pakistan (August 15, 1947), Burma (January 4, 1948), and Ceylon (February 4, 1948) saturated the air with the kind of anticipation that heralds the arrival of a new moon in a festive month. Britain was aware that with the political developments in South Asia, the spasms of decolonization would soon run rampant in the Black people's continent. It was judicious that Whitehall was planning in the reality of the time, explicitly positioning the Commonwealth as a successor to the empire.[45] The grand idea was to leverage the international forum to address the urgent economic and postwar sociopolitical problems within the UK and its dominions.

More than in any other region of the world, African decolonization politics presented the most significant challenges. In principle, the succeeding prime ministers of Britain, from Neville Chamberlain (1937–1940) to Clement Richard Atlee (1945–1951), brought pressure to bear on the Foreign Office to discreetly prepare ahead for the decolonization movement. Atlee increasingly embraced "the need for consultation on the spot by Ministers," although he was nostalgic as Churchill not to bear the toga of the British prime minister who dissolved the British Empire.[46] Unlike the Asian territories, the British settler colonies of South Africa, Northern and Southern Rhodesia, and Kenya harbored many Europeans who had sworn to resist the African quest for self-determination.[47] Because of the abysmal race relations in these territories, the indigenous people were anxious to jettison the cloak of second-class citizens the colonizers threw on them.

Unfortunately, the political situation in Southern Africa would be further troubled by crisis despite Whitehall's efforts to improve things with the royal visit of 1947. Prime Minister Jan Christian Smuts' designs and intents for inviting the King were visible and, in some ways, paralleled the King's personal and political motives for the African tour. The British Establishment conceived royal tours in the postwar period to promote imperial relations and recapture relevance in the postwar order. The King wanted to personally thank the empire's subjects and the Commonwealth for their loyalty and support during the war.[48] Equally important was the continued economic support from the colonies and dominions as Britain wrestled with postwar austerity. To demonstrate appreciation for the Union's wartime role and perhaps stave off republican ambitions in South Africa, the King paid tribute to those South African service members and veterans.[49]

On his part, the South African prime minister, General Smuts, planned to leverage the royal visit for electoral victory and strengthen ties with Britain. But the urgent questions of the period were not about colonial notions of royalty and personal political puffery. Instead, the national and international concerns were about gross human rights abuse, racial segregation, and the Union's seizure of South West Africa (Namibia).[50] On each of these issues, British authorities demonstrated conflicting views. Philip Murphy is apt in noting that in the broader context of Central African affairs in the 1950s, the Commonwealth Relations Office (CRO), which also coordinated Britain–South Africa relations, exhibited an evident "sympathy for the concerns of European settlers." However, the Colonial Office was more sensitive toward African political hopes. By implication, the opposing camps defended incompatible policies, especially what loyalty to the Crown portended for the colonial territories in the postwar period.[51]

It is striking that *The Economist* of May 10, 1947, weighed in on the meaning of the royal visit in the framework of dominion in disunity, concluding that the Union of South Africa was in apparent conflict. It observed that even in regular times, the leaders, "for no common purpose animates the three major racial divisions—Africans, Europeans, and Indians. But the blow to its prestige administered by the United Nations had accentuated and increased its internal dissensions."[52] The paper cautioned that the celebratory tour could produce the wrong signal in light of the region's emerging political trajectories.

To worsen issues, the United Nations failed to address South Africa's presence in South West Africa since 1915 or support civil rights agitation by Indians. Instead, the UN silence corroborated the British Establishment's attitude, described by Miss White as "just a new measure of appeasement to white settlers."[53] On February 21, 1947, *The Passive Resister*, the mouthpiece of the Indian National Congress of Natal Province, called for a boycott of the royal tour because of what the Asian community perceived as the practice of racial discrimination with impunity in South Africa.[54] A week later, the newspaper announced that all Indians would boycott the royal visit; it declared that any Indian who participated was not a true Indian.[55]

Putting all these together, it was predicted that the nationalists' projected success in the 1948 elections would truncate the tour's royal charm and circumstance. Indeed, the election's outcome ushered in a system of apartheid—

state-sanctioned segregation and discrimination—that diminished South Africa's international stature.[56]

Contrary to the outcome of events, Smuts calculated that strong ties between Britain and South Africa would strengthen or even reinvent South African national identity. In other words, entangled with the positive sides of the royal visit were the racial ideology of the time and the politics it accentuated. In the British idiom, royalty resonated with the minority English-speaking tribe of South Africa, but it held different meanings for the Dutch Boers, indigenous Africans, and Indians. *The Passive Resister* underscored this point by stating, "As far as the oppressed peoples of the Union are concerned, the visit of Their Majesties has made no difference to their plight. They have to continue with the struggle against the policy of racial oppression."[57]

Thus, navigating the murky politics of race, resource extraction, and African freedom in the settler territories and other parts of the empire posed a severe challenge in the postwar era. On March 7, 1947, Mary A. B. Atlee, sister to the British prime minister, congratulated the Student Labour Federation on organizing a student petition to the King, drawing attention to racial discrimination in South Africa.[58] The letter, signed by five hundred students from fifty-three universities and colleges in the British Isles, was presented at Buckingham Palace on Friday, April 4, 1947, for onward dispatch to King George VI in South Africa.[59]

Mindful of the political realities of the time, Britain's Labour Government under Prime Minister Atlee was privy to the Cape Town discourse. The speech's implicit philosophical ideas represented the Atlee government's official strategy to calm the frayed nerves the war caused across the globe. Elizabeth was not in South Africa for her birthday fêtes per se. As the Igbos of southeastern Nigeria often say on occasions of emergency, "When something greater than the farm threatens, the farmer foregoes the harvest."[60] Britain's national or corporate interest was an urgent priority over any individual or partisan interests in the immediate postwar era. Princess Elizabeth acknowledged the obvious with the exhortation, "We must not be daunted by the anxieties and hardships that the war has left behind."[61]

Soon after he came to power, Prime Minister Atlee saw a pressing need to conduct his government's internal and external affairs to align voters' aspirations. He inserted Elizabeth's face over colonialism's ugly records, worsened by the global conflict that claimed 75 million lives. As Sarah Gertrude Millin wrote in *The Spectator* in 1947, the royal tour "sweetened" South Africa's atmosphere. The royals "were modest, lovable, so anxious to please, so eagerly pleased."[62] In other words, the birthday announcement in South Africa unveiled a new royal brand—Atlee's parody, a forewarning for the painful demise of Britain's African Empire. The most significant paradox of the time was the prime minister's ascension, the introverted son of Henry Atlee, a city lawyer. The hawkish Churchill described Atlee as a "sheep in a sheep's clothing" and "a modest man who has a lot to be modest about" but loathed his successor's inclination to global peace.[63]

With a better understanding of the political context of the 1947 royal African tour, it is now appropriate to turn to the substance of Elizabeth's speech in Cape Town. Deciphering the proclamation as a discourse analysis is crucial to understanding Britain's decolonization plan and Elizabeth's future role as the Commonwealth's leader.

Discourse Analysis and the Cape Town Speech

Discourse scholarship, with roots in European studies in the 1980s, denotes an approach to interpreting the implicit meanings of vocal, written, or semiotic expressions, including sign language and kinetic communication. The object of interpretation is to decode what Samuel Obeng calls "voice-prints" in conversational interactions.[64] Conversational analytics interrogates the idioms of a communicative performance or event and, thus, provides whole meaning and coherence beyond the semantics of speech, sentences, relations of power, and intentions. Discourse analysis has been vital in studying history, politics, linguistics, and literature as a procedural and analytical tool to decipher meaning and reasoning frames.

Elizabeth started her Cape Town address, purportedly written by Dermot Morrah, *The Times* of London journalist, by thanking her numerous well-wishers worldwide.[65] While she acknowledged that the occasion was supposed to be a happy day in ideal circumstances, Elizabeth quickly admitted that she had a cumbersome task ahead: "This is a happy day for me, but it is also one that brings serious thoughts, thoughts of life looming ahead with all its challenges and with all its opportunity."[66] To be sure, the consequential considerations of the time were apparent. Although the Allied Powers were victorious, the British Empire had lost the peace when the war plunged its grip on the extensive global imperial holdings in jeopardy. The concepts of nationalism, democracy, liberalism, human rights, self-determination, feminism, and socialism permeated the colonies like a plague. Historians know that ideas are like bullets; they travel fast and far once fired. Undeniably, "challenges" and "opportunities" were the defining attributes of decolonization in the postwar era. The transition from imperial control to African freedom posed a world of unpredictability. However, gracious and intelligent management of the process promised unlimited opportunities for the colonizer and the colonized.

Jan Blommaert and Chris Bulcaen have argued that "discourse is socially constitutive as well as socially conditioned."[67] Before Cape Town, if anyone had doubted Elizabeth's suitability for the throne, her (or rather the speechwriter's) intelligent articulation of the global events and prediction of the way forward left few in doubt that there could not be a better future Commonwealth leader. The vision enunciated in the speech, which ranks at the same level as Dr. Martin Luther King Jr.'s "I Have a Dream" dialogue, was deliberate, humbling, and inspiring. Letters from Sir Alan Lascelles, the former courtier to King George VI, support this assertion. Lascelles, who later served Queen Elizabeth II, noted, "For a child of her years, she has got an astonishing solicitude for other people's comfort; such unselfishness is not a normal characteristic in that family."[68] However, one must be cautious about the speech, considering her age, inexperience, and the hidden agenda of the powers that be.

Deploying discourse as an analytical tool means conducting a forensic investigation of grammatical structure and vocabulary, speech acts, prosody, coherence, and intertextuality. These four discourse elements "link a text to its context."[69] In Elizabeth's case, the central focus was on the UK's future as an imperial power and the aftermath of the empire's end. "As I speak to you today from Cape Town, I am six thousand miles from the country where I was born. But I am certainly not six thousand miles from home. Everywhere I have travelled in these lovely lands of South Africa and Rhodesia, my parents, my sister, and I have been taken to the heart of their people and made to feel that we are just as much at home here as if we had lived among them all our lives."[70]

With those eloquent words describing the Africans' hospitality toward the royals, the princess made a compelling case for a universal family of races bound by a shared historical experience. The racial and political realities of South Africa made the request more urgent, meaningful, and coherent. For a world emerging from the dark cloud of fascism in Italy and Nazism in Germany, Elizabeth's appeal to the richness of a hybrid of peoples and cultures resonated with many around the world, especially in South Africa and the US where Black bashing persisted as part of the national culture.

About South Africa in particular, *The Economist* noted that before the royal ship, HMS *Vanguard*, had even departed its base in Portsmouth, the oppressive minority government in South Africa "had been arraigned at the bar of the Nations and publicly reprimanded for its policy towards its colored population." This report corroborated a meeting at the Grand Parade in Cape Town in late February, attended by over four thousand. The officials emerged from the conference with a resolution demanding the government implement the UN's decision.[71] The writer reminded the world that King George VI was visiting not only an ancient foe but "also a country whose people had been made angry and resentful, hurt and conscience-stricken, or even openly triumphant—according to their several outlooks."[72] For the political minorities, triumphalism was an expectation of change from the albatross of White domination. For the White supremacists, triumphalism was continuing racial privileges. In fact, Jan Smuts was unapologetic in decrying the possibility of equality: "If there was no discrimination in the world, where would we be? There must be discrimination; you cannot run amok with a word like equality."[73]

The princess called for racial tolerance within the dialectics of privilege and oppression. The imperatives of open-mindedness became more critical in the awareness that Britain had played a central role in planting multiculturalism within its extensive dominions. Unsurprisingly, King George VI echoed a similar sentiment in his October 21, 1947, speech to the House of Lords. "The present obstacles to cooperation and understanding between the peoples of the world have strengthened the determination of My Government to support the United Nations and to seek by that means to promote the mutual trust and tolerance on which peaceful progress depends."[74]

Further scrutiny of Elizabeth's speech reveals the intersectionality of language and liberty. Obeng's theory of language and freedom unearths the connection between linguistics/language philosophy, law, and politics. Taking cues from Isaiah Berlin's works on freedom,[75] Obeng contends that liberty is a philosophical, legal, and political concept, and language expresses freedom and its associated ideas.[76] In this context, it was good news for the colonized world that Elizabeth, the Crown's future inheritor, was not looking to the horrid past. Yet, instead of appreciating the emphasis on liberty, Smuts's mind was stuck in the dark alleys of domination and perilous military rivalry. Smuts came across as a train driver heading backward at high speed—that is, in his reckless and barefaced decision not to allow the royals to decorate the deserving African veterans.[77]

Aware of Smuts's racialist designs, Elizabeth categorically voiced her predisposition toward a future of multiculturalism and cooperation appropriated with friendship, peace, and respect among nations, races, and peoples. She articulated these ideals in familial terms: "That is the great privilege belonging to our place in the worldwide Commonwealth—that there are homes ready to welcome us in every continent of the earth. Before I am much older, I hope I shall come to know many of them."[78] Here, the princess implied that she knew little about Africa before the visit. However, as we have seen with college students' study abroad courses in contemporary times, spending six weeks in a foreign land can teach a visitor a lot.

For Elizabeth, the 1947 royal tour was a compelling education on Africa. She did not see Trevor-Roper's armchair imagination of a continent that was nothing more than "darkness" and "the meaningless gyrations of barbarous tribes in picturesque."[79] Instead, the princess witnessed firsthand a people ravaged by colonial racism and knew instantly that this was indefensible. Notes in the private diaries of Alan Lascelles, the King's counselor, recorded that the royals felt intense sadness about the race problem of South Africa.[80] In a moving tribute to his father in 1952, Elizabeth portrayed King George VI as a "symbol of steadfastness." She continued to say that the King "never wavered in his faith that with God's help, the cause of freedom would prevail. The friendliness and simplicity which so endeared him to his peoples during the trials of war were the fruit of a life-long interest in his fellow-men and of a human sympathy."[81]

Ben Pimlott has argued that Elizabeth's contact with South Africans was a compelling formative experience that led her to develop a particular interest in the region's affairs. And she remained sympathetic to the South Africans' cause even when the political climate was challenging. The common assumption is that the Queen's "disapproval of Margaret Thatcher's stance on sanctions against South Africa in the 1980s, for example, confirmed the idea that the monarch, as head of the Commonwealth, stood apart from mere governments on such questions."[82] In her speech, the princess also promised to visit the continent often to learn more about the people, their needs, and their aspirations.[83] She kept that promise to the letter.

Another import of the Cape Town speech was Elizabeth's decision to speak for the new generation—the global youth—especially those from the Southern Hemisphere. Indeed, the world could not have found an ideal advocate for freedom had the British Establishment granted her the right to free speech and free will. The emergent postwar/postcolonial generations of Africans were not the same as their enslaved, colonized, and exploited ancestors. The older generation suffered immense emotional, physical, and material traumas at the self-important Europeans' hands. In 1952, Elizabeth disclosed that she learned from her father his "great affection" and "understanding of young people, which led him, soon after the First World War, to start the camps for boys from all walks of life."[84] Thus, Elizabeth's speech demonstrated a clear sense of place and time.

After the Second World War, Africa was poised for a world rescued from colonialism's shackles. While the legendary Queen Victoria was the warrior queen and colonialist extraordinary, Elizabeth, as the Cape Town speech demonstrates, wanted to be the agent of peace and freedom. In this context, the *Belfast Telegraph* of June 1967 called Elizabeth the "Queen of Independence."[85] The postwar period's African youth reminds us of today's African youth—their fledging desire for freedom remains sacrosanct.

Perceptively, Elizabeth spoke to the emerging African nationalists' feelings and causes. "Although there is none of my father's subjects from the oldest to the youngest whom I do not wish to greet, I am thinking especially today of all the young men and women who were born about the same time as myself and have grown up like me in terrible and glorious years of the Second World War."[86] The juxtaposition of "terrible" with "glorious" in the description of the war was deliberate. It represented Elizabeth's sensitivity and consciousness about the diverse audience and the struggle between conservatism and liberalism in the transition period that must lapse for future change to materialize. Of course, the princess knew nothing was glorious about the war, but veterans of the Allied Forces were listening—therefore, she did not want to come across as condemnatory—a position that would have caused some damage to the royal brand.

The closing part of the Cape Town dialogue was more significant than the rest. The princess's polite and personal demeanor sharply contrasted with the colonial officers' violent and murderous conduct. Elizabeth sought the permission of the young and colonized Africans to speak as their representative henceforth: "Will you, the youth of the British family of nations, let me speak on my birthday as your representative? Now that we are coming to manhood and womanhood, it is surely a great joy to us all to think that we shall be able to take some of the burdens off the shoulders of our elders who have fought and worked and suffered to protect our childhood."[87] In simple terms, the princess acknowledged the sacrifice made by Churchill's generation and, at the same time, asked them to yield authority and future leadership.

Still, the deliberate interjection of gender (manhood and womanhood) and antitheses of old and young, privilege and deprivation, mirror what Norman Fairclough and others have identified as "discourse-as-social-practice." The opposites of concepts represent hegemonic processes and counterhegemonic trends engendered by centuries of colonial violence and oppression. In the context of Elizabeth's speech, Fairclough's work allows us to understand hegemony as concerning "power that is achieved through constructing alliances and integrating classes and groups through consent so that the articulation and articulation of orders of discourse is correspondently one stake in the hegemonic struggle."[88]

The question arises as to how the Africans received the Cape Town speech. Based on their needs, the emergent African nationalists welcomed the princess as a partner and, concerning her request, to serve as their spokesperson. However, a more revealing response came on the heels of communication by King George VI in May 1947, soon after returning to London. In the London Guild Hall speech, the King said that "the mass of the African people have gained and are gaining immeasurably in health, happiness, and prosperity by their context with white civilization and well assured."[89] *The Passive Resister*, a popular mouthpiece of the antiapartheid movement, angrily pounced on the statement, questioning who it was that assured King George VI that all was well for them. The newspaper concluded that if it was General Smuts who volunteered the "assurance," then "it was hardly necessary for him [the King] to have visited the Union."[90]

The context of the local newspaper's reaction captures the educated Africans' high hopes of Her Majesty in the 1950s and 1960s. The Africans expected the Queen to depart from the past policies of appeasement to the White minority elite in Africa and lend voices to future events like the Mau Mau and Suez Canal crises. The Africans wanted Elizabeth to denounce apartheid in Southern Africa (including the Nyasaland Emergency) and, later, the exile of Kabaka Mutesa II of Uganda and the Nigerian-Biafra crisis in Nigeria. For the African youth, implicit in Elizabeth's gesture to speak on their behalf was the expectation that the princess had voluntarily assumed a role as the chief advocate of decolonization and freedom. However, there were layers of ambiguity in both the speech and its ending.

In addressing the postwar generation, Elizabeth did not elaborate on the strategies to assume some of the burdens of transition from her British elders' shoulders. It is crucial to note that as the British Establishment proxy, it was beyond her power to explain the speed and method of action toward decolonization or an agenda to collaborate with the African nationalists toward that purpose. For the African nationalists, nothing short of an immediate end to racial oppression and political autonomy would be enough. More important, there was a miscommunication in Elizabeth's political power in the postwar era. Was the princess prepared to work in the spirit of urgency requested by the Africans or the slower approach to decolonization desired by the conservative elements at Whitehall?

It is conspicuous that while the Cape Town discourse implied it, there was no explicit mention of the word "freedom" throughout the speech—whether a slip of the pen or a measured oversight is open to speculation. Considering that Elizabeth spoke to the global audience about the future of "our imperial family," an educated guess is that it was deliberate. In 1947, there was no immediate indication that King George VI would soon die and leave the throne for his daughter. In other words, the question of immediate freedom from colonialism was neither in Elizabeth's view nor power. In 1945, Churchill declared before Parliament that "the Atlantic Charter is a guide and not a rule," adding, "We mean to hold our own," in a clear rejection of President Roosevelt's position.[91] Thus, Elizabeth's omission or silence on the word "freedom" soon caught the attention of the growing ranks of African nationalists across the continent. The coming decade and a half, when most parts of Africa started regaining political freedom, tested the true promises of the Cape Town speech or lack thereof.

Three significant developments in South Africa, the Rhodesias, and Kenya tested the weight of Elizabeth's pledge to serve as the chief advocate of African freedom. How would she respond to the imperial powers' attempts to entrench instead of retreat from Africa? Could she speak or act without due consultation with the pro-imperial actors in the British government?

The 1947–1952 Interval

The five-year interval between Elizabeth's speech in 1947 and her ascension in 1952 was painful because several unfolding events on the continent showed that the ideals she envisaged were heading in the opposite direction. It is vital to emphasize that as a self-appointed advocate for oppressed peoples, Princess Elizabeth was yet to assume a position of authority or influence over Britain's African policies. As long as King George VI held the Crown, Elizabeth was merely expressing her wishes as a future monarch. In other words, she had no direct voice in Britain's political affairs and overseas territories.

At the time of her Cape Town speech, Egypt remained the only independent nation among the British African colonies. While the drum of freedom got louder, Britain moved slowly toward implementing reforms and even tried to delay decolonization by sending conflicting signals in some areas. The apparent rationale for the delay was the dire economic problems the war created in Europe. The conflict left the European economies in shatters and the various governments in a state of desperation. *The Passive Resister* alluded to the conundrum of exploitation and the promise of freedom in May 1947, observing that the African continent has immense and untapped wealth with vast deposits of rich minerals, including uranium. Exploiting this mineral might restore the British pound to its historical position as an arbiter of world destinies.[92]

Indeed, Britain considered African resources vital in rebuilding the postwar economy. A speech by King George VI in the House of Lords on October 21, 1947, captured the imperative of delaying decolonization: "My Government will continue to devote their earnest attention to securing from overseas the essential foodstuffs and raw materials for My people. They will do all in their power to find new sources of supply, and they will seek to enter into further long-term agreements with overseas countries. A measure will be laid before you designed to promote the expansion of production of all kinds within the Empire."[93]

Thus, Europe's weak economies severely threatened Africa's freedom in the postwar era. This problem engendered a political crisis in several colonies and continued for a long time. In South Africa, the 1948 elections that brought the Afrikaner Nationalist Party into government set a dangerous trend in the opposite direction of the freedom and equality Elizabeth had emphasized in Cape Town. The May 1948 election results proved that self-serving political calculation was daring and counterproductive in such a restive global climate. As Churchill found out in Britain's postwar polls, Smuts's ploy to play the race card by pandering to Britain's close relationship was causal to his defeat in the elections. The United Party's loss to Daniël François Malan's Afrikaner Nationalists Party took the segregation train to a new height, as apartheid was part of the party's election promise. It ushered in the long, dark years of racial oppression and its convoluted notion of social order. Instead of seeking a rapid change from segregationist policies to an evolution of an "imperial family" where all peoples would live as equals, South Africa reinforced its bigoted socioeconomic and political ideology. The apartheid system ran amok against the country's Black and Colored communities.

In the British protectorate of Northern Rhodesia (Zambia) and self-governing Southern Rhodesia (Zimbabwe), an ill-advised British policy created the Central African Federation. The Union, established in August 1953, comprised the Rhodesias and Nyasaland (Malawi) under White settlers' control, with the governor-general as Her Majesty's representative.[94] While this was a vexing outcome for the Africans, the African Affairs Board's creation appeared optimistic. The board, established on August 1, 1953, assumed the responsibility for protecting Africans' rights. In response, Nyasaland traditional chiefs sent a delegation with a petition signed by 120 chiefs to Queen Elizabeth II directly because the British Conservative government rejected their petition, which argued that the federation violated the terms of the 1890s treaties signed during the European scramble for Africa.

The episode is a unique case in which the African rulers, who arrived in London in January 1954 (assisted by Dr. Hasting K. Banda, a Nyasaland native and representative of the African National Congress), erroneously believed that the Queen's power superseded the elected British government. But the conservative government of Prime Minister Churchill and Secretary of State to the Colonies Oliver Lyttelton frustrated the delegation's mission. As Geoffrey Traugh aptly notes, the chiefs supposed that the Queen would understand their petition as a plea from one traditional ruler to another. But they were sent home without an audience with the Queen because the British lawmakers wanted it, but Elizabeth took the blame.[95]

The Federation of Rhodesia and Nyasaland survived for a decade. Malawi and Northern Rhodesia, which became Zambia after independence on October 24, 1964, remained protectorates against the status of Southern Rhodesia as a self-governing entity. With the world rejecting colonialism in the 1950s, African nationalists pressured Britain to decolonize. Eventually, on December 31, 1963, the federation's dissolution paved the way for Northern Rhodesia and Nyasaland to become independent in 1964 as Zambia and Malawi. In 1965, the minority White elite in Southern Rhodesia unilaterally separated from British control and declared Rhodesia a sovereign state under White rule.

In Kenya, the old problems associated with colonial capitalist exploitation persisted. The Kikuyu, a handful of Kamba, and their allies took to armed resistance against colonial exploitation under the banner "Kenyan Land and Freedom Army," also known as Mau Mau. The colonial authorities placed Kenya under an emergency from October 1952 to December 1959. In December 1953, fifty-six men accused of killing Chief Luka (a loyalist) and his family were found not guilty. Instead of admitting that lack of evidence led to the exoneration of those on trial, Judge Clive Salter, who presided over the Special Emergency Assize Courts, turned the not guilty verdict into a moment of imperial jingoism. The judge told those on trial, "They will well be advised to remember for the rest of their lives that they owe their acquittal in this case to the standards of justice which our Lady the Queen commands shall be preserved throughout her Realms."[96]

Considering that the Lari murders (one of the several occasions in which the freedom fighters killed their African opponents) happened soon after Elizabeth's coronation, it would have been judicious for the colonial officials to leave Her Majesty out of the controversial court trials of December 1953. The same court sitting a few days before had pronounced a guilty verdict against

Figure 2.2: Kenya African Riffles hunting the Mau Mau Rebels. (The Imperial War Museum, collection no. 4905-03, public domain)

twenty-seven defendants, but Judge Salter was furious that there was insufficient evidence to condemn all fifty-six men under custody to death.[97]

Early in October 1953, Jomo Kenyatta, blamed by the British for the uprising, was arrested and handed a seven-year sentence despite his limited role in the rebellion. Dedan Kimanthi, the senior military and spiritual leader of the movement, was arrested in 1956 and hanged. Hundreds of other fighters lost their lives, and the lucky were bundled into detention camps. Petitions from Mau Mau detainees at Embakasi, Manyani, routinely called attention to unabating acts of cruelty at the prisons. One of the complaints, dated April 6, 1957, included a vivid picture of torture, starvation, and jamming wooden objects into the prisoners' anus. The petition enjoined the governor to send officers who understood "the Queen's Government Laws."[98] This outcome underlines an unintended negative consequence of the Elizabethan decolonization game plan. Other related complaints of January and March 1957 addressed to the governor had questions about the camp's commandant's nationality. The victims described the security men's actions as "completely out of orders and laws of Queen Elizabeth the II."⁹⁹ This depiction indicates the Africans' belief that their oppression or freedom rested in Her Majesty's hands. The beating to death of eleven Mau Mau detainees at the Hola camp in Kenya in February 1959 reinforced the belief that African lives did not matter and that Her Majesty's Government could care less about justice and freedom.¹⁰⁰ At the end of the rebellion, however, more Africans gained the right to participate in the political process as part of the program toward Kenya's independence in December 1963.

The death of Ndungu wa Gacheru (the coordinator of the May 1954 Mau Mau attack on the Treetops hotel where the royals lodged in 1952) in June 2013, provided an occasion for the Kenyans to revisit the uprising. Ex-Mau Mau officer Theuri Njugi Kimbo recalled that most of them "were frustrated with landlessness in the African reserves, and only our parents were paid wages for working in the European farms. We were idle, nursing pent-up anger while the colonialists seemed not to care about radical reforms."¹⁰¹

In the end, Elizabeth's Cape Town speech did not immediately move the pendulum of decolonization. Still, it set the agenda for the Commonwealth of Nations under her leadership and allows scholars to underline the dubious interjection of "Her Majesty's Government" on policy decisions scripted by Whitehall. However, the implicit values announced during the Cape Town speech were inspiring and provided hope for African nationalists. In the 1940s and 1950s, the Africans in British colonies were, for the first time, allowed into the Legislative Council based on representation.¹⁰² After her ascension, floods of risky political situations exacerbated by growing demands confronted the Queen as decolonization gathered traction across the continent. The slow pace of reforms created tensions between the educated elite and the colonial officials. This tendency worsened during the Cold War and caused severe anxiety among the colonial powers and the United States. The communists were fishing in troubled waters in Africa, and the Americans were restless about it. How did Queen Elizabeth respond to the urgent politics of African freedom during the Cold War? And how did the British Establishment and other royal stakeholders prepare the young Queen to react to the politics of the East-West ideological rivalry in the context of decolonization?

CHAPTER 3

THE COLD WAR: AFRICAN "RADICALS" AND HER ROYAL STATELINESS, 1953-1961

> The wind of change is blowing throughout the continent of Africa; whether we like it or not, the growth of national consciousness is a political fact.[1]
>
> —Harold Macmillan, 1960

> Danger is part of the job. If I were to cancel now, Nkrumah might invite Khrushchev, and they wouldn't like that, would they?[2]
>
> —Queen Elizabeth II, 1961

One of the most significant adversaries the Western world faced in the postwar era was the communist ideology threatening Western lifestyles. Arthur Schlesinger Jr. categorized the East-West duel as a "mortal antagonism between two rigidly hostile blocs."[3] The rivalry, marked by the arms race, propaganda, alliance making, proxy wars, censorship, petty bickering, covert missions, and fanaticism, attained its most poisonous height between 1953 and 1963 when obsessive ideologues led the three principal combatants: the United States, Union of Soviet Socialist Republics (USSR), and United Kingdom.

From 1953 to 1964, the USSR's Nikita S. Khrushchev accelerated the arms race by threatening to "bury" the United States and its allies.[4] Dwight D. Eisenhower, whose doctrine was to destroy the Soviet threat at all costs, was the United States' president from 1953 to 1961.[5] His successor, John F. Kennedy (r. 1961–1963), authorized the disastrous CIA-led Cuban insurgency (aka the Bay of Pigs) against Fidel Castro. In the UK, the combative Sir Winston

Churchill, who used the "Iron Curtain" analogy to describe Soviet aggression, spearheaded the Allies' diplomatic front against the Soviets before returning to power in 1951. On March 5, 1946, at Westminster College in Fulton, Missouri, Churchill invoked the phrase after Nazi propagandist-in-chief Joseph Goebbels to describe the emergent world order.[6] He harshly condemned the way of life the Soviets propagated, claiming that "an iron curtain has descended across the [European] continent."[7]

The focus period is highly relevant because it coincided with the New Elizabethan Monarchy's first decade. Ascending the throne in 1952, the Crown was under Prime Minister Churchill's direct political tutelage, with all that portends. The postwar superpower rivalry affected Africa's self-determination struggle and the postwar Commonwealth goals. Three critical questions are pertinent to comprehend Elizabeth's actions and inactions: What political decisions were in the Crown's control within the British government structure and Cold War interests? What were the constraints of the Cold War in consonance with her Cape Town promise of advancing freedom for the colonized people? How do we know?

To proceed, it is critical to reinstate that under the British constitution, the colonial territories' administration was hypothetically under the Crown. She must sign off every major decision or policy executed by the Colonial Office, which oversaw all the empire's affairs in cooperation with the Commonwealth Relations Office. In other words, the Colonial Office apprised Elizabeth of all Parliamentary resolutions related to decolonization. However, her consent was a formality in a system where the House of Commons exercised control over domestic and foreign affairs. That formality was even more consequential in a system where overzealous colonial officials often overstepped their authority's bounds by pursuing policies contrary to London's official position. Elizabeth, whom the elected politicians expected to eschew partisanship within this complex decision-making milieu, often was a mere rubber stamp for high-stakes political decisions.

Other constraints beyond national politics and wayward colonial servants' antics impinged on the Queen's duties. The US Cold War foreign policy interests greatly affected Britain's postwar foreign policy, mainly in its African colonies. The UK emerged from the war owing the United States a considerable debt.[8] Besides playing a pivotal role in the Allied victory, the United States' $4.34 billion ($27 billion today) loan pulled the United Kingdom out of a recession cloud that enveloped the economy after the war.[9] The situation was so dire that MP Oliver Stanley of Bristol West described it as the victory price: "Strange as it may seem, we are sitting here today as the representatives of a victorious people, discussing the economic consequences of victory."[10]

The point is that while the American overtures brought the two countries into a rock-solid friendship, the expectations of shared strategic interests between the allies truncated everything else, even when such collaborations became inconvenient for either side. A good example was the Anglo-Egyptian relationship that led to the Suez Canal Crisis in the 1950s. Peter Hennessy correctly observed that Prime Minister Churchill was the most forceful imperial preservationist in the postwar period. He was driving Britain's geopolitical position, and the thought of "disposing of parts of the British Empire, not even the base in the Suez Canal Zone" was far from his sight.[11] When America disagreed with the UK on Egypt, Churchill wrote Eisenhower, "If at the present time, the United States indicated divergence from us in spite of the measure of the agreement we had reached after making so many concessions, we should not think we had been treated fairly by our great ally."[12]

America's encroachment into Britain's foreign policy affected Elizabeth's postwar African and Commonwealth affairs because she had to play along with Britain's US policy, which sometimes conflicted with the Commonwealth's prerogatives, especially promoting reciprocal socioeconomic and political exchanges.[13] With the Cold War intensifying in the 1950s, when decolonization was in top gear, US curiosity in Africa rose to an unprecedented level. This sudden shift in attention had nothing to do with America's intent to engage with the new postcolonial state in reciprocated cultural, political, security, and economic exchanges. Instead, US strategic goals articulated in terms of a zero-sum game were the driving motive. The Americans interpreted their foreign policy gains as Soviet Russia's setbacks and vice versa. Political leaders in Washington, DC, calculated this prerogative as anything necessary to curb the USSR's growing presence in Africa.

Queen Elizabeth II's young age and bond with Churchill presented another layer of limitation to her exercise of liberal political free will.[14] Understanding this relationship's nuances is crucial to appreciating its impact on the Sovereign's engagement with Africa. Churchill, a die-hard royalist, had uncommon respect for Elizabeth. When she was two, he had foreseen Elizabeth's future leadership skills at Balmoral Castle. The elder statesman remarked that she "has an air of authority and reflectiveness astonishing in an infant."[15] Like other Britons, Elizabeth had grown up crediting Churchill with saving Britain from "Hitler and his mighty German military machine."[16]

The wartime leader, whom the Queen knighted in 1953, was not just an influencer of his era; he was to the Western bloc what Khrushchev was to the Eastern bloc during the Cold War. After his first prime minister stint ended in 1945, Churchill's second tenure started when the sitting prime minister, Clement Atlee, lost power in a snap election on October 25, 1951.[17] Less than four months later, Elizabeth ascended the throne at age twenty-five. This twist of fate saw Churchill serving as the Crown's political foster father.[18]

Raised to respect her elders and patriarchal authority, it was difficult for Elizabeth to question Churchill's belligerent political antics, even when in conflict with her beliefs. To the Queen, Churchill became an adopted father, a tribal elder, a trusted family friend, and a supporter. Churchill extolled her in his address to the Commonwealth Parliamentary Association (CPA) a few days before Elizabeth's coronation in 1953: "Here today we salute fifty or sixty Parliaments and one Crown. It is natural for Parliaments to talk and for the Crown to shine. The oldest here will confirm that we are never likely run short of Members and Ministers who can talk. And the youngest are sure they will never see the Crown sparkle more gloriously than these joyous days."[19] Churchill then reminded the nation about the weight of duty Elizabeth would shoulder in the postwar era: "Well do we realize the burdens imposed by sacred duty upon the Sovereign and her family. All round, we see the proofs of the unifying sentiment which makes the Crown the central link In all our modern changing life, and the one which above all others claims our allegiance to the death."[20] These were not mere words of flattery; it was an overt reminder to the nation of why the stakeholders had chosen Elizabeth and of the collective expectations of her to live up to the sacred duties of her reign and the brand she represented.

Churchill continued his new monarch's great branding promotion at Elizabeth's coronation on June 2, 1953. In coded terms, he reiterated the royal and regal image of the Crown's brand:

> Let it not be thought that the age of chivalry belongs to the past. Here at the summit of our worldwide community is a lady whom we respect because she is our Queen and whom we love because she is herself. "Gracious" and "noble" are words familiar to us all in courtly phrasing. To-night they have a new ring in them because we know they are true about the gleaming figure whom Providence has brought to us and brought to us in times where the present is hard and the future veiled.[21]

By the time a declining health condition forced Churchill aside from politics on April 5, 1955, he had schooled the Queen through the British constitution and the Crown's interaction with the people (the brand community), the cabinet, and the Parliament (the brand stakeholders). Churchill also gave her a look into international politics and diplomacy, including anticommunist consciousness.[22] Elizabeth's biographer, Nicholas Davis, underlined that Churchill drilled Elizabeth on responding to happenings worldwide as "her teacher and professor, her guide and mentor, educating her in the ways of the world."[23]

Churchill shaped Elizabeth's unalloyed commitment to British and Western interests, which left her more resolved to defend Britain if need be with her life. She reinforced this avowal explicitly during her coronation oath: "The things which I have here before promised, I will perform and keep. So help me God."[24] At the same time, the Queen reminded the world that she looked forward to service that would adapt to the future: "My coronation is not the symbol of power and a splendor that are gone, but a declaration of our hopes for the future."[25] This line resonates with her promise in Cape Town to serve the imperial family as a future spokesperson.[26] It was also consistent with her pledge in 1952 after King George VI passed: "I shall always work as my father did throughout his reign, to advance the happiness and prosperity of my peoples, spread as they are all the world over."[27] In a Christmas message from Auckland, New Zealand, in 1953, Elizabeth informed the world, "I want to show that the Crown is not merely an abstract symbol of our unity but a personal and living bond between you and me."[28]

The distance between the "living bond" promise and decolonization/Cold War political reality was the British Establishment's antics. Before Elizabeth was the task to balance national expectations with those of the African future under the Commonwealth. How did the Queen fare with this tricky challenge? A proper assessment of her performance starts with revisiting the African context.

Decolonization, Monarchical Authority, and Cold War Politics

In Africa, in the 1950s, the Cold War tensions escalated as the United States scrambled to wrestle control of the continent from what Washington, DC., perceived as the Soviet ideological offensive. In his inauguration address on January 20, 1953, President Eisenhower spent much time highlighting the Soviet dangers with the principles of engagement that would guide his foreign policy. He put all options on the table, including the possibility of another war of even greater magnitude if required to push back the Soviets. "Abhorring war as a chosen way to balk the purposes of those who threaten us, we hold it to be the first task of statesmanship to develop the strength that will deter the forces of aggression and promote the conditions of peace."²⁹ These words reechoed Churchill's July 1, 1945, plans to preemptively attack the Soviet Union.³⁰

The ideas Eisenhower and succeeding US presidents implemented for tackling the Soviet Union's presence on the African Cold War battlefront affected the continent in many ways, including the decolonization contours Britain had to navigate. African nationalists profoundly pressured the Allied Powers to comply with the "freedom" and "self-determination" promises made during the war. The moral dilemma in which the Africans caught the Western powers triggered a chain of events the monarch was unprepared to deal with.

One significant development was the Central African Federation (CAF), established on August 1, 1953.³¹ The British Parliament passed the bill barely a couple of months after Elizabeth's coronation and despite a clear understanding of the political and economic implications for the Union for self-government.³² In solid terms, Lord Altrincham (John Grigg) voiced his worry about the timing. With the "tremendous wave of unrest, suspicion, fear, and ambition running throughout Africa," he argued, "no one who is not *a political idiot* would fail to recognize that most important fact."³³ From the economic angle, Altrincham underscored that the bill would result in the concentration of "all wealth, all promise of wealth and practically all production of wealth in the white areas, and poverty would be concentrated in the native areas."³⁴

The bill's passage, despite the potential to entrench racial divisions, highlights curious questions about Her Majesty's participation in and understanding of the imports or consequences of Whitehall's policies related to Africa in the 1950s and 1960s. As Andrew Marr underscored, the story deserves a detailed examination because "it throws up hard questions about Britain's role in Africa, the decolonization project, and the Queen's own position as Head of the Commonwealth."³⁵ The federation endorsed by London failed to find a middle ground between the White supremacists in the South African region and the increasing rank of African nationalists and Marxist ideologues.³⁶

It cannot be overstressed that this political permutation was incendiary when the African nationalists in Southern Rhodesia, like Robert Mugabe, Joshua Nkomo, and their comrades, were keen to end colonial domination in all its manifestations. It is essential to also add that the nationalist leaders in the northern territories were more opposed to the federation early on than the Southern Rhodesia cohorts like Nkomo, for whom it meant little at first. The Union was a significant shift for Northern Rhodesia and Nyasaland, now under a tiny White settler minority to the south, and was strongly frowned upon by the Northern Rhodesian African nationalists. A feature of the federation to which the Africans attached little or no emotion was the African Affairs Board, instituted by Whitehall as an afterthought to safeguard Africans' interests, especially discriminatory legislation. While the federation's economic potential was clear, the Union's political risks in the era of decolonization were high.

Britain understood that Black majority rule was inevitable but decided to go slowly with decolonization, particularly in Southern Africa. For ten years, CAF existed with the Queen's image on its postage stamps and currency. CAF's flag incorporating the Union Jack was a stark reminder that the Cold War got into British leaders' heads and muffled the self-determination imperative. In December 1954, some in the Commonwealth Secretary's Office even suggested that the CAF be admitted "to full Commonwealth membership" if the Gold Coast (Ghana) attained that status.[37] With help from communist China, African nationalists in Southern Rhodesia, Northern Rhodesia, and Malawi fought the Union. The dissolution of the CAF came on December 31, 1963, and Northern Rhodesia and Nyasaland became independent entities under White minority control the following year. Therefore, the elusive quest for an inclusive democracy continued.

Ian Douglas Smith, the prime minister of Southern Rhodesia from 1964 to 1979, decided to play the communist card with UK prime minister James Harold Wilson to win his support. Smith promised to move Southern Rhodesia to majority rule after implementing universal education. In other words, Smith played down the urgent issue concerning voting rights, suggesting that he did not consider Africans' enfranchisement a good idea when he proclaimed in 1976 that Blacks would vote in one thousand years.[38] However, Smith added that decolonization would be possible after the final defeat of any communist guerrillas and rebels, pretending to be oblivious that oppression was the cause of communist inclination. Wilson never believed Smith's dubious promises, and Queen Elizabeth rejected Smith's political gamble that outraged the African majority in the Commonwealth. Her Majesty's position on the Rhodesian question demonstrates that the Commonwealth took precedence for the Queen when toxic actors like Ian Smith crossed paths with the group's family principles. Buttressing her stand in 1953, Elizabeth declared that "the Commonwealth bears no resemblance to the Empires of the past." She reiterated, "It is an entirely new conception, built on the highest qualities of the spirit of man: friendship, loyalty, and the desire for freedom and peace."[39]

In a turn of events that Lord Chancellor Elwyn Jones described as "an act of rebellion against the Crown," the White minority elite in Southern Rhodesia took a unilateral assertion of autonomy from the UK in 1965.[40] Smith timed the

Unilateral Declaration of Independence (UDI) on November 11, at 11:00 am London time, to remind Britain of Southern Rhodesia's role in the two world wars. Elizabeth ignored the "Queen of Rhodesia" Ian Smith imposed on her.

A week after Smith announced the UDI, Queen Elizabeth decorated the governor of Rhodesia, Sir Humphrey Vicary Gibbs, with a Knighthood of Grand Cross of the Royal Victorian Order. Although Gibbs declined to be part of the UDI, he was also intensely loyal to Rhodesia. Consequently, critics, such as Manuele Facchini, condemned the timing of the award. Those with a different view praised it as indicating a further rejection of Ian Smith's illegal action.[41]

Simultaneous with the crisis in Rhodesia, Queen Elizabeth and her ministers wrestled with the insubordinate stance of Kabaka Mutesa II of Buganda, whom Governor Andrew Cohen bundled into exile to London on November 30, 1953. MP A. Fenner Brockway admitted that Mutesa's actions emerged from two genuine concerns shared among Buganda's people. The first was the fear that the East African Federation may follow the CAF's disaster. The second was that "Uganda, which has been traditionally and historically an African State, may cease to be an African State."[42]

The Ugandan crisis showed that decolonization was a response to various contested issues. These included emotions triggered by socioeconomic changes and the spread of ideas in the colony. When Governor Cohen arrived in Uganda in 1952 with new ideas for decolonization in tune with the changing times, he needed to carefully consider handling the personal relationship implied in the British colonial partnership with Mutesa. In readiness for political transition, Cohen expanded the Legislative Council to accommodate election of "30 instead of 20 African members."[43] He also encouraged the rise of political parties in response to the anticipated elections for self-government.

Ordinarily, the policies introduced by Cohen should have encouraged more cooperation from the Buganda people. However, Cohen's inadequate assessment of Mutesa's private schemes in the transition program was a flashpoint that troubled his liberal policies.[44] Mutesa disclosed that he was upset because the governor had ignored his role in the transition program. Cohen's "plan for a unitary state could not include me," he argued. He "failed to see that I enjoyed the total support of my people." The kabaka accused Cohen of deciding to destroy his influence "perhaps by discrediting me or by more drastic means."[45]

Her Majesty's role in escalating the conflict leading to Mutesa's exile further highlights the often contradictory and confusing challenges of balancing the Cold War ideology, colonial preservationists' interest, and the Commonwealth movement for a monarch barely five months on the throne.[46] The crisis accentuated the Crown's delicate task of accommodating the interests of the old guards—the imperial preservationists versus the liberal advocates of decolonization. At a State House meeting in Kampala on November 27, 1953, Cohen had asked Mutesa to accept Her Majesty's Government's demands of obedience and pledge of support for Buganda's status as "part of the Uganda Protectorate."[47] The kabaka's refusal to comply led Cohen to seek and obtain deportation permission from Elizabeth ahead of a follow-up meeting on November 30, 1953. Once the flight to London was airborne,[48] Colonial Secretary Oliver Lyttelton informed the House of Commons that Mutesa's authority as monarch had been withdrawn because of his refusal to obey Her Majesty's orders.[49] In reality, the colonial secretary made the case for exile and asked the Queen for her endorsement. Lyttelton reminded the House that the 1900 Anglo-Buganda Agreement required the kabaka to "cooperate loyally with Her Majesty's Government" in the kingdom's organization and administration. "The Kabaka has recently repudiated these obligations."[50]

From the preceding, two facts are clear: Elizabeth signed off on Mutesa's deportation as advised by Lyttleton and Cohen without duly considering the ramifications of the Colonial Office's advice. The hasty decision betrayed Her Majesty's principle of due consultation and her pledge to depart from the past culture of colonial bullying. Given the House's reaction—such as by J. Griffiths, who described the incident as "grievous news from a Colony which has shown so much progress and advance"—not even the House of Commons was duly consulted before the deportation.[51] Second, and more grievous, the exile implicates the burden of complicity one may lay on a naïve twenty-seven-year-old's signature vis-à-vis the personal conduct of colonial officers, who often abused their powers. MP Brockway alluded to the fact two days after the exile's announcement: confessing his respect for Cohen, Brockway concluded that "the events which have taken place indicate that even in Colonies where we have the more progressive Governors today they cannot keep abreast with the tempo of African advance within the framework of the present colonial administration."[52]

In Buganda, the exile turned Mutesa into a nationalist martyr. The latent trade unions, separatists, anticolonial sentiments, communist elements, and even his rivals like the Bunyoro chief and the Catholic Church rallied behind the local chieftain to set off and sustain a prolonged period of protests that paralyzed the order of government for several months. Writing to the secretary of state for the colonies on May 30, 1954, a frustrated Governor Cohen explained that he had to reimpose a state of emergency in Buganda after the expiration of the first enforced from November 30, 1953, to March 31, 1954 "so that the Government can carry out its first duty of maintaining law and order."[53] The Ganda-educated elite supported their kabaka with deputations at home and in London, pressuring the Colonial Office to rescind the deportation.[54]

While Uganda was roiling in the decolonization crisis, Whitehall sent the Crown on what could pass as an apology call to reassure Ugandans that prosperity was coming. With immense economic potential, the colony held that self-importance as East Africa's jewel, as reflected in Her Majesty's Owen Falls hydroelectric opening in Jinja. The British built the dam to control the Nile River and provide a reliable power source for Uganda's infrastructure.[55]

The three-day royal visit started with a twenty-one-gun salute at the Entebbe airport. From the receptions to the event in Jinja, the itinerary through western Uganda's cultural sights reminded the informed onlookers about Mutesa's banishment. During his welcome address, Sir P. N. Kavuma, OBE, the senior regent of Buganda, voiced his sorrow about the kabaka's absence. As usual, Her Majesty diplomatically evaded the question by twisting her reply into a Commonwealth vision of development that the completed dam would bring: "It is a great pleasure to ... be able to include a visit to Uganda in our Commonwealth tour ... gathering as a unity of purpose." Governor Andrew added, "If we maintain a spirit of harmony, unity and enterprise the Owen Falls Dam will open new horizons of opportunity and prosperity for Uganda and all who live in it."[56]

For Mutesa's enemies, the tour planned as a distraction from the ongoing decolonization crisis was a success, an honor, and a source of pride for the country. This was symbolized by Elizabeth's signed portraits given to the native rulers of Tooro, Ankole, and Bunyoro. Otherwise, the royal trip was nothing more than Cohen's public relations stunt and political hype. Mutesa disclosed while exiled that he was "deeply against" the royal visit because the Queen's popularity would distract attention from his predicament.[57]

The security problems in the Buganda region compelled the royal schedule to exclude visiting Kampala, the commercial capital, home to the prestigious Makerere University and the Buganda Kingdom's capital. The security situation in neighboring Kenya brought about by the Mau Mau rebellion was an additional concern for the royal visit. There were specific intelligence reports that a female Mau Mau operative would attempt to assassinate the Queen on Ugandan soil.[58] In the meantime, Her Majesty's presence in Uganda demonstrated one of the many occasions in which the Colonial Office attempted to ameliorate bungled policy decisions with the face of a beautiful Queen.

After two frustrating years of unrelenting protests, the new secretary of state for the colonies, Alan Lennox-Boyd, approved Mutesa's return and reinstatement. The colonial authorities dropped an East African Federation idea to secure Mutesa's cooperation in the decolonization program. They allowed Mutesa to appoint and dismiss his chiefs (Buganda government officials).[59] Mutesa, in turn, accepted "the Principle of the Protectorate as a Unitary State."[60]

While the exile and homecoming of Mutesa increased nationalist sentiments, it also provoked resentment among those tired of Buganda's national political domination. Divided into their specific interests, all Buganda elite Establishment opponents were ready to work together to overturn the power equation. In 1960, Milton Obote, a northern Lango ethnic group politician, founded a new party, the Uganda People's Congress (UPC). The UPC was a coalition of all those outside the Roman Catholic–dominated Democratic Party (DP) resentful of Bugandan hegemony. More critically, regionalism (a form of decentralization) was approved for northern Uganda, while it was not extended to the southern part.

One of the significant issues discussed at the London Conference of 1960 was the incompatibility of continued Bugandan autonomy and a stable unitary government.[61] Failing to compromise, the summit deferred a decision on the structure of the envisaged self-government. The British concluded plans for elections in March 1961 for an eighty-two-member National Assembly as part of the "responsible government" it wanted to implement before formally granting independence.[62]

In Buganda, the "King's Friends" called for a total boycott of the proposed election unless the British guaranteed Buganda's autonomy. Only the DP's Roman Catholic Church supporters participated, securing twenty out of the twenty-one seats allotted for Buganda. While the DP held the preponderance of seats, they had a minority of 416,000 votes against the UPC's 495,000. Benedicto Kiwanuka, the leader of DP, assumed the position of chief minister of Uganda.

Upset with the outcome of the elections, the Ganda separatists formed a new movement called Kabaka Yekka (KY). In a communiqué following the election, the movement's leaders declared, "Nobody can ever have a supreme position over the Kabaka on Buganda soil. Also, in Buganda, no one or body of people can ever make laws for the Kabaka's observance."[63] The KY welcomed the recommendations of a British commission that proposed a future federal form of government. Resolute in upstaging DP's control of national politics, Obote's UPC reached out for an alliance with Mutesa and the KY. In other words, Obote agreed to the idea of a special federal status that allowed the kabaka power to appoint Buganda's representatives to the National Assembly. The deal guaranteed the UPC a tactical advantage over the DP at the polls.

Additionally, the alliance secured a ceremonial but symbolic post of the head of Uganda's state, Mutesa. The new UPC-KY coalition led Uganda to independence on October 9, 1962. Mr. Obote became the prime minister. A year later, Mutesa assumed the country's first executive president.[64] His presidency lasted until 1966, when the military deposed him at the behest of Obote. Financially broke and alcoholic, Mutesa died in 1969 during his second exile in London.[65] In words that could serve as his epitaph, Mutesa lamented that "The bread of exile whether eaten at the Ritz [Hotel] or in a Café in Bermondsey [Square Hotel] is always bitter."[66]

What role did the Queen play in the welfare of Mutesa during the crisis? The direct answer is evident in the pattern of colonial servants' choices in Africa and how the Colonial Office justified these policies using the royal brand. As argued, recognizing an error or regret made the Crown embark on the April 1954 visit to Uganda. A similar sentiment explained Her Majesty's invitation of Mutesa to Buckingham Palace in 1954. Queen Elizabeth also conferred him a knighthood in December 1961.[67] Peter Gukiina later wrote in *Uganda: A Case Study of African Political Development* that "it was common gossip in my home and school area that while in exile the Kabaka was hosted in Buckingham Palace, where he was seduced by Queen Elizabeth II but had refused her."[68] In reflecting on this rumor, Crawford Young noted that its symbolic content resides in "the personification of Buganda" and its "superior role, dramatized by the intrusion of the sexual motif."[69]

A similar romantic motif was associated with Mutesa's grandfather and the British monarch when he attended Queen Victoria's coronation on June 28, 1838. Michael G. Schatzberg's study *Political Legitimacy in Middle Africa* reveals that the standard idea that power induces changes in behavior and is often met with resistance differs in its Central Africa context, where it has more to do with consumption than transformation. "Power concerns the capacity to consume, or the ability 'to eat'" as often encountered in local idioms and discourses. Correlating food, corruption, sexuality, size, and power as aspects of politics and everyday life in contemporary Africa, Schatzberg concludes, "one is powerful if one can 'eat'; the more one eats, the more powerful one becomes."[70] Ridiculous as they are, these baseless rumors of romantic overtures between Bugandan and British royals would last beyond Mutesa and continue with the theatrical exchanges between Queen Elizabeth and General Idi Amin in the 1970s.

The Queen-Nkrumah Foxtrot Dance

A widely discussed Anglo-African relations incident during the Cold War was the stately dance between Queen Elizabeth II and President Kwame Nkrumah in Ghana's capital, Accra. Before 1957, when Ghana became the first British Sub-Saharan African colony to gain independence, the Queen visited Nigeria in 1956 to confer with the Nigerian elite, fighting over the appropriate handover date.[71] Three years earlier, the powerful sultan of the defunct Sokoto Caliphate overturned a motion at the London Conference for Nigeria's independence in 1956 on the premise that his Hausa-Fulani ethnic group was not ready for self-government until further notice.[72] The incident shook the nation's unity as the nationalists in southern Nigeria threatened to go it alone without the north, which would have meant southern secession.

During the 1956 royal visit to Nigeria, the Queen traveled across the country, inspecting hospitals, educational facilities, dance and sporting events, and other ceremonies. She conferred the title "Queen's Own" on the Nigeria Regiment when the Royal West African Frontier Force (RWAFF) was dissolved.

Governor Sir James Robertson had described the three-week royal visit to Nigeria as "a personal triumph for The Queen and The Duke of Edinburgh: in the face of their charm and sincerity."[73] However, the importance of this victory becomes explicit in the understanding that it was also part of the move to ensure that the allure of communism did not take over Nigeria's postcolonial statehood. In a letter from C. E. Eastwood to Sir C. Jeffries dated May 30, 1955, the official had addressed what he termed the "most difficult situation in the Eastern" part of the country. He reminded Jeffries about Mr. Lyttelton's earlier promise of Nigeria's self-government in 1956. "This declaration in terms was unconditional, but it seems to me that no human declarations are in fact, unconditional. If, for instance, a wholly anarchist, communist or fascist form of government emerged in any or all of the Regions, H.M.G. would presumably not feel bound by this declaration."[74] Ultimately, the royal tour brought some calm to Nigeria and left an intense desire among Ghanaians to host the Queen in Accra in 1957 during the independence celebration. But the visit was delayed until November 1961.[75]

Ghana's independence was momentous; because of Nkrumah's strong commitment to Pan-Africanism, Accra became the political capital of Africa's anticolonial movement. Nkrumah was undoubtedly the most influential African figure and "a key man in world politics."[76] The United States sought to win Nkrumah's friendship to obtain a firm diplomatic foothold on the con-

Figure 3.1: Kwame Nkrumah and Dwight D. Eisenhower, Washington DC, 23 July 1958. (Photograph by Warren K. Leffler; retrieved from the Library of Congress)

tinent. This desire explains why President Eisenhower invited Nkrumah on a state visit to Washington, DC.[77]

During the visit of July 23–26, 1958, in his characteristic candor, Nkrumah expressed the general need for more understanding among the US government's officials about Africa's needs and problems. He also cited a similar sentiment shared by President Bourguiba of Tunisia.[78] President Eisenhower took Nkrumah's message literally without realizing that, while relating Bourguiba's words, the Ghanaian president also expressed his views about US-Ghana/African relations—the Africans' economic needs.[79] On Nkrumah's mind was the Volta River Electricity Project, which he had hoped the United States would help finance through foreign direct investment rather than a grant. Nkrumah envisioned the Volta hydroelectric project as the cornerstone of his massive industrialization program in Ghana.[80]

Perhaps more critical during Nkrumah's visit were issues not discussed: the existing racial relationship between White Americans and African Americans, which troubled Nkrumah more than everything else. Kevin Gaines informs us that in a discussion in March 1957, Nkrumah had told Dr. Martin Luther King Jr. that he "would never be able to accept the American ideology of freedom until America settles its own internal racial strife." This confidential discussion inspired King to trust Nkrumah's leadership ability "to meet the challenge ahead."[81] In other words, the line of conflict between Nkrumah and the United States was marked on the sands of history before the emergence of the postcolonial state and its entanglement with the American Cold War interests.

Despite his American education, Nkrumah became a communist ideologue who envisaged harnessing socialism's principles to reconstruct a postcolonial model nation in Ghana. The paradox of this resolve is evident in light of Nkrumah's initial vision of liberty he wanted to bring to Africa. Nkrumah later wrote in *Ghana: The Autobiography of Kwame Nkrumah* that he had adopted the Statue of Liberty as a symbol of inspiration on his way home from the United States after his studies in 1945: "You have opened my eyes to the true meaning of liberty. I shall never rest until I have carried your message to Africa."[82] For Nkrumah, the Statue of Liberty inspired him to free his country and Africa from colonial domination. The context in which this original inspiration was lost to a communist ideal is a flashpoint in the discourse on US-African relations.

It is essential to add that America's sensitivity to its European allies and former colonial overlords in Africa shaped a good part of its African foreign policy. Queen Elizabeth, addressing the United Nations Assembly in New York on October 21, 1957, discussed the UN's purpose and intersection with the Commonwealth: "This Assembly was born of the endeavors of countless men and women from different nations who, over the centuries, have pursued the aims of the preservation of peace between nations, equality of justice for all before the law, and the right of the peoples of the world to live their lives in freedom and security." The United States appreciated this message at a time when staving off communist overtures was a matter of priority. The Queen noted: "Time has, in fact, made the task of the United Nations more difficult than it seemed when the terms of the charter were approved in San Francisco twelve years ago. We are still far from the achievement of the ideals that I have mentioned, but we must not be discouraged. The world's peoples expect the United Nations to persevere in its efforts."[83]

Queen Elizabeth II also pointed out that the ten Commonwealth countries, including Ghana, the only Sub-Saharan African nation at the meeting, constituted "a free association of fully independent states" with "widely different histories, cultures, and traditions. Common ideals and hopes, not formal bonds, unite the members of the Commonwealth and promote that association between them, which in my belief, has contributed significantly to the cause of human freedom." Elizabeth further underscored that the Commonwealth nations saw their continuing association as "an essential contribution to world peace and justice."[84] All these were consistent with Elizabeth's Cape Town proclamation. She was ecstatic to have Ghana in the Commonwealth, which also reflected the provisions of the "Ghana (Consequential Provision) Bill" of May 17, 1960, passed by the House of Commons.[85]

In his address before the Fifteenth General Assembly of the United Nations in New York on September 22, 1960, President Eisenhower enthusiastically welcomed the newly independent African nations to the "commonwealth of nations." He addressed the challenges before the world as the new countries emerged from decades of colonial rule. "We can strive to master these problems," he stated, "for narrow national advantage or we can begin at once to undertake a period of constructive action which will subordinate selfish interest to the general well-being of the international community." Of particular interest was Eisenhower's comment about eradicating outside interference in the internal affairs of African countries: "Outside interference with these newly emerging nations, all eager to undertake the tasks of modernization, has created a serious challenge to the authority of the United Nations."[86] As evident with Ghana and elsewhere in Africa over the period, the various European colonial powers were privy to US actions and inactions.

By 1961, Nkrumah had become increasingly agitated, given the slow pace of decolonization and the obstacles confronting his vision of a United States of Africa with an African military high command. A December 5, 1961, dispatch from Sir A. Snelling to Mr. Duncan Sandys, the Commonwealth secretary-general, noted, "Even in Colonial days, Nkrumah's view was that the independence of his country was meaningless unless linked up with the total liberation of Africa."[87] Snelling expressed fears that the Russians were increasingly gaining a solid foothold in Ghana. As Snelling noted, the Russians came to Accra during Ghana's independence celebrations in March 1957, aiming to forge diplomatic relations with Ghana. Two years later, the Russian ambassador arrived in Ghana, and within the first six months, he had organized "trips for influential Ghanaians to Moscow, Tashkent and Samarkand on a scale undreamt of by us."[88] Although the Anglo-Ghana relations remained strong, Britain and its allies were in pain that some of the speeches Nkrumah made during the Moscow trip damaged the West. Additionally, Nkrumah secured technical assistance and a £15 million development loan from Russia.

Simultaneously, Nkrumah's most significant problem at home was his dictatorial leadership style, which increasingly became a topic of public discourse in 1952.⁸⁹ Snelling counted this development as severe friction between Britain and Ghana, complaining that "there is no longer any significant Parliamentary Opposition" in Ghana.⁹⁰ Yet, there is evidence that the British government was not alarmed by Ghana's trend toward one-party rule. In a message dated October 11, 1962, sent to R. W. H. du Boulay in Washington from J. Chadwick in the Commonwealth Relations Office, the latter declared that they "need not have too many qualms," adding that "this is typical African manifestation and one with which we must learn to live if only because Westminster democracy is not automatically suited to African conditions."⁹¹

As his critics in Ghana expressed their worries about Nkrumah's authoritarian leadership style, he became a sitting target of local and foreign adversaries as he stoked anti-British and US feelings. Nkrumah's socialist speeches and writings about moving Ghana closer to Russia and away from Britain and America further generated anxiety among the Western leaders. Hence, the Americans began to devise plots to remove Nkrumah from power, including sponsoring local decedents to seize power through violence, if necessary.

In the interim, the British authorities developed a robust diplomatic strategy with the Crown, scheduling a state visit to Ghana. While the preparations for the trip concluded, there were reports of bomb explosions in Accra. On the eve of Her Majesty's arrival in Accra, Minister of Interior and Local Government Kwaku Boateng went on the radio to allege that recent events had revealed that "there was an organized body planning to sabotage the smooth administration of the country. *The Ghanaian Times* of November 9, 1961, carried a statement from Boateng calling on "all Ghanaians to be security officers."⁹²

Disturbing as the news from Ghana was, Harold Evans, Prime Minister Harold Macmillan's press secretary, noted in his diary the Queen's "indignance" at the idea she might not make the journey because of security concerns.⁹³ Elizabeth requested that the House of Commons not "show a lack of moral fiber in this way." This decision prompted her heroic comments to Prime Minister Harold Macmillan: "I am not a film star. I am the head of the Commonwealth—and I am paid to face any risks that may be involved. Nor do I say this lightly. Do not forget that I have three children. Danger is part of the job. If I were to cancel now, Nkrumah might invite Khrushchev, and they wouldn't like that, would they?"⁹⁴

It is vital to reflect on why, for Elizabeth, the choice of possible harm in Ghana was a lesser risk than the "moral" danger of Khrushchev landing in Ghana. Worried like most Britons, the archbishop of Canterbury, Arthur Michall Ramsey, offered a special prayer for the safety of the royals as the

Figure 3.2: Kwame Nkrumah and J.F. Kennedy, Washington DC, 1961. (Abbie Rowe, White House Photographs. John F. Kennedy Presidential Library and Museum, Boston)

party was airborne.[95] But who were those who would be unhappy if she had scuttled the trip? It would not be hard to see that the Americans and Harold Macmillan's cabinet were the powers-that-be the Queen wanted to avoid their ire. On October 28, 1957, Macmillan informed the cabinet that after Russia's launch of Sputnik prompted his visit to the United States, both countries had signed an "interdependence."[96] Lord Home, the Commonwealth secretary, was troubled because the US and his country's renewed bond may upset some Commonwealth members. However, Lord Home acknowledged the importance of Anglo-American relations and called for the best policy to handle it.[97] Immediately after Queen Elizabeth had left Ghana on November 20, 1961, an obviously relieved Macmillan called President John F. Kennedy to express his excitement: "I have risked my Queen; you must risk your money." In response, Kennedy acknowledged Queen Elizabeth's "brave contribution" and made good on his promise.[98] In other words, Elizabeth took the risk to please her people, and the UK and the United States agreed that President Kennedy would approve funds for Ghana's hydroelectric project if the Queen made the crucial meeting with Nkrumah.

The thought of ignoring the likely scenario of the Crown and president of Ghana cruising in an open-roof Rolls Royce and terrorist bombs detonated in Accra was reminiscent of Churchill's risk-taking Cold War politics with his US allies. In response to a letter from Churchill dated October 19, 1961, a month before the Ghana trip, Macmillan had admitted his worries about the timing:

> The Ghana problem is indeed a difficult one. It is a great tragedy that this visit did not take place when it was originally planned over a year ago, for then things were calm. Unfortunately, it had to be postponed owing to The Queen's baby. Now there is the dilemma to which you refer. If the visit were cancelled and The Queen continued her tour of Sierra Leone and Gambia, that would be tantamount to dismissing Ghana from the Commonwealth.[99]

Like the royal visit to Uganda amid the Mau Mau rebellion in neighboring Kenya, the Ghana episode corroborates the assertion that Churchill successfully inducted the Queen into his Cold War victory-by-all-means philosophy. Both trips were in the interest of the royal brand. The idea was that securing the Commonwealth was paramount, and propaganda was critical in winning the war. At the same time, Her Majesty had, in an address to Parliament on October 31, 1961, reiterated her desire to see "the improvement of relations between East and West," which she stated was "a primary object of [her] Government's policy."[100]

Debating the Ghana trip timing in the House of Commons on November 8, 1961, some members, especially Viscount Alexander of Hillsborough and Lord Rea, questioned the rationale for the risks involved.[101] Lord President of the Council and Minister for Science Viscount Hailsham tried to persuade the few dissenting voices in Parliament that all was well for the trip, based on privileged information.[102] According to Hailsham, the government had determined that the Accra explosions "do not indicate any intention by those concerned to perpetrate acts of violence during the Queen's visit, which would endanger Her Majesty's safety. We have, therefore, no reason to fear that this journey will involve any special and additional risk to Her Majesty's safety."[103]

It reveals that the nobleman shared the opinion that the cancellation of this visit, as some suggested, would disappoint the Ghanaians. That option, he argued, "would seriously impair the invaluable contribution made by Her

Majesty's journeys towards the strengthening of the ties which bind together the many peoples of the Commonwealth."[104] Hailsham concluded, "Her Majesty's Government has therefore advised the Queen that she should proceed with her visit to Ghana.[105] The Queen embarked on the eleven-day trip to Ghana in November 1961, hoping that the favorable publicity it would generate "would be a boost for the Commonwealth."[106]

The trip's high point was a popular Ghanaian highlife step between the Queen and Nkrumah, revisited as a "foxtrot ballroom dance" in a BBC One documentary, "The Queen: Her Commonwealth Story," which premiered on March 25, 2018. The documentary reiterated that the tour was to promote the Commonwealth and Western ideals. *The Telegraph* portrayed the trip as one of those occasions "where deference faltered," asserting that British policy-makers mandated Her Majesty to adjust to a shifting geopolitical landscape.[107] Macmillan was informed by British intelligence on the ground that "Nkrumah has not wholly sold out to the Russians." However, the prime minister firmly believed, "If Ghana was thrown out of the Commonwealth, Russia will move in."[108] Snelling corroborated this sentiment when he stated that Nkrumah was "not a Communist and will not become a slave of the Russians unless he is thrown by the West into their arms."[109]

The dance stealing the royal visit of 1961 requires more attention. The available records are silent on why the particular dance genre was selected. A traditional African dance style (with the Queen wiggling her waist) would have turned more heads worldwide in a country where highlife music was born. Instead, the chief dancers favored a hybrid of Afro-Western styles. However, it is essential to accurately note that the dance was to a highlife by a famous vocalist Cab Quay (born Nii-lante A. k. Quaye). The Takoradi Broadways Dance Band, led by a Nigerian Sam Obote, rendered the words of the specially composed song, "Happy Welcome to Ghana Queen Elizabeth of Ghana."[110]

The African highlife is parallel but not exactly the same as the foxtrot that emerged in the African American nightclubs in the 1920s as part of the Great Migration and the Black artistic revolution of the Harlem Renaissance. The American foxtrot, credited to Fred Astaire and Ginger Rogers, combines quick and slow steps, thus allowing dancers more suppleness in motion.[111] Like the waltz, the smooth step movement defines its counterclockwise steps. Vernon and Irene Castle popularized the dance, named after the American dance teacher Harry Fox.

The 2018 documentary reported that the Queen ended her tour on November 20, 1961, with a dinner speech during which she jokingly lamented how her pregnancy caused her to delay the trip.[112] But Elizabeth had earlier made the joke on November 10, 1961, that Andrew, born on February 19, 1960, would, in the future, "be able to come here himself and perhaps make amends for the inconvenience he caused. My elder children are following this journey, and we shall have a lot to tell them when we get home."[113] This was in response to Nkrumah's toast to the royals that "the wind of change blowing through Africa has reached a hurricane proportion." But he assured the Queen that no matter what the wind brings, his "personal affection for Her Majesty and His Royal Highness will remain unaffected by that hurricane."[114] In her response, the Queen described Ghana's membership in the Commonwealth as "a positive symbol of an association of equals in which disagreement was possible without any member losing "one iota of its sovereignty and individuality." Adding, "many people have said many things about this Commonwealth of ours. We know that it is a group of equals; a family of like-minded peoples, whatever their differences of religion, political systems, circumstances, and races, all working together for the peace, freedom, and prosperity of mankind." The monarch concluded by calling on all to "be generous in the interpretation of one another's feelings and intentions. Let us not doubt one another's intentions."[115]

Ghanaian historian Nat Nunoo-Amarteifio explains how significant and graceful the Elizabeth-Nkrumah dance was, as a mark of respect to Nkrumah for the Queen of England "to put her arms around him." He added, however, that with Ghana threatening to leave the Commonwealth and possibly embrace communism, it "was a gallant decision" on the Queen's part to be in Ghana. If she had not, the Commonwealth faced the threat of "bad publicity," becoming "an almost white-only club." Britain wanted to cement Ghana's loyalty to the bloc.[116] Similarly, Siofra Brennan noted that the Queen's effort "was significant" in that the privilege of dancing with the Queen moved Nkrumah to "turn his back on the Soviets."

However, it was not the dance per se that swerved Nkrumah's loyalty to the Commonwealth. As Nkrumah disclosed during the royal tour, the secret was the personal envoy the Queen sent to inform Nkrumah about the pregnancy and her invitation to the Ghanaian leader to visit the royal family's Balmoral Castle home two years earlier in 1959.[117] Thus, when Brennan declared Her Majesty's trip to Ghana a success, he forgot the most critical factor to that success: it was neither the dance nor the gifts exchanged between the two leaders. Instead, it was the humble, cheerful, and genuine spirit Queen Elizabeth demonstrated throughout the eleven-day tour.[118] A letter to the editor of *Evening Times* by one E. Kolay-Amos from Djorshe, Accra, captured it all: "I liked the way she

[Queen Elizabeth] took a keen interest in everything. All of this is wonderful and is bound to prove beneficial to us in our struggle. No wonder Accra went gay for her."[119] Nkrumah further demonstrated his happiness and personal connection with Elizabeth and the royal family by giving "Prince Charles with one of his most prized boyhood gifts of a bow and quiver full of arrows."[120]

Contrary to the popular opinion about Nkrumah's socialist inclination, it is vital to note that, like most of his African peers, Nkrumah's priority was promoting Pan-Africanism and freedom from colonial subjugation. There is no clear evidence to conclude that he intended to align himself with the Eastern or the Western bloc.[121] Rather, Nkrumah sought to play off one bloc against the other to benefit his country. This point was known to the British policymakers, as Lord Brand pointed out in 1961: "The African States ... They all want money. What is Mr. Nkrumah going to do in the Commonwealth? Mr. Nyerere, of Tanganyika is very unhappy because he could not get from the British Government quite what he hoped to get. But we have not the money to give them."[122] Indeed, the trip's outcome played a role in securing the US funds for the Volta River Project, which was more critical in restraining Nkrumah from relying on Soviet aid. In other words, the Nkrumah-Elizabeth dance was insignificant without the development funds.

In addition, there was no evidence of Prime Minister Harold Macmillan being surprised at the royal dance. David Cannadine has noted that the elite of British politics rigidly controlled Queen Elizabeth's life. As with the Nkrumah saga, she was therapy for radical African leaders seized by the communist bug. The Queen "helped preserve post-imperial connections with and between former British colonies."[123] Macmillan was delighted at the overall success of the royal visit, and his famous "Wind of Change in Africa" speech before the South African Parliament on February 3, 1960, was prompted by "Nkrumah's suggestion that Britain should make a declaration of policy."[124] Macmillan called on those opposed to the wind of change blowing throughout the African continent to accept that "this growth of national consciousness is a political fact."[125]

Nkrumah's grand plan to forge all parts of Africa into one country under the communist banner conflicted with America's interests, and increasingly the successive American governments interpreted Nkrumah's policies and actions to mean Ghana's gravitation to the Soviet bloc. This perception and the tension it generated at home and overseas became fraught with grave complications. Ultimately, America's clandestine activities in Ghana with British support demonized Nkrumah and culminated in a coup d'état that toppled his administration on February 24, 1966, while he was in Vietnam on a peacemaking mission.[126]

Whether the royal trips to Uganda and Ghana fully accomplished their goals remains debatable. What is vital is that these trips provided a blueprint for Her Majesty's engagement with the postcolonial African state. The idea was for the sovereign to promote her brand in Britain's interest by meeting the new African elite and the people. When the Queen was indisposed to travel, a royal family member usually took her place. Despite the challenging political climate in which British leaders inserted her, a favorable opinion circulated across Africa for various reasons. Elizabeth's calm, humane, and genuine persona was the mystique that endeared her to ordinary Africans.

In Nigeria, which gained independence on October 1, 1960, a positive image of Elizabeth traveled across the country as the people's "Queen of Nigeria." Because the birth of Andrew made it inconvenient for the Queen to attend Nigeria's independence celebration on October 1, 1960, Princess Alexandra stepped in.[127] The more levelheaded Nigerian nationalists used the occasion to thank Her Majesty and Britain for their "partnership." Nigeria's prime minister, Sir Abubakar Tafawa Balewa, KBE, expressed gratitude for the country's "friends in the Colonial Office" for establishing the basis of an enduring British-Nigerian alliance and the entire Commonwealth realm.[128] The prime minister thanked Princess Alexandra of Kent for conveying Her Majesty's cordial message.[129]

Whitehall encouraged the Crown's diplomatic tours to Africa because of their efficacy in connecting friendships and moderating the nationalist crisis. The royal tours to Uganda, Nigeria, and Ghana restrained situations that could have spiraled out of control. The tours are part of the decolonization story, a continuation of the royal branding matrix that has been more or less ignored in the extant literature. Further exploration of the purpose, diverse nature, and mixed results are required.

CHAPTER 4

HER MAJESTY'S AFRICA TOUR-DE-FORCE: FEASTING WITH THE OBEDIENT, THE NOBLE, AND THE NONCONFORMIST, 1961–1989

While Cold War politics threatened Africa's dreams of freedom in the immediate postwar era, the future Her Majesty aspired for the continent was sometimes misplaced, disrupted, or lost. Her successful trip to Nkrumah's Ghana in November 1961 encouraged more tours.[1] Between November 25, 1961, and November 9, 1989, when the Berlin Wall collapsed, the Queen completed ten African trips related to the Commonwealth and British government agendas. Additional trips to non–former British territories involved Ethiopia, Sudan, Algeria, Tunisia, and Morocco—all in 1965.

The royal visits were potent in soothing Anglo-African relations for a new beginning. The goals were to secure African nations for the Commonwealth, stop the spread of communism, promote a more humane Britishness, and stimulate a better European appreciation of the Africans. Klaus Dodds and David Robison have noted that the royal tours of the empire were considered critical in strengthening the colonies' attachment to Britain, the Crown, and, by extension, the realm. David Cannadine adds that the trips made the Crown "truly imperial, and the empire authentically royal."[2] In the 1950s and 1960s, the Queen and Winston Churchill understood that the visits would help Elizabeth fortify her monarchy and leadership of the Commonwealth.[3] Elizabeth's presence on the ground brought her into direct contact with ordinary Africans and, of course, the new men with the reins of power.

Until the Cold War thawed in 1989, the Commonwealth served to steady control of the crisis that engulfed the empire in a rapidly changing bipolar world order. Queen Elizabeth's position made her the protagonist in the crisis contiguous to decolonization. British politicians and the Commonwealth Relations Office set forth a mission to use the association to conquer Africans' hearts and minds, especially the new elite, and in the words of Sir James Robertson, "to provide an answer to Communist activities."[4]

In a study of the postcolonial African state, A. H. M. Kirk-Greene observed that the African leaders' characteristics, ideologies, excesses, eccentricities, conspicuous lifestyles, and the often brutal manner of their deaths were subject to "scholarly analysis and intellectual typologizing."[5] Kirk-Greene overlooked that stereotyping was a problem of the Cold War, central in decolonization politics. Placing the Africans into separate classes constituted part of the Colonial Office's broader practice of paternalism and its designs to handpick "responsible" Africans or those docile enough to inherit the postcolonial state. In Nigeria, an explicit colonial edict outlawed the employment of communist elements and "other undesirables in government positions, especially in Eastern Nigeria."[6] This policy was not limited to Nigeria. In August 1955, F. E. Cumming-Bruce, an adviser to the Gold Coast governor on external affairs, had sent a letter to Sir G. Laithwaite expressing the apprehension that "the Nkrumah Government, if in power after independence, will be inclined to assert its independence of British apron-strings in various ways, some of which may be embarrassing."[7] Cumming-Bruce's concerns speak to the broader anxiety to bar those disobedient to the empire from power positions. The plan's implementation evolved as a political discourse with the shifts in the treatises and actions of colonial officials. The exponents aimed to reformulate notions of nationality in socially conservative ways sensitive to gender and colonial obedience.

Within the dialectics of colonial obedience and gender empowerment, British lawmakers inserted Elizabeth as the symbol and chief envoy of the desired change and unity under the new Commonwealth. The expectation of being modest required those considered radical nationalists such as Nnamdi Azikiwe and Kwame Nkrumah to realign their ideas to at least somewhere in the center. The Foreign Office exercised suppleness to allow the rebellious progenies of the empire to reenter the obedient mold as a sine qua non for postwar cooperation, peace, and change. Nothing demonstrated this flexibility more than Azikiwe's transformation from a radical critic of the empire to the first governor-general of Nigeria from 1960 to 1963, when the country became a republic.[8]

The drivers of the African nationalist landscape were mixed in ethical and pragmatic terms. Some of the political elite of this period were beautiful in learning, status, and heart. This class of Africans was often recognized with prestigious empire titles and awards. These awards were so important to the humble and Anglophile recipients that during the first day of her royal visit to Sierra Leone, the local newspaper, *Daily Mail* of Saturday, November 25, 1961, reminded its readers with pride that the first African to be knighted was Sir Samuel Lewis, KCMG.[9] Radical West African press derided those Her Majesty honored with the Order of the British Empire as "Obedient Boys of the Empire (OBE)."[10] The critics loathed the Anglophiles for their ideological conventions, personal comportments, and advocacy for Africa's future relationship with the retreating imperialists.[11]

Among the new elite were those, such as Idi Amin of Uganda, who were often unconventional in their thoughts, outward displays of power, inclination to theatrical behaviors, political rhetoric, and material acquisitions. Dealing with the various manners of individuals raised under the colonial milieu was like paddling a small canoe in a troubled sea. The task revealed the best in Elizabeth as a diplomat, monarch, and custodian of Western civilization.

It is challenging to cover Elizabeth's numerous African tours in a study of this nature. Highlighting a few examples of her encounters with each category of African leaders provides insights into what the tours accomplished in postwar diplomacy and postcolonial social reengineering. A chronological account of the story needs to be clarified. It makes sense to start with the obedient before the noble and the nonconformists.

The "Obedient Boys of the Empire" (OBE)

From November 25 to December 1, 1961, Queen Elizabeth proceeded on her first visit to Sierra Leone in her husband's company. The Freetown experience is vital because Her Majesty, as the original Queen of Hearts, exhibited the best of her down-to-earth nature in reaching out to the poor and the rich.[12] Six months earlier, when Sierra Leone celebrated its independence on April 21, 1961, Elizabeth was absent for medical reasons. Prince Edward, the Duke of Kent (first cousin of the Queen), represented her during the independence festivities.[13]

The November trip was Her Majesty's second landing in a West African country within two weeks, and the next stop in the journey was The Gambia. The British Parliament had endorsed the late 1961 West Africa trips with the confidence that Elizabeth would make a massive impression on the people. "I am confident that wherever Her Majesty goes, be it the Gambia or the newly independent Sierra Leone, or Ghana, a tumultuous and warm-hearted welcome will await her."[14] Elizabeth held the Queen of Sierra Leone's role from April 1961 (when it was admitted to the Commonwealth) to April 1971, when it became a republic.[15] By its place as the freedom colony, founded in the eighteenth century by British philanthropists, the West African nation occupies a unique place in Afro-British relations.

Freetown, the country's capital, was not just symbolic of the dramatic inverse sail of slave journeys; it was the first sociopolitical community solely dedicated to building a new Afro-Western culture on African soil. The founders conceived it on freedom, liberty, and egalitarianism principles. In the settlement, the émigré (or Krio) and the indigenous people of Sierra Leone (Mende, Temne, Sherbro, and others) either relived or met Western-style education for the first time. They also blended Protestant Christianity with Islamic and indigenous forms of religiosity. The new settlers further experienced the pressures of monogamous marriages, European dressing styles, work ethics, and wealth accumulation through commerce.[16] Joseph Tracey explains that Charles McCarthy, who served as the colony's acting governor in 1814, had conceived Sierra Leone as a base for extending the advantages of civilization into Africa's interior.[17]

By Elizabeth's visit, the founders' high expectations of Sierra Leone still needed to materialize among its diverse citizens. However, the Colonial Office favorably viewed its first prime minister, Sir Milton Margai (a medical doctor who graduated from Newcastle University), as a moderate nationalist. In the scheme of safe investment of the postcolonial state, Margai was found worthy of entrusting Sierra Leone's leadership in his hands. Parliamentary papers related to the plan for the formal handover of power in the colony reveal the British policymakers' robust support for Margai. After a trip to Sierra Leone in 1960, Secretary of State to the Colonies Iain Macleod extolled Margai's leadership. He reported to the House of Commons that everybody he met in the colony during his trip "was in favor of independence, even though some of the simple people are not quite sure exactly what it will mean."[18] The secretary dismissed an allegation by the opposition that Margai would stifle future democratic elections in the country: "We were not, and could not be, convinced by the statement that it was Sir Milton Margai's intention never to have elections again and to establish a one-party state."[19] Macleod pointed out that Margai could not have such a plan and, at the same time, "recommended to Her Majesty that Sir Maurice Dorman be the Governor-General." He argued that if Margai had ideas to stifle democracy, "he would not have asked such a distinguished former Governor and so devoted an adherent of the parliamentary democratic system which we have in this country to become the Governor-General."[20]

Macleod's endorsement of Margai was corroborated by John Eric Drummond, the minister of state for colonial affairs. The Earl of Perth recalled his impression of meeting "the Doctor" in the 1950s:

> I was very much struck not only by his [Margai's] moderation and his charm but also by his wisdom, which had in it a certain firmness of purpose. We have seen that firmness of purpose over the years as he has been leading his country to this end, which will be finally given effect on April 27 [1961] next when Sierra Leone is to become independent. I feel that it is a country which will be well launched under his guidance and the guidance of others of his Cabinet. I beg to move.[21]

Macleod assured the House of Commons that equally moderate and competent officials surrounded Margai. For instance, he congratulated Sir Maurice Dorman as the governor-general. He described Mr. Lightfoot Boston, the colony's speaker of the House of Representatives, "as an eminent constitutional lawyer, a stout guardian of democratic liberties, and "a great believer in the principles of British common law."[22] Macleod spoke about the future of democracy in the colony, describing Margai as displaying a special love of village life and culture. He "goes out and serves his people with his own hands. As he told me with pride and evident satisfaction, he often delivers babies in the bush with his own hands, for he is a gynecologist trained in Newcastle. I am sure that he appreciates and values a thriving life on the land."[23]

Margai, Dorman, Boston, and others occupying important leadership positions in Sierra Leone represent examples of the Whitehall's identification and branding of neocolonial African partners, which favored those moderate and docile among the emergent African nationalists and postcolonial leaders. They were all honorees of Her Majesty's Medal of the Order of the British Empire for their loyalty to the empire.[24] Indeed, the *Daily Mail* splashed a reminder on its front page: "Our country is always referred to in official quarters at Whitehall, London, as "Ancient and loyal Sierra Leone."[25] In his study of colonial Zimbabwe, Michael Oliver West noted the struggle between the use of "Native honorifics" and the European ones. While the former was considered "to create ill-feeling among the Europeans," a change to the latter, such as using 'Mr.' on envelopes, was viewed as a matter of etiquette."[26] In many African countries, European titles were forms of imperial conformity and control.

In Freetown and elsewhere, during the royal visit, the Africans who received the regal awards paraded their accolades with pride. They tried to distinguish themselves from the vast crowd who welcomed the royals with flowers, cheers, dances, and twenty-one-gun salutes from the Royal Army regiment. The gatherings comprised schoolchildren, the underprivileged, and so on. Seeing the local kings and queens brought to the event by their subjects on hammocks was more ludicrous. The London *Observer* of November 16, 1961, focused more on the atmosphere of love and respect: "When the Britannia was moored, [Sierra Leoneans] gathered at her stern, some in real danger of being crushed, bumping wildly together, and the ceremonies at the quayside (named H.M. Queen Elizabeth II) were conducted against a cheerful background of strident shouting and the occasional song."[27]

The excitement was genuine and confirmed the importance of Elizabeth's outreach to ordinary Africans in the Anglo-African reorientation project.[28] The mayor of Freetown, who welcomed the Queen with a gold key to the city, wore red robes and cocked an English municipal hat. He told Elizabeth that the "key would unlock the hearts of the people."[29] As with Her Majesty's three-week trip to Nigeria in 1956, there was the Bo Durbar, stilts, hunters' guild, devil dancers, and several other masquerades and dance troupe ceremonies. The performances set the royals on the edge of their seats: "My husband and I have been greatly moved by the great welcome you have given us," the Queen told the crowd in appreciation. "Many of these we have met have had to travel long distances. We want them to know how glad we are to see them and meet them. I shall not forget your kindness and hospitality."[30] At the graduation ceremony at Fourah Bay College on November 30, 1961, the Queen paid special tribute to Prime Minister Margai:

> Sierra Leone can count itself truly fortunate that before gaining independence, she had found herself a leader, wise, experienced, and devoted to her people. To you, the Prime Minister, more than any other person, gets the credit for quickening the political consciousness of Sierra Leone and uniting her people. Yours is a record of selfless service and singular achievement that will always stand as an inspiration to your country.[31]

The next day, the Duke of Edinburgh visited the Guma Valley Water and Electric project commissioned by Britain. Initially, Britain did not plan to fund the project. Still, as several developmental infrastructures were built in the late colonial and early postcolonial eras, the Cold War rivalry figured in. In July 1955, MP John Tilney inquired from then secretary of the colonies Henry Hopkinson about the total cost and funding source for the Freetown hydroelectric project. On learning from the secretary that the estimated cost was £1,469,410, Tilney argued that because the project was of "a strategic content for the Atlantic Alliance," it would be unreasonable to saddle the impoverished nation with the budget. He charged Hopkinson to consider possibly using a defense aid grant to cover the cost.[32] The British government completed the dam without cost to the Sierra Leone government.

The Queen spent the second day in Sierra Leone, making her visit for all. She was graceful and charming as she toured villages and schools, including the historical Fourah Bay College (founded in 1827), where she conferred the students with degrees. Elizabeth visited hospitals, agricultural facilities, and diamond mines. These sites were critical to ensuring the expected new democratic and prosperous beginning for Sierra Leone. When Secretary Macleod visited the country in December 1960 to assess the sociopolitical capital for democracy sustenance, he found vibrant cooperative associations: "It has 400 societies, with 24,000 members and a staff of 135."[33] Macleod noted that civil society groups were essential in Sierra Leone's democratic development:

> I do not think that one can exaggerate the potential importance of this movement in improving agriculture, in developing a sense of community, and in providing a training ground for democracy; for democracy is by no means only a process of electing members of a Legislature: it must be practiced in daily life to become deeply rooted in any nation. The same applies to trade unions. The mineworkers' union, whose leaders we met and many of whose members we met, too, seemed to us to be in good shape. Its Secretary, I understand, is at present at Ruskin College, Oxford, following a course of training for his important duties.[34]

At the Freetown stadium, Her Majesty unveiled new colors to the Royal Sierra Leone Regiment. The replacement aligned with the country's new flag, depicting Elizabeth's position as the Queen.[35] The original colors of the Royal West African Frontier Force (RWAFF), comprising Nigeria, Ghana, Sierra Leone, and The Gambia, were based on the Union Jack. The abolishment of the RWAFF on July 1, 1956, allowed each of the four governments to take control of their separate armies.[36] During the ceremony at the Freetown stadium, the imam of the Muslim Congress blessed the new colors: "In thy holy name, O! Allah, most gracious, most merciful." The Roman Catholic bishop of Freetown, the president of the United Christian Council, and the Anglican bishop of Freetown took turns offering prayers.[37]

The most memorable part of the Sierra Leone royal tour was recognizing and promoting women's rights in tune with the postwar ideals, which aligned with the new Commonwealth values. During Macleod's visit in late 1960, he noted an intricate connection between Sierra Leone women and the "cooperative movement," which successfully engenders women's interest.[38] He concluded that these associations and the women, in general, were vital to "improving agriculture, in developing a sense of community and in providing a training ground for democracy."[39] Macleod noted that one-third of the 300 students at the Fourah Bay College in 1961 were women. The unprecedented trend was contrary to a colonial system that consigned African women to vocational studies and home economies. The expectation was that Elizabeth would show interest in women's affairs.

Gender diplomacy played out in two significant ways during the royal visit. First, Elizabeth honored Madam Woki Massaquoi, paramount chief of the Gallinas Perri, as a Member of the British Empire.[40] Along with Madam Ella Koblo Gulama of Kaiyamba Chiefdom, Elizabeth also awarded Madam Massaquoi the Queen's Medal for Chiefs.[41] Precolonial Mende and Sherbro peoples of Sierra Leone have a tradition of empowering women with the highest power positions. In 1787, Queen Yamacouba of Sherbro was one of the document's signatories when the Freetown treaty was made. Two other reigning female chiefs from Sherbro and Mende signed peace agreements with the Europeans and the new settlers.[42] Colonial records further show that in 1914, there were eight Mende female paramount chiefs and two others from Vai and Krim, including the famous Soma "Mammy" Yoko of Gbo chiefdom.[43]

The second event that mirrored women's empowerment during the Crown's visit concerns what a British Pathé newsreel of 1961 described as "the essential Africa" parading for "Mrs. Queen." The newsreel referred to a group of young women who treated the royals to the best African dances. The performers appeared topless in traditional attires, as it was the custom. Some European officials pretentiously thought it inappropriate to display any form of nudity before the sovereign. The objection's details remained muted until 1965 when the same troupe landed in the United Kingdom for the 1965 Commonwealth's Arts Festival. Several British dailies had a fit with headlines screaming with protests.[44]

The print media's demurrals contradicted the implicit philosophy of cultural diversity espoused by the Commonwealth of Nations. In his opening speech to the first Advisory Council meeting at Buckingham Palace, the Duke of Edinburgh reminded the audience that the association might share similarities in science and almost all the fields of cooperation, "but it's in their cultures, almost alone, that the differences exist. And a country's culture, after all, is what it's remembered by."[45] Ian Hunter, the director-general of the

1965 Commonwealth Arts Festival, reiterated the sentiment in his speech to the joint meeting of the Society's Commonwealth Section with the Royal Commonwealth Society on March 25, 1965:

> If you cast your mind back over the great civilizations, they are remembered on the whole for their cultures. And therefore, I feel, and a lot of others feel with me, that the cultural aspect of the Commonwealth in the exchange of ideas of the mind, of art performances, art forms, painting, is a very necessary aspect of building up understanding between the various countries; and with understanding comes what I think is the most important ingredient of all, which is respect.[46]

To the royals' credit, they did not reinforce the colonial officials' cultural stereotypes. The Queen and the Duke welcomed the Sierra Leone women dancers' cultural heritage. As Radhika Natarajan noted, their presence at the festivities was a "two-way process of legitimation with the participants in the festival that spoke to a long history of the monarchy's role in empire, changing political circumstances demanded new modes of encounter." The festival served in "fracturing imperial forms of looking and representation," which remains the broader goal of the Commonwealth and Elizabeth's tour-de-force. The association aims to harness diverse opinions and expressions, including political desires, open new horizons of learning, and international participation. Standing behind the dancers, the monarchy encouraged the old and the new orders to "meet at the Commonwealth Arts Festival, allowing for a reengagement with an association rooted in an imperial past, but promising an equitable future."[47]

Sierra Leone's experience with decolonization and conformity to colonial obedience reflected the broader trend in British Africa. In Nigeria, The Gambia, Tanganyika (Tanzania), Kenya, Uganda, Sudan, Nyasaland (Malawi), Basutoland (Lesotho), Bechuanaland (Botswana), and so on, African moderates and those who embraced the British tutelage enjoyed robust Foreign Office support and goodwill. In Nigeria, for instance, the Northern People's Congress leader, Sir Alhaji Tafawa Balewa, KBE, inherited the reins of power on October 1, 1960, without a national election.

Like Margai, Secretary Iain Macleod had a great admiration of Balewa compared to the three region premiers—the Sardauna of Sokoto (North), Chief Obafemi Awolowo (West), and Dr. Nnamdi Azikiwe (East). While Macleod labeled Azikiwe as "the same doctor who, in my day, was the stormy petrel of Nigerian politics and who, today, is the respected President of the Senate," he joined the Right Hon. Member for Middleborough, East, Mr. Marquand, in paying special tribute to Balewa. He described the federation's first prime minister as "one of the outstanding statesmen of the day, whether in Africa or elsewhere. I feel certain that under his guidance, the future of Nigeria can be well assured."[48] The colonial secretary was simply reechoing similar sentiments held by colonial officials in Nigeria and the colonial office. For instance, on February 20, 1959, M. G. Smith stated that Balewa "has displayed remarkable wisdom and statesmanship in his capacity and there is good hope that it will be he who leads the country [Nigeria] into independence."[49]

Later, Macleod grudgingly recognized the father of Nigeria's nationalism, Herbert Macaulay, but called him "a stormy petrel"—an individual who heralds trouble. Similarly, he saw Dr. Azikiwe as "a little irresponsible in his manner" in the earlier days but agreed, "He was a very great, magnetic leader" who "made a considerable impact on the thought of Nigerians for the liberation from aliens." However, to Balewa, he assigned the virtues of prudence and patience, concluding that under his guidance, Nigeria's future "can be well assured."[50]

While British leaders joggled the African nationalists into categories of their choice as the empire unraveled, one individual was in a class of his own—Ethiopia's Emperor Haile Selassie I.

Tour-De-Triumph Meets Noble Selassie

The self-styled "Conquering Lion of the Tribe of Judah," "Elect of God," and "King of Kings" positioned himself for global recognition after the Second World War.[51] After surviving many trials, Selassie, in his terms, successfully transformed indigenous political systems into modern ones. He demonstrated as much pride in the local institutions as Elizabeth did in her British origins. The self-importance of the emperor came from mutually reinforcing spiritual and temporal bases instituted in myths and legends.[52] Ethiopia alone staved off outright European colonization and stood as a source of inspiration for all the oppressed people of African descent. In the spiritual realm, scholars of the *Kebra Nagast* remind us that Selassie was a direct progeny of Menelik I, the son of the biblical King Solomon and Queen of Sheba. In other words, Selassie was a descendant of King David.

The divine lineage conferred the emperor with a sort of messianic spiritual aura. Gizachew Tiruneh argues that the primary purpose of the *Kebra Nagast*, written by the Monophysite Christians in the fourteenth century, was "to perpetuate the reign and prestige of Ethiopian monarchs as descendants of King Solomon, and the guardians of Judeo-Christianity."[53] In 1955, Emperor Selassie accentuated the significance of the *Kebra Nagast* in the country's revised constitution. "The Imperial dignity shall remain perpetually attached to the line of Haile Selassie I, a descendant of King Sahle Selassie, whose line descends without interruption from the dynasty of Menelik I, son of the Queen of Ethiopia, the Queen of Sheba, and King Solomon of Jerusalem."[54]

Selassie's genealogy and Ethiopia's success at colonial resistance had won respect for Ethiopia in the community of nations. There was high anticipation for Her Majesty's visit because Selassie genuinely appreciated Britain's role in Ethiopia's liberation from Benito Mussolini's Italian fascists in 1941. The Italian invaders had put the East African country under unimaginable pain with poison gas and aerial bombardment. The Anglo-Ethiopian relationship had formed during Selassie and his family's exile in a country house near Bath, Somerset, Britain, from May 9, 1936, to May 5, 1941.

In 1954, Emperor Selassie visited London under Prime Minister Winston Churchill. The sovereign, Duke of Edinburgh, Queen Mother, Churchill, and other officials gave him a warm reception.[55] Before Selassie's arrival, Lord Macpherson reminded the House of Commons that the emperor's visit afforded Britain an opportunity "to endeavor to negotiate a treaty of trade and friendship with this rapidly progressing country." He noted that "during the recent visit of the Emperor to the United States, a pact of a similar nature was negotiated" and that he "was rather disappointed that the Americans had stolen a march on us in that respect."[56] In principle, the House of Commons requested Her Majesty to treat Selassie with royal fanfare "so that the visit of the Emperor will mark in practical fashion the beginning of a closer and even more friendly association between us."[57]

Thousands of Britons and the African diaspora in England cheered the emperor at Whitehall and Trafalgar. Her Majesty remarked in her welcome speech, "I would like to think that in England, you would always feel at home."[58] The emperor generously expressed his indebtedness to the monarchy and the British people in response. Elizabeth honored Selassie with the prestigious Knight of the Garter, Britain's most exclusive chivalry order. Only a handful of individuals outside Western Europe, including the King of Nepal, Jang Bahadur Ranaji, held a similar honor.[59] The Queen also conferred on the emperor's son, the Duke of Harar, the emblem of a Knight Grand Cross of the Victorian Order. The emperor's military uniform was very Western: dark blue, heavily encrusted with gold lace, his chest alight with stars and orders' insignia.[60]

Figure 4.1: Emperor Haile Selassie I and Queen Elizabeth II, Buckingham Palace, 1954. (AP News; public domain)

In return, the emperor gave the Queen the Chain and Order of the Seal of Solomon, established by Emperor Yohannes IV of Ethiopia in 1874 as the highest imperial honor. To the Duke of Edinburgh, he gave the Chain of the MOM Exalted Order of the Queen of Sheba, instituted in 1922 by Emperor Zawditu. During the reception at Buckingham Palace, the Queen continued her praise: "Under your inspiring leadership, the Ethiopian people have made truly remarkable progress since the war. I am very proud of the part my country played in the liberation of Ethiopia, together with your own patriot forces."[61] In response, Selassie talked about the long years of bitter, enforced absence from his kingdom. He cherished Britain's royal friendship and the British people who sustained him and his people over the period: "Such friendship and loyalty have earned our imperishable gratitude."[62]

It was not by coincidence that the October 1954 trip to the United Kingdom was part of Selassie's first six other visits to the United States. The emperor symbolized the Cold War struggle as he consistently stood on the Western side. As President Dwight D. Eisenhower's guest, Selassie had embarked on a two-month-long trip that covered over 7,000 miles of North America. His rallying call for collective security (in June 1936) to the League of Nations as the Second World War approached remains a historical signpost in the League's history. Selassie contributed troops to the UN mission to the Korean War in 1950–1953 to ingratiate Ethiopia to the United States. Ethiopia enjoyed particular respect in the United States. It signed the United Nations Declaration on January 1, 1941, and contributed to the UN founding conference in San Francisco in 1945.[63]

The royal visit of February 1–8, 1965 (aka Tour-of-Triumph) to Ethiopia was a response to Selassie's tour of Britain ten years earlier.[64] Selassie treated Queen Elizabeth and Prince Philip to a kind reception in Addis Ababa.[65] Ever flamboyant in ceremonial garb, the emperor arrived at the airport to welcome the royals decked in the uniform of a field marshal and a lion's mane helmet. As the royal motorcade passed through the short distance to the Jubilee Palace in Addis Ababa, Elizabeth's attention caught "two huge gilded aluminum lions erected in her honor."[66]

The planning of the eight-day trip was as elaborate as it was royal, merry, and entertaining. With 60,000 waiting to welcome the Queen, the security forces closed the traffic hours before the regal aircraft landed in Addis Ababa. A band of amblers among the ecstatic crowd carried ceremonial spears. At a midpoint on the drive from the airport, the royals moved from their car to a chariot pulled by six white horses, which the *Ethiopian Gazette* of February 1, 1965, said came from the stable of the famous Emperor Ferdinand Maximilian, the archduke of Austria and Emperor of Mexico (d. June 19, 1867). A hundred horsemen from the imperial guards flanked the royal motorcade on all sides. The bodyguards wore heavy lion's mane helmets. With the jubilant crowd clapping a rhythmic welcome and drums thumping, driving to the Emperor's palace took about an hour. Equestrians cantered among the group with extended "lions' manes stuck to their hairs."[67]

The emperor treated Queen Elizabeth to a state banquet in the old palace. In the gardens was Selassie's pet lion, Tojo, symbolizing the Lion of Judah's land. Across from the palace where the royal guests spent the night was the Organization of African Unity's Addis Ababa headquarters. Since 1963, when the organization came into existence, African leaders had routinely gathered here to condemn colonial rule and strategize on a liberation plan for Southern Africa, including Southern Rhodesia, Northern Rhodesia, and apartheid South Africa. A banner across the road incongruously proclaimed, "Long live the friendship between Great Britain and Ethiopia." Behind the palace were streets named after three British generals—Archibald Wavell, Orde Charles Wingate, and Alan Cunningham. These officers commanded the Kenyan East African forces that liberated Ethiopia from the Italian occupation forces.[68]

As *The Guardian* reported in February 1965, with the royal visit, the Ethiopians saw Britain as a liberator and a great country rather than a colonialist. The contrast between colonizer and liberator cannot be more dramatic. Ethiopia demonstrated its enthusiasm and fascination with being imperial, with a vast majority of the soldiers at the airport adorned with the British African Star, a services medal founded by Britain on July 8, 1943, in honor of British and Commonwealth forces who participated in the North African front from June 1940 to May 1943 during the Second World War. Throughout the busy week, the focus was primarily on the country's ancient glories. Elizabeth spent a night seeing Gondor, the old city capital. She also visited the new landmarks, including the vast Tendaho cotton estates built by Britain's entrepreneur Mitchell Cotts and British shareholders.[69]

Like in Sierra Leone and elsewhere, Elizabeth's presence in Ethiopia prompted positive discourses on gender. One particular incident was Elizabeth's entrance into the Aksum Cathedral, housing the Ark of the Covenant (or Tabot in Ethiopia). As with the Hebrew tradition, the Ethiopian Coptic Church also barred women from the Holy of Holies, where the Ark resides. The emperor waived this tradition to admit Her Majesty.[70] Inspired by this event, *Ethiopia Herald*, Addis Ababa's only daily newspaper, inaugurated a page dedicated to women's matters. The paper thanked Elizabeth for showing interest in the industry and patronizing the arts. Her Majesty's dress on the day of arrival was also the paper's discussion topic. Her buttercup yellow coat and petal hat were a source of luster to the admirers.

Overall, the Queen's visit to Ethiopia was a positive diplomatic operation in many ways. It obscured most Ethiopians' frosty memory of the British monarchy before 1941. In public speeches throughout the tour, no one recalled the past unfortunate events when Emperor Theodore felt slighted in correspondence with Queen Victoria and later committed suicide during a British punitive expedition on his Abyssinia kingdom.[71] The enthusiasm for the royals belonged to a happy era—the age of Queen Elizabeth II, the branding mark of the new global Britain.

Like the 1954 meeting in the United Kingdom, Elizabeth's Ethiopian tour was marked with gifts and an exchange of pleasantries. Historians know that political gift-giving is filled with personal intentions, nuances of power and authority, motives, noise, secrecy, and symbolism. Elizabeth brought a racehorse, Robespierre, to Selassie as a mark of the envisioned new Afro-Anglo relationship. The horse, one of her favorites, signified courage, freedom, attachment, and mutual respect. Selassie, in turn, honored Elizabeth with a ceremonial horse race in honor of the Queen's particular fascination with horses. Here, we see a degree of the common characteristic of courage and interest in horses between the two leaders. The horse is widely seen as a loyal companion in battle and is often part of folklore, history, and myth-making.

Selassie also gave Elizabeth a gift in the form of a golden tray. Generally, gold is associated with glamor, grandeur, prosperity, and wealth—both royals shared these characteristics. The famous Armenian jeweler Bedros Sevadjian designed the thirty-pound artifact, curated with pure gold from the Adola Mines in southern Ethiopia. The gift, now on display at Buckingham Palace, forms part of a royal exhibition containing other presents received by Her Majesty from around the world.[72] Selassie also gave Elizabeth a screen-printed cotton headscarf made by the Cotonificio Barattolo in Asmara, Eritrea, as a sign of social distinction.[73]

Doing Hide-and-Seek with "Dear Amin"

Kirk-Greene's typology of the postcolonial African leaders placed Uganda's Idi Amin Dada Oumee at the eccentric center.[74] When the former army commander under President Milton Obote shot his way to power in a military coup in 1971, many Ugandans welcomed him as a political savior. Mr. Obote had become the prime minister at independence on October 9, 1962, and soon became an autocrat.[75] His crackdown on the opposition sent Kabaka Mutesa II, the Buganda monarch, into a second exile in 1966. Mutesa died in exile in London in 1969, and Amin cashed in on the widespread outrage following the kabaka's death to seize power.[76]

A member of Uganda's Kakwa group, with little formal education, Amin once said, "Sometimes people mistake the way I talk for what I am thinking. I never had any formal education—not even a nursery school certificate. But, sometimes, I know more than PhDs because, as a military man, I know how to act; I am a man of action."[77] The self-styled "Conqueror of the British Empire," he awarded himself the Victoria Cross, the highest British honor. He enlisted in the colonial army in 1946, battled against the Mau Mau uprising in Kenya, and was the boxing champion of Uganda from 1951 to 1960.[78] Amin's friendship with President Obote after independence in 1962 earned him a rapid rise through the ranks. He was Obote's instrument of terror against domestic opponents. One who rides on the tiger must prepare to pay the price when the beast gets hungry. Obote was about to dispense with the army chief when Amin executed a preemptive coup in January 1971.[79]

In 1985, a livid British lord, Viscount Buckmaster, in retrospect blamed his country for enabling Obote and destroying Kabaka Mutesa. The miscalculation, he pointed out, intensified Obote's "controls and paved the way for Amin's bloodless coup of January 25, 1971."[80] A few hours after the Amin coup upstaged Obote while at a Commonwealth conference in Singapore, *The Daily Telegraph* of January 26, 1971, applauded Amin and pugnaciously tried to tie the Commonwealth conferences' continued relevance with removing what the author called "undesirable rulers." According to the paper, the number of such rulers "overthrown as a result of their temporary absences, as has now happened to Dr. Obote of Uganda, would thereby be increased."[81] The influential *Financial Times* of London trailed in a similar line to vote Amin "Man of the Week" in the days following his power grab. *The Daily Telegraph* described the coupist as "a welcome contrast to other African leaders and a staunch friend of Britain." *The Times* paid an identical complement.[82]

Meanwhile, suspicions circulated that the US CIA, the British Foreign Office through MI6, Kenya's Intelligence Service, and the Israeli Mossad sacked Obote.[83] If there was any doubt about Britain's role in the coup, Foreign Secretary Alec Douglas-Home's report, received from Bruce Mackenzie, the MI6's Africa operative a day after, dispelled all suspicions: "The way is now clear for our high commission in Kampala to get close to Amin."[84] In his assessment of Amin's first six months in office, R. M. Slater wrote to Douglas-Home:

> Amin is a man the people can understand. His humble origin, direct speech and simple faith in God, apparently free from any bigotry, tell in his favour. His manifest enjoyment of the lighter side of his 'meet the people' campaign—the dancing and other forms of entertainment on which money has been freely spent—is an endearing trait. His courage commands respect; he takes no visible security precautions, even in areas where hostility might be expected.[85]

While perceptions of Obote changed as his behavior became more violent and erratic, the truth was that the West demonized Obote as "a dangerous Socialist" because he persistently criticized all forms of imperialism, including the apartheid system in South Africa.[86] Early in 1970, a dispatch from Kampala to London spoke to the growing suspicion between the government and Britain. The report blamed the situation on "the attitude taken in Britain towards Sir Edward Mutesa and his family." According to the dispatch, "after the Kabaka had left Uganda, the reporting of Ugandan events by the BBC and the London Press were perhaps understandably but all too frequently based on reports—often malicious and always tendentious—issued by the entourage of the former Kabaka."[87]

This explains why Obote's ouster from power became a divisive issue within the Organization of African Unity. A dispatch to Douglas-Home dated February 3, 1971, noted:

> It is clear that the Uganda situation is tending to divide the Black African Governments into two groups; the so-called "progressives" who clearly see the usurpation of Dr. Obote's presidency as damaging to the African community and damaging also to their claim to represent the people of Africa in the matter of British arms sales to South Africa in particular; and the 'moderates,' none of whom has yet felt able to recognize General Amin, though secretly sympathetic to him.[88]

Despite profiting from Britain's discontent with Obote's rule and support from the various Western governments, Amin soon revealed that he was no one's obedient boy: "I am just a professional soldier with a concern for my country and her people."[89]

Idi Amin ruled Uganda by coercion. The world ascribed to him an emblem of cruelty and violence. This attribute contributed to Amin's diminishing empathy with Africans, who joined the call for human rights in Uganda. The human rights violations posed a challenge to the Commonwealth. Although the association believed in noninterference in member nations' domestic affairs, its commitment to freedom and the rule of law was sacrosanct in the decolonization agenda. However, the association failed to suspend or expel Uganda from the bloc.[90] Amin remained in power for almost a decade, practicing unbridled madness. An estimated 300,000 died under the dictatorship.[91]

Amin's encounter with the British monarch remains one of the most bizarre exchanges in Commonwealth history. A commentator described the relationship as "a payback from the spirit world for colonial officials' wrongs to Kabaka Mutesa II."[92] Declassified papers from the National Archives reveal the need for Britain's continued support with arms and funds, which brought Amin to London in 1971. However, the exchanges between the dictator and the

Figure 4.2: President Idi Amin at the United Nations, New York, 1975. (Photograph by Bernard Gotfryd; retrieved from the Library of Congress)

monarch overshadowed everything else. Reading between the lines shows that Queen Elizabeth had diplomatically encouraged Amin's friendship in the hope that he would conform to good behaviors as part of the Commonwealth family.

On July 13, 1971, General Amin had lunch with the Queen at Buckingham Palace before meeting with Foreign Secretary Sir Alec Douglas-Home.[93] Soon, the joke circulated that the Ugandan leader had made an impromptu vote of thanks after lunch:

> My Majesty Mr. Queen sir, horrible ministers and Members of Parliament, invented Guests, ladies under gentlemen. I hereby thank you completely, Mr. Queen, sir, and also what he has done for me and my fellow Uganda who come with me. We have really eaten very much. And we are fed up completely; and also very thanks to you

keenly open up from all windows: so that those plenty climates can come into lunch. But before I go back to my country with a plane from the Entebbe airport of London, I wish to invitation you, Mr. Queen, to become home to Uganda so that we can also revenge on you. [*sic*]⁹⁴

Although this manner of speech was part of Amin's character, one may question whether this episode really happened—especially given the conspicuous media blackout of the address in London.⁹⁵ The curious question throws into relevance John Balmer's deduction that the Crown is managed as a corporate entity with royal, regal, relevant, responsive, and respected branding credentials. In this context, it makes sense to erase and forget the Elizabeth-Amin meeting with silence; the negative publicity linked to the Ugandan dictator's antics did not fit into the positive side of the "Royal Branding Mix."⁹⁶ Abraham Demoz reminds us that Queen Victoria retrospectively ordered her officials to destroy copies of her August 8, 1898, recorded messages to Emperor Menelik, although the text of Menelik's reply (also in a voice recording) was preserved in the Windsor Library.⁹⁷ While one may not want to speculate on the exact reason for Victoria's decision, it is evident that the royal branding culture predated Queen Elizabeth II's time.

Regarding Elizabeth's encounter with Amin at Buckingham Palace, Andrew Rice's study of murder and memory in Idi Amin's Uganda recalls that the dictator intentionally addressed the Queen's husband as "Mr. Philip" instead of adequately recognizing him as the Duke of Edinburgh.⁹⁸ The joke continued that during the after-lunch speech in 1971, Amin promised Elizabeth that she would "eat a full cow" in Kampala, filling "up your stomach" that she would have difficulty walking. "Even when you want to rest at night, I will make sure that you sleep on top of me" so that she would enjoy "all the gravity of fresh air." The Queen later inquired from the journalists present what Amin had said, and they replied that it was in a language similar to English, but that was all they could say.⁹⁹

Then, Her Majesty's Office sent Amin a Christmas postcard through the Foreign Office in December 1971. These exchanges happened before the details of Amin's horrific acts at home came to the knowledge of the outside world.¹⁰⁰ Consequently, Elizabeth altered her perception of Amin and became more cautious about their relationship. She took precautions to avoid endangering the British lives in Uganda.¹⁰¹

In January 1972, Amin invited the Queen to the tenth anniversary of Uganda's independence in October. "It would do my government a great honor," he wrote, "if Your Majesty could grace these celebrations with your presence in the company of your husband and the rest of your family."[102] The invitation prompted Sir Alec Douglas-Home to warn of the Queen's difficulties dealing with a "Commonwealth head of government known to be a murderer."[103]

On August 4, 1972, General Amin announced the expulsion of about fifty thousand Asians from Uganda so that Ugandans could be "fully independent" and "take control of their economy."[104] "If anyone is found painting himself with black boot polish, disciplinary actions will be taken against him," decreed Amin.[105] Those ejected included thousands of British passport holders.[106] On October 23, 1972, Douglas-Homes told Parliament that perhaps the best use of "the Commonwealth was to influence people who go astray." But he stressed that General Amin's actions "have been totally inconsistent with any civilized standard of behavior."[107]

The expulsion upset the Queen, so she was disinclined to send a proposed Independence Day message to the East African country. She rescinded her decision after a Foreign Office staff cautioned that British citizens in Uganda could face Amin's wrath if he felt slighted. In heeding the advice, the Colonial Office sent a brief message expressing the Queen's good wishes to Ugandans—without mentioning Amin.

> Dear Mr. President,
> Thank you for your message of 10th January, delivered by your Minister of Defence. I reciprocate your good wishes and read with pleasure what you said about the relations between our countries.
> I am very grateful for you asking me to attend the celebrations of the Tenth Anniversary of Ugandan Independence on 9th October 1972. I am most disappointed that my commitments at that time will prevent my accepting your invitation.
> I take this opportunity of wishing all success to your celebrations and to Uganda and its people throughout 1972.
> I am your good friend,
> Elizabeth R.[108]

On December 30, 1974, after contact with a Scottish nationalist organization urging revolution against Britain, President Amin wrote a telegram to prominent world leaders, including the Queen, Prime Minister Harold Wilson, UN Secretary-General Kurt Waldheim, the Soviet leader Leonid Brezhnev, Chairman Mao Zedong of China, Colonel Gaddafi of Libya, and others. The letter alleged, "The people of Scotland are tired of being exploited by the English. For a long time, England has thrived on the energies and brains of Scotland." Amin claimed, "The leaders of the Scottish Provisional Government have also asked me to inform you that they are fed up with English discrimination both within and England itself and in countries like South Africa and Rhodesia."[109]

The 1974 face-off was another provocation in the list of others from Kampala. Amin turned around while encouraging the Scottish rebellion, offering to solve the Ulster question. In January 1975, he sent a letter to Her Majesty indicating his intent to visit Britain that summer. In the memo now remembered as the "Honeymoon Message," Amin stated his plan to visit Scotland, Wales, and Northern Ireland to see the "people who are struggling for self-determination and independence from your political and economic system. As a revolutionary leader, I am prepared, when necessary, to advise on various liberation fronts and on ways and means of defeating not only real but also imaginary imperialism, racism, and economic serfdom."[110]

Amin asked that the Queen use her influence to arrange a meeting with the Asians of British nationality that he booted out of his country because of his "unequivocal determination to rid Uganda of economic slavery and loyalty to corruption."[111] The dictator added that the Asians' presence "in Uganda was perpetually identified with systemic looting of our economy and a concerted effort to voraciously subject and frustrate efforts and intents of the black man to shape his own economic, political, cultural, and social destiny."[112] Amin concluded his provocative letter by deriding the British economy and hoping "there would be a steady and reliable supply of essential commodities because I know that your country is ailing in many fields. I look forward to meeting you, Your Majesty."[113]

On June 19, 1975, Queen Elizabeth again found herself in an unenviable position to send a personal message to Kampala. A week earlier, Amin had refused to acknowledge a letter from Prime Minister Harold Wilson relating to Denis Cecil Hills, a British professor from Midland, incarcerated in Uganda. Amin's attitude toward Wilson portended serious danger for Mr. Hills in particular. Elizabeth's appeal was urgent to save Hills and another Briton from Amin's firing squad. Because of Amin's minor mention in an unpublished manuscript entitled *The White Pumpkin*, a military tribunal in Kampala found Mr. Hills guilty of treason.[114] There was a controversy over the circumstances surrounding the arrest of the professor. Kampala believed he was a British spy "working for a U.S. government security force."[115] But a Kampala civil court had cleared him of any wrongdoing earlier. The same tribunal acquitted Stanley Smolen, the second man, of hoarding cooking oil and detergent packets. Reports from Kampala said that Amin had congratulated Smolen on his release—thereby raising hopes in the Foreign Office "that clemency will now be shown to Mr. Hills."[116]

However, Amin had different ideas; he wanted to use Mr. Hills as a ransom to negotiate a stop to "malicious propaganda" about him in the foreign press, and to secure the expulsion of Ugandan dissidents in Britain and the British supply of some military vehicle parts.[117] Ironically, the parts were needed for the fifty-one vehicles Britain sent to Uganda soon after the 1971 coup to enable Amin to consolidate power. One of the two British army officers who carried the Queen's dispatch to Kampala was colonial King's African Rifles Commander Sir Chandos Blair. In his company was retired Major Ian Grahame, Sergeant Amin's regimental commander. The dictator requested the latter's presence as a precondition for releasing Denis. In a frantic response to the unparalleled ten-day ultimatum issued by Amin, the Queen ignored the standard protocol with her plea.[118]

In *the New York Times* in June 1975, Joseph Miller concluded that it was evident that Amin's "intention over the fate of the two Britons was to retaliate by humiliating the British, and at the same time, gain some practical advantage."[119] In the end, the dictator did not release the captive willfully. It took Kenya's seizure of military equipment shipped to Uganda from Russia to facilitate Hills's release. Kampala swapped Hills's freedom for the consignment on July 10, 1975.[120]

However, the trauma of the interchanges between Amin and Elizabeth lingered. In 1977, there were heightened fears among British officials that Amin would attempt to join the Commonwealth Heads of Government Meeting in London in the company of his wife Maryam and son Moses.[121] He had declared, "I do not want to be controlled by any superpower. I consider myself the most powerful figure in the world, and that is why I do not let any superpower control me."[122] As the conference was about to open on June 8, 1977, a report credited to Ugandan radio, apparently released to generate disquiet in London, claimed that Amin was flying to London through Libya with a contingent of 250 people comprising "dancers" and "supporters." In response to a warning that there was no space in the hotel for so many people, Amin declared they would all stay at Buckingham Palace.[123]

Amin's undesired presence at the meeting prompted a frenzy of objections and warnings from the British press and government officials. For example, the *Daily Mirror* of June 8, 1977, screamed, "Out with Idi Amin," although "the Commonwealth cannot wash its hands of Uganda any more than Idi Amin can wash the blood from his."[124] Meanwhile, British officials set up security and immigration alerts across neighboring countries, including Scotland, Belgium, and France, asking these countries not to allow Amin to enter Britain through their territories. British officials also designed a detailed plan, comprising an antiterrorist squad to arrest Amin at the airport.[125] Revisiting the story recently, *The Daily Squib* argued that although Amin did not eventually attend the conference, he caused quite a stir in London. The effectiveness of his game in rattling Buckingham and Whitehall confirms what the *Aberdeen Press and Journal* described as a "sinister new move in Amin's cat-and-mouse game with government."[126]

Ultimately, Amin's absence at the Commonwealth meeting was the main story of the year, so Queen Elizabeth remained troubled about the likelihood he would come for the June 1977 Thanksgiving Service at St Paul's Cathedral.[127] Lord (Louis) Mountbatten, former viceroy of India, disclosed that he inquired from the monarch why she appeared a bit worried. In response, Elizabeth said she was pondering "how awful it would be if Amin were to gatecrash the [Thanksgiving] party." With a laugh, the Queen said she planned to use the City's Pearl Sword to strike him on the head.[128]

For a monarch who had met with all manner of leaders worldwide with courage and dignity, it was apparent that the thought of Idi Amin having lunch with her again was a severe source of uneasiness. Hannah Furness wrote in the *Daily Telegraph* in 2013 that it revealed "how seriously the Queen took the potential threat posed by the Ugandan dictator."[129]

This assessment of Her Sovereign's royal tours to Africa in the immediate postcolonial era captured how the Cold War continued to affect international relations. Although Elizabeth made several visits to the continent from late 1961 to the end of the Cold War in 1989, two of them were discussed in detail. Also covered was Idi Amin's wish to host the Queen in Uganda—an impossible request to grant given the dictator's nonconformist behaviors. The royal trip to Sierra Leone in November 1961 was memorable because of Elizabeth's genuine interest in the lives of ordinary Sierra Leoneans. The journey to Ethiopia in early 1965 was exemplary on the part of the Ethiopian emperor, who successfully reinvented the institution and restored its respect along modern lines.[130]

Queen Elizabeth's experience with General Idi Amin is not just a sad reminder of the consequences of British colonial rule in East Africa. It implicated the errors of postcolonial paternalism and neocolonialism. The new African leaders who tried to resist neocolonial control were often demonized and marked for elimination. The fate of Nkrumah in Ghana and Obote in

Uganda are just a few examples where Britain, in conceit with its Cold War allies, subverted the offending postcolonial leaders. However, historians must underline Her Majesty's patience and sense of humanity in dealing with Amin. Where her ancestors, like Queen Victoria, would have used disproportional violence to humiliate the African kings, Elizabeth handled Amin with tolerance, humor, and understanding.

The royal tours were priceless in creating a new era of Afro-Anglo relations. While the colonial order represented an association of unequal partners, Queen Elizabeth's leadership in the postcolonial era left a more lasting and positive impression among the African masses. Through her visits and acquaintance with the Africans, the Queen prioritized the imperatives of amicable African politics and encouraged youth development, women's empowerment, and cultural exchanges without making these initiatives about herself. The Queen had a crucial role in instilling stability and peace in the Commonwealth through her leadership skills and diplomatic influence.[131] The association's milestones and the various cultural horizons it fostered under the Queen deserve closer attention.

CHAPTER 5

MAJESTIC MILESTONES: THE COMMONWEALTH AND AFRICA'S DEVELOPMENT

> We have been fortified in our faith that in the Commonwealth of Nations, we have a powerful force for cooperation in the promotion of peace, prosperity, and equity within and amongst peoples across the globe.[1]
>
> —President Nelson Mandela

> I feel enormously proud of what the Commonwealth has achieved, and all of it within my lifetime.[2]
>
> —Queen Elizabeth

At the 2015 Commonwealth Heads of Governments Meeting (CHOGM) in Malta, the Queen reflected on its achievements since 1949—evidently, her handover notes: "The sixty-six years since then have seen a vast expansion of human freedom: the forging of independent nations and new Commonwealth members, many millions of people sprung from the trap of poverty, and the unleashing of the talents of a global population. I have been privileged to witness this transformation, and to consider its purpose."[3]

In recognizing human freedom as the most prominent legacy in this mission accomplishment speech, the Queen offered a subtle cue to her 1947 birthday promise in Cape Town, "If we all go forward together with an unwavering faith, a high courage, and a quiet heart, we shall be able to make of this ancient commonwealth, which we all love so dearly, an even grander thing—more free, more prosperous, more happy and a more powerful influence for good in the world—than it has been in the greatest days of our forefathers."[4]

As a field of academic discourse, studies on the postwar Commonwealth have ignored the intersection between Elizabeth's African mission, the postcolonial state's development needs, and Whitehall's Commonwealth plan as a placeholder for a dying Empire. Melanie Torrent blamed the manifest dearth of scholarly interest on the "whiggish myth" that Britain had always been honest with self-government.[5] Kathleen Paul adds that while the postwar Conservative leader Winston Churchill entered the Second World War to evade being associated with the British Empire's demise, his Labour Party counterparts such as Clement Atlee, Ernest Bevin, and Herbert Morrison equally espoused parallel thoughts after the war.[6] Assessing the Tory and Labour party rhetoric from Harold Wilson's rise in 1964, Philip Murphy concluded that Britain's bond with the Commonwealth member nations has been marginal.[7]

Torrent, Paul, Murphy, and others provide some analytical lenses into the trials of Elizabeth's Commonwealth journey. Whitehall's manifest disinterest in Africa's postcolonial development allows for an appreciation of the Crown's devotion to the cause.[8] As the mother of a nation whose children had cut their teeth using *nkamanya* (brute, shameless, and unapologetic force) to rob others, Elizabeth believed in the Commonwealth as a path to remedy some colonial ills. Her belief derives from a consciousness that the unchaining of peoples from the humiliations of domination is the key to unity, economic development, and peace—a resonance of Her Majesty's 1953 vow "to that new conception of an equal partnership of nations and race."[9]

An estimate of Elizabeth's Commonwealth leadership conjures the norms and theories of her African mission vis-à-vis the imperatives of royal branding in a fast-changing world. The discourse also fits into the colonial reparations dialogue. But the pertinent argument, as the Malta conversation embodies, is that after six decades of pursuit, the Crown's African mission begs for closure. The Africans may feel different, as indicated by the slough of anger erupting after her death. The question is whether the dissonance between colonial exploitation and reparation activism diminishes or even mortifies the royal Commonwealth mission. Besides its adaptation as a vestige of colonialism, African leaders have clung to the Commonwealth for several reasons. *The African Report* of March 10, 2021, noted that the association serves as a forum for conflict resolution and to lobby donors and actors like the United Kingdom, Canada, India, and others.[10]

Torrent, Dan Halvorson, and others remind us that understanding the nuances of the Commonwealth undercurrents is essential as a decolonization concept. It personifies various things for the diverse stakeholders—a forum to rebrand the royal institution in the postwar order; an imperial creation to shelter, expand, and save Britain's power and influence while securing White Dominions' political autonomy and regional security; and an actor in its own right to end colonial forms of domination worldwide. On Australia's relationship with the British Empire in Southeast Asia, Halvorson discloses that before 1965, the Aussie elite considered it an obligation to aid Britain in the orderly decolonization of the Straits Settlements, Malayan Peninsula, and British Borneo Territories. A similar course of action demonstrated by White settlers in Southern Africa demystifies the narrative that a Cold War ideology of anti-communism explains a slew of racialized sentiments Whites held toward genuine decolonization within the organization.[11]

Despite the many idioms, arcs, and curves of the Commonwealth decolonization project, Her Majesty, in the end, built an inclusive and unified organization where Africans could play a vital role and appropriate political and economic autarky even with the British government's politics of subterfuge. Looking past Whitehall's decolonization plots and the virtual spaces and patterns of domination and dependence beyond the Colonial Office's closure in 1966 allows us to transcend the Manichean worlds of the colonizer and the colonized. Elizabeth piloted the Commonwealth ship through the treacherous waters of the Cold War, the sociospatial deprivations of apartheid, and the worst of Africa's bloody postcolonial conflicts, including the Nigeria-Biafra civil war of 1967–1970. Reflecting on these, Krishnan Srinivasan notes that from 1947, the Commonwealth's focus "has been on adjusting to new relationships within a framework in which past hostilities can be forgotten, and cooperation and consultation on both political and economic affairs can be fostered."[12]

Standing up for freedom, unity, and cooperation in an often contentious and fragile international arena where political realism and anarchy are the norms of engagement requires actions on the political and economic fronts. While the former was contentious, the association's economic initiatives proved less divisive. The group placed financial assistance at the center of member nations' development with the Colombo Plan for South and Southeast Asia in Sri Lanka in January 1950.[13] The Caribbean Aid Program, built on the theory of regional economic units as enablers of industrialization and other economic progress, followed eight years later in 1958.[14] As African countries broke the chains of colonial rule, CHOGM launched the Special Commonwealth African Assistance Program (SCAAP) in 1960.[15] A balanced assessment of the Commonwealth's achievements starts with the group's many challenges and setbacks. The association's records show Elizabeth's works, challenges, voice, passion, and dedication to the global family.

Challenges and Setbacks

Elizabeth's Commonwealth successes foreground many setbacks and sometimes divided opinions. For instance, when President Gamal Abdel Nasser of Egypt triggered the Suez Canal crisis on July 6, 1956, by nationalizing the strategic waterway, Britain abandoned the virtue of consultation with the member nations. It acted in tandem with its strategic interests and Cold War allies France and Israel. Prime Minister Anthony Eden voiced Britain's outrage against Nasser to the House of Commons, first on July 29 and again on August 2, 1956: "No arrangement for the future of this great international waterway could be acceptable to Her Majesty's Government which would leave it in the unfettered control of a single power. Which could, as recent events have shown, exploit it purely for purposes of national policy."[16] The reference to "Her Majesty's" objections to any arrangement for peace became a sticking point throughout the crisis. While it unfairly portrayed the Crown as the hand behind the neocolonial foreign policy, the war it provoked cast a dark shadow on the British frame of mind concerning Africa's freedom.

Feeling slighted by this development, India and Sudan threatened to leave the Commonwealth, while Canada and Australia openly expressed their disappointment. An apprehensive MP Major Patrick Wall had warned, "The future of the Commonwealth was at stake."[17] MP H. R. S. Crossman cautioned that Britain must consider the Africans' opinion of the crisis because "the British Government seems to be indulging in hectoring and bullying behavior. To them, the British Government looks like a great European, and the Egyptians look like little fellows who are being bullied. We had better get it clear how we look to the rest of the world."[18]

As the Suez Canal conflict ended with US diplomatic intervention, after a week of war and 3,200 deaths, meaningful steps toward rethinking Afro-Anglo relations came with Ghana's independence on March 6, 1957, and its admittance to the Commonwealth. To the displeasure of the White minority regime in South Africa, Ghana's admission was a source of discord within the group.[19] Although the apartheid leaders grudgingly agreed to Ghana's membership, President Daniël François Malan suggested in 1957 that it would be better to accord Ghana an inferior status. This idea would have created an "inner circle" comprising countries owing allegiance to the Crown. The "outer circle" would consist of those emerging nations who chose to become republics.[20] South Africa dropped this proposal when Johannes G. Strijdom succeeded Malan in 1958. However, Strijdom was as racially driven as his predecessor. Three years before his election, Sir P. Liesching had written to Sir S. Garner, UK high commissioner in South Africa, warning, "It would be even more difficult to handle with Mr. Strijdom's government than it would have been if Malan had remained in power."[21]

Like Malan, Strijdom snubbed formal diplomatic relations with the new African nations because he "needed the time to think about it carefully."[22] Reporting about his Africa tour to the cabinet in February 1960, Prime Minister Harold Macmillan lamented that the South African ruling party's racialist Oedipus syndrome or "doctrinaire policy" on race relations was a severe problem for Britain. "It would be a tragedy," he warned, "if South Africa's links with the Commonwealth were weakened by reason of differences of opinion on that question." Macmillan bemoaned that South Africa's exit would be economically detrimental to Britain and the Commonwealth because of its strong and flourishing economy.[23] A month later, one of the worst acts of apartheid repression occurred.

The Sharpeville Massacre

The Sharpeville killings of March 21, 1960, which led to sixty-nine deaths, were a police response to a peaceful protest against oppressive pass laws in a Black township. The incident obligated the Commonwealth to decide between support for the African state or the apartheid government. In siding with the Africans, MP John Stonehouse charged that the UK Parliament must demonstrate that the Commonwealth is constructively purposeful in response to the incident. He pressed that steps must be taken to strengthen unity within the association, including adopting a Commonwealth Convention in line with similar European Convention of Human Rights principles.[24]

Stonehouse was one of many who were troubled about the Commonwealth's future after Sharpeville. Early on March 1, 1960, *The Times* of London reported that several top officials, including A. Creech Jones, Jeremy Thorpe, Robert Exon, William Manchester, A. J. Ayer, Hugh Gaitskell, James Griffiths, and Donald Wade, signed a letter demanding the termination of South Africa's Commonwealth membership. On March 28, 1960, a week after Sharpeville, Prime Minister Jawaharlal Nehru of India told the Indian Parliament that the non-White people in South Africa "are practically prisoners" and compared it to the situation in the Nazi régime. The prime ministers of Canada and New Zealand also spoke out strongly against the South African regime's methods in response to the demonstrations. They requested the inclusion of the incident on the agenda of the Commonwealth Prime Ministers' Conference hosted by

Figure 5.1: Queen Elizabeth II and the Prime Ministers of the Commonwealth Nations, Windsor Castle, 1960. (John G. Diefenbaker Centre, Saskatoon, Canada, image number JGD1300; British Government, public domain)

Britain in March 1961. Nigeria immediately cut trade relations with South Africa.[25] In the face of these mounting pressures, South Africa suddenly withdrew from the Commonwealth on October 5, 1961, after an all-White referendum.[26] Frank Hayes noted that the withdrawal was long a republican agenda within Afrikaner nationalism that aimed to evade being held accountable by the Commonwealth.[27]

The association's stand against state-sponsored racism was a signpost in the modern notion of the Commonwealth. The new African nations' membership in the organization gave it much-needed vitality. As *British Documents on the End of the Empire* reveals, the overriding question for Britain was "whether to offend the rest of the world by pursuing policies toward South Africa conditioned by our economic and defense stakes there, or whether to take the calculated risk of offending South Africa in order to improve our position elsewhere in Africa."[28] Ghana's Commonwealth presence was conceived as a solution to rampant nationalism in Africa and an anodyne answer to the dilemma of undoing the empire in a manner satisfactory to British investments, prestige, and conscience.[29]

However, Whitehall continued appeasing the minority White rulers in South Africa at the risk of poisoning unity within the Commonwealth. British economic interests often took precedence over Hendrik Verwoerd's chauvinistic postures. But, by developing their relationships with the UN's member countries and strategic geo-regional blocs, the new African states shared their views on causes, sometimes at odds with the United Kingdom. A notable example was the Organization of African Unity's support for the freedom of Namibia, Zambia, and Zimbabwe from White minority domination.[30] The Biafra question in Nigeria caused deep disaffections within the OAU and the Commonwealth.

Nigeria-Biafra Civil War

To a great extent, economic considerations explain Britain's poor handling of the Nigeria-Biafra civil war of 1967–1970, prompting *The Times*'s comment that the secession raised Britain's dilemma of "antagonizing both sides in Nigeria" by remaining mute.[31] The civil war emanated from interethnic struggles for political power and resource control among the emergent Nigerian elite. Like other crises that troubled Commonwealth unity, Biafra mirrored the British colonial experiment's sad outcome in West Africa.[32] At Nigeria's independence in 1960, the international community anticipated it to be a shining example of democracy and Africa's prosperity. This expectation faded when violent interethnic politics became a humanitarian crisis in the country's eastern region. In 1968, a visitor to the area, which announced its secession on May 30, 1967, gave an eyewitness account of life. The Queen Elizabeth Hospital in Umuahia, the largest healthcare facility in the region, admitted 1,800 patients for kwashiorkor (severe protein deficiency) in a single day. In contrast, eighteen such cases occurred in 1963. At a nearby military hospital, the chief surgeon disclosed that physicians operated without anesthetizing their patients because of an acute shortage of medical supplies.[33]

The international dimension of the war proved that the notion of a "civil war" is a myth; there are always multiple foreign involvements.[34] Biafra's leader, Colonel Emeka Ojukwu, elevated Biafra's foreign dimension and peril with his revolutionary soliloquy. In particular, the June 1, 1969, discourse, known as the "Ahiara Declaration" in Biafra parlance, was Ojukwu's radio broadcast intended to bolster diminishing morale in Biafra. In its resentful, confrontationist, boastful, and romantic tone, the message turned counterproductive as it incorrectly portrayed the struggle as anti-West and anti-Soviet. In response, the USSR and Britain increased their support for the Nigerian federal government, while Egyptian pilots employed by the Nigerians flew bombing raids across Biafra.

Figure 5.2: Starving Woman from the Biafra War. (Photograph by unknown Centre for Disease Control and Prevention employee (Dr. Lyle Conrad?); Public Health Image Library (PHIL) Image #6874, public domain)

Outside assistance arrived for both sides in the war, but the nature of support was unbalanced. The Biafrans received humanitarian aid from agencies like the Red Cross, Caritas, individuals, and foreign governments, including France, Haiti, Ivory Coast, Ireland, and Israel. Biafra's receipts differed from the vast supplies of weaponry, hardware, technical, and logistics support, mostly flowing from Britain and the USSR, to the federal side.[35]

Within the Commonwealth, Tanzania, and Zambia called for an immediate end to the conflict that claimed over 1.5 million Biafran lives. In Britain, strident opposition to Prime Minister Harold Wilson's anti-Biafra policies gained momentum between 1968 and 1969. Peter Sedgwick has noted that the British Left did little to save Biafra from the stranglehold of British self-interests, especially Nigeria's oil.[36] The anger ensuing from Wilson's policy was channeled toward Queen Elizabeth II—another instance of the royal branding mix going awry. On November 25, 1969, John Lennon, of the legendary Beatles, returned his Member of the Order of British Empire award to Queen Elizabeth in protest to "Britain's involvement in the Nigeria-Biafra thing." In a statement to the press, Lennon condemned Britain's role in Biafra's plight.

I "Really shouldn't have taken it [the award]," he said. "Felt I had sold out. I must get rid of it, I kept saying, I must get rid of it. So, I did. Wanted to get rid of it by 1970 anyway."[37]

A year before Lennon, the two most influential Igbo men of the time returned their similar awards to the Queen. Two-division world boxing champion Richard Ihetu, aka "Dick Tiger," who was honored with a medal as a member of the Order of the British Empire (OBE) in 1963, returned the award to the Queen of England in 1969 in protest against British support of the Nigerian government in the civil war. In January 1968, Tiger joined the Biafran army to defend his people under a genocidal onslaught. "I know this is really a forgotten war as far as the rest of the world is concerned. No one cares about Africa." He argued that if his people did not fight back, it would be "genocide like they did to the Jews. They are out to kill all of us."[38]

Similar beliefs motivated his Igbo comrade, Sir Francis Akanu Ibiam, a staunch Anglophile and supporter of the British monarchy, to return a similar award to Elizabeth. An Igbo medical doctor trained in Scotland, Ibiam had espoused the doctrine of mutual partnership between the colonial government and Nigeria as a member of the legislative committee appointed to review Richard's constitution. He advocated for "step-by-step" decolonization, rejecting rushed processes: "I am not prepared to be rushed. I am not prepared to be told that we want self-government."[39] For his loyalty to the empire and contributions to missionary work, education, and politics, Her Majesty bestowed Ibiam with the OBE in 1951. During her visit to Nigeria in 1956, the Queen added the Queen's Coronation Medal to Ibiam's impressive honorary records.[40]

Dr. Ibiam served as governor of Eastern Nigeria and World Council of Churches president when Nigeria drifted into anarchy.[41] He bluntly expressed his disappointment in the Nigerian state, Britain's partisan role in the war, and Her Majesty's inaction or nonintervention. In August 1967, Ibiam sent a letter to Queen Elizabeth denouncing all the awards he had received from the monarch: "I threw my knighthood along with Francis, my English name at them."[42] Ibiam considered it "illogical and hypocritical" to keep his knighthood from the same Britain that was "backing the Federal troops with munitions."[43] As he explained in an interview in 1986, Ibiam came to a new awakening in dropping his English name, Francis: "I had to change it when I came to myself. I am an African and do know that names mean a lot."[44]

In Germany, The Netherlands, France, and Belgium, the Catholic Church, led by the Holy Ghost Fathers and the Spiritans, an influential French Order within the Catholic Church, mounted pressure on Europe to save the

Biafrans.⁴⁵ The European public perceived the war in religious terms as persecuted Christian Biafra versus a Leviathan Muslim Hausa-Fulani-led Nigerian government. In an era during which the West and East habitually disagreed on most issues concerning international politics, the question becomes critical as to why the superpowers were united in their objection to Biafra. Despite human rights abuses by the Nigerian state, Britain and Russia were more concerned that secession in the unstable postcolonial world order posed a severe strategic danger to the superpowers' vested economic, political, ideological, and cultural interests.⁴⁶ In *No Easy Row for a Russian Hoe*, Maxim Matusevich noted correctly that when Biafra was not an ideological partner and would lose the war, the Soviets went with the more vital Nigerian government force.⁴⁷

Additionally, the Commonwealth and the Organization of African Unity (OAU) shared a similar principle of noninterference in the member nations' internal affairs. Thus, at multiple levels, Biafra threatened the OAU and Commonwealth's internal cohesion and unity. Critical debates in the House of Commons showed that Prime Minister Wilson was more interested in the profits of the war's market economies. The crisis allows for a deeper reflection on Her Majesty's culpability or lack thereof in the conflict that greatly saddened several individuals and nations. On August 16, 1967, a month after secession, MP John Tilney had written to the *Daily Telegraph* suggesting that Britain should "either endeavor to get the Commonwealth to send troops to keep the peace while arbitration is enforced among the warring states, or remain out of internal squabbles."⁴⁸ Wilson, a Labour prime minister, ignored this idea, and there was no direct word about Her Majesty's stand.

One wonders how much influence the Queen had over a government policy driven by the economic advantage or "profit and loss policy." This is especially true with the discovery of Nigeria's colossal oil deposits in 1958, where British Shell BP had heavily invested. Wilson inherited a severe problem when he took office in 1964 with a £400 million deficit and persistent union strikes. He devalued the currency and identified trade as one of the strategies for economic recovery. On July 17, 1968, MP Denis Healey argued in defense of the arms trade with Nigeria, which Belgium, France, and The Netherlands had discontinued on moral grounds. Healey urged the House "to consider the value of the contracts and the interests in them of some Members' constituents."⁴⁹ In response, historian Margery Perham decried this manner of self-interest in a rejoinder in *The Times* of August 17, 1968, as "the same arguments used in defense of the slave trade."⁵⁰

Second, one may question Britain or the Commonwealth's power over now sovereign Nigeria. In a subsequent letter to *The Times*, Perham addressed this question. She contested that Britain may have no control over Nigeria, but it "has the historical, cultural and economic links which, if used with wisdom and generosity, might at this juncture help to bring this hideous war to an end and promote the first steps towards a unified Nigeria and a reconstructed Biafra."[51] Indeed, the famous novelist Chinua Achebe corroborated the point when, in 1968, the British Commonwealth Relations Office dismissed Biafra's agony as propaganda.[52] The official response from the Commonwealth remains in the Igbo/Biafra memory today as a betrayal.

Another revelation is that Elizabeth shared a close relationship with Harold Wilson, the first Labour prime minister and the first MP close to her age. To what extent this bond affected the Nigeria-Biafra conflict may remain a matter of speculation. Still, it is unconstitutional for the Queen to override popular Parliament decisions. The standing law of noninterference in exercising monarchical authority is the angle the Crown's critics often fail to appreciate. MP John Lee alluded to this misunderstanding when he charged that "Her Majesty's Government have aligned themselves with the [Nigerian] Federal Government to the extent of supplying them with arms. We are, therefore, held to be involved." Nonetheless, Lee noted that although Wilson's actions were "an Executive act," the policy could have failed if "it were known that the majority of hon. Members here were against it."[53] In other words, most MPs endorsed Wilson's anti-Biafra, profit-first policy. Indeed, British economic interests went further than the lucrative arms contracts from the Nigerian government. Individuals such as MP John Tilney also confessed their vested personal business benefits: "I ought to declare an interest," Tilney told the House of Commons on March 13, 1969. "I am a director of a company with large trading interests in Nigeria and the old Eastern Region, with a fleet which operated on the river which now forms no man's land between what is Ibo-land and the West of Nigeria."[54] The many Tilneys in positions of power were responsible for the fate of Biafra.

The Rhodesia Crisis of 1968

While Rhodesia remained a problem for Africa and the Commonwealth for many years, the 1960s were particularly trying as voices of dissent in the Commonwealth greeted Britain's handling of Rhodesia's intransigent posturing. *The Illustrated* of June 19, 1965, expressed serious concerns that even the most trusted anticommunist African leaders, such as Sir Albert Margai of Sierra Leone, had joined with the African nationalist radicals during the 1965 conference in their condemnation of British Southern Rhodesia policy. Margai vehemently decried the Wilson government's reluctance to impose sanctions on Southern Rhodesia with the statement, "We are concerned with the ending of subjugation in Commonwealth Africa and the liberation of all Africans."[55]

One of its many acts of unwillingness to change from minority oppression was demonstrated on March 6, 1968, when the illegal White regime summarily executed Africans—an act Wilson decried as "in defiance of the exercise of the Royal Prerogative of Mercy."[56] The victims opposed Rhodesia's unjust pass laws, segregation, and denial of political rights. Against widespread African anger, Wilson counseled the House of Commons not "to make light of what these issues and these passions could mean for the future, indeed, for the survival of the Commonwealth, or Britain's standing and influence in the world."[57]

The event of 1968 that continued to 1979 was another provocation episode within the broader racial oppression in the entire Southern African region. Although Elizabeth did not weigh in on the incident, she found occasions to reiterate the imperative of freedom, love, and oneness within the Commonwealth family. In her 1970 Christmas message, Elizabeth reinvigorated her 1947 vows by declaring that she was "thinking of rather a special family—a family of nations—as I recall fascinating journeys literally to opposite ends of the world."[58] Northern Rhodesia (Zambia) and Southern Rhodesia (Zimbabwe) gained independence in 1964 and 1980, respectively, but racial disharmony persisted in South Africa until the release of Dr. Nelson Mandela from prison in 1990 and his subsequent election in 1994.

Reassessment, Repurposing, and Transformations

The problems apartheid created for the Commonwealth would have spiraled out of control but for the reforms beginning in 1965 under the Crown. The changes resonated with Elizabeth's postwar vision of "marching together."[59] One of the period's innovations was the establishment of the Commonwealth Institute in 1962. Earlier in 1958, the Marquess of Lansdowne, echoing Her Majesty's government's position in the House of Lords, outlined that the institute would promote the British Empire's commercial, industrial, and educational interests.[60] In 1964, at the behest of Kwame Nkrumah, an independent secretariat at Marlborough House was added "to coordinate the members' dealings with one another, and to facilitate academic, professional and informational exchanges on a larger scale than the Commonwealth Relations Office had been able to do."[61] The subsequent Commonwealth Festival of Arts proposal the House of

Commons presented on behalf of Her Majesty's government in 1963 through Mr. Duncan Sandys, the secretary of the Commonwealth and for the colonies, was approved by the lawmakers for 1965.[62] These and other initiatives turned the association from a British-dominated Commonwealth to a more representative body. More important, the members saw common values as a guide to cooperation and a framework for conflict action.

To further their cause, the Singapore CHOGM meeting, chaired by Prime Minister Lee Kuan Yew in January 1971, adopted its core principles: racial equality, liberty, democratic norms and participation, decolonization and self-determination, elimination of global disparities in wealth, and peace through international cooperation.[63] With Elizabeth's endorsement, these ideas remained on Commonwealth agendas throughout the 1970s. However, the association sometimes overlooked antidemocratic and human rights abuses such as Idi Amin's excesses in Uganda. As illustrated below, this oversight continued because Cold War politics often interfered with the association's programs until 1989.

In anticipation of a post–Cold War era, the Commonwealth began reassessing its goals and strategies in a fast-changing world. It welcomed the new prodemocratic social movements and revolutions in Latin America and Eastern Europe, reinforcing the global acceptance of democratic values. The group also perceived change in apartheid regimes in South Africa and Namibia as a priority.[64] In October 1971, Mr. George Thomson conveyed Her Majesty's and the Commonwealth's objection to a proposed arms sale to South Africa on the pretense of helping deter the Soviet presence in East Africa. Thomson had asked the British government to cancel the deal "in Britain's interest," reiterating that Britain would offend the Africans and the Commonwealth if the sale proceeded.[65] Although the 1971 CHOGM meeting inaugurated the Commonwealth Fund for Technical Cooperation (CFTC), it could only partially harness its poverty reduction and fairer trade goals until the Cold War ended. Conceived to help build local capacity, the CFTC was positioned to promote cooperation, empowerment, and development by funding experts from one country to assist another. For instance, for the 1973–1974 financial year, the CFTC budgeted £1.5 million for technical assistance to developing countries.[66]

In 1979, with Prime Minister Margaret Thatcher in attendance, CHOGM adopted the Lusaka (Zambia) Declaration on Racism and Racial Prejudice. "We, the Commonwealth Heads of Government," will work together to eradicate "all forms of racism and racial prejudice."[67] In April 1979, Rhodesian security warned Queen Elizabeth of a possible bomb attack from African guerrillas when she visited Lusaka (Zambia) for the group's meeting. However, a Buckingham Palace official responded: "It was a matter for the government to advise the Queen on security. She will act on that advice." The Foreign Office, echoing Thatcher, added, "At the moment, we feel that if it is safe for forty Commonwealth heads of state to go to Lusaka, there is no reason why the Queen shouldn't attend."[68] The response and CHOGM's antiracism position elevated the group to the world stage as a champion of the principle of racial equality.

Subsequent declarations expanded the Commonwealth's readiness to engage in diverse transnational partnerships. The Melbourne Declaration of 1981, among other things, reaffirmed the association's collective belief that, irrespective of gender, all humans should "live in ways that sustain and nourish human dignity." In fact, as its secretary-general, Shridath Ramphal, emphasized, "Commonwealth is the negation of Empire." The Melbourne meeting saw it as an obligation on all states to respect their own and the people of all other nations.[69]

The Goa Declaration of 1983 in India shared concerns for international security by condemning the rampant acquisition of nuclear arsenals as a threat to human civilization and calling for a return to a peaceful approach to conflict resolution and cessation of "the illegal use of force."[70] The Nassau Declaration on World Order in 1985 reechoed the concerns of the Goa meeting. In alignment with Her Majesty's visions, the leaders reaffirmed a collective commitment to seeing a world without constant recourse to disorder and competitive power but demanded respect for the rights of all nations and peoples for lasting socioeconomic progress and peace.[71]

The Vancouver Declaration on World Trade, a bold shift to other urgent global concerns with a less political texture, started to gain priority in 1987. The pledge to stop counterproductive protectionist measures within the Commonwealth trade zone aimed to avoid the risk of exchange rate instability, indebtedness, development crisis, and the inability to develop countries to service debt.[72]

At the 1989 gathering in Malaysia, the leaders pressed on with the econometrics of partnerships and the environmental question. The summit saw sustainable development, including establishing new and better techniques in integrating the environmental dimension in economic decision making, as critical.[73] In 1990, the Third Meeting of Commonwealth Ministers in Canada articulated the crux of the 1991 Harare (Zimbabwe) CHOGM summit by focusing on women's issues and the Structural Adjustment Program (SAP).[74] Her Majesty's position on women and gender equality was revealed through the calls for meaningful reforms granting women unhindered rights to land, finance, and other resources to "contribute to, and benefit from productive activity in a market economy."[75]

The Harare Declaration, coming soon after the end of the Cold War, elaborated on the Elizabeth-led Commonwealth's new path. In a scathing rejoinder, the *Dundee Courier* of October 16, 1991, wondered aloud, "What on earth is Britain's monarch and the leader of its government doing in darkest Africa when parliament has just begun, and domestic affairs are gathering momentum in the run-up to the general elections?"[76] The answer to the question is the premium the Queen placed on the Commonwealth and its principles and works. The Harare conference reiterated Her Majesty's views of human rights as the foundation of democracy and development and equality of all human beings regardless of gender, race, color, creed, or political belief. The leaders also professed support for empowerment through education and participation and equity or fairness in the relationships between nations: "Neither the big nor the small nor those in between; ... should either dominate or feel marginalized."[77] The association proclaimed other values, including protecting vulnerable groups, promoting democracy, and citizens' participation in decision making. It adopted future development approaches based on sustainability, diversity of views, and perspectives in national and international forums. CHOGM identified dialogue, cooperation, consensus, and peace building as the basis for progress.[78]

Since 1991, the Harare Declarations have served as a catalyst for one of the goals Elizabeth vowed to promote through the Commonwealth—namely, more robust intergovernmental cooperative actions—including technical assistance among member nations. Such cooperation has provided the proper structure for some nongovernmental bodies that comprise the "informal Commonwealth": the CPU Media Trust, Commonwealth Forestry Association, Commonwealth Human Rights Initiative, Royal Commonwealth Society, Commonwealth Resounds, Commonwealth Fashion Council, Commonwealth Equity Network, and Institute of Certified Management Accountants. A good account of the Commonwealth's achievements in the post–Cold War era requires a retrospective assessment of its extensive and diverse outreach programs.

Political Freedom and Victories

Elizabeth's Commonwealth may have accomplished more in the economic sphere than in the political sphere, as exponents of globalization hold.[79] But one must remember Kwame Nkrumah's dictum, "Seek ye first the political kingdom and all things will be added to it."[80] Kenneth Grundy contends that the Nkrumah aphorism was fundamental for three reasons. First, the normative idiom of the political kingdom symbolized the view of empirical reality as a political struggle. Second, his approach to tackling underdevelopment in Ghana turned the mainstream Western attitude on its head. For Nkrumah, underdevelopment is a political question rather than an economic matter. Third, it was Nkrumah's conviction that policy alternatives (including financial solutions) would sprout to resolve Ghanaian and African problems within the political realm.[81] Her Majesty bought into the Nkrumah vision by using the association to support Africa's political freedom and economic and technical cooperation through membership in the Commonwealth.

In 1996, President Nelson Mandela repeated the Nkrumah view in his Commonwealth valuation. The former South African leader noted that Africans' trust in the Commonwealth evolved over time, resting squarely on freedom from all remnants of colonial domination, including dismantling apartheid in South Africa.[82] Extending the point in line with the colonizer-colonized discourse, John Holmes argues that the postcolonial African state's emergence was a watershed in Anglo-African relations. African membership in the Commonwealth increased emphasis on "consultation as a virtue" within the association.[83] Consequently, the Crown ceases to count as the constitutional center but as its symbolic head. Elizabeth's commitment to the association strengthened her leadership. As a result, the aggressive aura of nationalism gave way to the concept of republicanism, which meant unity and freedom in this context.[84] Hence, B. Vivekanandan views the Commonwealth as "the living symbol of man's genius adapted to the new and changing environment."[85]

In the Commonwealth's evolution as a democracy watchdog, consultation and consensus transcend mere platitudes. The 2007 CHOGM recognized that sustainable development is impossible without democracy and good governance. The group affirmed "the importance of leadership that embraces the Commonwealth's fundamental values and that is tolerant and encouraging of innovation, creativity, and diversity."[86] In her address at the occasion in Kampala, Uganda, the Queen explained that the theme of the meeting, "Transforming Societies," underscored that unity and cooperation are the keys to success for member nations: "No single society has achieved perfection, and there is no single recipe for success."[87] The association's moral compass as a democracy advocate continues to emphasize unity and development through aid to multiparty democratic transitions to democratic elections and postelection monitoring in Kenya, Tanzania, Nigeria, The Gambia, and Malawi.

Africa's Commonwealth presence facilitated the rise of the continent's regional economic blocs. Although apprehensive of compromising their newfound freedom within regional associations, African nations embraced regional cooperation within the framework of Pan-Africanism, believing that unity would hasten socioeconomic progress. This idea materialized the Commonwealth "Lagos Plan" initiative, modeled after the Colombo Plan, as a model for regionalism in the continent.[88]

The Economic Victories

At the beginning of 2012, the authoritative *African Business Magazine* offered an extended discussion on "The Commonwealth's Essential for Africa's Growth," focusing on the strategic emphasis from the political to the economic.[89] Most member nations have become developing markets—Nigeria, Ghana, South Africa, and Kenya. As the global economy remains volatile, the prediction is that some African economies will stand the shock and grow over the coming years.

The group's approximate population of 2.4 billion in 2020 constitutes a powerful trade zone. From an estimated $4 trillion in 2012, the member nations' GDP grew to $10.3 trillion in 2017. By March 2020, the GDP of member nations was $13 trillion, representing 14 percent of the world's GDP.[90] Further growth would depend on the group's reactions to the setbacks brought about by the COVID-19 pandemic, which became prominent in March 2020, and the effects of the Ukraine-Russian conflict that broke out in February 2022.[91]

So far as the Commonwealth offers trade as the ultimate benefit for membership, Africa and Britain's global influence in the wake of Brexit relies heavily on the group's economic belt. James McBride has noted that critics have described the Commonwealth as an outdated remnant of colonialism with funding encumbrances, powerless over human rights abuses, and withering British global influence. Yet, it holds importance despite some members' objections to Britain's withdrawal from the European Union. Proponents of Brexit anchored their optimism on the Commonwealth's economic growth rates. While the EU attained 2 percent growth, the Commonwealth's financial performance grew at a 4.4 percent average over the past four decades. In fact, some large Commonwealth economies, such as India, have achieved 7 percent annual growth.[92]

Simon Constable of *Forbes* magazine makes an excellent point that Britain could achieve more economic success through the Commonwealth if managed well.[93] While this optimism hinges on the member nations' consumer indexes, the association's aura and goodwill are the socioeconomic capital that will carry Britain through the unpredictable future. The organization has forged robust partnerships beyond member nations through the Hub and Spokes project. The initiative provides expert advice on trade to government departments and economic groups in Africa, the Caribbean, and Pacific countries. The underlying goal is to offer full service within the entire Commonwealth network.

The services available under the Hub and Spoke have been extended to the Organization Internationale de la Francophonie and the European Commission through a wide range of training, advice, and policy assistance with trade negotiations at all levels, including the World Trade Organization. Additionally, the Commonwealth has helped create collaborations with the African Union and the Economic and Monetary Community of Central Africa, comprising Cameroon, the Central Africa Republic, Chad, the Republic of the Congo, Gabon, and Equatorial Guinea.

The growing membership of other African, European, and Asian countries not part of the former British Empire attests to its potential for socioeconomic partnerships. Mozambique, Cameroon, Mauritius, and Rwanda's memberships in the organization serve as examples of what this transnational entity holds in stock for countries genuinely interested in reforms that will bring about political and economic progress to their citizens. This development vindicates Elizabeth's proposition of the new self-image of the organization as a business model when the Commonwealth Business Council (CBC) was founded by CHOGM in 1997.[94] The CBC lobbies the private sector to participate meaningfully in international trade and investment. It aims to facilitate greater investment flow "to developing member countries through schemes like the Commonwealth Private Investment Initiative.[95] However, its liquidation as an entity in 2014 was a severe concern for members of most Caribbean countries.

Going forward, the Commonwealth must resuscitate the CBC because of its success with foreign direct investment (FDI) among member nations. In 2007, President Museveni of Uganda reiterated that the members' long-lasting relationship depends on three key aspects; investments, trade, and tourism. Driving home his point, Museveni noted that "Foreign Direct Investment (FDI) is a good way of spreading prosperity globally. FDI has helped China become the second-largest economy in the world."[96] Theoretically, FDI flows into a country's economy depending on socioeconomic and political conditions: democracy, an independent judiciary, a free press, education, gender equality, and access to health for women and the less privileged. Although China's success defies these conditions, the 1991 Harare Summit reiterated these preconditions for socioeconomic progress and higher living standards among members.[97]

The Commonwealth provides a forum for pooling ideas, experience, humanitarian service, and technical assistance. Technical support from member nations with similar values and goals is vital in Africa. President Museveni reiterated this point on June 16, 2017, at an event in Uganda marking Queen Elizabeth's ninety-first birthday. Museveni thanked Britain for assisting Uganda in its recovery process, which began with refurbishing the Owen Falls Dam, built in 1954. With British aid, the capacity was increased from 150 to 180 megawatts.[98] Britain commissioned similar projects in Ghana, Nigeria, Kenya, Sierra Leone, Sudan, and The Gambia.

Tropes of Culture: Education, Natural Conservation, Arts and Leisure

There are several elements to the concept of cultural promotion and wildlife conservation on the continent under Elizabeth's leadership. These have intricate links with Africa's socioeconomic, political, and cultural spheres. The connection is found in the Charter of the Commonwealth, which, among other things, strives to protect the environment, promote sustainable development, and provide access to health, education, food, and shelter. The charter further advocates for youth and gender equality in the organization.[99] This echoes the substance of Her Majesty's 2007 call on governments, communities, and all peoples to pay "fresh attention" to "young people who make up nearly half of the Commonwealth population."[100]

Education

Education is one of the Commonwealth's principal areas that has left a lasting footprint on member nations' labor development. In September 1958, the Commonwealth Ministers at the Trade and Economic Conference in Montreal, Canada, discussed the need for educational cooperation. The conference reviewed arrangements to facilitate collaboration among member nations on education, technical education, and teacher training.[101] The Commonwealth Scholarship Commission recognized the educational needs of the former colonies in the postwar era and immediately launched the scholarship scheme in July 1959 at the first Commonwealth Education Conference at Oxford.[102] The House of Commons approved the July 15–29 meeting to "work out detailed arrangements for the new scheme for 1,000 Commonwealth scholars and fellows."[103]

Under the scheme, member governments offer generous scholarships and fellowships to member countries' citizens to pursue educational degrees and professional research in the awarding nation. These awards have totaled an average of 750 per annum. Established in 1965, the Commonwealth Secretariat oversees the organization's educational programs. Its demand-driven educational policies ensure that learners within the member countries have access to quality education irrespective of gender and social background. The secretariat takes extraordinary measures to support marginalized groups in countries with discriminatory policies toward the less privileged. These principles align with the association's mandates, prioritizing access to health, education, food, and shelter as central to sustainable development.[104]

To better serve the Commonwealth citizens' changing educational needs, the secretariat developed a four-year strategic plan (2013/2014 to 2016/2017) to help the new generation.[105] These included the Professional Standards Framework for Teachers and School Leaders. Several African countries, such as Botswana, Kenya, Mauritius, South Africa, and Swaziland, have adopted this pilot plan. The School Leaders Capability Framework, established by the Commonwealth Consortium for Education and Secretariat, is now implemented in Ghana and Namibia. Botswana, Uganda, and Kenya are instituting policies based on the secretariat's Guidelines for Quality Education Provision to Nomadic Communities for Africa and Asia. These are communities where the majority of school age came from predominantly pastoral farming and animal herding. Because of their constant movement, they need more opportunities for formal school education.[106]

The secretariat's close relationships with member nations' policymakers facilitate meetings of education ministers from different countries. Members share ideas on best practices in implementing education according to the mandated criteria through this forum. The nineteenth Conference of the Commonwealth Education Ministers in the Bahamas in June 2015 deliberated on the Commonwealth Ministerial Group's recommendations on the Development Framework for Education to ensure Performance, Paths, and Productivity.[107]

Natural Conservation

One of the most impactful but often neglected contributions of Her Majesty to East African economic growth is natural conservation. After her first visit to Kenya in 1952, Elizabeth retained an active interest in nature and the wildlife abundant on the continent. The Treetops Hotel in Aberdare National Park, Njeri, Kenya, became a tourist attraction after Her Majesty stayed there.[108]

The Biosphere Reserve, named in honor of Elizabeth's advocacy for wildlife conservation, oversees Uganda's wide range of habitats and landforms—rivers, lakes, swamps, tropical rainforests, grassy plains, savanna woodlands, wetlands, and volcanic craters. The core parts of the reserve serve as a research laboratory and for conservation education and biodiversity monitoring. Uganda's scenic landforms and large animal species in the savannah and rainforest zones are tourist magnets and second-leading income earners. In 2001, for instance, tourism brought in more than $163 million—representing 25 percent of Uganda's foreign earnings and 7.5 percent of its GDP.[109]

David Mackenzie's *The Empire of Nature* underscored that colonial interest in wildlife and hunting in Africa emerged as a facet of British culture, mainly European.[110] According to Robert Stafford, hunting down animals became a metaphor for European dominance over nature and the conquered people. Thus, the "colonial frontier became a hunting frontier, and subduing the empire's faunal inhabitants provided both paradigm and training for imperial rule and racial domination."[111] The colonial culture has proved resilient in the postcolonial era. Visitors are attracted to Uganda for the elephants, buffalos, lions, chimpanzees, hyenas, leopards, hippopotamuses, and many other species that comprise over six hundred native and migrant birds. A Ministry of Tourism, Wildlife, and Antiquities study in 2013 revealed that leisure and cultural tourists spent 30 to 100 percent more than others who come to the country for different reasons. The result has reinforced the government's plans to increase the tourism sector's economic contribution through market promotion. Out of the 1 million tourists that visited in 2013, 50 percent spent at least one night in Uganda.[112] In 2018, the Uganda Tourism Board reported over 1.7 million visitors, surpassing the 1.4 million tourists that brought $1.35 billion into the nation's economy in 2017. The 2020 target was $2.7 billion before the coronavirus turned the industry upside down.[113]

Similar records from Kenya show that the tourism industry netted $1.6 billion in 2019. The data revealed that over 2 million tourists visited the country in 2019, 1.16 percent over 2018.[114] Statistics from South Africa indicate that tourism contributed $8.3 billion, or 2.8 percent of its overall GDP. This figure increased to $8.59 billion in 2019.[115] In 2018, Botswana's tourism industry grew by 3.4 percent, above the African average of 3.3 percent. The sector accounted for the country's 8.9 percent employment or about 84,000 jobs. The report shows that the industry contributed $2 billion to the country's $18.3 billion GDP in the same year.[116]

Specifically, Queen Elizabeth nurtured her grandchildren's interest in preserving Africa's biodiversity. Between June 15–19, 2010, Prince William and Prince Harry made stops in Botswana and South Africa. The Botswana trip was on behalf of Tusk Trust, an NGO dedicated to wildlife protection. The royals visited Lesotho to promote Sentebale, an NGO Prince Harry cofounded with Prince Seeiso of Lesotho in 2006. Sentebale focuses on helping children and orphans in Lesotho. William and Harry completed their tour with a visit to Cape Town, South Africa, where they watched England play Algeria in the 2010 World Cup soccer match.[117]

Given Rebecca Clay's warning that the multitude of Africa's environmental issues has left the continent in chaos, the economic benefits of the royals' interest in conservation and environmental matters in Africa defy simple monetary interpretations.[118] David Western has underscored the importance of international collaboration in rescuing Africa from the urgent conservation issue.[119] On September 24–30, 2018, Prince William returned to Africa as patron of the Tusk Trust. The trip took him to Namibia, Tanzania, and Kenya. In December 2018, when President Girma Wolde-Giorgis of Ethiopia died, Queen Elizabeth sent a condolence message to Ethiopians, praising the former leader as a champion of environmental protection, whose presidency brought considerable growth and development to Ethiopia, including "an important contribution to environmental issues."[120] Protecting the tropical environment is critical to Africa's future as a bulwark of human and natural resource reserves. Slowing down desertification, sustaining the burgeoning tourism industry, and facilitating sporting and other recreational activities are also critical.

Arts and Leisure

In 1930, Hamilton, Canada, hosted the maiden Commonwealth Games, then the British Empire Games. The game concept goes back to 1891 when Mr. Ashley Cooper suggested an English-speaking sports festival every four years. The idea, published in *The Times*, materialized in "The Festival of Empire" 1911 as part of King George V's coronation festivities with the UK, South Africa, Canada, and Australia competing in the three events—swimming, boxing, and athletics. Finally, at the Olympic Games of 1928 in Amsterdam, Canadian journalist Melville Marks Robinson, aka Bobby Robinson, convened a meeting of Commonwealth representatives at the Olympics. He emphasized the imperative of a Commonwealth Games as a bridge to the Olympics.[121]

About 400 athletes from 11 countries participated in 59 events at the 1930 Games. Over the years, the games have continued every four years and have undergone transformations in name, size, and prestige. In 1954, it was called the British Empire and Commonwealth Games, and in 1974, the title changed to the British Commonwealth Games. In 1978, the Commonwealth

Games' current title was adopted at the Edmonton Games in Canada. As a rule, competitors at the games must be citizens or residents of member countries or a member country's dependency. An African government has yet to host the games because of the high costs.[122]

The events are more than sports competitions; they constitute a compelling force connecting transnational friendships and unity among competing nations. As Queen Elizabeth pointed out in the 1970 Scotland Commonwealth Games, the sporting festival offers the member nations a rare opportunity: "Never before has there been a group of independent nations linked in this way by their common history and continuing affections."[123] This purpose is central to the Commonwealth's core values and principles of equality, humanity, cooperation, and destiny. In her 2014 Commonwealth Day message, the Queen spoke about the twentieth Commonwealth Games in Glasgow—referring to the games as part of the "Team Commonwealth" quest to "build a brighter, united future in which every one of us can play a part and share in the rewards."[124] The Commonwealth Games return to Birmingham in 2022, marking the first on British soil since Brexit.

There are political and foreign policy considerations connected with hosting the Commonwealth Games. First, it projects the host nation into the global spotlight. After the Olympics and World Cup Soccer, the Commonwealth Games comes third as the most-watched television spectacle. For a wealthy host country, the benefit of elevated media attention with millions of television viewers worldwide outweighs the monetary costs. It also provides a platform for aggrieved members, especially the African and Asian nations, to express their objections to issues in world politics.

A good example is the apartheid struggle in South Africa—the Commonwealth Games offered antiapartheid activists the platform to protest against member nations that retained official contacts in the now-defunct system.[125] David Black and Janis van der Westhuizen have explored how state and non-state actors have leveraged sports politics of sports in the convergence of international relations. The authors used nine comparative case studies, including South Africa, "to underscore the degree to which issues related to identity, inequality and power shape states' interest in, capacity for and strategic engagement with the process of hosting major sports."[126] Indeed, during the Commonwealth Games in Scotland in 1986, African countries, joined by Malaysia, threatened to boycott unless Britain enforced tougher economic sanctions on South Africa. After South Africa transitioned to a democratic system, it rejoined the Commonwealth in 1994.[127]

In many ways, Elizabeth has touched her admirers' lives worldwide on the broader resonance of cultural production. In Africa, the monarch popularized the simple cotton gown as the standard dressing style among the youth in terms of simplicity and modesty. Royal curator Eleri Lynn told *People* magazine in 2020 that in the 1930s, Elizabeth wore matching floral dresses that demonstrated "certain thriftiness, which we know is still there today."[128]

In a parallel story, Clare Coulson of *The Telegraph* notes that Elizabeth's childhood velvet-collared jackets, shiny Mary Janes, and sweet cotton attires set a standard for formal dressing that has endured until today. This is particularly true in Africa, where in the 1950s through the 1980s, the simple gown with girded short arms was fashionable, and female civil servants went to work dressed in skirts and collared jackets.[129]

Many African first ladies copied Elizabeth's style; the royal fashion sense also caught the admiration of African politicians. Her wedding gown's thirteen-foot train, later in the early 1960s, inspired Nigeria's flamboyant finance minister, Festus Okotie-Eboh, to modify his traditional Itshekiri dresses into thirteen-foot spectacles. During her 1956 trip to Nigeria, the assumption was that gifts of dresses during the royal fanfare at Enugu would please the Queen and her sister Margaret.[130]

In 1957, when Ghana celebrated its independence, "Elizabethan II fashion" was a popular topic among African women. When it was announced that Her Majesty would be represented by the Duchess of Kent, Ghanaian socialites turned their attention to the attires the Duchess would bring to Accra. On February 28, 1957, a day before the independence celebration, the *Daily Graphic* wrote: "Saturday is the day for which the women of Ghana have been waiting. For years, they have read the fashion magazine and gazed upon pictures of her. And oh, how they admired her dress sense."[131] When the Queen eventually visited Ghana in 1961, the *Ghana Times* of November 14 reported that "everyone asked what was she wearing." Gifts to Her Majesty included a gold brooch from Major-General S. J. A. Otu, Ghana's defense chief, and a traditionally woven Kante textile material from Minister for Education A. J. Dowuona-Hammond. At the Young Women's Christian Association hostel, the monarch showed keen interest in the traditional textile style, including the *oduku* headgear and *kpen*, worn an inch below the knee, as the women paraded various colorful customs.[132]

It is also remarkable that the traditional West African strip-woven, indigo-dyed country cloth started adapting after Her Majesty visited Sierra Leone in 1961. Woven from the native silk-cotton tree, the textiles are produced in long strips and sewn together to create a more considerable material. Sierra

Leone's female paramount chief, Mabaja I of Bagbwe chiefdom, owned a sample of the textile now reserved in the British Museum as a relic of Elizabeth's historic visit in November 1961. The government spread the fabric produced by Gbokowa of Ngarlu on the floor like a carpet for the royal dais at Bo. The "UPP Party cloth" was initially designed to commemorate the Queen's canceled tour in 1959. The cloth carries the Queen and Prince Philip's portraits in floral-bordered circular frames superimposed over the background of buildings in London and Freetown.[133]

Elizabeth's attire transformed throughout these long decades, but she remained consistent with dignity. Her regular clean-cut coats, flashy hats, pearls, jersey gloves, sturdy footwear, and handbags captured the times rising above them. Yet, her quest for women's empowerment remained strong. She illustrated this with the theme of the 2011 CHOGM event, "Women as Agents of Change." During her opening ceremony speech, the Queen spoke to women's societal position as a reminder of an unlocked potential, which "encourages us to find ways to allow all girls and women to play their full part. We must continue to strive in our own countries and across the Commonwealth to promote that theme in a lasting way beyond this year."[134]

Her Majesty's tours of Africa often involved elaborate musical and dance displays. When she visited Nigeria in 1956, it was all singing and dancing from Lagos and Enugu in the south to Kaduna in the north.[135] Like the Nigerian troupe that greeted Her Majesty at the airport in London in 1956, on her way to Ghana in 1957 for the independence celebrations, the Duchess of Kent, Princess Alexandra, was greeted at the London airport by Gold Coast drummers in colorful national dress. The troupe played the "talking drums" and performed sendoff dances in honor of the Duchess.[136] The dance between Elizabeth and Nkrumah in November 1961 is well known, but the waltz she performed with Prime Minister Milton Margai in Freetown during her 1961 visit has received less attention. It is also vital to note the enthusiasm the African tours generated in the music industry. Steve J. Salm and Toyin Falola remind us that King Bruce, Ghana's famous highlife maestro, left a legacy with the song "The Queen's Visit" that he made in honor of Queen Elizabeth soon after independence.[137] The song begins:

> This is the day five million Ghanaians will go gay.
> Queen Elizabeth and Prince Phillip will be here on that special day.
> We'll drink and dance the whole day and put on Kante fine on that Thursday, 12th November, 1959.
> May God bless this fine Thursday when our Ghana will go gay.

The lyric, which Bruce wrote in 1957 in anticipation of Her Majesty attending Ghana's independence celebrations, continued to inform the audience that Ghanaians have been yearning for this day. "The Queen has come at last to Ghana from the United Kingdom."[138]

In contemporary art, Queen Elizabeth II inspired many artistic representations. Her ascension to the throne in Kenya was commemorated with wooden elephant horns artwork erected in 1952 on Arap Moi Avenue, Mombasa. In the indigenous society, "ivories were used to document culture."[139] The artifact's land has been transformed into a Uhuru Garden, a tourist attraction. The art objects, updated with aluminum in 1956 and a model elephant in 2017, are now a tourist center. Filmmakers pay the National Museum of Kenya $1,000 daily to film the objects.

When the Queen visited Nigeria in 1956, the famous Nigerian artist Ben Enwonwu Africanized the Queen's official portrait. As his son Oliver recalled, Enwonwu was "credited with inventing a Nigerian national aesthetic by fusing indigenous traditions with Western techniques and modes of representation."[140] Naima Mohamud notes, "Enwonwu took creative liberty with the Queen's lips and made them fuller, creating controversy in the British art world. Although the Queen publicly endorsed the sculpture, critics of the art did not appreciate the image's Africanizing idea.[141]

In British West Africa, the term "Queen's English" (and "King's English" when there is a King) denotes a symbol of the best-educated and cultivated individual. This view is the opposite of the widely spoken variant called Pidgin English in Ghana, The Gambia, and Nigeria, and Krio in Sierra Leone and Liberia. Those privileged with Oxford or Cambridge educations use their "Queen's English" to appropriate a certain status above the less privileged. Afua Hirsch observes that "a backlash is growing against the old mentality of equating a British accent with prestige. Now the practice has a new acronym, LAFA, or 'locally acquired foreign accent,' and attracts derision rather than praise."[142] In other words, the admiration for Queen's English persists. However, it is often associated with the highly educated and the *been-to*—a derogatory term for those abroad, especially the West African graduates of prestigious British and American educational institutions.

Overall, Elizabeth's most impactful achievement remains making the New Elizabethan Age not about herself but rather the people she has worked to improve their conditions worldwide. During the celebration of the Queen's sixty-third year on the throne, Simon Perry stressed that the public expected a special occasion, but the Queen approached it with a "business as usual" attitude. Elizabeth reminded her audience, "Inevitably, a long life can pass by many milestones; my own is no exception."[143] In *The Real Elizabeth*, Andrew Marr added that modesty has been Elizabeth's unique attribute.[144] Throughout her reign, Elizabeth suppressed the self-ego in realizing the stakeholders' expectations of her as a symbol of unity, peace, and human dignity. She saw her place as the commonwealth leader to build a bridge between the violent colonial past and a free and equal future. These duties required Elizabeth to tailor her words not to insult or degrade others but to motivate and bring about a positive end.

In 2015, *Forbes* magazine explored leadership lessons the world can learn from Elizabeth, starting with responsibility and "astounding poise." Another lesson is the virtue of being quiet and steady. As a brand, the Queen evaded controversial speeches, public policy, and "self-revealing interviews."[145] Again, she avoided making leadership about herself. Early in 1953, Elizabeth disabused attempts by admirers extolling her reign as a New Elizabethan Age. "Frankly, I do not myself feel at all like my great Tudor forbear, who was blessed with neither husband nor children, who ruled as a despot and was never able to leave her native shores."[146]

Elizabeth's Commonwealth mission has ended, but the enormous problems of colonialism linger on the continent. It is a legitimate debate for Africans to argue that her mission was unaccomplished at a time when many languished in poverty. It is also a valid point that through her Commonwealth leadership, Africa has recovered from some political and socioeconomic losses. Though the gains are miniscule compared to the Europeans' colonial looting, Elizabeth did not and could not have paid back what the Europeans stole from Africa. It makes sense for Whitehall to use the post-Elizabeth Commonwealth to expand the transnational partnership with a "rediscovery of Africa" spirit to keep Her Majesty's Commonwealth legacy and spirit alive.

CHAPTER 6

KING CHARLES III AND AFRICA'S COMMONWEALTH FUTURE

Addressing the Commonwealth Heads of Government Meeting (CHOGM) in 2018, H.M. Queen Elizabeth II announced her decision to transfer the organization's headship to her son, Charles, the then Prince of Wales (now King Charles III). She expressed the hope that the Commonwealth will endure in providing strength and opportunities to future generations of member countries under her son—per the vital work her father, King George VI, initiated in 1949.[1] The summit anticipated the leadership change. At age ninety-two in 2018, Elizabeth was right about a handover, but some members needed clarification on whether Charles was the rightful successor. After a retreat at Windsor Castle, the CHOGM proclaimed that the "next head of the Commonwealth shall be His Royal Highness Prince Charles, the Prince of Wales," who became King Charles III on September 8, 2022.[2]

The intent here is to examine King Charles's Commonwealth leadership potentials and risks in light of Africa's needs and hopes. This is crucial because, although the decolonization project under Her Majesty's brand came short of Africans' expectations, the Commonwealth remains vital in the enduring quest to make right the wrongs of imperialism. A day before Queen Elizabeth announced her departure, Prince Charles stood before the heads of government, touting his credentials and readiness to walk in his mother's shoes. He reminded the audience that he has been an integral part of the association since childhood.[3] Royal birthright may have made Charles part of the postwar Commonwealth history; his capability to lead is a fair question, however, especially concerning the questions that preceded his ascension in 2022.

Doubts about King Charles's monarchy and Commonwealth leadership succession emanated primarily from his tragic marriage to Princess Diana. At his wedding in 1981, the British prime minister, Margaret Thatcher, and the entire Parliament shared with the country "the Prince of Wales's obvious happiness and joy in the bride." They looked forward to a future where the couple would play an increasingly prominent part in Britain's life. The House declared that the couple "will inspire the same loyalty, respect, and gratitude as Her Majesty and Prince Philip."[4] The people's immense affection and admiration toward Charles suffered a discourteous setback after the royal union crashed against the standard expectation.

Following Princess Diana's death in August 1997, Charles strived to rebuild his image, respect, and leadership credibility.[5] Historians Philip Murphy and Daisey Cooper have ultimately suggested that the royal Commonwealth brand should end after Queen Elizabeth II because of the lack of a viable candidate: "The interests of the Commonwealth would be best served if the post of Head of the Commonwealth ceased to exist at the end of Her Majesty's reign."[6]

Murphy and Cooper were concerned with what they described as the organization's "lack of a really commanding figure" and the dearth of a "charismatic" individual among the royals to ably succeed the Queen.[7] They believed monarchists should protect Queen Elizabeth II's sterling records from the unknown under King Charles. This anxiety echoes a similar sentiment concerning the African postcolonial state's ability to run real parliamentary democracy under the Crown. Hence, Whitehall encouraged the emergent states to adopt the republican constrictions. Several ministers and the Commonwealth Relations Office's officials differed with the Colonial Office and other exponents of pragmatic conservatism in the decolonization period. Like Murphy and Cooper, the royal officials wanted to shield the Crown from what they regarded as the embarrassment of the African states switching from retaining the monarch as head of their governments to a republican constitution. As a result, the advocates of royal reputation protection, like Assistant Under-Secretary A. W. Snelling, spoke out against what he perceived as "the incorrigible paternalism of the Colonial Office." Snelling then asked, "How can the man-in-the-bush on the Niger Delta [modern Nigeria] be expected to adopt our sophisticated notions of the role the Queen in reality plays?"[8]

A similar mindset led to the call to end the Commonwealth headship in the post–Elizabeth II period. The 2018 London CHOGM summit allowed Charles to defend his candidature and dispel fears that he would end up sulking over his mother's accomplishment. Charles impressed upon the summit the imperative of renewing the bonds that hold the member nations so that the group would find some "practical solutions to their problems" and give life to the collective aspirations.[9] He pledged to pursue the group's goals and seek answers to overriding problems. If rightly interpreted, those avowals came across as Charles's Commonwealth manifesto or action guide—that is, to carry on with his mother's "inspiring leadership" and Commonwealth principles and ideals of freedom, unity, and equality.[10]

The questions surrounding the post-Elizabeth Commonwealth's future will persist for a while—until the new sovereign's doubters start to see specific results. The leadership poser transcends royal birthright. As Charles alluded to, the privilege of knowing the Commonwealth's complex history since 1949 is a genuine advantage for the organization's leadership but not sufficient qualification standing alone. The matter concerns management skills and visions, the ability to tackle tasks as they come, and, as Elizabeth has done, function as a transformative leader. King Charles or his future successor would be expected to serve as the custodian of the Commonwealth's principles and values and inspire the admiration and trust of a broad range of transnational actors and stakeholders with diverse interests, needs, and intents. In the royal branding mix idiom, the Establishment expects King Charles to reassure Britons that their national interests are safe under his leadership. The Africans are desirous to know if the new King will be able to solve real issues that matter—war, antidemocratic ideologies, human rights and women's rights, hunger, and unemployment.

In perspective, King Charles stepped into the Commonwealth's headship during threats from within and without. With Brexit's twists and turns in the age of COVID-19, Russia's military aggression in Ukraine, and nuclear threats, the job ahead is more onerous. In *The Empire's New Clothes*, Philip Murphy debunked the notion held in government circles that the Commonwealth will provide a bonanza of trade and investment as a better alternative to Brexit's economic losses. Instead, Murphy considers the institution irrelevant and diagnoses its present pomp and circumstance as a symptom of imperial amnesia. His future vision of the Commonwealth is to escape from the British Empire's shadow to become "an organization based on shared values, rather than a shared history."[11]

Murphy's prescription is in order—although it came two years before COVID-19 changed so much on the world stage. It is also noteworthy that Murphy's doubts about Charles may have been influenced by many developments—real and fictional—often celebrated in the newspapers. Two examples will illustrate this fact. On October 18, 1992, the *Daily Express* of London carried a misleading and unsubstantiated story about "Charles's rift with the Queen."[12] After Charles's separation from Princess Diana, the report claimed he was at war with his mother. The story claimed that the quarrel had gone to the point that Charles snubbed the Queen at the Balmoral annual family gathering. However, a rebuttal to the publication by a Buckingham official, Richard

Aylard, revealed that the entire story was fictional; Charles was at the family gathering for "six consecutive days."[13] This episode represents a common misunderstanding about the royal family that has lingered for a long time.

A similar incident in 2006 that raised questions about Charles's leadership preparedness was the implications of the "Prince Charles's Hong Kong journal," which revealed his worry over the terms of Britain's handover of Hong Kong to China in February 2006.[14] Prime Minister Tony Blair's government attempted to use Charles's position on the handover to cast him in a bad light before the British public. However, Charles acted within the constitutional convention, allowing the monarch to support and warn the nation's government. Charles's depiction of the deal as "the Great Chinese Takeaway" has become relevant today as China gears toward the seizure of Hong Kong and Taiwan. Then, Charles had predicted that China would one day violate the handover agreement.[15]

As the COVID-19 pandemic's economic impact and the Russian-Ukraine conflict unfold, the United Kingdom must look beyond Charles's previous periodic advocacy convictions. Instead, it should leverage the Commonwealth's shared values to support its post-Brexit economic aspirations and strategic goals. Ghana's president, Nana Addo Dankwa Akufo-Addo, underlined at the UN Assembly on September 22, 2022, "The West needs Africa, and Africa needs the West."[16] In essence, the Commonwealth's post-Brexit fate is tied to Africa's future and vice versa. Like the uncertainties surrounding the postwar decolonization era, the group's stability and peace remain paramount in overcoming the new world order's challenges and pushing ahead the rediscovery of a twenty-first-century vision of "Global Britain."[17]

Acknowledging Queen Elizabeth's extraordinary gift of composure amid upheavals, Philip Murphy told *The Telegraph* that Elizabeth had proved her mettle in holding countries together and creating a serene atmosphere between heads of state. Murphy concluded that with "unparalleled knowledge" of the organization, the Queen handled diplomatic matters just "by virtue of being there."[18] Elizabeth played the globalist role and promoted multiculturalism without losing consciousness of the group's diverse and distinct needs.

The assertion here is that there are no overriding reasons to scrap the British monarchy's leadership of the organization in the twenty-first century or to believe that King Charles will serve it no practical purpose. If the Commonwealth under the Crown had been disbanded in 1952 after King George VI, the world would have lost the organization's glories under Elizabeth. King Charles remains the best leader regarding maturity, age, global influence, and knowledge of the organization's intricate nature. He holds the potential benefit of leadership longevity that even democratically elected heads of government do not often have.

The critical question is whether the new King can unite the Commonwealth, stimulate collaborative economic synergies, and serve as a peace ambassador to Africa and the world. Does he have the persona and charisma that inspires and instills strength in conflict? Will he provide diplomatic, moral, and material assistance to the nations in a world often fraught with predatory designs and the conflict endangered by the zero-sum approach to international relations? How do historians know? These questions are only sometimes answerable precisely. The strategy is to examine them in light of Africa's future by reflecting on the ways and means that made Her Majesty successful. The ensuing discussions are in two broad themes, starting with the imperative of political unity and democratic governance.

Commonwealth's Unity and Democratic Order in Africa

As with his mother's tenure, sustained unity is at the core of the Commonwealth and Africa's future under King Charles. For Africa and the entire association, the prospect of harmony resides in two pillars: stable Commonwealth governance and beneficial transnational cooperation. Operational leadership prospers with dispassionate and positive motivation. As a reciprocal process, followers must accept the leader and work with him. As this study reveals, the Commonwealth has weathered many crises, specifically connected with the freedom and welfare of the postcolonial state, because member nations voluntarily accepted Elizabeth's authority. From the 1950s through the 1970s, several problems rattled the association's unity—the Suez Canal skirmish, the Rhodesia question, apartheid in South Africa, the Nigeria-Biafra conflict, and the responses to the numerous incidents of dictatorships in postcolonial Africa. Still, the group's capacity to resolve these issues made it more relevant.

The later high-profile challenges that affected the organization and Elizabeth's philosophy of unity comprised Nigeria's suspension in 1995 under General Sani Abacha, Zimbabwe under President Robert Mugabe in 2003, and The Gambia under President Yahya Jemmeh in 2013. In each case, human rights violations and attempts to stall democratic orders were at the heart of the conflicts. In Nigeria, the Commonwealth acted against the military dictatorship after General Abacha executed the environmental activist Ken Saro-Wiwa and eight others on November 10, 1995.[19] The killing brazenly violated the principles endorsed by Queen Elizabeth and the CHOGM in the Harare Declaration. The Gambia received the hammer after the ex-dictator, Yahya Jammeh, called the Commonwealth a "neocolonial" institution because the group opposed his authoritarian tendencies. Jammeh's disdainful comments poisoned The Gambia's relations with the outside world. The country's readmission in 2018 came after Adama Barrow's electoral victory and Jammeh's exile to Equatorial Guinea.[20] Nigeria and The Gambia remind us about the vital relevance of the Commonwealth leadership that is firm and, at the same time, flexible.

Under Charles's watch, the organization looked forward to welcoming back Zimbabwe at the canceled 2020 CHOGM initially scheduled for June 22–27 in Kigali, Rwanda.[21] Zimbabwe was suspended in March 2002 for breaking the inherent principles of the Harare Commonwealth Declaration. As with Nigeria and The Gambia, the Commonwealth indicted Zimbabwe for violating principles of democracy, human rights, and the rule of law; the CHOGM signed these into law under Her Majesty's leadership on October 21, 1991.[22]

For nearly forty years, Zimbabwe was under Mugabe, who started in 1980 with respect as the president of a country once referred to as the "breadbasket of Africa."[23] He maintained a good relationship with the Queen and the Commonwealth. But after two decades, Zimbabwe entered into a period of instability as Mugabe fought the opposition to keep the reins of power at all costs. From 2000, when the West objected to his new land redistribution policy that evicted more than four thousand White commercial farmers from their farms, Mugabe resorted to defiance and confrontationist postures, including demeaning comments against the Commonwealth and the Queen. To retain power, Mugabe's Zimbabwean African National Union (ZANU) party stirred up interracial and interclass conflict by arbitrarily confiscating White farmers' parcels of land, sponsoring political jobbery, and brigandage. These trends escalated the precarious White-Black relations, and ZANU perpetrated electoral violence from 2002 through 2011.[24]

Despite the general outcry and sanctions Western nations imposed on Mugabe's government, it took over eighteen years to turn Zimbabwe's perilous trajectory. This change was only possible after Mugabe's eventual exit from power in November 2017. The country's suspension from the Commonwealth saw Zimbabwe increasingly gravitate to China for economic and political support. Consequently, there is a need to revisit the effectiveness of sanctions and suspensions in addressing dictatorships, human rights abuse, and antidemocratic tendencies in Africa or elsewhere. The economic and political sanctions against Zimbabwe did little to effectively and speedily rebuild internal and external relations or enhance the principle of unity and equality within the Commonwealth.

The point here is that the record of evidence has shown that imposing a blanket sanction on an entire country to remedy the wrongs of dictators has not always produced the desired result. Similar to Zimbabwe, the Commonwealth suspension of Nigeria under Abacha's dictatorship proved counterproductive because nothing changed in Nigeria until Abacha's demise in 1997. Again, the conundrum of sanctions against apartheid South Africa did not alter the sociopolitical designs of apartheid leaders like P. W. Botha in South Africa. In each of these cases—Zimbabwe, Nigeria, and South Africa—women, children, and the poor suffered the economic brunt of international sanctions.

It is realistic to predict that obnoxious and antidemocratic regimes will persist in Africa. The former British territories, including Nigeria, Zimbabwe, South Africa, and other member nations, have vital roles to play in the post-Brexit and post-COVID-19 pandemic Commonwealth. This fact suggests that under King Charles, the association should develop a more efficacious formula or strategy for addressing dictators within its fold. Rethinking the pariah state strategy for a more result-oriented and less acrimonious process will be vital.

As the Commonwealth continues to incorporate the former French African territories like Cameroon and Rwanda, it is auspicious to consider the dangers Francophone dictators pose to the Commonwealth's future and Her Majesty's legacy. In President Paul Biya's Cameroon, which joined the Commonwealth in November 1995, incessant clashes between the government and the opposition have turned into a bloody conflict between the Anglophone minority and Francophone majority.[25] In Rwanda, which joined the Commonwealth in November 2009, the former guerrilla leader, President Paul Kagame, who does not speak French, has been in power since 1994 with no sign of leaving soon. His bogus 99 percent electoral victory in 2017 ensured he would remain in power until the next polls in 2024.[26] Cameroon and Rwanda's political trajectories mirror a disturbing trend of a resurgence of authoritarian movements on the African continent. Between 2014 and 2015 alone, dictatorial tendencies and human rights abuses escalated in several areas, threatening Africa's previous years' democratic political gains.

Another potential source of trouble for the Commonwealth as Rwanda's membership deepens will come from neighboring Burundi. Rwanda and Burundi have had a history of ethnic-based conflicts and genocidal practices between their Hutu and Tutsi populations. While Tutsi are the majority group in Burundi, Hutu are the majority in Rwanda. The future of political stability and economic progress in the Great Lakes Region will be determined mainly by the dynamics of Hutu-Tutsi relations in both countries and the Commonwealth's response under King Charles.[27]

The history of interethnic rivalry and autocratic resurgence in the Great Lakes region speaks to those in several African countries that continue to evince more democratic backsliding. The emerging dynamics implicate the challenges of democracy and good governance, which the Commonwealth aspires to promote on the continent. Overall, both the 2015 and 2017 Mo Ibrahim Democracy Index Reports highlight the problem of "more widespread declines in [political] participation and human rights" abuses in Africa. The reports concluded that over a third of African countries are backsliding on democratic governance.[28]

The question persists whether a King Charles–led Commonwealth could thwart authoritarian manipulations in Africa. Moreover, some critics have questioned the King's capacity or openness to modern ideas that will power the Commonwealth successfully in the twenty-first century. Does the King understand the multicultural, multiracial nuances of the organization, or should member nations turn to someone who fits into the modern leaders' ideals? In truth, King Charles's commitment to democratic ideals is undoubted; the question is whether he is too liberal, as US Senator Rick Scott implied by disputing the rationale for his visit to Cuba in 2019.[29] In response, Sir Alan Duncan, the UK minister of state for Europe and the Americas, wrote, "We believe that the best way to promote human rights and encourage a Cuba that fully respects fundamental freedoms is through practical diplomacy, such as with this visit."[30]

King Charles III has reaffirmed his belief in consultation and dialogue as central to change and peace in a multicultural setting. His mother successfully demonstrated a willingness to meet and dialog with dictators, including the Soviet Premier, Mikhail S. Gorbachev, in December 1988. Charles hopefully learned the virtue of open and friendly discussion from his mother, who later visited Moscow in 1989 in what *The Washington Post* branded "Gorbachev's Royal Coup."[31]

Addressing the scientific community's beef with the new King is vital. In May 2000, Oxford University genetic biologist Richard Dawkins penned a scathing article in the *Sunday Observer*, warning Charles not to ignore science. The op-ed responded to Charles's Reith Lecture on various themes, including science and God and the dangers of genetically modified food and the biosphere.[32] Expectedly, scientists such as Dawkins responded angrily to the lecture: "Your embracing an ill-assorted jumble of mutually contradictory alternatives will lose you the respect I think you deserve. I forgot who it was who remarked: 'Of course, we must be open-minded, but not so open-minded that our brains drop out.'"[33]

The controversial lecture highlights two apparent differences between the Queen and her son: the Queen avoided the dangers of divisive speeches. And despite her position as the custodian of the Church of England, the Crown treaded cautiously with religious dogmas. As a Prince, Charles's philosophical convictions concerning God and science, which also drew reproaches from some members of Parliament, were delivered unapologetically. The London *Express* of August 25, 2018, carried an opinion that his "outspoken views, including those on religion, mean that his ascension "could trigger a national debate between the Church of England and the state."[34] However, the report added that the backlash is less about him promoting God's supremacy over science and deviating from a longstanding tradition in the royal family of being the custodian of the Church of England. Instead, Charles declared himself "the defender of all faiths."[35]

Thus, some public condemnation of the vexing Reith Lecture stemmed from its inclination for religious inclusion—something liberals and some politicians sometimes dislike. Charles's appeal for a return to spirituality as a guide to human endeavors resonated with the conservatives, but his perception of "excessive" scientific rationalism as an affront to "the Creator" was received by his critics as a direct attack on science.[36] For all his troubles, Gilbert Rose branded Charles "the Duke of Darkness."[37] Such name-callings negate the noble cause of environmental conservation, supported by science, which the Prince of Wales has embraced as the chief global advocate.

How King Charles's ethical beliefs mesh with the themes of "Delivering a Common Future: Connecting, Innovating, Transforming," chosen for the rescheduled 2020 CHOGM summit, is as good as anybody's guess. However, unlike the science themes, the ongoing dialogue on governance and the rule of law, information and communication technology, innovation, youth, environment, and trade are perhaps less controversial.[38] The issues that will make or mar King Charles's tenure as the Commonwealth's head will continue to evolve in the local and international economic milieu where socioeconomic and political alterity are high.

Brexit, the Commonwealth, and Africa's Economic Diplomacy

In an interview with Benita van Eyssen in April 2018, Asmita Parshotam, a South African Institute of International Affairs researcher, spoke on various African and Commonwealth issues. In response to a question on the significant advantage of membership for African countries in the group, Parshotam stated that trade and investment top the list.[39] In Parshotam's view, higher education opportunities, connected with labor development in member nations, come next on the list. Trade, investment, and higher education opportunities are directly associated with labor development, environmental preservation, and a higher standard of living.

It is irrelevant to revisit whether securing the political kingdom in Africa comes before the economic paradise, which echoes the chicken and egg adage. Modernization theorists correlate economic growth with democratic consolidations for several reasons. In *Political Man*, Seymour Lipset found a strong relationship between a stable democracy and a country's economic development level or modernization.[40] The correlation is also with other political systems, including monarchical and totalitarian regimes. With enough money to buy off the opposition and sustain loyalties, politics and leadership usually run with a soft tone. Modernization theorists presume that with "greater access to education, improved communications, and the shifting of people from the slumbering 'traditional' rural sector economy to the vibrant 'modern' industrial sector," ethnic consciousness will give way to national consciousness.[41] Lipset saw variables such as urbanization, industrialization, per capita income, and the level of education as harbingers of democracy.[42] The lower class's interests are better secured in an economically viable state, allowing very slim chances for the underprivileged to turn to opposition or counter ideologies. This illuminates some critical reasons why heated competition for power in Africa is sometimes too difficult to moderate.

What is paramount here is recognizing that African countries are in the same financial predicament as Britain following the coronavirus pandemic's economic consequences and the plethora of economic implications of the Ukraine-Russia war. If the world ignores the consequential economic crisis, it will lead to political dysfunctions. Before March 2020, when the COVID-19 outbreak in China became a global health crisis, Africa's fate was less close-knit than Britain's. While the virus has made many economies vulnerable worldwide, Brexit has increased Britain's need to project its image as a global player with its own rights rather than as part of the European Union. The desire to leverage its political influence to achieve economic stability is a task the UK needs Africa to accomplish.

King Charles, the new Commonwealth head, was in a similar position to Queen Elizabeth II in the immediate postwar era when Britain's economy could not carry the national demands and the African colonies' massive expectations. Like in the 1950s and 1960s, when African countries were gravitating toward the Eastern bloc in search of help to kick-start their economies, Africans are going the same route in the twenty-first century in search of opportunities to transcend centuries of international exchanges that have perpetuated poverty and undermined developmental infrastructure on the continent. Again, as in the immediate postwar period, the UK needed US assistance to weather the storm.

The projection is that the Commonwealth economic bloc will fill in some of Brexit's gaps. The data indicates that Nigeria, the most prominent African economy, is a big player in intra-Commonwealth trade. After South Africa, the UK is Nigeria's second-largest trading partner, with annual bilateral exchanges of £3.8 billion. As the chairman of the Commonwealth Enterprise and Investment Council, Lord Marland of Odstock noted at the 2018 London Commonwealth Business Forum that with a total GDP of about $480 billion, Nigeria is not only one of Britain's post-Brexit trading allies but also offers UK investors significant opportunities. In 2015, Nigeria had a positive trade balance of $8.26 billion, with $47.8 billion in exports against imported $39.5 billion in imports. Overall, 30 percent of Nigeria's exports pass through the Commonwealth market, with India buying 50 percent. Nigeria and South Africa represent about 70 percent of Commonwealth African trade.[43]

However, as the world's leading economy, US support would greatly help facilitate Britain's economic and trading engagements with Africa. The challenge remains to deal with a problematic partner in the United States. Under President Donald Trump, it was not assured that the US might provide the kind of support the UK expects, but Joe Biden's presidency may help the Anglo-African cooperation. To echo Parshotam, Africa has moved on from both the postwar and immediate postcolonial eras. The global village is closer than ever, with new and powerful states and multinational actors vying for power and influence worldwide. The UK has to contend with renewed strength to retain its relevance as a global power.[44]

China's robust economic grip on Africa is a critical factor that deserves considerable thought. Over the past three decades, the Asian giant has systematically forged close financial relationships with African countries. While China's successes highlight one of the shortcomings of the Commonwealth, it emerged on the heels of the vacuum created by the former European colonial powers. At the end of colonial rule, the new states faced the onerous responsibility of organizing social, economic, and political activities and struggling to create a unified nation. Besides, US actions and inactions in Africa since the end of colonial rule made African economies vulnerable to manipulations from without.

Within the search-for-survival frame came the inclination of African leaders to look toward China for economic partnership. For the Africans,

China offered something neither the Commonwealth nor the European colonial legacy had provided: the opportunity to work together as partners, not in a master-servant or superior-inferior relationship.[45] The African-Sino collaboration, which began to take shape in the 1960s, outpaced the Commonwealth economic project in the late 1980s following a thaw in the Cold War.[46] Africa's abundant natural resources are critical to China's continued economic growth.[47]

Nonetheless, there is more to this exchange than some critics are willing to admit today. Scholars realize that the "global hunt for energy," as David Zweig and Jianhai Bi described, does not fully explain China's rapport with its African allies.[48] We now acknowledge the "allure of the Chinese model," predicated on mutual partnership and respect for the indigenous elite, and connected with the "greater historical context" where "Cold War rationales have evolved towards convergence of economic interests."[49]

From a geopolitical standpoint, China's emergence as a new force in Africa has diminished the influence of the former colonial powers as never before.[50] The African countries have perceived China's presence as a counterhegemonic force in a geopolitical arena under the sway of the Western powers for several centuries. This is evident in China's ability to clinch bilateral relations with several African countries. How the Commonwealth under King Charles will respond to the evolving dynamic remains an intriguing test of his leadership. In pursuing its own economic interests, China has constructed a post–Cold War vision that projects its newly found global power.[51]

Theoretically, the nature of Afro-Sino relations today has led to the adoption of concepts such as the "rediscovery of Africa."[52] China commemorated this rediscovery in 2000 by founding the Forum on China-Africa Cooperation to increase aid to Africa significantly.[53] Anja Manuel has noted that while China was the largest recipient of Asian Development Bank and World Bank loans in the 1980s and 1990s, "in recent times, China alone loaned more to developing countries than did the World Bank."[54] The Chinese initiative has since blossomed, reaching $163 billion in 2011 alone. It is worth noting that the Commonwealth's sanctions on African countries—Nigeria, Zimbabwe, and The Gambia—pushed them into China's hands during times of crisis.

China's African policies cover many areas, including youth empowerment and other sundry goals the Commonwealth had set in the Harare Declaration. The implication for the Commonwealth and the former European colonial powers is that China's African rediscovery ideology confronts a convergence of geopolitical issues, including economic aid, development and underdevelopment, emancipation from neocolonialism, and solutions to citizens' aspirations.

This newfound focus arrived when Africa's economies experienced severe deterioration, engendered partly by foreign exploitation, civil conflict, mismanagement, and corruption. This aligns with the world capitalist system paradigm, as articulated by Immanuel Wallerstein: the developed Western nations aim to drain resources from the peripheral African economies to the core economies.[55] The failed "Structural Adjustment Policies" the World Bank and the IMF imposed in the 1990s did not help the African economies. On the contrary, Africans saw these Western-owned international credit houses as neocolonialist apparatuses.[56] The lessons learned from this experience are how Africans have tried to assert their new priority goals in the New Global Age.

China's successes in Nigeria, Zimbabwe, Kenya, and others offer some perspective on Africa's rediscovery, which holds a severe lesson for the United Kingdom and the Commonwealth. First, it is instructive that China modeled its multi-billion-dollar modern railway project in East Africa after the uncompleted British colonial East African narrow-gauge line.[57] China's East African project agreement signed in 2014 stipulated that the railway line would run from Mombasa to Nairobi, extending to Uganda, Rwanda, Burundi, and South Sudan. In the spirit of its win-win slogan, China is financing 90 percent of the project's costs as part of its One-Belt-One-Road initiative.[58]

Whether Britain is suited to compete with China in Africa depends on two critical factors. One is securing Africa's crucial readiness for collaboration. The consent will depend on the strategies deployed by the Commonwealth to wrestle control from China. The other factor is US readiness to work with Britain and the Africans in a multilateral framework. President Biden must amend President Trump's "America First" foreign policy to accommodate a multilateral approach to support trade deals with African nations and Britain in the American mutual trade plans.

Although China's economic interest is expanding in Africa, not all hopes are lost for Britain and the Commonwealth. The politics of the COVID-19 pandemic offers the Commonwealth and Britain an opportunity for an African policy reset. This is the right time to do some catch-up. China's role in the pandemic and racist attacks on African immigrants in China have led many African governments to rethink Afro-Sino relations.

UK and Commonwealth immigration policies will also determine their likely success in securing Africa's trust and partnership. Britain and the United States share similar views today of strict cross-border movement. However, the Commonwealth member nations, especially those from the developing regions, sharply differ in opinion from the US and British immigration policies, though they oppose Brexit. The immigration issue figures prominently in the same breath with economic revival, higher education opportunities, labor growth, and tighter cooperation among the Commonwealth nations. How would the Commonwealth under King Charles balance immigration restrictions with harnessing the Commonwealth's market's full potential? It seems contradictory that the pro-Brexit exponents will kick against the EU's open border and market policies and then embrace open borders with Commonwealth member nations from Africa, the Caribbean, and Asia.

How Britain navigates through its immigration/border politics is critical to the Commonwealth's economic and political framework. Unfortunately, immigration is a complicated issue to find consensus on within the EU and the Commonwealth; it will remain a divisive topic for a long time.

Within Africa, migrant labor creates deep animosity between South Africa and other countries, especially Nigeria, Zimbabwe, and Zambia, whose citizens have found the host country a popular destination. Reporting on the recent waves of xenophobia in South Africa, Jon Bornman disclosed that citizens of Thokoza (a Black township of East Rand) pointed to mass unemployment as a justification for "evicting migrant neighbors and setting ablaze their belongings in the streets." The antimigrant mob claimed that they "were just sanitizing the area."[59] The Thokoza incident resulted in over one hundred African migrants' deaths in South Africa between 1994 and 2020.[60]

Whatever steps the Commonwealth chooses to address the migrant labor question must include a plan to create "pockets of prosperous Europe" in different African regions to provide opportunities for the African youth. The agenda for King Charles's Commonwealth tenure is full. The future will tell how much he or his successor can tackle. But whatever happens, Africa must be central to any post–Elizabeth II royal branding permutations.

CONCLUSION

This examination of H.M. Queen Elizabeth II's role in Africa's decolonization and the postcolonial state's progress since the late 1940s contextualized her headship of the postwar Commonwealth. The transnational association was repurposed by Britain to absorb the shocks of a dying empire, guard national interests, and project a sober postempire image. The account unfolds with Elizabeth's Windsor family upbringing at a time of fundamental change, tracing the complex and diverse forces that fashioned her brand—values, priorities, goals, and African policies under the control of the British Establishment. With forty-six African countries under colonial rule at the end of the Second World War, fusing the continent's future and the new monarch's paths was a fait accompli.[1]

At age twenty-one in 1947, Princess Elizabeth announced her leadership mission and guiding principles in Cape Town, South Africa, and, as providence may have it, observed her final rites of passage in Njeri, Kenya, where she got the news of her succession to the throne in 1952. These events intertwined Elizabeth's monarchy and the continent's future in ways scholars can no longer downplay in decolonization studies. Any explanation of the British African empire's end and the postcolonial state's growth without Elizabeth's role is a faux pas.

What are the revelations of Her Majesty's relationship with the Africans? What does this multipart connection illuminate about monarchy and the British Empire traditions, the African decolonization drive, and the postwar Commonwealth mission?

Monarchy: Changing Times and the Empire Brand

Because "tradition," as Thomas Spear has argued, is a multifaceted discourse in which past historical events are constantly reinterpreted in the eyes of the present, rethinking Elizabeth's place in the broader scheme of empire culture and authority system is vital to evaluating her African records.[2] For perspective, in 1947, Elizabeth had beckoned on the Africans to allow her to serve as their "representative"—a request that came across to the nationalists as her will to collaborate in the fight for colonial freedom and racial equality. The princess then declared the readiness of her generation to assume some of the burdens of leadership "off the shoulders" of the old guards at Whitehall and Colonial Office. She reminded the global community that the ultimate prize of the Second World War was freedom; the postwar imperative, she stressed, remains the "defense of liberty." The resolve to protect liberty and freedom underlines her famous line about how the British Empire saved the world and how it had to save itself. Elizabeth's manifestation of time and space highlighted her appeal to citizens and subjects to march forward "together" with quiet hearts, high courage, and "an unwavering faith." The Princess stressed that these values would help elevate the new Commonwealth to "an even grander thing"—higher levels of freedom, happiness, prosperity—and exert a more "powerful influence for good in the world—than it has been in the greatest days of our forefathers."[3]

From the preceding, it is evident that Elizabeth came to the decolonization expedition with the best intentions for the colonized people. But she was oblivious then that her presence in the process was London's late colonial invention to diffuse and delay the independence movement for as long as possible. The clashing plot to use Elizabeth to achieve hidden national interests and at the same time project her monarchy as a messianic mission under an empire brand that embodied manipulation, exploitation, and oppression was like the Frankenstein story in which the negative repercussions of science and technology became a matter of thought after the fact.[4] Elizabeth's time was entirely dissimilar to Queen Victoria's era (the beginning of European imperialism in Africa and Asia) when the Crown indulged in global recognition as an imperial brand.[5] To the conscientious, the legend of "Her Majesty's Government" as a decolonization brand would imply an unending nightmare, hampering freedom, justice, and racial equity. Whitehall's poor judgment cultivated the apotheosis of cynicism that muddled Elizabeth's African relations as colonialism became obsolete in the postwar era.[6]

The point of the matter is that Britain misjudged the enormous damages of its colonial practices and the resolve of Africans to regain their independence. Caroline Elkins attributed this miscalculation to the self-indulgence of Britons that metonymic colonial violence epitomized their nation's cultural superiority.[7] The blinkered outlook explains the self-defeatist and contradictory royal mission Whitehall assigned to Elizabeth. In a review of Caroline Elkins's *Legacy of Violence: A History of British Empire*, Angus Mitchell reiterated that the maintenance of empire was "a project of information management, surveillance, cognitive dissonance, and Orwellian doublethink. Secret state agencies created an alternative moral universe functioning outside law and democracy."[8] By implication, the colonists forgot that they could not realize an Elizabethan sainthood in a whorehouse that was British colonialism in Africa.

From her 1947 birthday speech, it is evident that young Elizabeth dreamed of addressing the low "moral universe" of empire with a gospel of freedom and welfare of the restive subject people.[9] But life as a carefree princess (when the speech was delivered) profoundly contrasted with duty as a British monarch. Her oath of office and the royal brand bound Elizabeth to service to Britain above all else. Flanked by the British patriarchal authority system in the metropole and the colonies, the royal stakeholders charged the Queen to be "responsive" (i.e., being accommodative to change) and "relevant" (i.e., being meaningful to Britain).[10] As John Balmer reminds us, a royal or "brand promise" attached to the Queen's brand incorporated sociocultural, economic, and political products managed by the "Farm"—a British colloquialism for Whitehall. The expectation of the Crown was "to be authentic, consistent, and valued by consumers and other stakeholders."[11]

A stark reality of the Crown's branding and the tasks attached to the position is the objectification of Elizabeth as a consumable product within the realm of empire politics and its Orwellian, unethical universe. The intersection between the amorality of colonial conduct and Elizabeth's quest for Africans' welfare is opaque, through which the prudent could see the dissonance of imperialism and a convoluted path to a royal messianic journey the Queen was set up for in 1952. Elizabeth was in reality a hostage, the proverbial sheep led to its slaughter: "In a way I didn't have an apprenticeship. My father died much too young, and so it was all a sudden kind of taking on, and making the best job you can."[12] The Queen had to wade through colonialism's alterations, secrecy, deceptions, lacunas, and imbalances colonial officials erected at every turn in Afro-Anglo relations. In this context, Her Majesty's mission conjures Leopold Bell-Gam's *Ije Odumodu Jere*, a story of adventure and civilizing mission in which Odumodu, the principal character, was exposed to all manner of dangers leading to a shipwreck on his way from Eko, Nigeria, to Saint Helena.[13] From this prism, Elizabeth's duty to a dying Empire became a dance of destiny, a devil's alternative—she could not have been more pro-African than pro-British and retained the Crown.[14]

The established frame of royal obedience to the nation and the nature of British political colonial culture meant that Elizabeth could not publicly rebuke race baiters like Andrew Cohen of Uganda, Jan Christian Smuts and P. W. Botha of South Africa, and Ian Smith of Rhodesia because such actions would not be "respected" (i.e., having the approval of the British people and government). For similar reasons, Elizabeth could not arbitrate between Whitehall and the "unruly" African progenies of the empire, such as the chiefs of Nyasaland opposed to the Federation, Kabaka Mutesa II and General Idi Amin of Uganda, Robert Mugabe of Zimbabwe, and Colonel Ojukwu and General Gowon who led Nigeria to a self-destruct in 1967.[15] Instead, the Queen must hide when the Africans needed her most or risk being "compromised," as Oliver Lyttelton, the Conservative colonial secretary, stated in 1953.[16] Elizabeth must see her life of service through the ontological optics of the royal brand as "a people with a Queen"—an abstraction radiating psychological effects, which allows for an appreciation of the emergence of influence from social relationships with specific social, ideological, and historical contents.[17] The ideology of royalty and soft power as a conveyor of friendship, influence, and change challenges the social psychology explanation of power as the capacity to influence based on resource and political control—especially under colonial rule.[18] More important, the path the Crown traveled accentuates a load of idioms in the postwar discourses of meanings of decolonization and freedom.

African Decolonization

Decolonization was a dense, swampy landscape of the imperial politics of inventions, deceptions, and hegemonic control in rapid flux. The diverse and unpredictable curves of Africa's struggle for independence led Frantz Fanon to describe the phenomenon as a disorderly historical movement to alter the world. Of particular interest is his idiomatic inference that the moment was "intelligible" except in the specific context that provides it with "historical form and content."[19] While addressing France's rule in Algeria, Fanon's view underlines Britain's imperial resourcefulness, which had no bounds in the quest for a dignified end-of-empire pursuit.

For the most part, Europeans' aptitude to manipulate subject people to seize and retain hegemony sometimes unfolded ad hoc—meaning that colonial policies and institutions were constantly created, modified, or repositioned as the needs demanded. Collaborating this view in 1958, eminent Africanist James Coleman stated that it would have been "very un-British" to do otherwise. According to Coleman, "the British, unlike the French, lean toward a pragmatic muddling-through approach to problems of state, especially those involving imperial or foreign affairs."[20] The insertion of Elizabeth in the politics of the empire's end offers an explanatory metaphor for the different outcomes of decolonization in the various British African colonies. In some places like Ghana, Nigeria, Tanzania, The Gambia, and Sierra Leone, decolonization ended more peacefully despite its chameleonic nature. The process was marked by reactionary executions in Kenya, Southern Rhodesia, Malawi, and South Africa. In other words, within the grand scheme of a noble end-of-empire chase, the Crown's role to hypnotize, to delude the African nationalists, and to stymie the native people's agency in decolonization could not and did not entirely bode well for Her Majesty's reputation at the end.

The course and outcomes of decolonization corroborate Ann Laura Stoler and Frederick Cooper's perception of Europe, a Machiavellian sociocultural and political scene, as a product of "its imperial projects." While Stoler and Cooper see colonial encounters as a consequence of "conflicts within Europe," Michael Collins adds that imperial projects, particularly concerning decolonization, were functions of the peripheral and metropole conflicts. The metropole-periphery dialectics also mirror the dire socioeconomic conditions in Europe and Africa after the war, which supposed that Her Majesty would help Britain slow down the tempo of decolonization. Any decolonization studies that omit the conflict between monarchy, postwar social reordering, and empire paint an incomplete picture, more because, despite her complex and marginal position, Elizabeth served to gratify the competing interests of conservative versus reformist lawmakers who decided what happened in the colonial territories.

Once Whitehall prefigured the Elizabethan postwar decolonization plot, every step the Crown undertook was scripted by the royal stakeholders in the high politics of the royal branding mix.[21] This fact contradicts the "balance sheet" lenses through which British historians often present decolonization as a benevolent project. The Crown was a tool for pretentious royal stakeholders and politicians seeking to turn an ugly colonial reputation into a narrative of normalcy, progress, and hope under the postwar Commonwealth.[22] Abundant evidence from official British records shows that the aim of Whitehall in the immediate postwar era was not to abandon the empire but to reinvigorate it. In this last-ditch effort, Elizabeth was activated as the mediator in the struggle between African freedom and a *retardataire* imperial revivalism.[23] Her Majesty's original visions for African freedom wavered in the renewed hegemonic scheme.

In creating and injecting Elizabeth into the decolonization scheme, the political Establishment aimed to control the process by entrapping the African leaders in utter misapprehension or mental confusion. Nothing epitomized the impact of Elizabeth on African decolonization more than the declaration of the people of Sierra Leone when the Queen and her husband arrived in Freetown in November 1961. *The Daily Mail*, claiming to speak on behalf of the people, wrote that the country is "happy" and will always be proud of its "association with Britain. It is one we are not ashamed of, rather, it is one we are proud of."[24] In this milieu, Maya Jasanoff described Elizabeth's patriotic duty for Britain as a "fixture of stability" in a time of immense upheaval. Ben Domenech's satire offered that the appropriate epithet for the Queen at the end of her life should read, "Colonizers lost one of their most beloved soldiers."[25]

While scholars of the British Empire and government officials continue to celebrate Her Majesty's achievements, they should also reevaluate the thought or official mind behind enlisting Elizabeth in the surreptitious decolonization game, which, when it became apparent, sullied the Crown's character among African nationalists. As a principal actor in moderating the Cold War tensions in the former British territories, her actions and inactions brought positive and negative consequences for the indigenous populations. But the adverse outcomes often precede political discourses—among them, the subversion of elected governments, inaction toward racial bigotry, and civil conflicts in Ghana, Nigeria, The Congo, South Africa, and other places. The era's geopolitical games troubled Africa's Commonwealth relations until 1989 when a thaw in East-West relations paved the way for apartheid's end in South Africa. Nelson Mandela's discharge from jail in 1990 and the subsequent presidential election in 1994 marked the dismantling of colonialism's remaining political enclave on the continent and a reset of Elizabeth's Commonwealth African mission for good.[26]

The British Commonwealth

The postwar British Commonwealth is analogous to the tortoise and the hare in the marketplace. Britain, the tortoise, and Africa, the hare, run on parallel tracks. While the hare is on a marathon and wants things to move quickly for good, the tortoise, with a bag of tricks, is not in a rush but on a series of calculated slow steps. Within this analogous worldview, one appreciates how the Commonwealth represents different things for diverse groups and stakeholders. For Britain, in the immediate postwar era, the Commonwealth served as a placeholder for the empire, pending a more convenient and honorable termination. For the Africans, it was a forum for emerging new nations where freedom, equality, and unhindered voluntary cooperation challenged imperial dependency.

Through the organization, Elizabeth helped Britain accomplish its goal to dissolve the empire on its own terms—particularly appeasing some complacent preservationists in Whitehall, inserting elisions on unfavorable colonial practices, defending Britain's Cold War interests, and projecting global influence. Rasheeduddin Khan has posed the rhetorical question of whether the postwar Commonwealth signifies a neocolonial architecture, a continuation of imperialism by other means, or the colonizer's entrapment to keep "the newly freed countries into newer forms of dependence."[27] Terry Evans and Viktor Jakupec offer a more sanguine viewpoint in conceiving the Commonwealth as a melting pot of modernization, dependency, and soft power.[28] Although Khan, Evans, and Jakupec provide essential perspectives on the place of developing nations in the postwar Commonwealth, Marcus Power has underlined African agency in the institution, using the case of Mozambique (a former Portuguese territory that joined the Commonwealth on November 13, 1995) to illustrate the broader and diverse connections between Africa and British charities, industries, and the Department of International Development based in London.[29]

Thus, despite being seen as a reformulation of the British Empire by crook and design, African agency in the Commonwealth cannot be discarded for a more attractive argument—that is, Britain's neocolonial bait for the emergent nations to remain in newer dependence systems. The Africans have held on to the organization because it represents a medium for political dialogue, conflict resolution, economic collaboration, and debt negotiations.[30] Of course, the immediate postwar world order differed from the post–Cold War order. Within the bipolar world system, the postcolonial state sought ways to navigate the constricted pathways to genuine socioeconomic and political freedom. In a restricted bipolar political mélange, the African political elite had engaged with hegemonic powers within the international systems in diverse ways, including seeking help from the Queen to sustain their newly won freedom.

Faced with decolonization challenges, the new African elite, who had sensed a grand conspiracy between British Conservatives and Labourites to stall decolonization, perceived Elizabeth as a symbol of motherhood—which in the African idiom connotes sacrifice; a custodian of love, fairness, and morality; a peacemaker; a mark of communal harmony; and a defender of truth, justice, and equity. These assumptions resonate with Michael Collins's argument that "empire and decolonization [were] bound up with a moral mission and continued to provoke questions about the legacies of empire."[31] The African leaders courted Elizabeth's intervention in urgent and often perilous decolonization crises, perhaps unmindful that she was not the super sovereign the prodigal colonial officials made them believe by often reciting the misleading dystopian maxim "Her Majesty's Government" as a colonial brand. Analogous to the biblical story of Esau and Jacob, where the patriarch Isaac heard Jacob's voice but held Esau's phony hand, the messenger's hand belonged to Elizabeth but Whitehall was the authentic voice of power.

Notwithstanding the turns and twists of decolonization and Whitehall's efforts to sabotage it, the post–Cold War Commonwealth has helped strengthen Africa's quest for sociopolitical autarky more than many are yet to fully acknowledge. Her Majesty never abandoned the group's ideals but continued to push for its growth and success. Its solid foundation for free enterprise and prosperity in the twenty-first century means that the best part of the association's story is yet to come as Britain untangles its European Union commitments to leverage the organization's market potential to project power and influence. The point has been made that in the post-Elizabeth order, the opportunity exists for Britain to reinvigorate its global leadership in a more positive direction with Africa at the center and, thus, strengthen Elizabeth's Commonwealth legacies with a win-win economic formula for the member nations. The task may be onerous, but Britain must not recreate the wheel; it only requires stealing China's "rediscovery of Africa" economic creed purporting profit for all partners. Considering its exploitative colonial history, skeptics may doubt Britain's intentions in the post-Elizabeth era. But Europeans should not underestimate the muse of historical consciousness among the African youth primed to uncover hidden agendas and actions—real or imagined as the expected new order unfolds.

African Historical Memory/Consciousness

This book has clarified the concepts and contexts of Her Majesty's relationship with the Africans. To bring this analysis to a logical end, an additional explanation of the love-hate overtone requires a modified element of game theory as a philosophical dynamic in international cooperation. Game theory explains how "*interacting choices* of *economic* [and *political*] *agents* produce *outcomes*" where the desired results "might have been intended by none of the agents."[32] Regarding the relationship between imperial Britain and its African holdings during decolonization, the game in play was the Elizabethan Commonwealth decolonization scheme formulated by the British Establishment. The rational actors comprised Whitehall, colonial agents, the African political elite, and the British and African public. The game's primary goal was to use Elizabeth to moderate the African nationalist movement while Britain micromanaged the process in alignment with a preconceived and convenient decolonization pace. The other intended purpose was to cultivate a serene and loving image of the Crown in Africa as the face of a new and more humane global Britain.

Ultimately, the game produced an unintended outcome—a manifest but unfortunate dislike for Elizabeth among the African majority—evident in rampant emotions following Her Majesty's death on September 8, 2022. From the Western world, where colonialism remains the history of European heroism, or what Shailja Patel, a Kenyan author, identified as the "mythmaking machine," emerged words of reproach to Africans' modest and legitimate rebuttals.[33] The critics miss the point that Africa's indignation at colonialism's misdeeds under the royal brand is an act of righteous anger. Patel argues persuasively that Africans reacting differently would reinforce the hypocrisy and double standards perpetuated by Whitehall. Sipho Hlongwane, a Johannesburg-based writer, asserts that Queen Elizabeth's choices (meaning her consistent loyalty and devotion to the British cause) in the last years of the empire could have been different—by tendering a genuine apology for colonial sins as King Willem-Alexander recently did on behalf of The Netherlands: "You can be born into that level of privilege and make different choices, then eat the consequences."[34]

Although many Africans were and are still respectful of the Queen, the more widespread adverse reaction to the Elizabethan monarchy speaks to a deeper issue in the broader sense of African historiography, historical memory, and historical consciousness. In qualifying Elizabeth as colonizers' "most beloved soldier," Jasanoff and Domenech's anectodical parodies underscore the pitfalls of an anachronistic mindset embedded in the former colonies and the ex-metropoles.[35] Anachronism, the temptation to use past actions of historical actors to judge those after them, is a common problem in historical studies. Elizabeth was not a colonizer; historical consciousness, Louis Jonker argues, does not mean anachronistic clinging to something that *never* existed or no longer exists; it connotes the capacity to see "the multidimensionality of interpretation."[36] In her study of postapartheid South Africa, Natasha Robinson observed that historical consciousness denotes how young people understand the legacy of historical injustice that shapes many of South Africa's defining questions.[37] About the Elizabeth question, Robinson illuminates how African youth today see the historical injustices of colonial rule vis-à-vis the postcolonial problematics as entirely dissimilar to the Western viewpoint.

Ultimately, the Elizabethan story is not about the wealth or privilege she may have relished while ordinary Africans were stewed in poverty and deprivation. It is not about her longevity or the blame she may deserve for what she did or did not do right. The story is about the Queen's fortitude to swallow the responsibility for Britain's colonial sins with uncommon equanimity and silence. Also, her courage and persistence to see the Commonwealth succeed despite Whitehall's deliberate efforts to destroy it is the character and strength of her African mission no one should underemphasize. Indeed, the Queen built an inclusive and unified organization where the Africans could play a vital role and appropriate political and economic autarky. Altogether, Elizabeth's burdens and fortes were interlocked: Churchill's unabating manipulations, suppressed voices, the virtual preventability of truths, the obscurity of facts, crime scene cover-ups, the planting of intellectual land mines, and misleading whispering galleries—all culminating into what Michel-Rolph Trouillot has branded "bundles of silences" that require unique processes to deconstruct.[38]

The paradigm of the royal branding matrix informs that Elizabeth's brand prescribed manners of behavior, among them imposed silences for continued patronage. The tensions of reward and punishment inherent in the royal brand reflect the relationship between sports personalities and multinational entities that sponsor their brands.[39] Regarding the Elizabeth brand and African history, her culture of silence in moments of conflict created an epistemological lacuna rather than a revelation of her complicity and culpability in the violence that marked Africa's decolonization. Arthur Chapman and Caitriona Ni Cassaithe have argued that silences in historical narratives are worrying because they erode legitimacy, contexts, and knowledge frames—thereby cultivating "a façade of homogeneity that promotes the othering of differences."[40] Elizabeth's culture of silence or inaudible voices in every moment of decolonization rapture left a severe elision in the history of Africa's nationalist struggles. In his illuminating study, *Concealed Silences and Inaudible Voices in Political Thinking*, Michael Freedman noted that while the silences of the past are open to interrogation and refutation, the hushed voices of the future pose problems of reach and fragility.[41] A substantial part of Elizabeth's records as the leader of the postwar Commonwealth's decolonization project may have died with her; the speculation into the unknown and the future will not end soon.

What is known for now is that Elizabeth completed her life journey as a British postwar lodestar, heroine, and savior. Unfortunately, many Africans see only an unkind, unscrupulous, and unapologetic colonizer. The notion persists on the continent that Elizabeth supported or, at best, remained silent about the brutal crackdown on Kenya's Uhuru (or Mau Mau). An anecdotal expression of this belief in Kenya was the burning down of the Treetops Hotel, where then Princess Elizabeth and Prince Philip spent some nights in 1952. As elsewhere, the colonial officials in Kenya often ignored the legitimate complaints of the Africans—which gave cause for the widespread negative perception of "Her Majesty's Government" in the country. But the global refrain was a mythical branding concept Whitehall sold worldwide as the legitimate hand behind its empire affairs. With the royal brand attribution, the Mau Mau brutal prosecutions left a bitter feeling against Elizabeth among that generation of Kenyans and their descendants.

Similar colonial servants' misbehaviors that shaped the Africans' view of Elizabeth include Uganda's Kabaka Mutesa II's deportation from 1953 to 1954. Governor Andrew Cohen's miscalculation remains a bitter lesson in colonial paternalism and African rebellion. The Suez Canal crisis (1956–1957) was one more show of force that many stakeholders in Africa, the Middle East, and the United States objected to. It was part of Sir Winston Churchill's geopolitical chess game embedded in the anti-Soviet/Cold War policies that left the African nationalists wondering about the meaning of freedom and self-determination the Allied leaders had promised their supporters during the war. As Derek Brown stated, many Britons in positions of power could not accept in the postwar era that Great Britain was no longer "a first-rate power." Although Prime Minister Anthony Eden succeeded Churchill in 1955, Eden was part of the older colonial generation, refusing to live with the postwar movements for freedom, racial equality, and decolonization.[42] The Southern Rhodesian Unilateral Declaration of Independence (UDI) of 1965 was an additional moment of decolonization rapture in which the Africans expected Her Majesty's intervention. It is indicting to recall that the push for the UDI by Winston Field, Southern Rhodesia's prime minister, had started in 1963, and although Evan Campbell, the high commissioner for Southern Rhodesia in London, had identified Field as a "stubborn old pig," Harold Wilson's government connived to "play this issue as long as possible."[43]

Parallel high-stakes political plays that ruined African lives in the millions and truncated the royal brand's reputation were behind the Nigeria-Biafra humanitarian crisis (1967–1970), for which critics accused Queen Elizabeth. John Lennon, Dick Tiger, and Francis Akanu Ibiam's decisions to return their respective British Empire titles speak to the dangers of perceptions and reactions as complex problems.[44] British journalist Fredrick Forsyth explains that Biafra was the making of Prime Minister Harold Wilson and David Hunt, the British high commissioner in Lagos, Nigeria (1967–1969). While Britain's economic interests guided Wilson's adamant attitude toward the war, Forsyth revealed that Mr. Hunt was an egomaniac who loathed Colonel Emeka Ojukwu, the ex-Biafran leader.

From a private discussion with Jim Parker, the British deputy high commissioner in Enugu in 1967, Forsyth concluded that Ojukwu's sin was his failure to bow before David Hunt, as did General Yakubu Gowon, the Nigerian military leader during a prewar meeting in Lagos.[45] Forsyth's inference is corroborated in a dispatch to London following the secession on June 6, 1967, where Hunt described Col. Ojukwu as "a drunkard and too proud ... motivated by "personal ambition.... He is a man who has a high opinion of his own talents and believes he is destined for the highest positions in the State." Hunt claimed no other military governor would have taken the same action except Ojukwu, whose radio and press propaganda machine made "him feel something like a Frankenstein."[46]

Biafra was a multidimensional separatist movement with foreign powers maneuvering for Nigeria's oil and other resources. The conflict intersected with Pan-Africanism, anticolonialism, Anglo-French rivalry, the military-industrial complex of arms dealers and gunrunners, personality conflicts, regional power blocs, and intraregional geopolitical power struggles. While the prewar encounter between Ojukwu and Hunt in Lagos cannot be held solely responsible for Biafra—by design, overzealous colonial officials like Clive Salter, David Hunt, and Andrew Cohen routinely created unfavorable images of Elizabeth in Africa. The remnants of these misconceptions about Elizabeth today betray the obvious: practitioners of African studies hesitate to analyze Her Majesty's African records to shed light on the complexities of her monarchy in African history beyond the realms of mythmaking and prejudices.

One could begrudge the truth that the Queen never held the powers the critics may ascribe to her as a sovereign.[47] Her devotion to the Commonwealth in the post–Cold War era proves that she never lost sight of her promise of Africa's welfare, though it was not and could not have been the Crown's primary mission under the coronation oath. Her post–Cold War Commonwealth legacies reinforce her belief that affection always triumphs over hate. Her historic twenty-first birthday speech illuminates Elizabeth's conviction that there was no retreat from the path of freedom and racial equality at a time that Whitehall failed to follow her values, instead conceiving the speech as a diplomatic doublethink for a significant and potentially postwar redistributive colonial state that achieved its goals through Orwellian-style propaganda and sovereign regulatory muscle.

Elizabeth's life history sheds light on gender empowerment, even decolonial feminism, from the standpoint of one of the most privileged females ever who lived most of her life in a man's world. Her story parallels Buchi Emecheta's *The Joys of Motherhood*, a tale of fortitude, bravery, and resilience cast in postwar Nigeria. As with Elizabeth (the matriarch of postwar Britain) the main character Nnu Ego's life journey revolved around her troubled children, through whom she earned public reverence. The novel depicts a moving aspect of Western feminism, gender oppression, sexual difference, and patriarchy's silencing of women. Parallel to what Elizabeth's demise conjures among the Africans, Ego's eventual end throws into relief Emecheta's sarcastic intention. For a hard-working matriarch who suffered immense abuse, loneliness, silencing, starvation, and penury—to the point that she several times considered suicide an escape—the elaborate and expensive funeral her children held in her honor underlined Emecheta's befitting allegory for the "joy of motherhood."[48]

While the Queen's material wealth sharply contrasts with Nnu Ego's penury, Elizabeth's exemplarity reiterates that women's empowerment is indispensable and should be pursued diligently without misplacing the message. Few queens in history matched her sense of fashion, beauty, self-esteem, and women's empowerment. Throughout her extraordinary life, Elizabeth lived up to that symbolism of the mother of modern Britain, whether we refer to a nation searching for a postwar direction or one that needed seven decades to process its empire's dysfunctions to interpolate into a people mortified by its history of *nkamanya*—violence and robbery.[49] The H.M. Queen Elizabeth II era has ended; the fascinating history of poise, steadfastness, love, open-mindedness, patriotism, and devoted service she spurred is a fountain of inspiration for leaders worldwide. Her critics and admirers should appreciate why the apple fell close to the tree and where the coconut at the top of it got its water. Her epitaph should read, "The most conscientious and humane European that ever set foot on African soil."

NOTES

Introduction

1. The African territories Queen Elizabeth II inherited from King George VI were Basutoland (Botswana), British Somaliland (Northern Somalia), The Gambia, Ghana, Lesotho, Nyasaland (Malawi), Mauritius, Nigeria, Sierra Leone, South Africa, Sudan, Swaziland, Uganda, Northern Rhodesia (Zambia), and Southern Rhodesia (Zimbabwe). Others were the mandate territories—Namibia, British Togoland (Western Togo), British Cameroon (Western Cameroon), and Tanganyika (Tanzania)—a region the United Nations seized from Germany after World War I. The status of mandated African areas is in the League of Nations Covenant, Article 22, signed on June 28, 1919. For a Parliament debate comparing the mandated territories' status with the colonies, see HL Deb June 21, 1922, vol. 50 cc1046–47, Status of Mandated Territories in Africa.
2. For this view of self-government held by British lawmakers like Hornsey Gammans, see HC Deb July 12, 1950, vol. 477 cc1430–91, Colonial Affairs, 1430; CAB 129/129, C(69)59, "The Value of the Commonwealth to Britain: Cabinet Memorandum by Mr. Bowden," April 24, 1967.
3. John Rawls, *The Theory of Justice* (Cambridge, MA: Harvard University Press, 1971); D. J. Bentley, "John Rawls: A Theory of Justice," *University of Pennsylvania Law Review* 121, no. 5 (1973): 1070–78.
4. Robert Nozick, *Anarchy, State, and Utopia* (New York: Basic Books, 1974); Friedrich A. Hayek, *The Constitution of Liberty* (Chicago: University of Chicago Press, 1960).
5. Kant's seminal work enthroned the basic idea of modern ethical thoughts—the supreme principle of morality. See Immanuel Kant, *Groundwork of the Metaphysic of Morals*, trans. H. J. Paton, 3rd ed. (1785; reprint New York: Harper & Row, 1964); Immanuel Kant, *Critique of Pure Reason*, trans. Norman Kemp Smith (1788; reprint New York: St. Martin's, 1965).
6. H. L. A. Hart, *The Concept of Law* (Oxford: Oxford University Press, 1961), 153–55; J. S. Mill, *Utilitarianism, Liberty, and Representative Government*, with an introduction by A. D. Lindsay (New York: Dutton, 1951), 51–80.
7. The passing of Her Majesty on September 8, 2022, saw an outburst of these long-held views. For details of this and others alike, see Real Ombuor, Rachael Chason, and Meena Venkataramanan, "In Former British Colonies, Ghosts of Past Haunt Mourning for

Queen," *Washington Post*, September 9, 2022; Abdi Latif Dahir, Lynsey Chutel, and Elian Peltier, "In Africa, the Queen's Death Renews a Debate about the Legacy of the British Empire," *New York Times*, September 6, 2022; Eniola Akinkuotu and Julian Pecquet, "Queen Elizabeth's Death Elicits Dueling Emotions in Many African Countries," *The Africa Report*, Paris, September 9, 2022; and Canisius Banda, "Queen Elizabeth Died: Her Empire Brutally Killed Africans," *Lusaka Times*, September 11, 2022.

8   Adom Getachew, *Worldmaking after Empire: The Rise and Fall of Self-Determination* (Princeton, NJ: Princeton University Press, 2019); Bruce Gilley, "The Case of Colonialism," *Third World Quarterly* (2017): doi: 10.1080/01436597.2017.1369037. Gilley's paper is no longer in circulation because of its crude and provocative glorification of colonialism.

9   CAOG 12/62, Royal visits: H.M. The Queen to Nigeria, 1956; CAB 21/5957. Visit by H.M. The Queen and Duke of Edinburgh to Ghana, Sierra Leone, Gambia and Liberia, November 1961; HL Deb December 7, 1961, vol. 236 cc159–63, Her Majesty's Return from West African Tour. For the Uganda tour of 1952 and other royal family visits to the East African nation, see Bamuturaki Musinguzi, "Reviewing Queen Elizabeth's Three Visits to Uganda," *Monitor*, Kampala, September 18, 2022.

10 CAB 21/5957, Visit by H.M. The Queen and Duke of Edinburgh to Ghana, Sierra Leone, Gambia, and Liberia, November 1961; CAOG 12/62, Royal visits: H.M. The Queen to Nigeria, 1956.

11 CAB 129/129, C(69)59, The Value of the Commonwealth to Britain: Cabinet Memorandum by Mr. Bowden, April 24, 1967.

12 Princess Elizabeth, Speech on Her 21st Birthday, Cape Town, South Africa, April 21, 1947 (hereafter, PE/CTS/SA). In the speech, the princess declared that colonial domination and wanton conflict would not be part of her reign.

13 Reggie Norton, a Gibraltarian, cited in *The Illustrated London News*, July 5, 1969. For more on how the Gibraltarians constructed their Britishness over the twentieth century, see the volume Andrew Canessa, ed., *Bordering on Britishness: National Identity in Gibraltar from the Spanish Civil War to Brexit* (New York: Palgrave McMillan, 2019), esp. 25; Stephen Constantine, "Monarchy and Constructing Identity in 'British' Gibraltar, c.1800 to the Present," *Journal of Imperial and Commonwealth History* 34, no. 1 (2006): 25; Klaus Dodds, David Lambert, and Bridget Robison, "Loyalty and Royalty: Gibraltar, the 1953–54 Royal Tour and the Geopolitics of the Iberian Peninsula," *Twentieth Century British History* 18, no. 3 (2007): 365–90.

14 Clyde Sanger, *Malcolm MacDonald: Bringing an End to Empire* (Montreal: McGill-Queen's University Press, 1995), 389–404, 410–16; Colin Baker, *Sir Glyn Jones. A Proconsul in Africa* (London: Bloomsbury Academic Press, 2000), 197–200.

15 John Johnson, ed., *Colony to Nations: British Administrators in Kenya 1940s-1963* (Banham, UK: Erskine, 2002); Harry Mitchell, *Remote Corners: A Sierra Leone Memoir* (London: Radcliffe, 2002).

16 Ashley Jackson, "Governing Empire: Colonial Memoirs and the History of H.M. Overseas Civil Service," *African Affairs* 103, no. 412 (2004): 478.

17 Sarah Stockwell, *The British End of the British Empire* (Cambridge: Cambridge University Press, 2018); *The British Empire: Themes and Perspectives* (Malden, MA: Wiley Blackwell, 2008). The earlier work's essays explored the British Empire's economic costs and benefits.
18 Denis Judd, *Empire: The British Imperial Experience from 1765 to the Present* (New York: Basic Books, 1998); Ronald Hyam, *Britain's Declining Empire: The Road to Decolonization, 1918–1968* (Cambridge: Cambridge University Press, 2007).
19 Vernon Bogdanor, *The Monarchy and the Constitution* (Oxford: Oxford University Press, 1995), 300.
20 Kwasi Kwarteng, *Ghosts of Empire: Britain's Legacies in the Modern World* (London: Bloomsbury, 2011), 390. Kwarteng argued that "the British Empire had nothing to do with democracy." Others who made a similar argument include Roger Southall's "Democracy in South Africa: Moving Beyond a Difficult Legacy," *Review of African Political Economy* 30, no. 96 (2003): 255–72; and Howard W. French, "Queen Elizabeth II Wasn't Innocent of Her Empire's Sins," *Foreign Policy*, September 12, 2022.
21 Ben Pimlott, *The Queen: A Biography of Elizabeth II* (London: HarperCollins, 1996), 111–19, 345–54, 466–69. The Diamond Jubilee edition, with a slightly amended title and a foreword by Lord Hennessey of Nympsfield Village, released twelve years later, did not overcome the limitations. See Ben Pimlott, *The Queen: Elizabeth II and the Monarchy* (London: Harper, 2012).
22 Robert Lacey, *The Crown: The Official Companion, Volume 1: Elizabeth II, Winston Churchill, and the Making of a Young Queen (1947–1955)* (London: Crown Archetype, 2017).
23 Andrew Marr, *The Real Elizabeth: An Intimate Portrait of Queen Elizabeth II* (New York: Henry Holt, 2012).
24 Walter L. Arnstein, "The Warrior Queen: Reflections on Victoria and Her World," Presidential Address delivered at the North American Conference on British Studies at Asilomar, California, on November 1, 1997.
25 David Cannadine cited in Tristram Hunt, Review of "Queen Elizabeth the Queen Mother: The Official Biography by William Shawcross," *The Guardian*, London, October 3, 2009.
26 Ronald Hyam, *Understanding the British Empire* (Cambridge: Cambridge University Press, 2010); Piers Brendon, *The Decline and Fall of the British Empire, 1781–1997* (New York: Vintage Books, 2010).
27 See Philip Murphy, *Monarchy and the End of Empire: The House of Windsor, the British Government and the Postwar Commonwealth* (Oxford: Oxford University Press, 2013).
28 Chima J. Korieh, *Nigeria and World War II: Colonialism, Empire, and Global Conflict* (Cambridge: Cambridge University Press, 2020).
29 Edward Owens, *The Family Firm: Monarchy, Mass Media and the British Public, 1932–53* (London: The University of London Press, 2019), 200; and Mark Connelly, *We Can Take It! Britain and the Memory of the Second World War* (London: Routledge, 2004), 28, 63.

30 Philip Murphy, "The African Queen? Republicanism and Defensive Decolonization in British Tropical Africa, 1958–64," *Twentieth Century British History* 14, no. 3 (2003): 245.
31 David Maxwell Fyfe, the Secretary of State for Home Department to the House of Commons, HC Deb March 3, 1953, vol. 512 cc193–257, Royal Titles Bill. See National Archives Kew (NAK)–Dominions Office, DO 177/84, Minutes by A.W. Snelling, September 5, 1958, enclosed in Cabinet Discussions on the Nigerian Constitutional Conference, 1958–1961.
32 Gordon Walker (MP), HC Deb March 3, 1953, vol. 512 cc193–257, Royal Titles Bill, 198.
33 See Report of the Commission of Rapporteurs, League of Nations (L.N.) Council DOC. B7/21/68/106 (1921), "The Right of Nations to Self-Determination," August 14, 1941. In the document, President Roosevelt and Prime Minister Churchill pledged to uphold the rights of all peoples to choose the form of government under which they woul live and to restore sovereign rights and self-determination to those "forcibly deprived of them."
34 HL Deb June 25, 1947, vol. 149 cc266–71, Colonial Development.
35 HL Deb June 25, 1947, vol. 149 cc266–71, Colonial Development, 267–68.
36 HC Deb November 14, 1929, vol. 231 c2242W, Colonial Development Act. See also T 161/291/S33978, 1–7, Minutes by Sir P. Waterfield and Sir R. Hopkins, November 26, 1928.
37 See HC Deb March 5, 1930, vol. 236 cc419–20, Colonial Development (Schemes); HC Deb April 18, 1931, vol. 251 cc1463–6W, Colonial Development Fund; and T 161/657/S34609/0358, Colonial Development, Minute by E. Hale, June 20, 1935.
38 HL Deb July 2, 1940, vol. 116 cc723–48, Colonial Development and Welfare Bill. Governor Bourdillon had earlier criticized this policy as applied to Nigeria: "It is needless to labour the futility of thus looking to African colonies to work out their own regeneration without material aid." See CO852/214/13, no. 1, Despatch from Sir B. Bourdillon to Mr. MacDonald, April 5, 1935.
39 This argument gained currency in several Parliamentary sessions. See HC Deb July 13, 1943, vol. 391 cc47–151, Colonial Affairs, 107; HC Deb July 12, 1950, vol. 477 cc1430–91, Colonial Affairs, 1430; and HL Deb February 2, 1955, vol. 190 cc905–19, Future of Colonial Affairs, 905–6.
40 Creech Jones, The Secretary of State to the Colonies to the House of Commons, HC Deb July 29, 1947, vol. 441 cc263–378.
41 HC Deb January 27, 1947, vol. 432 cc621–23, Their Majesties' Visit to South Africa, 621–22.
42 PE/CTS/SA, Cape Town, South Africa, April 21, 1947. It is crucial to remember that this was Princess Elizabeth's first visit outside the UK. See Harriet Mallinson, "Queen Elizabeth II: Monarch's First Trip Abroad Was to This Country before Prince Philip," *Express*, London, January 19, 2019.
43 H.M. Queen Elizabeth, "A Speech by the Queen at the Commonwealth Heads of Government Meeting in Malta," Valletta, Malta, November 27, 2015.

44 See Jonathan Moore, "The Transformation of the British Imperial Administration, 1919–1939" (PhD diss., Tulane University, 2016), 57; and Margaret Gannon, "The Basle Mission Trading Company and British Colonial Policy in the Gold Coast, 1918–1928," *Journal of African History* 24, no. 4 (1983): 512.

45 See CO 533/471, Minute by Flood, 1936; Anthony Clayton and Donald Cockfield Savage, *Government and Labour in Kenya 1895–1963* (London: Routledge, 2012), 184; and David Anderson, *Histories of the Hanged: The Dirty War in Kenya and the End of Empire* (New York: W. W. Norton, 2005), 172. See HC Deb November 30, 1953, vol. 521 cc780–88, Kabaka of Buganda (Withdrawal of Recognition), 783; and Frederick Forsyth, "Buried for 50 Years: Britain's Role in the Biafran War," *The Guardian*, January 21, 2020.

46 In specific response to Buganda's situation, *The Spectator* of December 4, 1953, told the British people that the chain of episodes represented the high level of distrust among Africans of the British government's intentions in the continent.

47 David Cannadine, "The Last Hanoverian Sovereign? The Victorian Monarchy in Historical Perspective, 1688–1988," in *The First Modern Society: Essays in English History in Honour of Lawrence Stone*, edited by A. L. Beier, David Cannadine, and James M. Rosenheim (Cambridge: Cambridge University Press, 1989), 129.

48 In pursuing this research, the present author contacted Buckingham Palace in 2017, seeking a one-on-one interview with the Queen to help put her direct voice on issues concerning her African engagement. The request was declined because "Her Majesty does not give personal interviews; it will not be possible to do as you ask." (Personal memo: Reply from Buckingham Palace dated October 26, 2017, and signed by Mrs. Georgina Seage, Senior Correspondence Office.). Cannadine alluded to encountering similar hindrances in his research on "the right to reign and the rights of women" in nineteenth-century Britain. See Arianne Chernock, "The Persistent Monarchy," *Public Books*, September 5, 2012, https://www.publicbooks.org/the-persistence-of-monarchy/.

49 John M. T. Balmer, "A Resource-Based View of the British Monarch as a Corporate Brand," *International Studies of Management and Organization* 37, no. 4 (2007): 20–44. Two years after this publication, Balmer doubled down on the perspective with a detailed analysis "chronicling the corporate brand" and its consequential duties, challenges, trials, and survival: "Scrutinising the British Monarchy: The Corporate Brand that Was Shaken, Stirred and Survived," *Management Decision* 47, no. 4 (2009): 639–75.

50 Some of these documents are now available in printed and electronic volumes. See Anne Thurston, *Records of the Colonial Office, Dominions Office, Commonwealth Relations Office, and Commonwealth Office—British Documents on the End of Empire* (London: HMSO, 1995). Philip Murphy and S. R. Ashton, *Central Africa: Crisis and Dissolution 1945–1958* (London: HMSO, 2005); Philip Murphy and S. R. Ashton, *Central Africa: Crisis and Dissolution 1958–1965* (London: HMSO, 2005); and David Goldsworthy, *The Conservative Party and the End of Empire, 1951–1957* (London: University of London Institute of Commonwealth Studies, 1994).

51 Nicholas B. Dirks, "Annals of the Archive: Ethnographic Notes on the Sources of History," in *From the Margins: Historical Anthropology and Its Futures*, edited by Brian

Keith Axel (Durham, NC: Duke University Press, 2002), 47, 62–63; Antoinette Burton, ed., "Introduction," in *Archive Stories: Facts, Fictions, and the Writing of History* (Durham, NC: Duke University Press, 2005), 2; Tony Ballantine, "Mr. Peal's Archive: Mobility and Exchange in Histories of Empire, in *Archive Stories*, 94, 95; Barbara Harlow, "Sappers in the Stacks: Colonial Archives, Land Mines, and Truth Commissions," *Boundary* 225, no. 2 (1998): 179–204; Arunima Datta, *Fleeting Agencies: A Social History of Indian Coolie Women in British Malaya* (Cambridge: Cambridge University Press, 2021).

52 PE/CTS/SA, Cape Town, South Africa, April 21, 1947.

53 In the company of her husband, Philip, Elizabeth was in Africa to receive a wedding gift from Kenyans before proceeding on a Commonwealth trip to Australia and New Zealand. In 1952, King George VI's illness compelled him to ask the princess to take his place.

54 *Time* magazine was apt in a 1952 cover story by noting that the Queen was oblivious to the fact. See "Foreign News: Elizabeth II," *Time*, February 18, 1952.

55 *Mombasa Times*, "Elizabeth Proclaimed Sovereign," February 7, 1952, 1.

56 The Official Gazette of the Colony and Protectorate of Kenya Special Issue) published under the Authority of His Excellency, the Governor of the Colony and Protectorate of Kenya, vol. LIV, no. 10, Nairobi, February 7, 1952.

57 *Mombasa Times*, "Where the Prince and the Duke Will Stay," January 16, 1952, 3; Joseph Karimi, "In Njeri: Memories of Queen's Visit Lives On," *The East African*, Nairobi, June 3, 2012. In May 1954, the Mau Mau freedom fighters led by Ndungu wa Gacheru burnt down the original Treetops Hotel. A second Treetops was built in 1957 opposite the original site. Although there was no evidence, there were attempts to link the Mau Mau with Communist Russia. See Correspondent Report, "Nationalism in Kenya: Influences Behind the Rise of Mau Mau," *The Times* (London), November 13, 1952.

58 For clarity, the Sagana Lodge is about 22 miles from the center of Mt. Kenya. The mountain occupies roughly 276 square miles and is approximately from the Lodge. The Kikuyu treated the mountain as a shrine and often ascended the peak to offer spiritual duties. In *Facing Mount Kenya*, Jomo Kenyatta recounts a legend about Mogai (Lord of the Universe), who created the big mountain "as his resting place." On the day of creation, Mogai took Kikuyu, the mythical forbearer, to the mountaintop, where he showed him the wonders of his nature and asked him to erect his homestead on the surrounding land. Then, before the Creator departed, he instructed Kikuyu to offer sacrifice and raise his hands in prayers toward the mountain of mystery anytime he was in need. See Jomo Kenyatta, *Facing Mount Kenya: The Tribal Life of the Gikuyu with an Introduction by B. Malinowski* (London: Mercury Books, 1961), 23. See also an engaging discussion by Louis S. B. Leakey, *The Southern Kikuyu before 1903* (London, Academic Press, 1977), 1–3; and John S. Mbiti, *The Concept of God in Africa* (London: SPCK, 1970).

59 See Caroline Howarth, "Representations, Identity, and Resistance in Communication," in *The Social Psychology of Communication*, edited by Derek Hook, Bradley Franks, and Martin W. Bauer (Houndmills, UK: Palgrave Macmillan, 2011), 130–31.

60 Jürgen Habermas, *The Theory of Communicative Action*, Vol. I: Reason and Rationalization of Society, translated by T. McCarthy (Boston: Beacon, 1984).
61 Jürgen Habermas, *Theory and Practice*, trans. J. Viertel (Boston: Beacon, 1973), chap. 1.
62 Jürgen Habermas, *Knowledge and Human Interests*, translated by J. J. Shapiro (Boston: Beacon, 1971).
63 Habermas, *Knowledge and Human Interests*, 168.
64 See Hugh Pope, "'She Elephant' Lends Weight to Zulu Peace," *Independent* (London), March 25, 1995; Simon Perry, "Ruling Great Britain," in "Queen Elizabeth II Special Issue," *Life Magazine*, December 1, 2022, 49.
65 Interview, John Kerubo, Mombasa, August 12, 2019.
66 The elephants are also gentle giants, a trait Elizabeth related to fellow Britons, Africans, Commonwealth citizens, and the world. The animals display great care toward their herd, offspring, and elders, access water used by other animals, disperse seeds, and encourage biodiversity. See Peter Ngugi Kamau, "Elephants, Local Livelihoods, Landscape Change in Tsavo, Kenya" (PhD diss., Louisiana State University and Agricultural and Mechanical College, 2017), 70.
67 Jim Corbett, cited in Philippe Oberle, *On Safari: 40 Circuits in Kenya: Rift Valley, Highlands, Mountains with 54 Pictures and 60 Sketches* (Nairobi: P. Oberle, 1991), 83; Megan C. Hills, "Royal Family Members in Africa: From the Queen and Princess Diana to Megan and Harry," *Standard* (London), September 27, 2019.
68 Miriam Ma'at-Ka-Re Monges, "Candace Rites of Passage Program: The Cultural Context as an Empowerment Tool," *Journal of Black Studies* 29, no. 6 (1999): 828.
69 Dona Richards, "The Implications of African America Spirituality," in *African Culture: The Rhythms of Unity*, edited by Molefi Keke Asante and Kariamu Welsh Asante (Trenton, NJ: Africa World Press, 1990), 211.
70 The precise hour transition depicted by King George VI's death and Elizabeth's succession to the throne was marked by an eagle sputtering from a tree close to the log cabin.
71 *Mombasa Times*, "Mombasa Goes into Morning," February 7, 1952, 5.
72 *Ugandan Herald* (Kampala), "Death of the King," February 7, 1952.
73 *Ugandan Herald* (Kampala), "Her Majesty at Entebbe," February 9, 1952; and *Mombasa Times*, "*Gothic* Is Likely to Continue to Australia," February 7, 1952, 5.
74 Private Communication Ochieng Mbalazi, April 29, 2019.
75 *Ugandan Herald* (Kampala), "Her Majesty at Entebbe," February 9, 1952; and *Mombasa Times*, "Gothic is Likely to Continue to Australia," February 7, 1952, 5.
76 *Ugandan Herald* (Kampala), "Her Majesty at Entebbe," February 9, 1957.

Chapter 1. The House of Windsor

1. Shailja Patel, cited in *The Washington Post*, September 12, 2022; Karine Delafosse, "The Death of Queen Elizabeth II Is a Reminder of the Pain of British Colonialism," *LocalToday*, September 12, 2022. Many British and American historians have raised a similar question on the proclivity to "myth and mythmaking" in history. See Henry A. Murray, "Introduction to the Issue 'Myth and Mythmaking,'" *Daedalus* 88, no. 2 (1959): 211–22.

2. Traugh has articulated this influence as an issue in Queen Elizabeth's career. See Geoffrey Traugh, "Apartheid by Another Name," *London Review of Books*, September 12, 2022. David Cannadine's "Churchill and the British Monarchy," *Transactions of the Royal Historical Society* 11 (2001): 249–72, is obviously one of the most informative works on stakeholders' royal mentoring and branding tradition. The alliance between Whitehall and the monarch goes back in time. See William M. Kuhn, "Ceremony and Politics: The British Monarchy, 1871–1872," *Journal of British Studies* 26, no. 2 (1987): 133–62.

3. Luise White, *The Comforts of Home: Prostitution in Colonial Nairobi* (Chicago: University of Chicago Press, 1990), 20; Margaret Zoller Booth, *Culture and Education: The Social Consequences of Western Schooling in Contemporary Swaziland* (Dallas: University Press of America, 2004), 123–25.

4. See Carle C. Zimmerman, "Family Influence upon Religion," *Journal of Comparative Family Studies* 5, no. 2 (1974): 1–16; Daphne C. Watkins, Chavella T. Pittman, and Marissa J. Walsh, "The Effects of Psychological Distress, Work, and Family Stressors on Child Behavior Problems," *Journal of Comparative Family Studies* 44, no. 1 (2013): 1–16. See David O. Sears, "Whither Political Socialization Research? The Question of Persistence," in *Political Socialization, Citizenship Education, and Democracy*, ed. O. Ichilov (New York: Teacher College, 1990), 69–97.

5. Charles-Louis de Secondat Montesquieu, *De l'Esprit des lois* [*The Spirit of the Laws*] (Geneva: Chez Barrillot and Fils, 1748); C. D. Broad, "Lord Hugh Cecil's 'Conservatism,'" *International Journal of Ethics* 23, no. 4 (1913): 396–97.

6. Edmund Burke, *Reflections on the Revolution in France*, ed. J. G. A. Pocock (Cambridge, MA: Hackert, 1987); John Gray, *Liberalism* (Milton Keynes, UK: Open University Press, 1995), 78. For instance, in 1839, as a backlash to the upheavals of the French Revolution, the Belgian National Congress insisted that constitutional changes would be guided by past and present experience and not by the dangers of "abstract speculations." See A. de Dijn, "A Pragmatic Conservatism. Montesquieu and the Framing of the Belgian Constitution (1830–1831)," *History of European Ideas* 28 (2002): 227–45.

7. Striking a fine line between conservative ideals, including openness to Africa's freedom, was vital to preserving the corporate brand Elizabeth was entrusted in 1952.

8. See Susan Fournier and Lara Lee, "Getting Brand Communities Right," *Harvard Business Review* (2008): 1–8; Daniel Korschun, "Boundary-Spanning Employees and Relationships with External Stakeholders: A Social Identity Approach," *Academy of Management Review* 40, no. 4 (2015): 611–29; Mahesh Subramony, "Service

Organizations and their Communities: Perspective and New Directions for Management Research," *Academy of Management Perspectives* 31, no. 1 (2017): 28–43.

9 The Role of the Monarchy (accessed on 1/16/2023 at https://www.royal.uk/role-monarchy#:~:text=The%20Sovereign%20acts%20as%20a,members%20of%20their%20immediate%20family). As with all corporate brands, there is the need to understand the monarchy from a stakeholder and customer perspective because the brand's legal ownership is entrusted to the corporation represented by the stakeholders. In contrast, emotional ownership (the actual value) resides with the community.

10 While Elizabeth's leadership preparation did not include an African curriculum, she gained direct knowledge of the Africans and their hopes in the late colonial and postcolonial eras through the Commonwealth and extended royal tours of the continent.

11 John M. T. Balmer, "A Resource-Based View of the British Monarch as a Corporate Brand," *International Studies of Management and Organization* 37, no. 4 (2007): 20–44; John M. T. Balmer, "Scrutinising the British Monarchy: The Corporate Brand that Was Shaken, Stirred and Survived," *Management Decision* 47, no. 4 (2009): 639–75.

12 HC Deb May 4, 1953, vol. 515 cc37–167, Central African Federation, 42; 83, 87. If Elizabeth felt ready to meet with the African chiefs despite Oliver Lyttelton's position, she did not say so publicly.

13 This notion of identity must be underlined, including imperialism, which the Crown robustly supported. British Broadcasting Service (BBC), "Queen Victoria: The Woman Who Redefined Britain's Monarchy," https://www.bbc.co.uk/teach/ks3-gcse-history-queen-victoria-monarchy/z73rnrd.

14 F. N. Forman, *Constitutional Change in the United Kingdom* (London: Routledge, 2002), 6–7.

15 Cahal Milmo, "The Independent Guide to the U.K. Constitution: The Monarchy," *Independent* (London), June 12, 2015.

16 Walter Bagehot, *The English Constitution Second Edition* (London: Chapman and Hall, 1867), 68. Before the book's publication, it was serialized in *The Fortnightly Review* (London) from May 15 to January 1967.

17 Frank Hardie, *The Political Influence of Queen Victoria, 1861-1901, 2nd edition* (1935 reprint, London: Frank Cass, 1938), 21. See William M. Kuhn, "Ceremony and Politics: The British Monarchy, 1871–1872," *Journal of British Studies* 26, no. 2 (1987): 134.

18 Clarissa Campbell Orr, introduction to *Queenship in Britain, 1660–1837: Royal Patronage, Court Culture, and Dynastic Politics*, ed. Clarissa Campbell Orr (Manchester: Manchester University Press, 2002), 7.

19 Walter L. Arnstein, "The Warrior Queen: Reflections on Victoria and Her World," Presidential Address delivered at the North American Conference on British Studies at Asilomar, CA., November 1, 1997.

20 Salisbury to the Queen, August 29, 1886, cited in Queen Victoria, *The Letters of Queen Victoria, 3rd Series: A Selection from Her Majesty's Correspondence and Journal Between the Years 1886–1901*, ed. George E. Buckle (London: John Murray, 1930), 193–94. See Richard Hart Sinnreich, "An Army Apart: The Influence of Culture on the Victorian British Army," in *The Culture of Military Organizations*, ed. Peter R. Mansoor

and Williamson Murray (Cambridge: Cambridge University Press, 2019), 177. John Charmley, *Splendid Isolation? Britain, the Balance of Power, and the Origins of the First World War* (London: Faber and Faber, 1999), 207; David Steele, "Salisbury and Soldiers," in *The Boer War: Direction, Experience, and Image*, ed. John Gooch (London: Frank Cass, 2000), 4.

21 Queen Victoria, cited in Marie Mallet, *Life with Queen Victoria: Marie Mallet's Letters from Court, 1887–1901* (Boston: Houghton Mifflin, 1968), 186, and Helen Rappaport, *Queen Victoria, A Biographical Companion* (Santa Barbara, CA: ABC-CLIO, 2003), 331. The government launched a propaganda campaign to gain public support for the war by leveraging *The Times*' massive readership of over 60,000 in 1899. George W. Potter, "How English Pro-Boer Newspapers Feed the War Flames," *The Times* (London), October 1, 1901, 5; "The Transvaal Crisis: Boer Brutality," *The Times* (London), October 7, 1899; "The Boer Rebellion," *The Times* (London), November 28, 1899.

22 National Archives Kew (hereafter NAK), Correspondence and papers relating to the Imperial British East Africa Company (IBEA), CO. File 1 A PP MS 1/IBEA/1/1A 1888-1889 [n.d.]. See D. A. Low, *Buganda in Modern History* (Berkeley: University of California Press, 1971), 36–37; Margery Perham, *Lugard, The Years of Adventure, 1858–1898* (London: Collins, 1956). See NAK, Letter from Wilson to Acting Commissioner, Entebbe Staff Correspondent Inward, vol. 1., A4 item II, 1895; Tarsis B. Kabwegyere, "The Dynamics of Colonial Violence: The Inductive System in Uganda," *Journal of Peace Research* 9, no. 4 (1972): 303–14.

23 Peter Gukiina, *Uganda: A Case Study in African Political Development* (Notre Dame: University of Notre Dame Press, 1972), 99; Letter from Mutesa King of Uganda to Queen Victoria, April 3, 1876.

24 Colonial Office (CO), Mr. Chamberlain to Queen Victoria, November 11, 1895; Queen Victoria, *Letters of Queen Victoria,* 572–73. In the telegraph, Chamberlain had requested permission to deploy "400 of your Majesty's West Indian troops from Sierra Leone, of 30 special officers, and 300 carefully selected men from your Majesty's Army in England, and of about 800 of the Haussa armed constabulary drawn from the Gold Coast and Lagos."

25 National Archives Ibadan (hereafter NAI), C&CC to Resident Benin 25-3-97. Ben Prof. 2/97. See also Ministry of Local Government and Chieftaincy Affairs Archives, Benin City (hereafter MLGA), H. F. Marshall (Assistant District Officer), "Intelligence Report on Benin City," August 12, 1939, WP 1080, 15. For a very engaging study of the expedition, see Osarhieme Benson Osadolor's "The Benin Royalist Movement and Its Political Opponents: Controversy over Restoration of the Monarchy, 1897–1914," *International Journal of African Historical Studies* 44, no. 1 (2011): 45–59.

26 Queen Victoria, *Letters of Queen Victoria,* 310–11.

27 Queen Victoria, *Letters of Queen Victoria,* 263. Harrington was the former consular officer at Zeila, the northwestern port of Somalia.

28 Ethiopia's cooperation with the Abyssinia Convention, which allowed the British imperial agents to secure Sudan for Her Majesty's control, was the magic factor.

See HC Deb June 10, 1898, vol. 58 cc1316–441, Class II, 1321; H. G. Marcus, "Ethio-British Negotiations Concerning the Western Border with Sudan, 1896–1902," *Journal of African History* 4, no. 1 (19630): 81–94.

29 *The Gazette* (London), March 8, 1902, 6; *The Illustrated London News*, July 7, 1902; Ham Mukasa, *Uganda's Katikiro in England* (London: Hutchinson and Co., 1904), 188.

30 H.M. Queen Elizabeth II Royal Archives (RA) VIC/ADDA27, Speech read by Queen Victoria in Council on the day of her accession, June 20, 1837.

31 Kathryn Hughes, "Gender Roles in the 19th Century," May 15, 2014. British Library. *Discovering Literature: Romantics & Victorians*. Accessed May 30, 2024. https://www.britishlibrary.cn/en/articles/gender-roles-in-the-19th-century/.

32 Jane Austen, *Pride and Prejudice with illustrations by Hugh Thomson* (London: Printed for T. Egerton by Military Library Whitehall, 1813), chap. 8.

33 Michael J. C. Echeruo's *In Victorian Lagos: Aspects of Nineteenth Century Lagos Life* (London: Macmillan, 1977), 67.

34 Parliamentary Archives (hereafter PA), HL/PO/PU/1/1918/7&8G5c64, Representation of the People Act February 6, 1918. Britain became a democracy following the Act of 1918. The law granted voting rights to all men aged twenty-one and above and women from thirty with a property qualification. An amendment to the Law in 1928 gave voting rights to all men and women over twenty-one. See PA, HL/PO/PU/1/1928/18&19G5c12, 1928 Equal Franchise Act.

35 Sarah Bradford adds that her mother's social status as a commoner made the prospect even less feasible. "Queen Elizabeth the Queen Mother—The Official Biography by William Shawcross," Review in *The Daily Telegraph* (London), September 18, 2009.

36 HL Deb December 10, 1936, vol. 103 c725, Abdication of King Edward VIII. See *The Sunderland Daily Echo and Shipping Gazette*, October 27, 1936, 1; *The Evening Telegraph* (London), December 12, 1936, 8.

37 See, for instance, "Mrs. Simpson, Friend of King, Seeks Divorce," *Chicago Daily Tribune*, October 5, 1936; "Many Peers Fear Marriage," *New York Times*, November 20, 1936. Prime Minister Baldwin informed the House of Commons that these inquiries caused his disquiet. See HC Deb December 10, 1936, vol. 318 cc2175–97, Members of the House of Commons, 2177; HL Deb December 10, 1936, vol. 103 cc725–34, Message from His Majesty.

38 For a cursory look at some of these letters, see Reverend Alan Don D.D. to Reverend J. E. Macrae, November 17, 1936. *Lang Papers: Coronation 1936–1938*. Lang papers vol. 22, Lambeth Palace Library, folio 405. And Cosmo Gordon Lang, *Lang Papers: Royal Correspondence, 1923–1945*, Lang papers vol. 318, Lambeth Palace Library, folio 105.

39 "King and Monarchy," *The Times* (London), December 2, 1936.

40 H.R.H. Edward Duke of Windsor, *A King's Story: The Memoirs of H.R.H. the Duke of Windsor K.G.* (London: Cassell, 1951), 372.

41 "The King and His Ministers Constitutional Crisis," *Daily Express* (London), December 3, 1936.

42 HC Deb December 10, 1936, vol. 318 cc2175–97, Members of the House of Commons, 2175; NAK, PC 11/1, extract from PC 2/599, Instrument of Abdication of Edward VIII, December 10, 1936.

43 King Edward VIII, Radio Address, December 11, 1936; "Instrument of Abdication" signed by King Edward VIII and his three brothers, Albert (later George VI), Henry, and George, December 10, 1936; *The Guardian*, "King Edward Renounces the Throne," London, December 10, 1936.

44 Edward cited in "A Child of England," in "Queen Elizabeth at 90," Special Edition, *Life*, April 1, 2016, 22.

45 Germany's Kaiser Wilhelm II was exiled to Holland on March 9, 1918. The Bolsheviks executed Russia's Emperor Nicholas II and his family soon after the armistice on November 11, 1918. In contrast, by supporting British troops, domestic ideals, and charity work, King George V won the hearts of Britons as a "symbol of all that was best in national life." See Theo Aronson, *Crown in Conflict: The Triumph and Tragedy of European Monarchy, 1910–1918* (Manchester, NH: Salem House Press, 1986), 39; *The Derby Journal* (London), December 4, 1936, 9; *The Sunday Post*, December 13, 1936, 1.

46 *Diamond Fields Advertiser*, Kimberley, South Africa, May 2, 1915.

47 T. Jack Thompson, "Prester John, John Chilembwe and the European Fear of Ethiopianism," *Society of Malawi Journal* 68, no. 2 (2015): 18–30; Ian Linden and Jane Linden, "John Chilembwe and the New Jerusalem," *Journal of African History* 12 (1971): 631.

48 CO 852/349/1, no. 18, Memo by E. Melville in reply to West African Students' Union, April 1940. The WASU memo to MacDonald was sent on March 1, 1940.

49 Peter B. Clarke, *West Africans at War, 1914–18, 1939–45. Colonial Propaganda and Its Cultural Aftermath* (London: Ethnographica, 1986), 25–29, 30; Fred Omu, "The Nigerian Press and the Great War," *Nigeria Magazine* 96 (1968): 45–46; Akinjide Osuntokun, *Nigeria in the First World War* (Atlantic Highlands, NJ: Brill Academic Publication, 1979), 67–71, 78–79; Jean Meyer, Jean Tarrade, Anne Rey-Goldzeiger, and Jacques Thobie, *Histoire de la France Coloniale. Volume 2 1914–1990* (Paris: Armand Colin, 1990), 79.

50 See *Gold Coast Leader*, May 9, 1925; *West Africa*, March 21, 1925; *Nigerian Pioneer*, April 17, 1925; RA EVIII PWH/PS/ VISOV/1925/AFSAM: Nigeria File.

51 Mr. Leopold Amery, Secretary of State to the Colonies, HC Deb July 27, 1925, vol. 187 cc65–190, Colonial Office, 74.

52 *Natal Mercury*, April 23, 1925; *Indian Opinion*, April 24, 1925; *Umteteli*, May 2, 1925; *Imvo Zanbantsundu*, May 5, 1925; Ralph Deakin, *Southward Ho! The Tour of the Prince of Wales to Africa and South America* (Philadelphia: Lippincott, 1926).

53 H.R.H. Edward Duke of Windsor, *A King's Story*; Philip Ziegler, *King Edward VIII* (New York: Knopf, 1991), 218.

54 Linda W. Rosenzweig, "The Abdication of Edward VIII: A Psycho-Historical Explanation," *Journal of British Studies* 14, no. 2 (1975): 102.

55 The Royal Marriage Act of 1772 stipulates that members must seek the monarch's consent for a legitimate marriage. The law prohibits any royal wedding in contravention of this rule.
56 Sarah Bradford, "*Queen Elizabeth the Queen Mother—The Official Biography* by William Shawcross," review, *Daily Telegraph* (London), September 18, 2009.
57 The *Derby Journal* (London), December 4, 1936; Tristram Hunt, "*Queen Elizabeth the Queen Mother: The Official Biography* by William Shawcross," review, *The Guardian* (London), October 3, 2009; Anne Sebba, *That Woman: The Life of Willis Simpson Duchess of Windsor* (New York: St. Martin's Press, 2011), 102, 221.
58 Peter Forest, "This Girl may be Queen Elizabeth II of England," *Britannia and Eve* (London), February 1, 1937, 8; Eliana Dockterman, "Elizabeth Didn't Expect to be Queen: Here Is How It Happened," *The Times* (London), June 18, 2018.
59 See William Shawcross, *The Queen Mother: The Official Biography* (London: Alfred A. Knopf, 2009). Simon Perry, "A Child of England," in "Queen Elizabeth at 90," Special Edition, *Life*, April 1, 2016, 23, 52.
60 Queen Mary responded to the suggestion that the children should leave for Canada for safety reasons. See Prime Minister Churchill to the Parliament, HC Deb September 17, 1940, vol. 365 cc121–38, War Situation, 136.
61 HC Deb September 17, 1940, vol. 365 cc121–38, War Situation, 136.
62 HC Deb September 17, 1940, vol. 365 cc121–38, War Situation, 136. See Hunt, "*Queen Elizabeth the Queen Mother.*"
63 RA, PS/PSO/GVI/PS/MAIN/04970, F. W. Ogilvie to A. Lascelles, October 19, 1940; "Princess Elizabeth Broadcasts," *Pathé Gazette*, October 17, 1940; *The Times*, October 14, 1940, 4; *The Sphere* (London), February 23, 1952, 304.
64 *Daily Telegraph*, April 22, 1942, 5; *The Times*, April 22, 1942, 6. For an engaging analysis, see David Cannadine, "The Context, Performance, and Meaning of Ritual: The British Monarchy and the 'Invention of Tradition,' c. 1820–1977," in *The Invention of Tradition*, ed. Eric Hobsbawm and Terence Ranger (Cambridge: Cambridge University Press, 1983), 157–63.
65 *The Scotsman*, April 21, 1947; "Queen Elizabeth II: Key Moments in Her Reign," *New York Times*, September 9, 2015.
66 Wilson Harris, "The Education of the Queen," *The Atlantic*, December 1943.
67 David Livingstone, *Livingstone's African Journal 1853–1863* (Berkeley: University of California Press, 1963); Hugh Trevor-Roper, "The Rise of Christian Europe," *The Listener* 70 (1963): 871. Trevor-Roper took pleasure in dismissing Africa as "the meaningless gyrations of barbarous tribes in picturesque but irrelevant corners of the globe."
68 Winwood W. Reade, *Savage Africa* (New York: Harper & Brothers, 1864). Not even Mary Kingsley's skewed travel journals were good enough to amuse and mentally tickle the princess's curiosity. See Mary Henrietta Kingsley, *Travels in West Africa* (London: Macmillan, 1897).

69   P. T. Barnum, *The Humbugs of the World: An Account of the Humbugs, Delusions, Impositions, Quackeries, Deceits, and Deceivers Generally, in All Ages* (New York: Carleton, 1866), 13.

70   Harris, "Education of the Queen"; Marion Crawford and Jennie Bond, *The Little Princesses: The Story of the Queen's Childhood by Her Nanny, Marion Crawford* (New York: St. Martin's Griffin, 2020).

71   Harris, "Education of the Queen."

72   *The Scotsman*, April 21, 1947, 5; *The Times*, April 21, 1944, 6; *Daily Mirror*, April 12, 1943, 5; *Daily Express*, April 21, 1943, 4; "Princess Elizabeth Second Subaltern," *Pathé Gazette*, April 19, 1945.

73   In the House of Commons, Prime Minister Atlee called on MPs to wish the King and his family a successful trip to support the Commonwealth. See HL Deb January 28, 1947, vol. 145 cc164–68, The Royal Visit to South Africa, 164–65.

74   Douglas Williams, "Royal Tour of South Africa," *The Courier-Mail*, Brisbane, February 3, 1947, 2.

75   See Hilary Sapire, "African Loyalism and Its Discontents: The Royal Tour of South Africa, 1947," *Historical Journal* 54, no. 1 (2011): 215–40.

76   Joanne Toor and H. G. Picknell, "The Proper Place of Propaganda," *Columbia Journal of International Affairs* 5, no. 2 (1951): 79. Propaganda was widely deployed in the war by the Allied and Axis camps. See Urvashi Gautam, "Image of the Enemy: German and British Propaganda in the Second World War," *Proceedings of the Indian History Congress* 73 (2012): 1099–106.

77   Tim Stapleton, "Letters from Burma: Views of Black Zimbabwean Soldiers during the Second World War," in *War and Peace in Africa*, ed. Toyin Falola and Raphael Chijioke Njoku (Durham, NC: Carolina Academic Press, 2010): 268.

78   *Bantu Mirror*, Bulawayo, September 16, 1939, 1. Open letter from Governor to Africans of Southern Rhodesia. See *Bantu Mirror*, Bulawayo, September 23, 1939, 1, for the Bulawayo meeting.

79   *Bantu Mirror*, Bulawayo, June 22, 1940, 1.

80   NAZ S726 W5/B/1-9, G.A. Bain, Report on Recruiting, September 21, 1945.

81   *Bantu Mirror*, Bulawayo, August 27, 1945, 8.

82   David Johnson, *World War II and the Scramble for Labour in Colonial Zimbabwe, 1939–1948* (Harare: University of Zimbabwe Publications, 2000), 32.

83   Ashley Jackson, *Botswana 1939–1945: An African Country at War* (Oxford: Oxford University Press, 1999), 31–32.

84   Peter McLaughlin, "Victims as Defenders: African Troops in the Rhodesian Defence System 1890–1980," *Small Wars and Insurgencies* 2, no. 2 (1991): 263. The voluntary service point explains why RAR recruiters said, "Those who wish to serve their King should apply." The overenthusiastic volunteers grumbled about delays in their deployment on overseas service. See *Bantu Mirror*, Bulawayo, August 9, 1941, 1; NAZ S726 SW 5/1-2 Lt. Colonel Wane to Defence Headquarters, December 4, 1941

85   Ashley Jackson, *The British Empire and the Second World War* (London: Hambledon Continuum, 2006), 187.

86 Nigerian National Archives Calabar (NNAC), Calprof 3/1/2353, Loyalty to the King and Government, 1939. See Chima J. Korieh, *Nigeria and World War II: Colonialism, Empire, and Global Conflict* (Cambridge: Cambridge University Press, 2020), 51, 63, 72–73.
87 *Gold Coast Times* (Accra), March 13, 1939, 1.
88 *West African Pilot* (Lagos), September 4, 1939, 3.
89 *West African Pilot* (Lagos), February 12, 1942, 1.
90 *The Nigerian Daily Times*, Lagos, April 1, 1939, 1.
91 Princess Elizabeth, Speech on her 21st Birthday, Cape Town, South Africa, April 21, 1947 (hereafter, PE/CTS/SA).
92 Hughes, "Gender Roles in the 19th Century," 1.
93 Prince Andrew and Prince Edward's birth in 1960 and 1964 marked the only children born to a sitting British Crown since Queen Victoria.
94 See HL Deb October 22, 1947, vol. 152 cc83–88, The Marriage of Princess Elizabeth: Address of Congratulation.
95 Christopher Wilson, "Palace Plot that Almost Stopped Her from Being Queen: On the 60th Anniversary of the Coronation," *Daily Mail* (London), May 31, 2013. See "Royal Fight: How Queen Elizabeth's Reign was Nearly Scuppered by Edward VIII," *Daily Express* (London), January 18, 2018; Christopher Wilson, "Secret Plot to Deny the Queen the Throne," *The Telegraph* (London), November 22, 2009.
96 *Mombasa Times*, "Mombasa Goes into Mourning," February 7, 1952, 5; *Ugandan Herald* (Nairobi), "Death of the King," February 7, 1952. For the initial planning of the trip, see NAK CO 967/63 Correspondence with Sir Philip Mitchell, Governor, about the possibility of visits to Kenya by the King and Queen and Princess Elizabeth and the Duke of Edinburgh, 1950. The Africa trip came at a risky period in the colony because of the violent Mau Mau nationalist movement, which worried officials about the royals' safety. For more on this story, see Best, "Day Princess Elizabeth Became Queen," 1; *The Sphere* (London), August 31, 1957, 16–17; *Lisburn Herald, and Antrim and Down Advertiser* (Antrim, Northern Ireland), January 3, 1953, 4.
97 See Supplement to the *London Gazette*, "Ceremonial of the Coronation of Her Majesty Queen Elizabeth II," November 17, 1953, 6223.

Chapter 2. Deconstructing the 1947 Cape Town Speech

1 Princess Elizabeth, Speech on Her 21st Birthday, Cape Town, South Africa, April 21, 1947 (hereafter, PE/CTS/SA). *The Scotsman*, Edinburgh, April 21, 1947, reported that the "Empire Broadcast" was Elizabeth's idea and that "she gave up one of her days at the Victoria Falls rehearsing and recording her speech." A diary kept by Captain Lewis Ritchie, who served as King George VI's press secretary, states that the speech broadcasted on the BBC from Cape Town as a live program was prerecorded on Sunday, April 13, 1947, at Victoria Falls Hotel, Rhodesia. "At 6 pm, Princess Elizabeth recorded her speech for the BBC. It was afterward played off for Her Royal Highness to hear and

was a great triumph." See Captain Lewis Ritchie, cited in Hannah Furness, "Uncovered: The Surprising Secret of Queen's Cape Town Speech," *The Telegraph*, London, September 17, 2018; *The Evening Telegraph*, August 1, 1947.

2   Viscount Addison, the Secretary of State for Dominion Affairs, to the House of Lords, HL Deb January 28, 1947, vol. 145 cc164–68, The Royal Visit to South Africa, 165.

3   Reiss Smith, "The Royal House of Windsor: King George VI and Young Elizabeth's South African Tour," *Express*, London, March 8, 2017.

4   See BBC, "Royal Tour of South Africa," Original Broadcast June 2, 1947.

5   The birthday present featured twenty-one large diamonds from Kruger. "The Queen calls these stones her 'best diamonds' and still wears them to this day." *Daily Telegraph*, April 21, 1947; *The Scotsman*, April 21, 1947. See Reiss Smith, "The Royal House of Windsor: King George VI and Young Elizabeth's South African Tour," *Express*, London, March 8, 2017.

6   Mr. William Gallacher to the House of Commons, HC Deb January 27, 1947, vol. 432 cc621–23, 622.

7   CO525/199, 44379/46 no. 1, Letter from Hastings K. Banda to Mr. Creech Jones, Nyasaland, June 14, 1946 [Nyasaland].

8   PE/CTS/SA, Cape Town, South Africa, April 21, 1947.

9   See Martin Thornton, *Churchill, Borden, and Anglo-Canadian Naval Relations, 1911–14* (New York: Palgrave Macmillan, 2013), 46.

10 See HC Deb March 2, 1911, vol. 22 cc551–52; HC Deb June 17, 1921, vol. 143 cc783–860; and HL Deb December 2, 1930, vol. 79 cc370–418.

11 HL Deb December 8, 1926 vol. 65 cc1315–38; and HL Deb July 6. 1960, vol. 224 cc1160–234, 1169–70.

12 The Belfour Declaration, 1926. Inter-Imperial Relations Committee Report, Proceedings and Memoranda E (I.R./26) Series, Secret E. 129, No. 129, November 1926 (Printed for Her Majesty's Britannica Government, 1926), 2. National Archives Ireland (hereafter NAI), No. 420. Preliminary note on the 1930 Imperial Conference by the Department of External Affairs (Secret and Confidential). Dublin, dated 1930. See Berriedale Keith, "The Imperial Conference of 1930," *Journal of Comparative Legislation and International Law* 13, no. 1 (1931): 26–42.

13 HC Deb November 23, 1931, vol. 260 cc48–51, Statute of Westminster Bill.

14 Statute of Westminster, 1931, 22 and 23 GEO.5, c.2 (3) CH. 4 (England: Printed by Swift (Printing & Duplicating Ltd., for Percy Faulkner, C.B. Controller of Her Majesty's Stationery Office and Queen's Printer of Acts of Parliament, 1931). See National Archives Kew (NAK), Cabinet Papers CAB 129/175/CP 55-9/b.

15 This occasion is generally seen as the birth of the modern Commonwealth. See the Commonwealth, "Our History," https://thecommonwealth.org/history. HL Deb April 28, 1949, vol. 162 cc126–31, Meeting of Commonwealth Prime Ministers, 126. Present at the one-week meeting were the prime ministers of the United Kingdom, South Africa, India, Pakistan, Australia, New Zealand, and Ceylon, and the Canadian secretary of state for external affairs.

16 John Flint, "Planned Decolonization and Its Failures in British Africa," *African Affairs* 82, no. 328 (1983): 390.
17 Richard Rathbone, ed., *British Documents on the End of Empire, Series B, Vol. 1 Ghana* (London: HMSO, 1992), 346–74. See Ritchie Ovendale, "MacMillan and the Wind of Change in Africa, 1957–1960," *Historical Journal* 38, no. 2 (1995): 455–77.
18 John D. Hargreaves, *Decolonization in Africa* (London: Longmans, 1988), 186–87.
19 John Darwin, *Britain and Decolonization: The Retreat from Empire in the Post-War World* (London: St. Martin's, 1988), 223.
20 Flint, "Planned Decolonization," 411.
21 Robert D. Pearce, *The Turning Point in Africa: British Colonial Policy 1938–1948* (London: Frank Cass, 1982), 1.
22 Pearce, *Turning Point in Africa*, 21, 34–36.
23 Jomo Kenyatta, *Facing Mouth Kenya: The Tribal Life of the Gikuyu with an Introduction by B. Malinowski* (London: Mercury Books, 1938).
24 Kenyatta, *Facing Mouth Kenya*, 197.
25 Robert L. Tignor, "Kamba Political Protest: The Destocking Controversy of 1938," *African Historical Studies* 4, no. 2 (1971): 249. See Robert L. Tignor, *Colonial Transformation of Kenya: The Kamba, Kikuyu, and Massai from 1900 to 1939* (Princeton, NJ: Princeton University Press, 1976).
26 See *Kenya Weekly News*, December 12, 1938. The overriding interest of the European settlers was the entire point of this government policy. The various newspapers published in colonial Nairobi, including the *Kenya Weekly News* and the *East African Standard*, carried news of the Kenya Legislative Council's debates. In the *East African Standard*, December 19, 1938, the newspaper had a piece where the Nairobi Chamber of Commerce opposed the government's decision to stop destocking.
27 CO 533/487, Temple to McDonald, October 28, 1938. See also *Manchester Guardian*, October 22, 1928; *Manchester Guardian*, January 4, 1939; and *Manchester Guardian*, January 13, 1939.
28 Lord William Malcolm Hailey, *African Survey: A Study of Problems Arising in Africa South of the Sahara* (London: Oxford University Press, 1938). Sponsored by the Colonial Office in 1938, the study provided a trove of data on colonial reforms. After the war, it would become a blueprint for British reform programs and African decolonization. See HC Deb December 7, 1938, vol. 342 cc1199–261, Colonial Policy; and HL Deb February 1, 1944, vol. 130 cc578–612, White Settlement in East Africa.
29 CO 847/13/47091/2 Minutes by Bushe, January 1939.
30 CO 847/13/47091/2 Minutes by Arthur James Dawe, January 19, 1939.
31 HC Deb June 7, 1939, vol. 348 cc437–99, Colonial Office, 453; CO 847/20/47139 at folio 1, and CO 323/1868 Pt II/9057 1A. See 847/20/47139, East Africa and Rhodesia, June 2, 1938. Speech by Mitchell in Kampala. The UK parliamentary committees are sublegislative bodies comprising several Parliament members from the House of Commons. Alternatively, they could consist of members from the House of Lords or a mix of both. As a duty, the appointees deal with particular areas or issues.

32   Kingsley Ozuomba Mbadiwe, *British and Axis Aims in Africa* (New York: Wendell Mallet and Company, 1942).
33   NAK, Cabinet Papers CAB 129/175/CP 55-9/b.
34   Lord Rowley to the House of Lords, HL Deb July 26, 1966, vol. 276 cc680–85, South Africa's Administration of South Africa, 681.
35   See Mbadiwe, *British and Axis Aims*, 162–70.
36   K. O. Mbadiwe, "Thank You Great Britain," Being Text of an Address, published in *West African Pilot*, Lagos, July 15, 1955, 1.
37   E. A. Ayandele, *The Educated Elite in Nigerian Society* (Ibadan: Ibadan University Press, 1974), 69–70, 73. Ayandele emphasized that for the educated elite, including "the so-called nationalists," loyalty to the British Crown was "an article of faith." Ayandele charged that "all educated elite, including those literature and scholarship we love to classify as nationalists, were collaborators with the British in that period of Nigerian history."
38   Mbadiwe, *British and Axis Aims*, 64–65.
39   Mbadiwe, *British and Axis Aims*, xxiv; Hollis R. Lynch, *K. O. Mbadiwe: A Nigerian Political Biography, 1915–1990* (New York: Palgrave Macmillan, 2012), 189.
40   Nwafor Orizu, *Africa Speaks*! (Enugu, Nigeria: Horizontal Publishers, 1990), 16. According to Lynch, at this point, Mbadiwe, Orizu, Ojike, Nkrumah, and others strongly felt that Africa had become its own interpreter. Hitherto, "the role of black spokesmen for Africa in the United States had been assumed by Afro-American and West Indian leaders such as W. E. B. Du Bois and Marcus Garvey." See Lynch, *K. O. Mbadiwe*, 188.
41   CO525/199, 44379/46, no. 1.
42   DO 35/6851 W.A.W.C. to Sir P. Liesching, [Possible Prohibition against Hastings Banda], Minutes by D. Williams and W. A. W. Clark, July 27, 1973.
43   Obafemi Awolowo, *Path to Nigerian* Freedom (London: Faber and Faber, 1947).
44   Derek Brown, "1945–51: Labour and the Creation of the Welfare State," *The Guardian*, March 14, 2001.
45   See HC Deb July 15, 1947, vol. 440 cc227–84, Indian Independence Bill.
46   Prime Minister Clement Atlee to Mr. W. R. Williams, HC Deb December 2, 1947, vol. 445 cc189–90, African Colonies, 190.
47   British Documents on the End of Empire Project (BDEEP), Vol. 9, *Central Africa Part I: Closer Association, 1945–1958*, ed. Philip Murphy (London: TSO, 2005), xxxiv–xxxv. It is essential to add that there was a significant difference among these territories as some, like South Africa and Southern Rhodesia, had settler governments, but others, like Kenya, did not.
48   See a similar view by Klaus Dodds, David Lambert, and Bridget Robinson, "Loyalty and Royalty: Gibraltar, the 1953–54 Royal Tour and the Geopolitics of the Iberian Peninsula," *Twentieth Century British History* 18, no. 3 (2007): 365–90.
49   NAK, Dominion Office Papers (hereafter DO) 119/1430, M/70/147, High Commissioner, Cape Town, to Secretary of State, Dominion Office, London, May 16, 1947. See William Shawcross, *Queen Elizabeth the Queen Mother: The Official Biography* (London: Macmillan, 2009), 610, 637.

50 "Students' Parliament against S.W.A. Incorporation," *The Passive Resister* (Johannesburg), April 8, 1947.
51 BDEEP, *Central Africa Part 1*, xxxi–xxxiv.
52 "South Africa and the British Empire: Divided Dominion: A Royal Tour of Great Significance," *The Economist*, May 10, 1947.
53 CO 1015/55, Minutes of a meeting with Anti-Slavery and Aborigines Protection Society, July 13, 1951. Present at the meetings were Mr. Griffiths, A. B. Cohen, and J. S. Gandee for the Commonwealth's Relations Office. D. Williams represented the Colonial Office in the discussion, including a member of the Aborigines Society, including C. W. W. Greenidge, W. H. Grey, Basil Brooks, and others.
54 "Boycott the Royal Visit," *The Passive Resister* (Johannesburg), February 21, 1947.
55 "Boycott the Royal Visit," *The Passive Resister* (Johannesburg), February 28, 1947.
56 "South Africa and the British Empire: Divided Dominion: A Royal Tour of Great Significance," *The Economist*, May 10, 1947.
57 "The Royal Visit," *The Passive Resister* (Johannesburg), April 11, 1947.
58 "London Students to Petition the King against Colour Bar," *The Passive Resister* (Johannesburg), March 7, 1947. See *Malaya Tribune* (Singapore), February 28, 1847 (Microfilm, Reel NL2140).
59 "Students from 53 Universities Petition the King," *The Passive Resister* (Johannesburg), April 4, 1947.
60 My grandmother, Nne Nkaru Anosike, often used this adage in emergencies.
61 PE/CTS/SA, Cape Town, South Africa, April 21, 1947.
62 Sarah Gertrude Millin, "The King of South Africa," *The Spectator* (London), June 19, 1947.
63 Winston Churchill, cited in Kristin M. Haugevik, and Atle L. Wold, "Churchill the Quotable," *British Politics Review* 4, no. 4 (2009): 11.
64 The voice print theory was first developed in Samuel Gyasi Obeng's "Conversational Strategies: Towards a Phonological Description of Projection in Akyem-Twi" (PhD diss, University of York, 1987). His subsequent studies expanded on the concept, as evident in Obeng, *Conflict Resolution in Africa: Language, Law and Politeness in Ghanaian (Akan) Jurisprudence* (Durham, NC: Carolina Academic Press, 2018), particularly in chapters on judicial discourse; Obeng, *Conversational Strategies in Akan: Prosodic Features and Discourse Categories* (Köln, Germany: Rüdiger Köppe Verlag, 1999); Obeng, "A Phonetic Description of Repair Sequences in Akan Conversation." *Text* 12, no. 1 (1992): 59–80; Obeng, "Pitch, Loudness and Turn Regulation in Akan Conversation," *York Papers in Linguistics* 15 (1991): 221–35; and Obeng, "Conversational Strategies: Towards a Phonological Description of Turn-Taking in Akan," *Journal of West African Languages* 19 no. 1 (1989): 104–20. See also Thomas Berg, "Is Voice a Suprasegmental?" *Linguistics* 23, no. 6 (1985): 883–916.
65 See Dermot Morrah, *Princess Elizabeth, Duchess of Edinburgh: The Illustrated Story of the Life of the Heir Presumptive* (London: Oldenus, 1950).
66 PE/CTS/SA, Cape Town, South Africa, April 21, 1947.

67 Jan Blommaert and Chris Bulcaen, "Critical Discourse Analysis," *Annual Review of Anthropology* 29 (2000): 448.
68 Alan Lascelles, cited in Hannah Furness, "Uncovered: The Surprising Secret of Queen's Cape Town Speech," *The Telegraph* (London), September 17, 2018. See also Hannah Furness, "Queen's Famous Speech Not 'Live,'" *The Herald* (London), September 18, 2018; and Maureen Waller, *Sovereign Ladies: Sex, Sacrifice, and Power—The Six Reigning Queens of England* (London: Macmillan, 2006), 460.
69 Jan Blommaert and Chris Bulcaen, "Critical Discourse Analysis," *Annual Review of Anthropology* 29 (2000): 448–49.
70 PE/CTS/SA, Cape Town, South Africa, April 21, 1947.
71 "Cape Meeting Demands Implementation of UNO Decision," *The Passive Resister* (Johannesburg), February 31, 1947.
72 "South Africa and the British Empire: Divided Dominion: A Royal Tour of Great Significance," *The Economist*, May 10, 1947.
73 "Catholic Paper Takes Gen. Smuts to Task," *The Passive Resister* (Johannesburg), February 28, 1947.
74 HL Deb October 21, 1947, vol. 152 cc1–5, The King's Speech, 3.
75 See Isaiah Berlin, *Four Essays on Liberty* (Oxford: Oxford University Press, 1969).
76 Samuel Gyasi Obeng, "Grammatical Pragmatics: Language, Power and Liberty in African (Ghanaian) Political Discourse," *Discourse and Society* 31, no. 1 (2019/20): 85–105; Samuel Gyasi Obeng, "Language and Liberty in Ghanaian Political Communication: A Critical Discourse Perspective," *Ghana Journal of Linguistics* 7 no. 2 (2018): 199–224. See Cecilia Sem Obeng and Samuel Gyasi Obeng, *Invisible Faces; Hidden Stories: Narratives of Vulnerable Populations and Their Caregivers* (Oxford: Berghahn Books, 2020).
77 Alan Watson, "Why the Queen Matters," *New York Times*, June 4, 2012.
78 PE/CTS/SA, Cape Town, South Africa, April 21, 1947.
79 Hugh Trevor-Roper, "The Rise of Christian Europe," *The Listener* 70 (1963): 871.
80 Duff Hart-Davis, ed., *King's Counsellor: Abdication and War: The Diaries of Alan Lascelles* (London: Weidenfield and Nicholson, 2006), 402.
81 Queen Elizabeth, "Queen's Tribute to Her Father," *The Yorkshire Observer*, October 22, 1955, 5.
82 Ben Pimlott, "Some Thoughts on the Queen and Commonwealth," *The Round Table* 87, no. 347 (1998): 303–5.
83 As the Commonwealth's leader, Queen Elizabeth has visited Africa more times than any foreign official or traveler, including legendary travelers such as Ibn Battuta and Marco Polo.
84 *The Yorkshire Observer*, October 22, 1955, 5.
85 *Belfast Telegraph*, June 20, 1967, 3.
86 PE/CTS/SA, Cape Town, South Africa, April 21, 1947.
87 PE/CTS/SA, Cape Town, South Africa, April 21, 1947.
88 Norman Fairclough, *Discourse and Social Change* (Cambridge: Cambridge University Press, 1992), 93.

89 "The King and South African Non-Europeans," *The Passive Resister* (Johannesburg), May 23, 1947.
90 "The King and South African Non-Europeans," *The Passive Resister* (Johannesburg), May 23, 1947, 2.
91 See HC Deb February 21, 1945 vol 408 c794. Churchill's statement was in response to a question from Mr. Petherick on whether Article 2 of the Atlantic Charter stated that colonial powers ought to consider the colonized people's freely expressed wishes for freedom or lack of.
92 "The King and South African Non-Europeans," *The Passive Resister* (Johannesburg), May 23, 1947.
93 HL Deb October 21, 1947, vol. 152 cc1–5, The King's Speech, 2.
94 NAK, CAB 129/57/45, Proposed Federation of Southern Rhodesia and Nyasaland by Salisbury, Swinton, Oliver Lyttelton, December 16, 1952.
95 HC Deb, May 4, 1953 vol. 515 cc37–167, Central African Federation; Nyasaland Delegation of Chiefs and Citizens, *A Petition to Her Majesty Queen Elizabeth II Against Federation, Issue 99* (Accra: African Bureau, 1953.); Geoffrey Traugh, "Apartheid by Another Nature," *London Review of Books*, September 2, 2022.
96 Clive Salter, cited in David Anderson, *Histories of the Hanged: The Dirty War in Kenya and the End of Empire* (New York: W. W. Norton, 2005), 172.
97 See Kenya National Archive (KNA), MLA 1/626, MLA 1/709, MLA 1/900, and MLA 1/1098, "Judgment," Criminal Appeals 988 and 989 of 1954, from Emergency Assize Criminal Case No. 584 of 1954 of the Supreme Court of Kenya at Nairobi. The evidence from the listed files provides proof of the torture that marked the trials. For a general critique of British colonial administration in Kenya, see Diana Wylie, "Confrontation over Kenya: The Colonial Office and Its Critics, 1918-1940," *Journal of African History* 18 no. 3 (1977): 427–47.
98 KNA, JZ 7/4/35, Embakasi Convicts to Commissioner of Prisons, April 6, 1957.
99 KNA JZ 7/4/36, Black Africans in Manyani Detention Camp to Governor, March 9, 1957. The petition mirrored one a couple of months earlier. See KNA JZ 7/4, The Black People of Kenya in Manyani Detention Camps to Governor, January 1, 1957.
100 CAB 120/164GEN 688/2nd Mig., Kenya Hola Detention Camp, Secret, June 8, 1969; and CAB 128/33, CC 43(59)1 Secret, folios 278, 179, 280, July 20, 1959. In his report before the cabinet, Sir Evelyn Barring, governor of Kenya, blamed the beating deaths on the camp superintendent, Mr. Sullivan. While Barring accused Sullivan of not providing proper oversight, he failed to denounce the African guards who killed the victims for refusing to work, reinforcing the notion that the Queen was behind these cruel acts.
101 Theuri Njugi Kimbo, interview with Wainaina Ndung'u, "Fearless General Who Shot Down British Warplanes," *The Standard* (Nairobi), June 26, 2013. Among the Kikuyu warriors, Mr. Gacheru remains a legend revered for "shooting down killer British bomb-dropping planes."
102 HC Deb December 8, 1943, vol. 395 cc951–52, Kenya (African Representation); and HC Deb May 4, 1953, vol. 515 cc37–167, Central African Federation.

Chapter 3. The Cold War

1. DO 35/10570, no.53, Harold Macmillan, "Wind of Change in Africa," Address by Mr. Macmillan to both Houses of the Parliament of South Africa, Cape Town, February 3, 1960. The Conservative Party politician served as prime minister between 1957 and 1963. In his response to Macmillan, Hendrik Verwoerd, South Africa's prime minister (1958 to 1966), remarked that a just course of African independence would also recognize justice for Africa's White man. See Hendrik Verwoerd, Response to the "Wind of Change" speech, to the South Africa Parliament, Cape Town, South Africa, February 3, 1960.
2. Constance Novis, ed., *Queen Elizabeth and the Royal Family: A Glorious Illustrated History* (London: Penguin Random House, 2015), 195.
3. Arthur Schlesinger Jr., "Origins of the Cold War," *Foreign Affairs* 46, no. 1 (1967): 22. Schlesinger disagrees with those who see the Cold War only as a "democratic alliance versus authoritarian bloc." For instance, Michael Wesley, "Interpreting the Cold War," in *Power and International Relations*, ed. Desmond Ball and Sharyn Lee (Canberra: Australian National University Press, 2014), 82.
4. Nikita S. Khrushchev, "We Will Bury You," Speech for Poland's Mr. Wladyslaw Gomulka Send-Off Reception, Polish Embassy, Moscow, November 18, 1956. CIA declassified File no. CIA-RDP73B00296R00020004, February 7, 1962. See *The Times*, "Ambassadors Work Out," London, November 19, 1956; and *Time Magazine*, "Murder Will Out," New York, November 26, 1956.
5. For a cursory exploration of this, see Dwight D. Eisenhower Public Papers of the President of the United States Dwight D. Eisenhower, 1957 (Washington. DC: U.S. Government Printing Office, 1958), 6–18.
6. Goebbels had written in *Das Reich*, his weekly tabloid, that if Germany and its allies should lose the war, "an iron curtain would fall over the enormous territory controlled by the Soviet Union, behind which nations would be slaughtered." See Joseph Goebbels, *Das Reich*, Berlin, February 25, 1945, 1–2; and Ignace Feuerlicht, "A New Look at the Iron Curtain," *American Speech* 30, no. 3 (1955): 186–89.
7. Prime Minister Winston Churchill, "Sinews of Peace or An Iron Curtain Has Descended," a Speech at Westminster College, Fulton, Missouri, March 5, 1946. Located at Churchill Press Photographs, Churchill Archive Center, Cambridge, CHPH 1A/FA/4A, Associated Press, 350. See *Time*, "This Sad and Breathless Moment," March 18, 1946.
8. The financial burden was so overwhelming that Lord Keynes told the House of Lords that Britain could not repay the debt. See HL Deb December 18, 1945, vol. 138 cc777–897, Anglo-American Financial Arrangements, 792.
9. It took Britain sixty-one years to repay the loan. See Philip Thornton, "Britain Pays Off Final Installment of U.S. Loan—After 61 Years," *Independent*, London, December 29, 2006. Announcing Britain's final loan repayment in 2006, Ed Balls, the economic

secretary to the treasury, acknowledged that the money "was vital support, which helped Britain defeat Nazi Germany and secure peace and prosperity in the postwar period."

10   See HC Deb December 13, 1945, vol. 417 cc641–739, Anglo-American Financial and Economic Discussions, 652–53.

11   Peter Hennessy, *The Prime Minister: The Office and Its Holder Since 1945* (London: St. Martin's, 2000), 205. See also Philip Ziegler, "Churchill and the Monarchy," in *Churchill: A Major Assessment of His Life in Peace and War*, ed. Robert Blake and William Roger Louis (New York: W. W. Norton, 1994), 187–98.

12   FO 371/102811, no. 372, June 12, 1953. See also *British Documents on Decolonization, Egypt Part II*, ed. John Kent, 61–62.

13   Sir Winston S. Churchill drew attention to this "special relationship" notion in his historic Fulton, Missouri, speech on March 5, 1946. The wartime British prime minister urged the Americans to avoid isolationism in the statement. Churchill characterized this relationship as a joint responsibility to foster military cooperation based on "kindred systems of society." Winston S. Churchill, "Sinews of Peace," in *Never Give In! The Best of Winston Churchill's Speeches*, ed. Winston S. Churchill (New York: Hyperion, 2003), 413–24. For a robust analysis of these relations, see Robert M. Hathaway, *Great Britain and the United States: Special Relations Since WWII* (Boston: Twayne, 1990); and Steve Marsh, "Personal Diplomacy at the Summit," in *Churchill and the Anglo-American Special Relations*, ed. Alan P. Dodson and Steve Marsh (New York: Routledge, 2017), 120–21.

14   Several studies have noted that Queen Elizabeth was a mentee of Sir Winston Churchill early in her reign. Just to mention but three, see Pelling Henry, *Winston Churchill* (London: Macmillan, 1974); Robert Rhodes James, ed., *Winston S. Churchill: His Complete Speeches, 1897–1963*, 8 vols. (London: Chelsea, 1974); and Eugene L. Rasor, *Winston S. Churchill, 1874–1965: A Comprehensive Historiography and Annotated Bibliography* (Westport, CT: Greenwood, 2000), 203–5.

15   Mary Soames, ed., *Speaking for Themselves: The Personal Letters of Winston and Clementine Churchill* (Toronto: Doubleday, 1998), 328. See Simon Perry, "A Child of England," in "Queen Elizabeth at 90," special edition of *Life*, April 1, 2016, 18–19.

16   See Nicholas Davies, *Elizabeth: Behind Palace Doors* (Edinburgh: Mainstream Publishing Projects, 2000), 87.

17   In 1950, Clement Atlee, the Labor Party's candidate, again beat Churchill in the general elections. However, in October 1951, Atlee was under pressure to ameliorate King George VI's anxiety that Britain could have a government change while on a Commonwealth tour scheduled to start in January 1952. The prime minister, whose Labour Party held a slim majority in Parliament, called for an early election. Although he won the popular votes, Churchill's Conservative Party garnered more seats in Parliament.

18   Meanwhile, out of power, Atlee continued to serve as the Labor Party leader until 1955. See Thomas P. Jenkin, "The British General Election of 1951," *Western Political Quarterly* 5, no. 1 (1952): 51–65; and Richard M. Scammon, "British By-Elections, 1951–1955," *Journal of Politics* 18, no. 1 (1956): 83–94.

19   Winston S. Churchill, *Never Give In! The Best of Winston Churchill's Speeches Selected and Edited by His Grandson Winston S. Churchill* (New York: Hyperion, 2003), 483–84.

20 Churchill, *Never Give In!*, 483–84; Winston S. Churchill, "The Crown and the Parliament," Speech at the Commonwealth Parliamentary Association Luncheon, St. Stephen's Hall, Westminster, March 27, 1953, published in Churchill, *Never Give In!*, 403–4. See Martin Gilbert, *Never Despair: Winston S. Churchill, 1945–1965* (London: Heinemann, 1988), 809.

21 Winston S. Churchill, "The Coronation of Elizabeth II: An Introduction to the Royal Broadcast," June 2, 1953, published in Winston S. Churchill, *The Unwritten Alliance, Speeches 1953–1959* (New York: Rosetta Books, 1961), 55.

22 See CO554/1177, no. 16 Assessment of Anti-Communist Propaganda: Memorandum by the UK Information Office in Gold Coast, April 23, 1956.

23 Davies, *Elizabeth: Behind Palace Doors*, 87–88.

24 Queen Elizabeth II, "The Queen's Coronation Oath," June 2, 1953, on BBC TV (available on https://www.youtube.com/watch?v=52NTjasbmgw). For a read on the coronation's glamor, see "The Queen Turns on the Lights," *Daily Express*, London, June 3, 1953, 1; and "River Mirrors London's Feu-de-Joie," *Daily Telegraph*, London, June 3, 1953, 1.

25 Queen Elizabeth II, Coronation Speech, June 2, 1953, published in Catherine Ryan, *The Queen: The Life and Times of Elizabeth II* (London: Chartwell Books, 2018), back page.

26 See Princess Elizabeth, A Speech on her 21st Birthday, Cape Town, South Africa, April 21, 1947.

27 Chris Slack, "The King Is Dead, Long Live the Queen," *Daily Mail*, London, January 9, 2012.

28 Queen Elizabeth II, Christmas Broadcast, Auckland, New Zealand, December 25, 1953.

29 Dwight D. Eisenhower, "Inaugural Address," Washington, DC, January 20, 1953.

30 Jonathan Walker, *Operation Unthinkable: The Third World War: British Plans to Attack the Soviet Empire* (Cheltenham, UK: History Press, 2013). In 1952, Churchill ordered an atomic bomb test to prepare for a potential war with the Soviet Union. See "Ship Vaporized in British Atomic Test," *The Times*, London, October 24, 1952. In a speech at the House of Commons, the prime minister called the explosion conducted in a frigate a "successful outcome."

31 The bloc comprised the self-governing colony of Southern Rhodesia (Zimbabwe) and the protectorates of Northern Rhodesia (Zambia) and Nyasaland (Malawi).

32 HL Deb July 7, 1953, vol. 183 cc270–347, Rhodesia and Nyasaland Federation Bill.

33 HL Deb July 7, 1953, vol. 183 cc270–347, Rhodesia and Nyasaland Federation Bill, 275.

34 HL Deb July 7, 1953, vol. 183 cc270–347, Rhodesia and Nyasaland Federation Bill, 278.

35 Andrew Marr, *The Real Queen Elizabeth: An Intimate Portrait of Queen Elizabeth II* (New York: Henry Holt, 2012), 188.

36 NAK, CAB 129/57/45, Proposed Federation of Southern Rhodesia and Nyasaland by Salisbury, Swinton, Oliver Lyttelton, December 16, 1952.

37 PREM 11/1367, CC 83(54)5, Commonwealth Relations: Cabinet conclusions on the report of the Official Committee on Commonwealth Membership, December 7, 1954.

38   Alan Cowell, "Ian Smith, Symbol of White Rule, Is Dead at 88," *New York Times*, November 21, 2007; Samuel M. Makinda, Review: "The Great Betrayal: The Memoirs of Ian Douglas Smith by Ian Smith," *Foreign Policy* 109 (1997–1998): 166–68.
39   Queen Elizabeth II, Christmas Broadcast, Auckland, New Zealand, 1953.
40   The Lord Chancellor (Lord Elwyn Jones) to the House of Lords, HL Deb November 9, 1978, vol. 396 cc423–635, Southern Rhodesia Act 1965 (Continuation) Order 1978, 427.
41   Manuele Facchini, "The 'Evil Genius,' Sir Hugh Beadle and the Rhodesian Crisis, 1965–1972," *Journal of Southern African Studies* 33, no. 3 (2007): 673–89; HC Deb November 18, 1965, vol. 720 cc1336–39, Rhodesia H.M. Governor, 1336; Ben Pimlott, *The Queen: A Biography of Elizabeth II and the Monarchy* (London: Wiley, 1996), 351.
42   Mr. A. Fenner Brockway to the House of Commons, HC Deb December 2, 1953 vol. 521 cc1229–86, Kabaka of Buganda (deposition), 1230.
43   NAK, CAB 129/71/38, Memo. Ugandan Protectorate by Alan Lennox-Boyd, 10 November 1954.
44   Carol Summers, "Local Critiques of Global Development: Patriotism in Late Colonial Uganda," *International Journal of African Historical Studies* 47, no. 1 (2014): 27. Summers has noted that Y. S. Bamutta, an abiding Ugandan activist, held a blatant "vision of patriotism as early as 1927, arguing that Buganda needed to be able to critique the government without being accused of being disloyal." For Bamutta, loyalty "was not to be found in following British suggestions."
45   Kabaka Mutesa II, *The Desecration of My Kingdom* (London: Constable and Company, 1967), 114–15; Henry Lubega, "How Kabaka Muteesa's Deportation Was Planned," *Daily Monitor* (Kampala), February 20, 2017.
46   See A. B. K. Kasozi, *The Bitter Bread of Exile: The Financial Problems of Sir Edward Muteesa II during his Exile, 1966–1968* (Kampala, Uganda: Progressive Publishing House, 2013).
47   See Ogola Wrong, "On Mutesa's Deportation," *The Independent* (Kampala), November 11, 2012.
48   "The Kabaka is now on his way to England by air." HC Deb November 30, 1953 vol. 521 cc780–88, Kabaka of Buganda (Withdrawal of Recognition), 782.
49   During the House of Commons meeting, the secretary for the colonies reported that the kabaka "stubbornly refused to move," HC Deb November 30, 1953 vol. 521 cc780–88, Kabaka of Buganda (Withdrawal of Recognition), 782.
50   HC Deb November 30, 1953 vol. 521 cc780–88, Kabaka of Buganda (Withdrawal of Recognition), 780. See Yoga Adhola, "Kabaka Muteesa Deported to Britain," *Daily Monitor* (Kampala), July 3, 2012.
51   HC Deb November 30, 1953 vol. 521 cc780–88, Kabaka of Buganda (Withdrawal of Recognition), 783.
52   HC Deb December 2, 1953 vol. 521 cc1229–86, Kabaka of Buganda (deposition), 1229.
53   NAK, CO 822/1150 11804, Inward Telegram to the Secretary of State for the Colonies by Andrew Cohen, 30th May 1954, 5; and FO, CO 822/1150 111804, "From Foreign Office to Certain of Her Majesty's Representatives," June 3, 1954, 27.

54 See Jonathan L. Earle, *Colonial Buganda and the End of Empire: Political Thought and Historical Imagination in Africa* (Cambridge: Cambridge University Press, 2017), 77–88; and Eridadi M. K. Mulira, EMKM/GEN/1/1. (Unpublished autobiography, University of Cambridge), 195.
55 NAK, Uganda: The Owen Falls Dam, Uganda. Inaugurated by Her Majesty the Queen, INF 10/370/9, 1954. See also Christopher Mason, Review of Moses Zikusooka's book documenting the Queen's last visit to Uganda, posted November 15, 2007; *Illustrated London News*, May 8, 1954, 24; *The Sphere* (London), May 8, 1954, 14; *Bradford Observer* (West Yorkshire), April 15, 1954.
56 *Uganda Herald* (Kampala), April 29, 1954; *East Africa* (Kampala), April 29, 1954; *The Observer* (Kampala), April 29, 1954; and NAK, Uganda: The Owen Falls Dam, Uganda, INF 10/370/9, 1954.
57 Mutesa II, *Desecration*, 131; *Bradford Observer* (West Yorkshire), April 15, 1954; *Uganda Herald* (Kampala), April 29, 1954.
58 *Uganda Herald* (Kampala), April 29, 132.
59 NAK, CAB 129/71/38, Memo. Ugandan Protectorate, 1954, 2.
60 NAK, CAB 129/129/70, Memo. The Kabaka of Uganda, September 9, 1954, 2.
61 FCO, 141/18410, Report of the Uganda Constitutional Conference, London, October 1961–62; Colonial Office (CO), Uganda: Report of the Constitutional Conference, 1961 and text of the agreed draft of a new Buganda Agreement initialed in London on October 9, 1961 (London: Her Majesty's Stationery Office, 1961).
62 CO, Uganda: Report of Constitutional Conference, 1961.
63 Kabaka Yekka, Communiqué, "What News in Buganda," 28 August 1961. See FCO 141/18392, Kabaka Yekka organization, monarchist political party, 1961.
64 NAK, Home Office, Ho 421/2 covering 01/01/1982–23/03/2000.
65 For a report on the death of Mutesa from alcoholic poisoning, see FCO 31/713, no 1. Uganda: valedictory Despatch from D. A. Scott1 (Kampala) to Mr. Stewart on the outlook for President Obote, January 26, 1970.
66 Mutesa II, cited in Kasozi, *Bitter Bread of Exile*, v.
67 For a report on the knighthood, see "Queen Confers Knighthood on Mr. Blundell and the Kabaka," *East African Standard* (Nairobi), January 1, 1962.
68 Peter Gukiina, *Uganda: A Case Study in African Political Development* (Notre Dame, IN: University of Notre Dame Press, 1972), 99.
69 Crawford Young, *The Politics of Cultural Pluralism* (Madison: University of Wisconsin Press, 1976), 226.
70 Michael G. Schatzberg, *Political Legitimacy in Middle Africa: Father, Family, Food*. (Bloomington: Indiana University Press, 2001), 38–41.
71 CAOG 12/62, Royal Visits: HM The Queen to Nigeria, 1956; CO 554/1178, no. 3, Inward Telegram no. 21 from Sir J. Macpherson to Mr. Lennox-Boyd on Implications of the Possible outcome of the Federal Elections, Minute by N. B. J. Huijsman. In the message, Macpherson reported that the "Success of N.C.N.C. in the West has severely shaken the North and, in particular, Abubakar Tafawa Balewa in whose mind the fear of

Southern domination by the North is always present." See also Correspondent Report, "The Queen in Lagos," *West Africa* (London), February 4, 1956, 100.

72 See CO 554/278, no. 29, [London Conference] Minutes CNC 18 (53) 1 & 2 of the Eighteenth Plenary Meeting of the Constitutional Conference, August 19, 1953. See Nigerian National Archives Kaduna, CO 554/965 Position of Ex-officio Members of the Northern Region Executive Council of Nigeria 1956–1957; National Archive Ibadan, NC/B10 Records of Proceedings of the Nigerian Constitution Conference held in London in July and August (1953). See the appendix on Self-Government (1956), 125–37.

73 CO 554/1159, no. 14, Despatch no. 17 from Sir J. Robertson to Mr. Lennox-Boyd Reporting on the Queen's Visit to Nigeria, April 9, 1956. CAOG 12/62, Royal visits: HM The Queen to Nigeria, 1956.

74 CO 554/1181, no. 12, Letter from C. G. Eastwood to Sir C. Jeffries on Morale among Administrative Staff in the Eastern Region [Extract from Minute by M. G. Smith, May 30, 1955.

75 CAB 21/5957. Visit by HM The Queen and Duke of Edinburgh to Ghana, Sierra Leone, Gambia, and Liberia, November 1961.

76 See Gertrude Parthenia McBrown, "Prime Minister Kwame Nkrumah," *Negro History Bulletin* 16, no. 5 (February 1953), 98, 115–16. The author described Nkrumah as an influential figure in world politics.

77 For the text of President Eisenhower's invitation, dated March 4, 1958, and Nkrumah's reply, see *Public Papers of the Presidents of the United States: Dwight D. Eisenhower, 1958* (Washington, DC: Government Printing Office, 1959), 211–13.

78 Memorandum of Conversation, No. 294 Prime Minister Nkrumah's Talk with the President, July 23, 1958. Eisenhower Library, Whitman File, International File. Secret. Drafted by Deputy Assistant Secretary of State for African Affairs Joseph Palmer 2d.

79 See Department of State, Central Files, 033.45J11/7–2458. A Memorandum of a conversation with Under Secretary of State Herter concerning Ghana's economic aims, Conference Files: Lot 63 D 123, Nkrumah Visit.

80 HC Deb December 11, 1956, vol. 562 cc229–326, Ghana Independence Bill, 263. For more insight on this project, see Central Intelligence Agency, Office of National Estimates, Staff Memorandum No.85-63, December 19, 1963, 10. Soliciting the assistance of Her Majesty in securing funds for the project was one of the main goals of Nkrumah during the royal visit. See "Royal Visitors Inspect Volta River Project Dam Site," *Evening News* (Accra), November 17, 1961; "Royal Visitors See Mode of Big Volta Dam at Akosombe, the Site of the Dam," *The Ghanaian Times* (Accra), November 17, 1961.

81 Kevin K. Gaines, *African Americans in Ghana: Black Expatriates and the Civil Rights Era* (Chapel Hill: University of North Carolina Press, 2006), esp. chap. 3, 81. See Lalbila Yoda, "The Influence of the USA on the Political Ideas of Kwame Nkrumah," *The Round Table: The Commonwealth Journal of International Affairs* 326 (1993): 187.

82 Kwame Nkrumah, *Ghana: The Autobiography of Kwame Nkrumah* (London: Nelson, 1957), 48. See David Lamb, *The Africans* (New York: Vintage Books, 1987), 286; and

Yekutiel Gershoni, *Africans on African Americans: The Creation and Uses of an African-American Myth* (London: Macmillan, 1997), 142.

83 Queen Elizabeth II, Address to the United Nations General Assembly, New York, October 21, 1957.

84 Queen Elizabeth II, Address to the United Nations General Assembly, New York, October 21, 1957.

85 See HC Deb May 17, 1960, vol. 623 cc1104–30, Ghana (Consequential) Provision Bill.

86 All quotes are in Dwight D. Eisenhower's Address before the Fifteenth General Assembly of the United Nations, New York, September 22, 1960.

87 CO 936/714, [Relations between Britain and Ghana, and the Communist Threat]: Valedictory Despatch (no. 37; CO print) from Sir A. Snelling to Mr. Sandys, December 5, 1961.

88 CO 936/714, [Relations between Britain and Ghana, and the Communist Threat]: Valedictory Despatch (no. 37; CO print) from Sir A. Snelling to Mr. Sandys, December 5, 1961.

89 For these discussions, see "Nkrumah not a Dictator," *Daily Graphic* (Accra), August 28, 1952; "Plot of Assassination by GOPA backed by Vested Interests," *The Ashanti Sentinel* (Kumasi), February 24, 1954; and Osei Akyeampong, "Who are the Dictators?" *The Ashanti Sentinel* (Kumasi), June 18, 1955.

90 CO 936/714, December 5, 1961.

91 FO 371/161361, no. 21, [Situation in Ghana and the Communist Threat]: Letter from J. Chadwick (CRO) to R. W. H. du Boulay (Washington), October 11, 1962.

92 "Assassins and Nation Wreckers doomed," *The Ghanaian Times* (Accra), November 9, 1961. The minister claimed that the government had seen evidence that these saboteurs had "received financial assistance from elsewhere."

93 "Mac: Sandys Saw a Friendly Crowd," *The Ghanaian Times* (Accra), November 9, 1961, stated that the British prime minister had confirmed to the Nkrumah government that the visit would proceed as planned despite the security concerns. This confirmation came on the heels of a trip to Ghana by the Commonwealth Secretary Duncan Sandys, who returned to London on November 8 after touring the West African country where he evaluated the security measures with Nkrumah. Sandys was quoted reporting that he saw "the unmistakable friendliness of the crowd" in Ghana.

94 All quotes are from *Queen Elizabeth and the Royal Family*, 195. See CAB 21/5957. Visit by HM The Queen and Duke of Edinburgh to Ghana, Sierra Leone, Gambia, and Liberia, November 1961; "Ghana: The Queen's Visit," *Time*, November 17, 1961; Hannah Furness, "The Queen's Plot to Bash Idi Amin over the Head with a Pearl Sword," *Daily Telegraph* (London), December 27, 2013; *Birmingham Daily*, August 13, 1961; and *Belfast Telegraph*, August 2, 1961.

95 "Prayers Said for Safe Journey," *The Ghanaian Times* (Accra), November 10, 1961.

96 CC 76(57), secret October 28, 1957, enclosure in CAB 128/31 pt. 2, folio 525.

97 PREM 11/2689, Home to Lloyd, top secret, May 21, 1958.

98 See Harold Macmillan, cited in William Shawcross, *Queen and Country: The Fifty-Year Reign of Elizabeth II* (New York: Simon & Schuster, 2002), 84; and Sally Bedell Smith, *Elizabeth the Queen* (New York: Random House, 2012), 159.
99 CO 967/400, [The Queen's Visit to Ghana] Letter from Mr. Macmillan to Sir Winston Churchill, October 19, 1961.
100 H.M. Queen Elizabeth to Both Houses of Parliament, HC Deb October 31, 1961, vol. 648 cc4–144, Queen's Speech, 4.
101 HL Deb November 8, 1961, vol. 235 cc364, The Queen's Visit to Ghana.
102 The privileged information Hailsham alluded to here is from Robert Jackson, chairman of the Development Commission, Ghana, 1956–1961. He was responsible for organizing the royal tour in 1961. See CO 967/400, [The Queen's Visit to Ghana] Letter from Mr. Macmillan to Sir Winston Churchill, October 19, 1961.
103 HL Deb November 8, 1961, vol. 235 cc364, The Queen's Visit to Ghana.
104 HL Deb November 8, 1961, vol. 235 cc364, The Queen's Visit to Ghana.
105 HL Deb November 8, 1961 vol. 235 cc364, The Queen's Visit to Ghana.
106 "What Happened When the Queen Visited Ghana," *The Daily Mail* (London), March 15, 2018.
107 Gabriel Tate, "The Queen: Her Commonwealth Story Showed a Global Admiration for Our Monarchy," *The Telegraph* (London), March 26, 2018. The itinerary for the royal visit listed the dance as highlife. See CAB 21/5957. Visit by HM The Queen and Duke of Edinburgh to Ghana, Sierra Leone, Gambia, and Liberia, November 1961.
108 CO 967/400, [The Queen's Visit to Ghana] Letter from Mr. Macmillan to Sir Winston Churchill, October 19, 1961.
109 CO 936/714, December 5, 1961.
110 "'Welcome' High Life: Her Majesty Dances at State House," *The Ghanaian Times* (Accra), November 20, 1961. Much has been told about the Elizabeth-Nkrumah dance but not the partnership between the Duke of Edinburgh and Madam Fathia, Nkrumah's wife.
111 Peter William Evans, "Astaire and Rogers: Carefree in Roberta," in *Hollywood and the Great Depression: American Film, Politics and Society in the 1930s*, ed. Iwan Morgan and Philip John Davies (Edinburgh: Edinburgh University Press, 2016), 124–38.
112 Tate, "The Queen: Her Commonwealth Story," March 26, 2018; and "Ghana: The Queen's Visit," *Time*, November 17, 1961.
113 "400 Guests Attend State Banquet," *Evening News* (Accra), November 11, 1961.
114 "Wind of Change Will Not Alter Affection for British Crown," *Evening News* (Accra), November 11, 1961.
115 H.M. Queen Elizabeth II, Ghana: A Vigorous Nation," Accra, November 11, 1961; Henry Tanner, "Ghanaians Hail Queen in Parade: Nkrumah Vows Continuation of Esteem for Elizabeth," *New York Times*, November 11, 1961.In the 2018 BBC documentary, Princess Anne draws attention to the fact that in the Cold War era, her mother was in the men's world by her position. By having the ability to deal with world leaders, Anne concluded that the Queen was "virtually unique," occupying a role as "an honorary man." See Tate, "The Queen: Her Commonwealth Story," March 26, 2018.

116 According to Nunoo-Amarteifio, the visiting British monarch paid tribute to the president by visiting his former high school. His view corroborates Sir D. Wright's correspondence with J. Chadwick. See FO 371/161361, no. 21, November 6, 1962; and CO 1027/382, no. 8, C.F.R. Barclay to British Representatives in Africa, November 9, 1962. The entire communications were about countering communism rather than the expulsion of Ghana from the Commonwealth.
117 "Asagyefor Recalls Best Kept Secret," *Evening News* (Accra), November 11, 1961.
118 See Tanner, "Ghanaians Hail Queen in Parade."
119 E. Kolay-Amos, Letter to the Editor: "A Royal Visit to Ghana," *Evening News* (Accra), November 18, 1961.
120 Siofra Brennan, "The Dancing Queen: Documentary Captures the Symbolic Moment the 35-Year-Old Monarch Danced Like a 'Good White Woman' with the President of Ghana in 1961 to Boost the Commonwealth," *Daily Mail* (London), March 27, 2018.
121 See CO 936/714, December 5, 1961, for more insights.
122 Lord Brand, HL Deb August 2, 1961 vol. 234 cc111–207, Britain and the Common Market, 146–47.
123 David Cannadine, "Royal Pains," *New York Times*, May 26, 1996, 7; and Philip Norton, *The British Polity* (London: Longman, 2010), 23.
124 See Ritchie Ovendale, "Macmillan and the Wind of Change in Africa, 1957–1960," *Historical Journal* 38, no. 2 (1995): 476.
125 Macmillan, "Wind of Change in Africa," Cape Town, February 3, 1960.
126 For a history of events ending with the coup, see U.S. Department of State, *Foreign Relations of the United States, 1961–1963*, vol. 21 (Washington, DC: Government Printing Office, 1995), 341–49.
127 CO 554/2479, no.4, [Political Situation] Despatch no. 31 from Sir J. Robertson to Mr. Macleod on the Political Situation in Nigeria, April 27, 1960. Initially, Princess Margaret, Queen Elizabeth's sister, was to represent her during the celebration, but her upcoming marriage made it difficult for her to travel.
128 Sir Abubakar Tafawa Balewa, *Mr. Prime Minister: A Selection of Speeches Made by Alhaji, the Right Honorable Sir Abubakar Tafawa Balewa, K.B.E., M.P., Prime Minister of the Federal Republic of Nigeria* (Apapa: Nigerian National Press, 1964). See also Correspondent Report, "The Queen in Lagos," *West Africa* (London), February 4, 1956, 100.
129 DO 177/8, no. 27, Independence Day Messages to the Federation of Nigeria: CRO Press Release, October 1, 1969.

Chapter 4. Her Majesty's Africa Tour-De-Force

1. The British Parliament welcomed these tours as a diplomatic strategy. I have adopted this phrase to capture Her Majesty's travels because the Colonial Office and the Foreign Office directed them with ingenuity and skill. The accomplishments of the trips, though mixed, were impressive. Discussions in the House of Commons show that the Parliament considered the royal travels very auspicious in sensitizing the West Africans and endearing them to the British course. See Iain Macleod (The Secretary of State for the Colonies) to the House of Common (hereafter HC), HC Deb March 22, 1961, vol. 637 cc391–440, Sierra Leone Independence, Order of Second Reading, 396.
2. Klaus Dodd, David Lambert, and Bridget Robinson, "Loyalty and Royalty: Gibraltar, the 1953–54 Royal Tour and the Geopolitics of the Iberian Peninsula," *Twentieth Century British History* 18, no. 3, (2007): 366.
3. Dodd, Lambert, and Robinson, "Loyalty and Royalty," 366; and David Cannadine, *Ornamentalism: How the British Saw Their Empire* (London: Allen Lane, 2001), 115–20.
4. CO 554/1159, no. 17, Despatch no. 43, From Sir J. Robertson to Lennox-Boyd on the Royal Tour, the Northern Region and the Amendment of Change to HMOCS.
5. A. H. M. Kirk-Greene, "His Eternity, His Eccentricity, or His Exemplarity? A Further Contribution to the Study of H. E. the African Head of State," *African Affairs* 90, no. 359 (1991): 163–87.
6. CO 554/856, no. 4, Letter from T. B. Williamson to R. F. A. Grey on Divisions of Power between the Federal and Regional Governments in the New Constitution, December 1, 1955; CO 554/1181, no. 2. [Eastern Region of the Colonial Service] Eastern Region, Minutes by W. L. Corell Barnes, Sir C. Jefferson, Sir T. Lloyd, and Mr. Hopkinson, October 18, 1954. See also CO /1181, no. 12, May 30, 1955.
7. PREM 11/1367 F. E. Cumming-Bruce to Sir G. Laithwaite, August 19, 1955.
8. Over this period, Azikiwe was the representative of Her Majesty in Nigeria. When a group of young people tore a poster with a portrait of the Queen close to Azikiwe's official residence, the *West African Pilot* owned by Azikiwe described the act as "the greatest insult to the Governor-General and the Queen." "Advertisement Mania Hits Lagos," *West African Pilot* (Lagos), December 7, 1960; and "Advertisement Mania Hits Lagos," *West African Pilot* (Lagos), December 8, 1960.
9. "Did You Know?" *Daily Mail* (Freetown), November 25, 1961, 5. Sir Samuel Lewis (1843–1903), a Krio mayor of Freetown Municipal Council, was a barrister by training.
10. The primary exponents of this view were Dr. Nnamdi Azikiwe and I. T. A. Wallace Johnson. See Stanley Shaloff, "Press Controls and Sedition Proceedings in the Gold Coast, 1933–39," *African Affairs* 71, no. 284 (1972): 241–63.
11. For an engaging read, see Fred I. A. Omu, "The Dilemma of Press Freedom in Colonial Africa: The West African Example," *Journal of African History* 9, no. 2 (1968): 280. And Shaloff, "Press Controls and Sedition," 241–63, Azikiwe and Johnson were once charged with treason for their fearless press activities.

12. This point was explicitly recorded by the local newspapers that covered the visit. The *Daily Mail*, for instance, noted that it was one of the Queen's "ambitions" to meet with the village people of Sierra Leone and watch them "cook their meals, dye clothes, and work at their crafts." See "She Is Here as Our Queen," *Daily Mail* (Freetown), November 25, 1961, 5.
13. HC Deb March 27, 1961, vol. 230 cc23–40, Sierra Leone Independent Bill, 38; *The Birmingham Post* (Warwickshire), September 5, 1959, 13, 28–29.
14. Sir Roland Robinson to the House of Commons, HC Deb October 31, 1961, vol. 648 cc4–144, Queen's Speech, 11.
15. See HC Deb March 22, 1961, vol. 637 cc391–440, Sierra Leone Independent Bill, 38; and "She Is Here as Our Queen," *Daily Mail* (Freetown), November 25, 1961, 5.
16. K. L. Little, "The Significance of the West African Creole for Africanist and Afro-American Studies," *African Affairs* 49, no. 197 (1950): 312.
17. Joseph Tracey, *An Historical Examination of Western Africa as Formed by Paganism and Muhammedanism, Slavery, the Slave Trade and Piracy* (Boston: Press of T. R. Marvin, 1845).
18. Iain Macleod, The Secretary of State for the Colonies, HC Deb March 22, 1961, vol. 637 cc391–440, Sierra Leone Independence, Order of Second Reading, 400.
19. Iain Macleod, The Secretary of State for the Colonies, HC Deb March 22, 1961, vol. 637 cc391–440, Sierra Leone Independence, Order of Second Reading, 400–401.
20. Iain Macleod, The Secretary of State for the Colonies, HC Deb March 22, 1961, vol. 637 cc391–440, Sierra Leone Independence, Order of Second Reading, 401–2.
21. The Earl of Perth, HL Deb March 27, 1961, vol. 230, cc23–40, Sierra Leone Independence Bill, 27–28.
22. Macleod, HC Deb March 22, 1961, vol. 637 cc391–440, 401–2.
23. Macleod, HC Deb March 22, 1961, vol. 637 cc391–440, 401–2.
24. For instance, Milton Margai was knighted by Queen Elizabeth II in 1959. See Christopher Fyfe, *A Short History of Sierra Leone* (London: Longmans, 1962), 178.
25. "The Queen and the Duke Are Here," *Daily Mail* (Freetown), November 25, 1961, 1.
26. Michael Oliver West, *The Rise of an African Middle Class: Colonial Zimbabwe, 1898–1965* (Bloomington: Indiana University Press, 2002), 30.
27. "Queen Causes a Frenzy in Freetown," *The Guardian* (London), November 26, 1961, reproduced as Patrick O'Donovan, "From the Observer Archive, 26 November 1961: Queen Causes a Frenzy in Freetown," November 23, 2013, https://www.theguardian.com/news/2013/nov/24/queen-causes-frenzy-sierra-leone-freetown.
28. British Pathé Newsreel (Hereafter BPN), *Drums for a Queen*, Record C, Reel 2, 1961.
29. BFI National Archives, "Sierra Leone Greets the Queen" (1961). For a detailed account of the 1956 Nigeria royal trip, see Correspondent Report, "The Queen in Lagos, *West Africa* (London), February 4, 1956, 100.
30. BPN, Record C, Reel 2, 1961 (available at https://www.youtube.com/watch?v=hqaSoBjD-N4).

31 H.M. Queen Elizabeth Speech, recording, BFI National Archives, "Sierra Leone Greets the Queen," Freetown, November 30, 1961. (Available on https://www.youtube.com/watch?v=9x_56-r8w0w).

32 Mr. Tilney to Mr. Hopkinson, HC Deb July 20, 1955, vol. 544 c366, Queen Elizabeth Quay (Cost). Tilney's point of reference about using the defense budget to cover Sierra Leone's project became the new priority as the Cold War intensified in the 1960s. See CAB. 134/1315, Note by Secretary of Cabinet on Cabinet Policy Review, top Secret, June 4, 1965, which reveals Britain's decision to "cover changes in domestic and overseas policy and adjustments in our defense programs" to stop the Soviet Union's infiltration into Africa.

33 Macleod, HC Deb March 22, 1961, vol. 637 cc391–440, 403.

34 Macleod, HC Deb March 22, 1961, vol. 637 cc391–440, 403.

35 *Illustrated London News*, December 2, 1961; *Illustrated London News*, December 9, 1961; Sesay Private Papers (hereafter S.P.P.), J. B. Blyden Jenkins-Johnson to Alhaji G. Sesay: re: Visit of Her Majesty, 4566/FC/292 10/10/61 (Freetown, 1961); and "Your Radio Program for Today and Tomorrow," *Daily Mail* (Freetown), November 25, 1961, 7.

36 Mr. George Wigg (Dudley) to the House of Commons, HC Deb June 25, 1958, vol. 590, cc564–74, Defence, West Africa, 264.

37 O'Donovan, "From the Observer Archive, 26 November 1961: Queen Causes a Frenzy in Freetown."

38 Macleod, HC Deb March 22, 1961, vol. 637 cc391–440, 403.

39 Macleod, HC Deb March 22, 1961, vol. 637 cc391–440, 403.

40 It is crucial to understand that these African leaders bore titles as kings, queens, and chiefs in the precolonial era. Under the colonial order, they were called paramount chiefs. See Ruth Finnegan and David Murray, "Limba Chiefs," in *West African Chiefs: Their Changing Status Under Colonial Rule*, ed. Michael Crowder and Obaro Ikime (Ile-Ife, Nigeria: Africana, 1970).

41 For a complete account of these awards, see Carol P. Hoffer, "Mende and Sherbro Women in High Office," *Canadian Journal of African Studies* (1972): 151–64.

42 Thomas Joshua Alldridge, *The Sherbro and Its Hinterland* (London: Macmillan, 1901), 166–68, 181. Alldridge, a colonial officer, provided a detailed account of these women in chapter 18, "Through the Hinterland Chiefs and Treaties." See also Christopher Fyfe, *A History of Sierra Leone* (Oxford: Oxford University Press, 1962), 486–87; 516, 529; and Joseph J. Bangura, *The Temne of Sierra Leone: African Agency in the Making of a British Colony* (Cambridge: Cambridge University Press, 2017).

43 Sierra Leone Government Archives (SLGA), *List of Paramount Chiefs, Their Chiefdoms, Character, and Sub Chiefs*. Collection Fourah Bay College, Freetown, Typescript, 1914; and SLGA, *Records of Paramount Chiefs*, Freetown, Typescript, 1899.

44 See, for instance, "Never in Trafalgar Square," *The Guardian* (London), September 9, 1965; "Dancers Refuse to Cover Up," *The Times* (London), September 11, 1965; and "The Duke Will Open Festival," *Yorkshire*, September 16, 1965; "The Commonwealth Arts Festival," *The Stage* (London), September 23, 1965, 16.

45   Duke of Edinburgh quoted in Ian Hunter, "The Commonwealth Arts Festival," *Journal of the Royal Society of Arts* 113, no. 5108 (1965): 606.
46   Ian Hunter, "The Commonwealth Arts Festival," a Speech at a Joint Meeting of the Society's Commonwealth Section with the Royal Commonwealth Society, Northumberland Avenue, London, March 25, 1965. Published in Ian Hunter, "The Commonwealth Arts Festival," *Journal of the Royal Society of Arts* 113, no. 5108 (1965): 605–11.
47   Radhika Natarajan, "The Commonwealth Arts Festival of 1965," *Journal of British Studies* 53, no. 3 (2014): 725. See "Commonwealth Arts Festival," *The Stage* (London), September 16, 1965, 26.
48   Iain Macleod, HC Deb July 15, 1960, vol. 626 cc1793–1846, Nigeria Independence Bill, 1807.
49   CAB 134/1303, AF (59) 5 CO Memorandum for the Cabinet (Official) African Committee (Extract), February 10, 1960; CO 554/048, Minute by M. G. Smith on Pressure from Alhaji Abubakar Tafawa Balewa for Self-Government on April 1960, May 15, 1960.
50   Macleod, HC Deb July 15, 1960, vol. 626 cc1793–846, 1818, 1826. Later, during his speech, Macleod paid exceptional special tribute to Dr. Azikiwe. He called him the "Nigerian unity and Nigerian democracy" champion since its conception and supported appointing him the governor-general of the newly independent Nigeria. "If that happens, it will be a worthy recognition of his contribution."
51   For a complete account of Emperor Selassie's names and titles, Conquering Lion of the Tribe of Judah Haile Selassie I, Elect of God, Emperor of Ethiopia, see "1955 Revised Constitution of Ethiopia, Chapter 1, Article II: "The Ethiopian Empire and the Succession to the Throne," Addis Ababa, Ethiopia, November 4, 1955, 1.
52   See Donald Levine, "Haile Selassie's Ethiopia: Myth or Reality," *Africa Today* 8, no. 5 (1961): 11–14. The author has questioned the integrity of these myths and legends.
53   Gizachew Tiruneh, "The Kebra Nagast," *International Journal of Ethiopian Studies* 8, no. 1–2 (2014): 51.
54   Conquering Lion of the Tribe of Judah Haile Selassie I, Elect of God, Emperor of Ethiopia, "1955 Revised Constitution of Ethiopia, Chapter 1, Article II: "The Ethiopian Empire and the Succession to the Throne," Addis Ababa, Ethiopia, November 4, 1955, 1.
55   *The Illustrated London News*, October 23, 1954; *Bradford Observer* (West Yorkshire), October 16, 1945; *The Sphere* (London), "Haile Selassie in London, October 23, 1954; "The Queen Welcomes the Emperor of Ethiopia," *The Birmingham Post*, October 15, 1954.
56   HL Deb July 28, 1954, vol. 189 cc232–316, Annex 1: Organization of the Base, 307.
57   HL Deb July 28, 1954, vol. 189 cc232–316, Annex 1: Organization of the Base, 308; *The Sphere* (London), October 30, 1954; *The Sphere* (London), October 23, 1954; *Illustrated London News,* England, October 16, 1954.
58   See H.M. Queen Elizabeth, Welcome Speech at Buckingham Palace, recorded in British Pathé, "Queen Greets Haile Selassie," 1954 (available at https://www.youtube.com/watch?v=46l17LlB6-M).

59 See W. F. Deeds, "Final Resting Place for the Lion of Judah," *Telegraph* (London), November 4, 2000; John Whelpton, *A History of Nepal* (Cambridge: Cambridge University Press, 2016); James McConnachie, Shafik Meghji, and David Read, *A Rough Guide to Nepal* (London: Rough Guides, 2012), 390. Ranaji was the Knight Grand Cross of the Order of Bath (GCB).

60 *The Birmingham Post* (Warwickshire), October 15, 1954; *The Illustrated London News*, Saturday, October 23, 1954.

61 Staff Correspondent, "Haile Selassie Now Knight of Garter," *Sidney Morning Herald*, October 16, 1954; and London, October 15, 1954; *The Sphere* (London), October 23, 1954; *Shields Daily News* (Northumberland), October 14, 1954.

62 *Shields Daily News* (Northumberland), October 14, 1954, 3. See also A.A.P. London, October 15, 1954.

63 Theodore M. Vestal, "Emperor Haile Selassie's First State Visit to the United States in 1954: The Oklahoma Interlude," *International Journal of Ethiopian Studies* 1, no. 1 (2003): 133–52.

64 "Royal Visit to Ethiopia," *Coventry Evening Telegraph* (Warwickshire), July 6, 1964; "Invitation from Haile Selassie Accepted," *Liverpool Echo* (Lancashire), May 27, 1964, 1.

65 British Pathé, "Tour of Triumph," London, 1965 (available at https://www.youtube.com/watch?v=J-2l0xzGSIU). See *The Birmingham Post*, February 2, 1965, 15; *Coventry Evening Telegraph* (Warwickshire), January 28, 1965, 50.

66 Clyde Sanger, "Ethiopia Welcomes the Queen," *The Guardian* (London), February 2, 1965. A reproduction of the story appeared on February 2, 2016. See *The Illustrated London News*, "Addis Ababa Pageantry Greets the Queen on Ethiopia Tour," February 13, 1965, 18.

67 Clyde Sanger, "Ethiopia Welcomes the Queen," *The Guardian* (London) February 2, 1965. A reproduction of the story appeared on February 2, 2016. *Illustrated London News*, "Addis Ababa Pageantry Greets the Queen on Ethiopia Tour," February 13, 1965, 18. For a detailed read of the era's politics, see Harold G. Marcus, *The Politics of Empire: Ethiopia, Great Britain, and the United States 1941–1974* (Lawrenceville, NJ: Red Sea, 1995).

68 Harold E. Raugh Jr., "General Wavell and the Italian East African Campaign," *Military Review* 63, no. 7–12 (1983): 54–66. See also Trevor Royle, *Orde Wingate: A Man of Genius 1903–1944 with Introduction by Andrew Roberts* (Barnsley, UK: Frontline Books, 2010), 178–202; and Jon Diamond, *Archibald Wavell: Leadership, Strategy, Conflict* (London: Bloomsbury, 2012), 30–40.

69 *Illustrated London News*, "Addis Ababa Pageantry Greets the Queen on Ethiopia Tour," February 13, 1965, 18; Sanger, "Ethiopia Welcomes the Queen," *The Guardian* (London), February 2, 1965.

70 British Pathé, "Tour of Triumph," London, 1965.

71 The House of Commons provided more than £2 million for the expedition. See HC Deb 26, November 1867, vol. 190 cc181–305, The Abyssinian Expedition, and HC Deb December 5, 1967, vol. 190 cc578–97, Paragraph of the Queen's Speech Relating to Abyssinia.

72 "Ethiopia: Golden Tray, Emperor Haile Selassie's Gift to Queen Elizabeth," Ethiopian News and Views (ECADF) (Addis Ababa), September 7, 2017.
73 See *Time*, "Ethiopia: A Wing on the Palace," London, February 12, 1965; British Pathé, "Royal Visit to Africa," February 2, 1965.
74 Kirk-Greene, "His Eternity, His Eccentricity," esp. 163–64, 178, 181.
75 National Archives Kew, Home Office, HO 421/2 covering 01/01/1982–23/03/2000.
76 In a long and emotional speech in the House of Lords, the Viscount of Falkland condemned British policy on Uganda. See House of Lords (HL) Deb December 4, 1985, vol. 468 cc137–98. For reasons advanced for the coup, see GAO 2/1971, General Administrative Order, No. 2.
77 See Barbet Schroeder, *Général Idi Amin Dada: Autoportrait [General Idi Amin Dada, A Self Portrait]* (Documentary History, DVD 90 minutes, 1974), produced by Jean-Francois Chauvel, Charles-Henri Favrod, and Jean-Pierre Rassam. See BFI NFTVA, "General Idi Amin: A Portrait," *People and Politics*, S. Hall (director), Thames Television, June 20, 1974.
78 For more on Amin's background, see Mark Leopold, *Idi Amin: The Story of Africa's Icon of Evil* (New Haven, CT: Yale University Press, 2021), 6–11; Idi Amin, president of Uganda, quoted in Thomas Patrick Melady and Margaret Badum Melady, *Idi Amin Dada: Hitler in Africa* (Kansas City, MO: Sheed Andrews and McNeil, 1977). See *Sunday Independent* (Dublin), October 10, 2004, 94.
79 E. A. Brett, "Rebuilding War-Damaged Communities in Uganda in the late 1980s," in *In Search of Cool Grounds: War, Flight, and Homecoming in Northeast Africa*, ed. Tim Allen (Trenton, NJ: African World, 1996), 206.
80 Viscount Buckmaster, to Her Majesty's Government, HL Deb December 4, 1985, vol. 468, cc1376–98, "Uganda."
81 *The Daily Telegraph* (London), January 26, 1971.
82 Michael Twaddle, "Anatomy of a Coup," *The Times* (London), February 3, 1971; *The Daily Telegraph* (London), January 26, 1971; and *Financial Times* (London), January 26, 1971.
83 For this allegation, see Lord Wigg to Her Majesty's Government, HL Deb. May 24, 1978, vol. 392 cc1013–34, Discovering Africa's Past. See "African Tyrant: The Truth About Amin," *Independent* (London), January 16, 2007; and Richard Dowden, "Revealed: How Israel Helped Amin Take Power," *Independent* (London), August 17, 2003.
84 Bruce Mackenzie to Alec Douglas-Home cited in Dowden, "African Tyrant," *Independent* (London), January 16, 2007.
85 FCO 31/1017, no. 59, The First Six Months of General Amin's government: Despatch from R.M.K. Slater (Kampala) to Sir A. Douglas-Home, August 6, 1971.
86 *Washington Post*, February 24, 1978.
87 FCO 31/713, no 1, Uganda: Valedictory Despatch from D. A. Scott (Kampala) to Mr. Stewart on the Outlook for President Obote, January 26, 1970.

88 FCO 31/1024, no 109 [Uganda]: FCO brief for Sir A. Douglas-Home on recognition of the new regime in Uganda following the overthrow of President Obote, Feb 3, 1971. See also FCO 31/1017, no 59, August 6, 1971.
89 Idi Amin, cited in Michael L. Martin, "The Ugandan Military Coup of 1971: A Study of Protest," *Ufahamu: Journal of African Studies* (1972): 114.
90 See Krishnan Srinivasan, "What Are Commonwealth Values? Traditional Ones: Against Aggression and Authoritarianism," *International Journal* 53, no. 4 (1998): 622–33.
91 See HL Deb 20 July 1983, vol. 443 cc1218–42, Human Rights Violation, 1236. See Leopold, *Idi Amin*, 216, 264; Henry Kyemba, *State of Blood: The Inside Story of Idi Amin* (New York: Putnam Publication Group, 1977). Kyemba, whose brother was killed by Amin, was a highly placed official of the dictator. For some insight on the place of women under Amin's rule, see Alicia Decker, *In Idi Amin's Shadow: Women, Gender and Militarism in Uganda* (Athens: Ohio University Press, 2014), esp. 100–110. Decker provides a vivid account of how Amin attempted to appropriate political hegemony and legitimacy by assembling and managing particular forms of femininity in which he positioned his wives as "mothers of the nation." 100.
92 Peter Ochieng, Correspondence, January 17, 2020.
93 See British Pathé, "UK: Uganda's President Amin Arrives at Buckingham Palace for Lunch, GY Buckingham Palace," 1971. The lunch at Buckingham Palace made a news splash in the British press. See *The Times*, "How Many Arms Does Uganda Need?" London, July 15, 1971; "Uganda May Seek Arms in Britain," *The Birmingham Post*, London, July 13, 1971.
94 This speech's text is widely circulated. See, for instance, Bernard Sabiti, *UgLish: Dictionary of Ugandan English, First Edition* (Kampala, Uganda: Jean-Claude Mugunga, 2014), 49. See Andrew Marr, *The Real Queen Elizabeth: An Intimate Portrait of Queen Elizabeth II* (New York: St. Martin's Griffin, 2013), 92–94.
95 My research in Kampala and questions among the locals, including newspaper houses concerning this, produced no concrete result. However, this is a popular joke in Uganda.
96 John M. T. Balmer, "A Resource-Based View of the British Monarch as a Corporate Brand," *International Studies of Management and Organization* 37, no. 4 (2007): 20–44.
97 Abraham Demoz, "Emperor Menelik's Phonography Message to Queen Victoria," *Bulletin of the School of Oriental Studies* 32, no. 2 (1969): 251–56.
98 Andrew Rice, *The Teeth May Smile, but the Heart Does Not Forget: Murder and Memory in Uganda* (New York: Henry Holt, 2009), 166.
99 See Sabiti, *UgLish*, 49; Tacu Poetry, *Symphony of Selected Poetry Volume 3* (Morrisville, NC: Lulu Publishing, 2008), 154; and Emmanuel Kabenlah Cudjoe, "Idi Amin's Letter to Queen Elizabeth Can Kill You with Laughter," *Africanews*, April 4, 2017.
100 Pompeo Porthouse, "If the Queen Launched with Idi Amin She Can Certainly Meet Trump," *The Daily Squib* (London), January 31, 2017.
101 Marc Horne, "The Queen's 'Good Friend' ... Idi Amin: Extraordinary Personal Sign-Off in Letter to Brutal Ugandan Dictator Revealed in Previously Unseen Archives," *Daily Mail on Sunday* (London), December 27, 2014.

102 Sam Waswa, "Archives: Letter Reveals Amin's Friendship with Queen Elizabeth," *Chimp Reports* (Kampala), December 28, 2014. A copy of the original letter signed by Her Majesty is available at https://chimpreports.com/archives-letter-reveals-amins-friendship-with-queen-elizabeth/.
103 Douglas-Home, cited in Adam Withnall, "The Queen 'Plotted to Hit Idi Amin with a Sword,' If He Visited Britain," *Independent* (London), December 28, 2013.
104 HC Deb 23 October 1972 vol. 843 cc768–70, British Passport Holders, 770. The number of those thrown out of Uganda has yet to be discovered. They actually include many Africans, as Parliamentary records show. Murphy put the Asian population at 80,000. See Philip Murphy, *Monarchy and the End of Empire: The House of Windsor, the British Government and the Postwar Commonwealth* (Oxford: Oxford University Press, 2013), 132.
105 See Ken Cooper, "The Rise of Amin from Cook (and L'Cpl) to General," *The Press and Journal*, July 2, 1975, 6.
106 See Sir Alec Douglas-Home to the House of Commons, HC Deb October 23, 1972 vol. 843 cc768–70, British Passport Holders, 770.
107 HC Deb October 23, 1972 vol. 843 cc770–733, Uganda, 772.
108 Marc Horne, "The Queen's Good Friend," *Daily Mail on Sunday* (London), December 27, 2014; and Adam Withnall, "The Queen's 'Plotted to Hit Idi Amin with a Sword,' If He Visited Britain," *Independent* (London), December 28, 2013.
109 See Mark Leopold, "'Print the Legend': Myth and Reality in the Last King of Scotland," in *Framing Africa: Portrayals of a Continent in Contemporary Mainstream Cinema*, ed. Nigel Eltringham (Oxford: Berghahn, 2013), 30–31.
110 "When Idi Amin Wrote to Queen Elizabeth II over Honeymoon" (republished) *NEWZ PCST* (Kampala), October 27, 2016 (http://newz.ug/when-idi-amin-wrote-to-queen-elizabeth-ii-over-honeymoon/).
111 "When Idi Amin Wrote to Queen Elizabeth II over Honeymoon."
112 "When Idi Amin Wrote to Queen Elizabeth II over Honeymoon."
113 Idi Amin Dada, "Economic Honeymoon Letter to Queen Elizabeth II," Kampala, January 1975. See *NEWZ PCST*, "When Idi Amin Wrote to Queen Elizabeth," October 27, 2016; Joseph Collins, "Queen in Personal Plea to Save Briton in Uganda," *New York Times*, June 20, 1975.
114 FCO 27 10 45 Z Confidential AL Anglo-Uganda Relations, "To Immediate/Certain Missions and Dependent Territories/Telno Guidance 149," July 27, 1976. Amin's anger stemmed from the BBC's negative comments on his government. Hills eventually published the manuscript that almost cost him his life: *The White Pumpkin First Edition* (London: Allen and Unwin, 1975).
115 British Pathé, "Ugandan President Amin Accuses Dennis Hill of Working for a Secret U.S. Government Security Force," CU Amin Speaks at Press Conference, New York, 1975.
116 FCO 27 10 45 Z, Anglo-Uganda Relations, July 27, 1976.
117 *The Birmingham Post*, "Amin Issues Ultimatum on Life of Midlander," June 11, 1975.
118 Collins, "Queen in Personal Plea."

119 Collins, "Queen in Personal Plea."
120 Office of the Secretary of State for Foreign and Commonwealth Affairs, PS/75/2 Department Series (DS/L) 599 no. 2, July 8–10, 1975. Document No. 15, Text of Press Conference at Entebbe Airport, July 10, 1975. See Document 16, "On Arrival from Kampala," Text of Press Conference at the Airport, July 10, 1975. See Conflict Resolution Document MID#1809, June 26–28, 1975. In Douglas M. Gibler, *International Conflicts, 1816–2010: Militarized Interstate Dispute Narratives, Volume I* (Lanham, MD: Rowman & Littlefield, 2018), 452.
121 Apollo N. Makubuya, *Protection, Patronage or Plunder? British Machinations and (B)uganda's Struggle for Independence* (Berlin: Cambridge Scholars Publishing, 2018), 345. The Commonwealth Heads of Government Meeting occurred in London June 8–15, 1977. Idi Amin did not attend, but he continued to harass Britons with his plans to attend. See Spencer Mawby, *The End of Empire in Uganda: Decolonization and Institutional Conflict, 1945–79* (London: Bloomsbury Academic, 2020), 78–81.
122 Idi Amin, quoted in Melady and Melady, *Idi Amin Dada*. See Idi Amin's self-bestowed titles, as reported in "A Clown Drenched in Brutality," *Sunday Times* (London), July 27, 2003.
123 See Nicholas Davies, "'Big Daddy Is on His Way': Next Stop London," *Daily Mirror* (London), June 8, 1977; John Simpson, "Security Panic over Idi Amin's Threat to Visit," *The Times* (London), March 19, 2013; Joseph B. Treaster, "Uganda Reports Amin Is Flying to London," *New York Times*, June 8, 1977.
124 "Out with Idi Amin," *Daily Mirror* (London), June 8, 1977.
125 Hannah Furness, "The Queen's Plot to Bash Idi Amin over the Head with a Pearl Sword," *The Telegraph* (London), December 27, 2013.
126 *Aberdeen Press and Journal*, June 8, 1977.
127 Porthouse, "If the Queen Lunched with Idi Amin She Can Certainly Meet Trump." *Aberdeen Press and Journal*, "Briton Faces Execution," June 10, 1977. It was also reported that Amin had requested the help of General Mobutu of the Congo-Zaire with transportation to London but was turned down. See "Mobutu Refused to Give Amin a Lift," *The Straits Times* (Kuala Lumpur), June 11, 1977. Again, this report is false because a week before, Ugandan Airways flight 707 from Entebbe landed at the airport in Essex with twenty-one passengers, including a newly appointed high commissioner designated for Canada. But Amin was not on the flight. See "Idi Will Be Guest of English Family," *Belfast Telegraph*, June 3, 1977.
128 Lord Mountbatten cited in Philip Murphy, *Monarchy and the End of Empire: The House of Windsor, the British Government and the Postwar Commonwealth* (Oxford: Oxford University Press, 2013).
129 Furness, "The Queen's Plot to Bash Idi Amin"; "Queen Elizabeth Planned to Hit Idi Amin, New Book Says," *The Economic Times* (London), December 28, 2013.
130 *The Telegraph* (London) shared a similar view: "Pomp, Ceremony and Haile Selassie's Pet Lions—The Most Memorable Royal Tours of Africa," September 24, 2018.
131 Murphy, *Monarchy and the End of Empire*, 2.

Chapter 5. Majestic Milestones

1   President Nelson Mandela, A Speech at the Banquet in Honor of Queen Elizabeth II, London, July 11, 1996.
2   H.M. Queen Elizabeth, "Speech by The Queen at the Commonwealth Heads of Government Meeting in Malta," Valletta, Malta, November 27, 2015.
3   H.M. Queen Elizabeth, "Speech by The Queen at the Commonwealth Heads of Government Meeting in Malta."
4   Princess Elizabeth, Speech on her 21st Birthday, Cape Town, South Africa, April 21, 1947 (hereafter, PE/CTS/SA).
5   Melanie Torrent, "A Commonwealth Approach to Decolonization," *Études anglaises* 65, no. 3 (2012): 348. An example of this narrative remains in John Flint's "Planned Decolonization and Its Failure in British Africa," *African Affairs* 82, no. 328 (1983): 389–411. Torrent's points had been made by others: J. Saville, *The Politics of Continuity: British Foreign Policy and the Labour Government 1945–46* (London: Verso, 1993); John Darwin, *Britain and Decolonization: The Retreat from Empire in the Post-war World* (New York: St. Martin's, 1988); Ritchie Ovenda, ed., *The Foreign Policy of the British Labour Governments* (Leicester, UK: Leicester University Press, 1988); Peter Weiler, *British Labour and the Cold War* (Stanford, CA: Stanford University Press, 1988).
6   Kathleen Paul, "'British Subjects' and 'British Stock': Labour's Postwar Imperialism," *Journal of British Studies* 34, no. 2 (1995): 233–76; Kenneth O. Morgan, *Labour in Power 1945–1951* (Oxford: Oxford University Press, 1984); William Roger Louis, *Imperialism at Bay* (New York: Oxford University Press, 1977); John Kent, *British Imperial Strategy the Origins of the Cold War, 1944–49* (Leicester: Leicester University Press, 1993).
7   Philip Murphy, "Britain and the Commonwealth: Confronting the Past, Imagining the Future," *The Round Table: The Commonwealth Journal of International Studies* 100, no. 414 (2011): 267–83. Murphy challenged the British government to engage more with the Commonwealth and demonstrate openness to those critical of its past. And given its practical and symbolic importance, he advised Whitehall to center the organization on British foreign policy.
8   As a reminder, Whitehall floated the postwar Commonwealth scheme to buy the time to manage the wind of change on its terms while colonial preservationists gradually acquiesced to the obvious that Britain's use of *nkamanya* or crude force to subjugate and dispose of the "colored" races is not a usual way of life. I have used this term in the context of the African agency. Regarding the Commonwealth as a political scheme, Malcolm MacDonald noted in 1947 that Britain was faced with the difficult task of transforming "the colored part of the Colonial Empire into a commonwealth of free of nations" after its success with the British selling colonies of Australia, New Zealand, Canada, and South Africa under White rule.
9   See the text of the Queen's 1953 Christmas message in "The Queen's Message to Her Peoples," *The Yorkshire Post and Leeds Mercury*, December 28, 1953, 5.

10 "The Commonwealth: Why Does It Exist and Does It Help Members?" *The Africa Report*, March 10, 2021, https://www.theafricareport.com/71058/the-commonwealth-why-does-it-exist-and-does-it-help-its-members/.
11 Torrent, "A Commonwealth Approach to Decolonization," 349; Dan Halvorson, *Commonwealth Responsibility and Cold War Solidarity: Australia in Asia, 1944–74* (Canberra: Australian National University Press, 2019), 6.
12 Krishnan Srinivasan, "What Are Commonwealth Values? Traditional Ones: Against Aggression and Authoritarianism," *International Journal* 53, no. 4 (1998): 623.
13 See International Bank for Reconstruction and Development, No. E.135b 67058, *The Colombo Plan*, prepared by Antonin Basch, January. 23, 1950, 1. The plan charged members of the Commonwealth to (1) draw up "a realistic and comprehensive six-year development plan" and (2) set up a bureau at Colombo to administer a technical assistance program with a budget of £3 million. See "Commonwealth Premiers to Meet Colombo," *Northampton Chronicle and Echo*, November 22, 1950, 4; E. E. War, "The Colombo Plan," *Australian Outlook* 5, no. 4 (2008): 191.
14 See Oswald Wilkinson Larcher, "The Politics of Canadian Aid to the Commonwealth Caribbean" (PhD diss., University of Waterloo, 1973), 90.
15 DO 193/79, no. 7, The Commonwealth and British Interest: Canada and the Commonwealth: Letter from E. J. Emery (Ottawa) to R. Walker, December 1, 1966. For an engaging account of Canada's role in the Caribbean development plans, see John Kenner, *A Forgotten Legacy: Canadian Leadership in the Commonwealth* (Bloomington: Trafford, 2011), 75–78.
16 Prime Minister Sir Anthony Eden made this clear at the House of Commons in 1956. See HC Deb July 30, 1956 vol. 557 cc918–21, Suez Canal, 919; HC Deb August 2, 1956, vol. 557 cc1602–43, Suez Canal, 1603; HC Deb, September 12, 1956, vol. 558 cc2–149, Suez Canal, 10.
17 Major Patrick Wall (Haltemprice, Hull), HC Deb, September 12, 1956, vol. 558 cc2–149, Suez Canal, 50.
18 Mr. H. R. S. Crossman (Coventry East), to the House of Commons, HC Deb, September 12, 1956, vol. 558 cc2–149, Suez Canal, 84–85.
19 PREM 11/1367 Letter from Sir P. Liesching to Sir S. Garner on the National Party Government and Its Attitude towards Commonwealth Membership for the Gold Coast, June 8, 1955.
20 PREM 11/1367 Letter from Sir P. Liesching to Sir S. Garner. Malan called this a "two-tier solution."
21 PREM 11/1367, June 8, 1955. See also CO 1030/437, no. 3 Letter from H. J. B. Lintott (CRO) to Sir P. Liesching (South Africa), August 2, 1957; and *The Observer* (London), January 25, 1955.
22 See *The Scotsman* (Edinburgh), June 19, 1957.
23 CAB 128/34, CC9(60)2, Report by Mr. Macmillan on His African Tour: Cabinet Conclusions, February 16, 1960.
24 HC Deb April 8, 1960, vol. 621 cc774–843, Union of South Africa (Racialist Policies), 779.

25 Jawaharlal Nehru cited in HC Deb April 8, 1960, vol. 621 cc774–843, Union of South Africa (Racialist Policies), 780.
26 *The Times* (London), March 1, 1961; *The Guardian* (London), March 16, 1961; and *Daily Telegraph* (London), March 17, 1961.
27 Frank Hayes, "South Africa's Departure from the Commonwealth, 1960–1961," *International History Review* 2, no. 3 (1980): 453–84.
28 CAB 129/114, C(63)106, Cabinet Memorandum, (Joint FO-CRO Paper), June 25, 1963. 291.
29 Ghana and Nigeria's emergence as new markets in the 1960s reinforced Canada, Australia, and India's role in reducing the Commonwealth's saliency as a British-owned club.
30 See Mohamed A. El-Khawas, "South Africa: A Challenge to OAU," *Africa Today* 24, no. 3 (1974): 25–41; Godfrey Mwakikagile, *Nyerere and Africa: End of an Era* (Pretoria: New African Press, 2010), 229.
31 Roy Lewis, "Britain's Danger of Antagonizing both Sides in Nigeria," *The Times* (London), May 31, 1967; and "Treaties Respected, Debt Honored," *The Times* (London), May 31, 1967.
32 In his recent study, Samuel Daly highlighted how crime incidents, skewed law administration, and other socioeconomic and political dysfunctions contributed to the conflict. See Samuel Fury Childs Daly, *A History of the Republic of Biafra: Law, Crime and the Nigerian Civil War* (Cambridge: Cambridge University Press, 2021).
33 "Nigeria: Agony in Biafra," *Time*, August 2, 1968; "Massacre of 2,000 Ibos Claimed," *The Times* (London), October 20, 1968. The report claimed that 2,000 were killed at Owaza village and 300 Uzuaku village by Nigerian troops. See Arua Oko Omaka, *The Nigerian Humanitarian Crisis, 1967–1970: International Human Rights and Joint Church Aid* (Madison, NJ: Fairleigh Dickson University Press, 2016), 62–63.
34 Elsewhere, I have underscored this point. See Raphael Chijioke Njoku, "Nationalism, Separatism and the Neoliberal Globalism: A Review of Africa and the Quest for Self-Determination since the 1950s," in *Secession as an International Phenomenon*, ed. Don Doyle (Athens: University of Georgia Press, 2010), 338–80.
35 Alain Rouvez, *Disconsolate Empires: French, British, and Belgian Military Involvement in Postcolonial Sub-Saharan Africa* (Lanham, MD: University Press of America, 1994), 147–49.
36 Peter Sedgwick, "The Appalling Silence and Inactivity of the British Left as Biafrans Face Death and Starvation from Socialist Workers," July 10, 1969, https://www.marxists.org/archive/sedgwick/1969/07/biafra.htm.
37 Gloria Emerson, "John Lennon Returns Award as a Protest," *New York Times*, November 26, 1969, https://archive.nytimes.com/www.nytimes.com/library/music/112669lennon-award.html; "John Lennon–Returning His MBE," *thebeatlesinterviews*, September 30, 2007, http://www.youtube.com/watch?v=6m0glhvwhdI.

38 "Dick Tiger Joins Biafra Army," *Biafra Telegraph*, January. 31, 1968; Dave Anderson, "Dick Tiger, 42, Nigerian Boxer Who Won World Titles, Dead," *New York Times*, December 16, 1971;

39 See David C. Nwafo, *Born to Serve: The Biography of Dr. Akanu Ibiam* (Ibadan, Nigeria: Macmillan, 1988), 149; and Okapni Nkama Jr., *Akanu Ibiam 1906–1995: A Compendium of the Humble Hero* (Enugu, Nigeria: Nkamedia Communications, 1995), 47.

40 See Agwu Kalu, *Dr. Ibiam: The Challenge of His Life* (Aba, Nigeria: Presbyterian Church of Nigeria, 1986), 72–73; Buch Opene and Adamson Momoh. "Ibiam: Apostle of Morality," *Times International* (Lagos), December 8, 1986, 12; Nwafo, *Born to Serve*, 103, 244.

41 Francis Akanu Ibiam, "What About Africa?," address delivered by His Excellency, the governor of Eastern Nigeria Sir Francis Akanu Ibiam, at the Third Assembly of the World Council of Churches, New Delhi, November 18–December 6, 1961, 3–4; 22.

42 These were the words of Ibiam on the denunciation of his British accolades. See his interview with Opene and Momoh, "Ibiam: Apostle of Morality," 11.

43 Agwu Kalu, *Dr. Ibiam: The Challenge of His Life* (Aba, Nigeria: Presbyterian Church of Nigeria, 1986), 39.

44 Opene and Momoh, "Ibiam: Apostle of Morality," 9.

45 Rouvez, *Disconsolate Empires*, 147.

46 The British Parliament cited this as a severe problem. See HC Deb 13 March 1969, vol. 779 cc1636–96, 1651–52. Sir F. Bennett says a successful Biafran breakaway would be the most significant fillip to tribal fragmentation throughout Africa.

47 Maxim Matusevich, *No Easy Row for a Russian Hoe: Ideology and Pragmatism in Nigerian-Soviet Relations, 1960–1991* (Trenton, NJ: Africa World Press, 2003), 105–13; Maxim Matusevich, "Ideology and Pragmatism: The Biafra War and Nigeria's Response to the Soviet Union, 1966–1970," *Nigerian Journal of International Affairs* 28, nos. 1–2 (2002): 97–138; Lasse Heerten and A. Dirk Moses, "The Nigeria-Biafra War: Postcolonial Conflict and the Question of Genocide," *Journal of Genocide Research* 16, no. 2–3 (2014): 169–203.

48 *Daily Telegraph* (London), August 16, 1967. See also HC Deb March 13, 1969, vol. 779 cc1636–96, Nigeria, 1638.

49 Mr. Denis Healey to the House of Commons, HC Deb March 13, 1969, vol. 779 cc1636–96, Nigeria, 1636–37.

50 *The Times* (London), August 17, 1968. Later, Margery abandoned the Biafra cause by joining the Commonwealth documentary series in dismissing Biafra's claims of genocide. See *The Times* (London), September 15, 1968.

51 Margery Perham cited in HC Deb March 13, 1969, vol. 779 cc1636–96, Nigeria, 1636–37.

52 Chinua Achebe, "Biafra's Reply," *The Times* (London), September 19, 1968.

53 HC Deb July 24, 1968, vol. 769 cc667–700, Adjournment Summer, 673.

54 John Tilney to the House of Commons, HC Deb, March 13, 1969 vol. 779 cc1636–96, Nigeria, 1637. In 1966, Mr. Tilney emphasized that it was a primary British interest

for Nigeria to remain united. See HC Deb, June 14, 1966 vol. 729 cc1225–26, 1226. In response, Mr. Bottomley had assured Tilney that Her Majesty's Government "would strongly deprecate any development tending to obstruct" the Nigerian government's effort.

55   Albert Margai, cited in "The Commonwealth Conference," *The Illustrated* (London), June 19, 1965, 14.
56   Prime Minister Eden made this clear in a 1965 brief at the House of Commons. See HC Deb September 12, 1956, vol. 558 cc2–149, Suez Canal, 10.
57   Prime Minister Harold Wilson to the House of Commons, "Rhodesia," HC Deb, March 27, 1968, vol. 761 cc1543–679, 1546.
58   "A Family of Nations—The Queen's Message," *Evening Express* (Aberdeen), December 25, 1970, 5.
59   PE/CTS/SA, Cape Town, South Africa, April 21, 1947.
60   HL Deb February 27, 1958, vol. 207 cc1047–78, Commonwealth Institute Bill, 1049. The institute was officially opened in November 1962. See *The Illustrated London News*, November 19, 1962, 761.
61   Kwame Nkrumah cited in "The Commonwealth Conference," *The Illustrated* (London), June 19, 1965, 14. The report states that Nkrumah's brilliant suggestion was "rapidly accepted" by his colleagues.
62   HC Deb November 28, 1953 vol. 685 cc457–58, Commonwealth Festival of Arts, 458. The "British Commonwealth Arts Festival" idea was the brainchild of the Canadian journalist Mr. Marks. See Stanley Marks, "Commonwealth Arts Festival: A Novel Plan from Canada," *The Stage* (London), September 24, 1953, 15.
63   Library of Commonwealth Document on "The Declaration of Commonwealth Principles, Issued at the Heads of Commonwealth Meeting in Singapore," January 14–22, 1971. Before the meeting, the organization was the "British Commonwealth." The 1971 conference was the first convened as CHOGM. It would mark the only CHOGM meeting held every two years that the Queen missed from 1971 to 2003.
64   "The Declaration of Commonwealth Principles." See Srinivasan, "What Are Commonwealth Values?" 623–24.
65   *Belfast Telegraph*, "Government Warned Again Over Arms," October 17, 1971, 2.
66   See Commonwealth Secretariat, *Commonwealth Information News Release* (London), 78/51, June 18, 1973.
67   CHOGM, "Lusaka Declaration on Racism and Racial Prejudice," Lusaka, Zambia, August 1–7, 1979.
68   "Bomb Fear for Queen," *Daily Mirror* (London), April 12, 1979, 4; "Ceasefire Bid to End Fears for the Queen," *Sunday Mirror* (London), July 1, 1979, 5.
69   CHOGM, "Melbourne Declaration," Melbourne, Australia, September 30–October 7, 1981; Shridath Ramphal cited in Des Wilson, "The Changing Commonwealth," *Illustrated London News*, September 1, 1981, 38.
70   CHOGM, "Goa Declaration of International Security," Goa, India, November 23–29, 1983.

71   CHOGM, "Nassau Declaration on World Order," Nassau, The Bahamas, October 16–22, 1985.

72   CHOGM, "Vancouver Declaration on World Order," Vancouver, Canada, October 13–17, 1987.

73   CHOGM, "Langkawi Declaration on the Environment," Kuala Lumpur, Malaysia, October 18–24, 1989.

74   See CHOGM, "Ottawa Declaration on Women and Structural Adjustment," submitted by the Third Meeting of Commonwealth Ministers Responsible for "Women's Affairs, Ottawa, Canada, October 9–12, 1990.

75   CHOGM, "Langkawi Declaration on the Environment," Kuala Lumpur, Malaysia, October 18–24, 1987; CHOGM, "Ottawa Declaration on Women and Structural Adjustment Program," Ottawa, Canada, October 9–12, 1990; and CHOGM, "Harare Declaration," Lusaka, Zimbabwe, October 16–21, 1991.

76   "Playing Happy Family," *Dundee Courier*, October 16, 1991, 12. When the writer acknowledged that Britain had used the Commonwealth to further its post-Empire global influence, he questioned whether it was worth the hassle for Britain and the Queen, who only spoke to the partners every Christmas.

77   CHOGM, "Harare Declaration," Lusaka, Zimbabwe, October 16–21, 1991.

78   CHOGM, "Harare Declaration," Lusaka, Zimbabwe, October 16–21, 1991.

79   For instance, Vaughan A. Lewis, "Commonwealth Caribbean Relations with Hemispheric Middle Powers," in *Dependency under Challenge: The Political Economy of the Commonwealth Caribbean*, ed. Anthony Payne and Paul K. Sutton (Manchester: Manchester University Press, 1984), 287. Vaughan's study was in connection with the Commonwealth of the Caribbean.

80   Kwame Nkrumah, cited in Godfrey Mwakikagile, *Africa at the End of the Twentieth Century: What Lies Ahead* (Dar es Salaam: New Africa Press, 2013), 14. See *Gold Coast Weekly Review* (Accra), July 20, 1955, as quoted in Martin L. Kilson Jr., "Nationalism and Social Classes in British West Africa," *Journal of Politics* 20, no. 2 (1958): 380.

81   Kenneth W. Grundy, "Nkrumah's Theory of Underdevelopment: An Analysis of Recurrent Themes," *World Politics* 15, no. 3 (1963): 440.

82   President Nelson Mandela, A Speech at the Banquet in Honor of Queen Elizabeth II, London, July 11, 1996.

83   John Holms, "The Impact on the Commonwealth of the Emergence of Africa," in "Africa and International Organization," special issue, *International Organization* 16, no. 2 (1962): 293.

84   India's admission to the Commonwealth in 1948 set the path for other African and Asian emerging nations to insert their freedom (which in this context stands for independence) and, simultaneously, be allowed in the association. See *Daily Telegraph* (London), April 23, 1949; "Playing Happy Family," *Dundee Courier*, October 16, 1991, 12. Then, the public opinion in Britain was on whether India would cooperate with the Commonwealth or break away.

85 B. Vivekanandan, "Commonwealth of Nations Today," *Indian Journal of Political Science* 35, no. 1 (1974): 13. "The Commonwealth Conference," *The Illustrated* (London), June 19, 1965, 14, shared this view.

86 CHOGM, "Kampala Declaration on Transforming Societies to Achieve Political, Economic, and Human Development, Kampala," Uganda, November 23–25, 2007. The declaration reiterated that of 2003 in Abuja, Nigeria. See CHOGM, "Aso Rock Declaration on Development and Democracy: Partnership for Peace and Prosperity," Abuja, Nigeria, December 3–8, 2003.

87 Queen Elizabeth II, A Speech by the Queen at CHOGM, Uganda, November 23, 2007.

88 Organization of African Unity, *Lagos Plan of Action for Africa's Economic Development, 1980–2000* (Addis Ababa: Organization of African Unity, 1980). The initiative emphasized a "regional approach based primarily on collective self-reliance" (4).

89 "The Commonwealth Essential for Africa's Growth," *African Business Magazine* (London), January. 19, 2012.

90 See World Bank, National Accounts Data, and OECD National Accounts Data Files, https://data.worldbank.org/indicator/NY.GDP.MKTP.CD; Eurostat Archives, EU-Commonwealth of Independent States CIS Statistics on GDP, March 10, 2017; Simon Constable, "How Britain's Empire Can Strike Back, Surpass the E.U.," *Forbes*, January 26, 2017.

91 A report published on June 12, 2020, showed that the UK GDP slowed by 5.8 percent in the first quarter and fell by 20.4 percent in April. See the Office of National Statistics, "GDP Monthly Estimate, U.K.," June 9, 2020 https://www.ons.gov.uk/economy/grossdomesticproductgdp/bulletins/gdpmonthlyestimateuk/april2020. See also Nigel Walker, Claire Mills, and Ben Smith, *The Commonwealth in 2020*, research briefing, UK Parliament House of Commons Library, March 6, 2020, https://commonslibrary.parliament.uk/research-briefings/cdp-2020-0052/#:~:text=There%20are%20now%2054%20countries,reach%20%2413%20trillion%20in%202020.

92 James McBride, "The Commonwealth of Nations: Britain and the Future of Global Britain," *Council on Foreign Relations*, March 2, 2020. For the Commonwealth members' objection to Brexit, see Ian Jack, "Britain Sees the Commonwealth as Its Trading Empire. It Is Sadly Deluded," *The Guardian* (London), April 7, 2018.

93 Simon Constable, "How Britain's Empire Can Strike Back, Surpass the E.U.," *Forbes*, January 26, 2017.

94 CHOGM, "The Millbrook Commonwealth Action Program on the Harare Declaration," Auckland, New Zealand, November 10–15, 1995.

95 Commonwealth Business Council, *Globalization: Policies, Strategies, and Partnerships Edited Papers of the Commonwealth Business Forum 2000* (London: Commonwealth Business Forum, 2000), 189. CHOGM, "The Millbrook Commonwealth Action Program on the Harare Declaration," Auckland, New Zealand, November 10–15, 1995.

96 The State House of Uganda (hereafter SHU), "President Museveni Toasts to Queen Elizabeth's Life," British High Commission, Nakasero, Kampala, June 17, 2017.

97 See CHOGM, "Harare Declaration," Lusaka, Zimbabwe, October 16–21, 1991.

98 SHU, "President Museveni Toasts to Queen Elizabeth's Life."

99 Charter of the Commonwealth Signed by Her Majesty Queen Elizabeth II (hereafter CC-HMQE), Head of the Commonwealth, Commonwealth Day 2013, 6–8. The charter aligns with the UN 2030 Agenda for Sustainable Development.
100 Queen Elizabeth II, a speech by the Queen at CHOGM, Uganda, November 23, 2007.
101 The Secretary of State for Commonwealth Relations (The Earl of Home), HL Deb July 2,1959, vol. 217 cc637–38, Commonwealth Education Conference, 637.
102 H. Lionel Elvin, "First Commonwealth Education Conference Oxford, July 1959," *International Review of Education* 6, no. 1 (1960): 79–82.
103 The Secretary of State for Commonwealth Relations (The Earl of Home), HL Deb July 2, 1959, vol. 217 cc637–38, Commonwealth Education Conference, 637.
104 CC-HMQE Commonwealth, Commonwealth Day 2013, 6. The Charter agrees with the UN 2030 Agenda for Sustainable Development.
105 Commonwealth Secretariat Strategic Plan, 2013/14–2016/17 (hereafter CSSP2013–2017), approved by the Commonwealth Secretariat Board of Governors, May 23, 2013.
106 See Republic of Kenya Ministry of Education, Policy Framework for Nomadic Education in Kenya, in collaboration with UNICEF, Mar 2, 2011; CSSP2013–2017, 43.
107 Government of the Bahamas, 19th Conference of Commonwealth Education Ministers, Nassau, The Bahamas, June 22–26, 2015.
108 See Paul D. Zimmerman, "Treetops Hotel, Not a Bit Posh, but It Attracts a Posh Clientele," *New York Times*, September 18, 1968. Eric Sherbrooke Walker built the facility, which sits at 6,450 feet and is within sight of Mount Kenya, in 1932.
109 Expenditure Survey Report 2001, Uganda Final Report. See Uganda Bureau of Statistics, *A Report on the Uganda Business Register, 2001/2002*. Uganda Bureau of Statistics, External Trade Statistics Bulletin Volume 1–2002, November 2002.
110 John M. Mackenzie, The Empire of Nature: Hunting, Conservatism and British Imperialism (Manchester, UK: Manchester University Press, 1988); D. Anderson and R. Grove, "The Scramble for Eden: Past, Present and Future," in *Conservation in Africa: People, Policy and Practices,* ed. David Anderson and Richard Grove (Cambridge: Cambridge University Press, 1987), 1–12.
111 Robert A. Stafford, review of *The Empire of Nature: Hunting, Conservatism and British Imperialism* by John M. Mackenzie, *British Journal for the History of Science* 23, no. 1 (1990): 122–24.
112 See World Bank Group, *Economic and Statistical Analysis of Tourism in Uganda*, Washington, DC: World Bank Group, 2013.
113 See "What the Ugandan Tourism Must Focus on in 2019," *East African Business Week* (Kampala), January 18, 2019.
114 Hon. Najib Balala, Tourism Sector Performance Report, Nairobi, Ministry of Tourism and Wildlife, 2018; Hon. Najib Balala, Tourism Sector Performance Report, Nairobi, Ministry of Tourism and Wildlife, 2019; and Jüergen T. Steinmetz, Kenya Tourism Performance Report, January 10, 2020.
115 Statistics South Africa, Statistical Release, *PO352.2 Domestic Tourism Survey Bi-Annual Report*, December 12, 2019.

116 Keith Jefferis, Sethunya Sejoe, and Kitso Mokhurutshe, "Economic Review, First Quarter," Gaborone, Botswana, January–March 2019. The report should have included the 2019 tourism economic trends.
117 For more on Sentebale, see https://www.royal.uk/sentebale.
118 Rebecca Clay, "A Continent in Chaos: Africa's Environmental Issues," *Environmental Health Perspective* 102, no. 12 (1994): 1018–23.
119 David Western, "Conservation Science in Africa and the Role of International Collaboration," *Conservation Biology* 17, no. 1 (2003): 11–19.
120 H.M. Queen Elizabeth, "A Message from The Queen to the People of Ethiopia," Bottom of Form, December 21, 2018, https://www.royal.uk/message-queen-people-ethiopia.
121 See K. S. Duncan, "The Commonwealth at Play," *Journal of the Royal Society of Arts* 124, no. 5239 (1976): 393.
122 See "Edinburgh Is Next Venue for Games," *Liverpool Echo*, August 8, 1966, 14; "Main Rival," *Reading Evening Post* (Berkshire), August 4, 1966, 16; "1970 Games Go to Edinburgh," *Coventry Evening Telegraph* (Warwickshire), August 8, 1966, 11.
123 "A Family of Nations—The Queen's Message," *Evening Express* (Aberdeen), December 25, 1970, 5.
124 Queen Elizabeth, Commonwealth Day Message from HM Queen Elizabeth II, March 10, 2014.
125 Muhammad Muda, "The Significance of Commonwealth Games in Malaysia's Foreign Policy," *The Round Table* 87, no. 346 (1998): 211–26.
126 David R. Black and Januaryis van der Westhuizen, "Editorial: The Neglected Allure of Global Games?" *Third World Quarterly* 25, no. 7 (2004): 1191; Aaron Baker, "Sports Films, History, and Identity," *Journal of Sport History* 25, no. 2 (1998): 217–33.
127 See Rob Nixon, "Apartheid on the Run: The South African Sports Boycott," *Transition* 58 (1992): 68–88; Douglas Booth, "Hitting Apartheid for Six? The Politics of the South African Sports Boycott," *Journal of Contemporary History* 38, no. 3 (2003): 477–93.
128 Eleri Lynn, quoted in Simon Perry, "Princess Diana's Famous 'Travolta' Dress in 'Isolation Room' amid Lockdown," *People*, New York, May 26, 2020.
129 Clare Coulson, "Queen of Style," *The Telegraph* (London), September 6, 2015.
130 See British Pathé, "Queen in Enugu," FILM ID#: 2532.14 1956. For an elaborate report on Okotie-Eboh's dramatic attires during the Queen's visit in 1956, see "Eyes on Nigeria," *West Africa* (London), February 4, 1956, 1.
131 Bankole Timothy, "Now the Way Is Clear," *Daily Graphic* (Accra), February 28, 1957, 5.
132 "She Admires a Present," *Ghana Times* (Accra), November 11, 1961; "She Is Showered with Petals," *Ghana Times* (Accra), November 13, 1961; and "A Kante Gift for His Wife," *Ghana Times* (Accra), November 13, 1961.
133 Object No: 202-9-6, Undetermined Artists, Sierra Leone, Factory printed cloth "Queen Elizabeth II," Cotton, dye, Freetown, 1961, Gift of Donald A. Theuer and Lilburne Senn, Smithsonian National Museum of African Art, Washington, DC.
134 Queen Elizabeth, "The Queen at the CHOGM Opening Ceremony," Perth, Australia, October 28, 2011.

135 Photographic Gelatin, "Dance in Honor of Elizabeth II and the Duke of Edinburgh, Kaduna, Nigeria," by Brian Blake, Kaduna, 1956, Registration No.: E004128/20.
136 "Talking Drums Will Be There," *Daily Graphic* (Accra), February 28, 1957, 1. For the Nigerian airport musical spectacle in honor of the Queen, see "Queen Sends Message of Appreciation to Nigerians Who Saw Her Leave for Lagos," *West Africa* (London), February 4, 1956, 122.
137 Steven J. Salm and Toyin Falola, *Culture and Customs of Ghana* (Westport, CT: Greenwood, 2002), 183.
138 King Bruce and the Black Beats, "The Queen's Visit," in Golden Highlife Classics, Retro3CD.
139 Raphael Abdumajad, interview with Mohamed Ahmed, in *Daily Nation*, Mombasa, July 7, 2019.
140 See "Nigerian Artists Opens Exhibition," *West Africa* (London), February 11, 1956; Naima Mohamud, "Ben Enwonwu: The Nigerian Painter behind 'Africa's Mona Lisa,'" *BBC News*, October 17, 2019, https://www.bbc.com/news/world-africa-50071212. Enwonwu was the first African artist to depict any European monarch's formal image.
141 Mohamud, "Ben Enwonwu."
142 Afua Hirsch, "Ghana Calls an End to Tyrannical Queen's English," *The Guardian* (London), April 10, 2012. See also Afua Hirsch, "Africa's Colonization of the English Language," *The Guardian* (London), January 29, 2020; and Rebecca English, "God don Butta my Bread! Prince Charles Drops Queen's English and Speaks in Pidgin during Speech in Nigeria," *Daily Mirror* (London), November 8, 2018.
143 H.M. Queen Elizabeth, cited in Simon Perry, "A Queen for All Times," in "Queen Elizabeth at 90," special edition of *Life*, April 1, 2016, 7.
144 Andrew Marr, *The Real Elizabeth: An Intimate Portrait of Queen Elizabeth II* (New York: St. Martin's Griffin, 2013), 319.
145 Geof Lostus, "Lead like Elizabeth II," *Forbes*, September 24, 2015, 53.
146 Queen Elizabeth II, Christmas Broadcast, Auckland, New Zealand, 1953.

Chapter 6. King Charles III and Africa's Commonwealth Future

1 H.M. Queen Elizabeth, Welcome Address to the Commonwealth of Heads of Government Meeting (CHOGM) (London), April 19–20, 2018. See Liam Doyle, "Royal Shock: Will Prince Charles Be Head of the Commonwealth? Is It Independent?" *The Express* (London), July 7, 2020.
2 CHOGM, Communique after Retreat (London), April 20, 2018. See Victoria Howard, "Prince Charles Will Be the Next Head of the Commonwealth, Leaders Decide," *Crown Chronicles* (London), April 20, 2018.
3 Prince Charles, Address to the Commonwealth of Heads of Government Meeting (CHOGM) (London), April 19, 2018. His Malta reference here is in connection with 1949. At age one and a half, Prince Charles accompanied the Queen to the

Southern European island nation while Parliament and King George VI announced the modern Commonwealth by signing the London Declaration. From 1949 to 1951, the Queen and Prince Philip lived in Malta while her husband was stationed in the island nation as a naval officer. See HL Deb April 28, 1949, vol. 162 cc126–31, Meeting of Commonwealth Prime Ministers.

4   The Prime Minister, Mrs. Margaret Thatcher to the House of Commons, HC Deb July 14, 1981, vol. 8 cc990–92, 991.

5   For a quick read of the world's mood after Diana died in 1997, see Telegraph Reporters, "Princess Diana: What Happened on the Night of Her Death," *Telegraph* (London), August 29, 2017. See also "Diana, Princess of Wales," *Time*, September 8, 1997; and Michael M. Simmons, *Queen of People's Hearts: The Time and Mission of Diana, Princess of Wales* (Scotts Valley, CA: Create Space, 2017).

6   Philip Murphy and Daisey Cooper, *Queen Elizabeth II Should Be the Final Head of the Commonwealth* (London: Commonwealth Advisory Bureau /Institute of Commonwealth Studies, 2012), 1.

7   Murphy and Cooper, *Queen Elizabeth II Should Be the Final Head of the Commonwealth*, 5.

8   Public Records Office (PRO) Kew–Dominions Office, DO 177/84, Minutes by A. W. Snelling, 5 September 1958, enclosed in Cabinet Discussions on the Nigerian Constitutional Conference, 1958–1961.

9   Prince Charles, CHOGM Address, April 19, 2018. Murphy has persistently argued that only Queen Elizabeth can lead the Commonwealth because she understands its relevance. See "Only the Queen Understands the True Value of the Commonwealth," *The Telegraph* (London), December 23, 2013.

10 King Charles III repeated this pledge in his first Republic speech on September 12, 2022.

11 Philip Murphy, *The Empire's New Clothes: The Myth of the Commonwealth* (London: C. Hurst and Company, 2018), x, 133, 135–38, 159.

12 *Daily Express* (London), October 18, 1992.

13 Richard Aylard, "*Daily Express* Article: The Following Points Are Relevant," reproduced in Jonathan Dimbleby, *The Prince of Wales: A Biography* (London: Little, Brown, and Co. 1994), 576–79.

14 Andrew Piarca, "Secret Thoughts of Prince Charles Released," *Irish Independent* (Dublin), February 23, 2006, 34.

15 See Stephen Bates, "Charles Claims Victory in Hong Kong Diary Case," *The Guardian* (London), March 18, 2006; "Prince Charles' Private Diary Is Now Public," *The Herald* (London), February 23, 2006; "A Breach of the Prince's Trust? Charles and the Great Chinese Takeaway," *The Independent* (London): February 23, 2006.

16 Nana Addo Dankwa Akufo-Addo, Address at the UN General Debate, 77th Session, New York, September 22, 2022.

17 See Bob Seely and James Rogers, *Global Britain: A Twenty-First Century Vision* (London: Henry Jackson Society and the Global Britain Program, 2019).

18 Philip Murphy, cited in Hannah Furness, "The Queen's Plot to Bash Idi Amin," *The Telegraph* (London), December 27, 2013. See also "Queen Elizabeth Planned to Hit

Idi Amin, New Book Says," *The Economic Times* (London), December 28, 2013; Philip Murphy, cited in Hannah Furness, "Commonwealth Has No 'Dirty Secrets,' Says Oxford Professor after Prince Harry Warns of Its 'Wrongs,'" *The Telegraph* (London), July 7, 2020. See also Philip Murphy, *Monarchy and the End of Empire: The House of Windsor, the British Government and the Postwar Commonwealth* (Oxford: Oxford University Press, 2013).

19   See Godwin Onyeacholam, "The Price of Democracy," *The Week* (Lagos), May 31, 1999, 8–13; and Aminu Tijani, "Abacha's Murder Incorporated," *Tell* (Lagos), July 19, 1999, 16–24. For an engaging read on the Abacha dictatorship, see Raphael Chijioke Njoku, "Deconstructing Abacha: Demilitarization and Democratic Consolidation in Nigeria After the Abacha Era," *Government and Opposition* 36, no. 1 (2001): 71–96; and "Killing Nigeria: Abacha's One Year of Pain, Decline, and Gloom," *The News*, November 21, 1994.

20   Foreign Staff Report, "Gambia Rejoins the Commonwealth after Democratic Election," *The Telegraph* (London), February 8, 2018. President Barrow reversed Mr. Jammeh's pullout of the group without any delays. See "The Gambia Rejoins Commonwealth after Five Years," *The Times* (London), February 9, 2018; and "Gambia Rejoins Commonwealth under New President, *Punch* (Lagos), February 8, 2018.

21   In a recorded message on June 25, 2020, Patricia Scotland, the Commonwealth secretary-general, announced the postponement of the CHOGM meeting due to COVID-19.

22   CHOGM, Harare Declaration, Issued at the Commonwealth Heads of Government Meeting, Harare, Zimbabwe, October 16–21, 1991. Those principles also affect gender equality and sustainable economic and social development.

23   See United Nations Human Rights Office of the High Commissioner, "Once the Breadbasket of Africa, Zimbabwe Now on the Brink of Man-Made Starvation, UN Rights Expert Warnes," Geneva/Harare, November 28, 2019.

24   See Ollen Mwalubunju and Elizabeth Otitodun, *State Reconstruction in Zimbabwe* (Cape Town: Centre for Conflict Resolution, 2011), www.jstor.org/stable/resrep05175. See also Robert I. Rotberg, "Africa's Mess, Mugabe's Mayhem," *Foreign Affairs* 79, no. 5 (2000): 47–61; Tonderayi Mukeredzi, "Zimbabwe's New Land Reforms Don't Go Far Enough," https://foreignpolicy.com/2019/07/31/zimbabwes; "White Farmer Killed in Zimbabwe," *The Guardian* (London), March 18, 2002; and Léa Kalaora, "Madness, Corruption and Exile: On Zimbabwe's Remaining White Commercial Farmers," *Journal of Southern African Studies* 37, no. 4 (2011): 747–62.

25   Danielle Paquette, "The Mystery of Paul Biya, Cameroon's Unusual Absent President: 'Sir, Are You Alive?" *Washington Post*, April 16, 2020. President Biya took office in 1982 and has been in power for thirty-eight years without stepping down.

26   Jason Burk, "Paul Kagame Re-Elected President with 99% of Vote in Rwanda Election," *The Guardian* (London), August 3, 2017. I owe immense gratitude to a friend and colleague who told me more about President Kagame. I was surprised when I learned from an acquaintance of President Kagame that he does not speak French. While Kagame has since acquired a little French-speaking skill, he was educated and spent formative years in Uganda. Kagame's relations with France have been terrible until very

recently. During the early 1990s, the French saw the RPF as an Anglophone force as it emerged among long-exiled Rwandans in Uganda.

27 Kagame's dubious "landslide" electoral victory mirrored his Congolese counterpart (Congo Brazzaville), President Denis Sassou Nguesso, who in March 2016 extended his thirty-two-year rule with an improbable third-term election victory. See Cono Gaffey, "Congo's Denis Sassou Nguesso Extends 32-Year Rule," *Newsweek*, March 24, 2016. During the election mired in fraud, the president ordered a communication blackout to prevent all mobile and internet communications. For Kagami's 2017 election, see James Munyaneza, "Kagame Wins Rwanda Poll by a Landslide," *The New Times* (Kigali), August 5, 2017. Clement Uwiringiyimana, "Rwanda's Kagame Wins Third Presidential Term by Landslide," *Reuters*, August 4, 2017. In the Democratic Republic of the Congo (DRC), President Joseph Kabila, who had held power for seventeen years, extended his tenure two years before stepping down on January 24, 2019, for Felix Tshisekedi. See AFP, "Joseph Kabila Maintains Suspense over Election Plans," *The East African*, July 20, 2018, https://www.theeastafrican.co.ke/news/africa/DR-Congo-Joseph-Kabila-maintains-suspense-over-plans/4552902-4672640-ua7kmnz/index.html.

28 Mo Ibrahim Foundation, 2015 Ibrahim Index of African Governance—Index Report, 2015, 4; Mo Ibrahim Foundation, 2017 Ibrahim Index of African Governance—Index Report, 2017, 13, 21, 28.

29 See Senator Rick Scott, "Open Letter to His Royal Highness, the Prince of Wales," Washington, DC, February 8, 2019. In the message, Senator Scott suggested Prince Charles should visit Florida instead.

30 RT. Hon. (Sir) Alan Duncan, MP (Foreign and Commonwealth Office [London]), to Senator Rick Scott (United States Senate, Washington, D.C.), February 19, 2019, https://www.rickscott.senate.gov/sen-rick-scott-prince-charles-trip-cuba-sends-wrong-message.

31 For the Queen-Gorbachev meetings, see David Remnick, "Gorbachev's Royal Coup: Her Majesty to Come Calling," *Washington Post*, April 8, 1989.

32 See HRH Prince, Charles, "Respect for the Earth—A Royal View," The BBC Reith Lectures, May 16, 2000.

33 Richard Dawkins to Prince Charles, an Open Letter, "The Prince and the Great Debate. Don't Turn Your Back on Science," *Sunday Observer* (London), May 21, 2000.

34 Latifa Yedroudj, "Prince Charles' Views on Religion Could Force Him to GIVE UP Throne—'ABDICATION,'" *Express* (London), August 25, 2018.

35 Yedroudj, "Prince Charles' Views on Religion." As hysterical as the report might sound, Prince Charles's views on religion and the state were not entirely different from those held by most members of the House of Lords. See HL Deb 22 May 2002, vol. 635 cc769–816, Church and State.

36 HRH Prince Charles, "Prince Warns of 'Playing God,'" *BBC News* (London), May 17, 2000.

37 Gilbert Ross, "The Prince of Darkness," American Council on Science and Health, New York, May 26, 2000.

38 See Editor, "Rwanda Confirms Hosting of CHOGM in 2020," *East African Business Week* (Kampala), September 25, 2019.
39 Asmita Parshotam, interviews with Benita van Eyssen, "The Commonwealth Still Relevant for Africa?" April 20, 2018, https://www.dw.com/en/the-commonwealth-still-relevant-for-africa-today/a-43474891.
40 Seymour Martin Lipset, *Political Man: The Social Basis of Politics* (London: Heinemann, 1960), 1–54.
41 Leroy Vail, "Introduction: Ethnicity in Southern African History," in *The Creation of Tribalism in Southern Africa*, ed. Leroy Vail (Berkeley: University of California Press, 1991), 1.
42 Seymour Martin Lipset, "Some Social Requisites for Democracy, Economic Development and Political Legitimacy," *American Political Science Review* 53, no.1 (1959): 69–105. See also Seymour Martin Lipset, "The Social Requisites of Democracy Revisited," *American Sociological Review* 59 (1994): 1–22.
43 Press Release, "Commonwealth Investment Council Chief Wants Nigeria as Post-BREXIT Trade Ally," *Premium Times*, Abuja, February 12, 2018; Chijioke Nelson, "What Global Investors Are Looking for in Nigeria," *The Guardian Business News* (Lagos), November 25, 2019; and Chinwendu Obienyi, "Good Infrastructure Will Turn Nigeria into Investment Hub –Marland, CWEIC Boss," *The Sun* (Port Harcourt), January 6, 2020.
44 Parshotam, "Commonwealth Still Relevant for Africa?" April 20, 2018.
45 See Toyin Falola and Raphael Chijioke Njoku, *United States and African Relations, 1400s to the Present* (New Haven, CT: Yale University Press, 2020).
46 Owei Lakemfa, "The African Road to China," *Vanguard* (Lagos), August 24, 2018.
47 Timothy S. Rich and Sterling Recker, "Understanding Sino-African Relations: Neocolonialism or a New Era?" *Journal of International and Area Studies* 20, no. 1 (2013): 61–76; and David Zweig and Bi Jianhai, "China's Global Hunt for Energy," *Foreign Affairs* 84, no. 5 (2005): 25–38.
48 David Zweig and Jianhai Bi, China's Global Hunt for Energy," *Foreign Affairs* 84, no. 5 (2005): 25–38.
49 Wei Zhang, "The Allure of the Chinese Model," *International Herald Tribune*, November 2006; and Rich and Recker, "Understanding Sino-African Relations," 61.
50 Anna Katharina Stahl, *EU-China-Africa Trilateral Relations in a Multipolar World: Hic Sunt Dracones* (New York: Palgrave MacMillan, 2017), 2.
51 Anna Katharina Stahl, "Fostering African Development, Governance and Security through Multilateral Cooperation between China and Western Donors: The Case of China-DAC Study Group," in *China-Africa Relations: Governance, Peace and Security*, ed. Mulugeta Gebrehiwot Berhe and Liu Hongwu (Addis Ababa: Institute of Peace and Security–Addis Ababa University, 2013), 79.
52 Emilian Kavalski, Review: *China's Struggle for Status: The Realignment of International Relations* by Yong Deng, *Europe-Asia Studies* 61, no. 8 (2009): 1499–1500.
53 David H. Shinn, "An Opportunistic Ally: China's Increasing Involvement in Africa," *Harvard International Review* 29, no. 2 (2007): 52–56; Jin Sato, Hiroaki Shiga,

Takaaki Kobayashi, and Hisahiro Kondoh, "How Do 'Emerging' Donors Differ from 'Traditional' Donors? An Institutional Analysis of Foreign Aid in Cambodia," *JICA Research Institute* No. 2 (2010): 3.

54 Anja Manuel, "China Is Quietly Reshaping the World," *The Atlantic*, October 17, 2017.

55 Immanuel Wallerstein, *The Modern World System I: Capitalist Agriculture and the Origins of the European World Economy in the Sixteenth Century* (New York: Academic Press, 1974), and Immanuel Wallerstein, *The Modern World System II: Mercantilism and the Consolidation of the European World Economy, 1600–1750* (New York: Academic Press, 1980).

56 Richard Drayton, "The Wealth of the West Was Built on Africa's Exploitation," *The Guardian* (London), August 19, 2005.

57 The colonial railway lines needed to be completed because of Britain's unwillingness to invest more funds in the project. See T 161/297/S34608, CP434 (25), East African Development Loan: Cabinet Memorandum by Mr. Amery, October 15, 1925. See also CAB 23/51, CM 50(25)7, October 23, 1925, and Cmd 2463, 1925, Memorandum by the Committee on Trade and Industry, on Transport Development and Cotton Growing in East Africa, 1924–25.

58 Yun Sun, "Africa in Focus: China and the East African Railways: Beyond Full Industry Chain Export," *Brookings*, Washington DC, July 16, 2017; Nicholas Muller, "Chinese Railway Remodeling East Africa," *The Diplomat*, Washington DC, January 25, 2019.

59 Jon Bornman, "Xenophobic South Africa: We Are Sanitizing," *New Frame* (Braamfontein), Johannesburg, July 31, 2020.

60 "South Africa: Attacks on Foreign Nationals," *Human Rights Watch*, April 25, 2019.

Conclusion

1 The forty-six count is determined based on the number of African countries that emerged between the 1950s and 1980s. It was not apparent that some of these states, as we know them today, would appear from the colonial order as sovereign entities. In 1947, only Ethiopia, Liberia, and Egypt were more-or-less independent nations.

2 Thomas Spear, "Neo-Traditionalism and the Limits of Invention in British Colonial Africa," *Journal of African History* 44, no. 1 (2003): 3. Spear's study is a tribute to Leroy Vail, who blazed the path in studying African colonial culture and its complexities. See Leroy Vail, ed., *The Creation of Tribalism in Southern Africa* (Berkeley: University of California Press, 1989).

3 Princess Elizabeth, Speech on Her 21st Birthday, Cape Town, South Africa, April 21, 1947 (hereafter, PE/CTS/SA). In the speech, the princess declared that colonial domination and wanton conflict would not be part of her reign.

4 For the original Frankenstein story, see Mary Wollstonecraft Shelley, *Frankenstein: Or the Modern Prometheus—The 1818 Text* (reprint; Oxford: Oxford University Press, 2009).

5 The British Broadcasting Service (BBC), the loudest propaganda voice under colonial rule, spoke for the British public when it credited the warrior Queen with rescuing the Crown's reputation from her royal uncles' misdeeds. See BBC, "Queen Victoria: The Woman Who Redefined Britain's Monarchy," https://www.bbc.co.uk/teach/ks3-gcse-history-queen-victoria-monarchy/z73rnrd.

6 As highlighted in chapter 2, we see this expression of cynicism in the public speeches and copious writings of African intelligentsia such as Jomo Kenyatta, *Facing Mouth Kenya: The Tribal Life of the Gikuyu with an Introduction by B. Malinowski* (London: Mercury Books, 1938); Kingsley Ozuomba Mbadiwe, *British and Axis Aims in Africa* (New York: Wendell Mallet and Company, 1942); Obafemi Awolowo, *Path to Nigerian* Freedom (London: Faber and Faber, 1947); Hasting K. Banda in CO525/199, 44379/46 no. 1, Letter from Hastings K. Banda to Mr. Creech Jones, Nyasaland, June 14, 1946 [Nyasaland].

7 Caroline M. Elkins, *Legacy of Violence: A History of British Empire* (New York: Alfred A. Knopf, 2022), 24.

8 Angus Mitchell, Review: *Legacy of Violence: A History of British Empire* by Caroline Elkins, *Journal of Colonialism and Colonial History* 24, no. 1 (2023), https://doi.org/10.1353/cch.2023.0002.

9 PE/CTS/SA, Cape Town, South Africa, April 21, 1947. In the speech, the princess declared that colonial domination and wanton conflict would not be part of her reign. This is different from how Angus Mitchell read the address: he interpreted a line from the speech on the princess devoting her life to the "service of the great imperial family" as an "innocent pride" in colonialism. See Mitchell, Review: *Legacy of Violence*, 1.

10 John M. T. Balmer, "A Resource-Based View of the British Monarch as a Corporate Brand," *International Studies of Management and Organization* 37, no. 4 (2007): 20, 28; John M. T. Balmer, "How the British Monarchy Became a Global Brand," *Highbrow Magazine*, May 30, 2023, 2; and John M. T. Balmer, "Scrutinising the British Monarchy: The Corporate Brand that Was Shaken, Stirred and Survived," *Management Decision* 47, no. 4 (2009): 647.

11 Balmer, "How the British Monarchy Became a Global Brand," 1–4. See Balmer, "Scrutinising the British Monarchy," 639–75; and Balmer, "A Resource-Based View of the British Monarch as a Corporate Brand," 20–44.

12 Queen Elizabeth II, to BBC in "Elizabeth R: A Year in the Life of the Queen," Directed by Edward Mirzoeff, released February 6, 1992.

13 See Leopold Bell-Gam, *Ije Odumodu Jere* (London: Longman, 1952). For an interesting analysis of Bell-Gam's Igbo language novel, see Mercy Nnyigide Nkoli, "Migration and Development in Africa: Lessons from *Omenụkọ* and *Ije Odumodu Jere*," *Journal of Popular Education in Africa* 3, no. 2 (2018): 15–26.

14 Being more pro-African under her oath of office would have amounted to national betrayal.

15 For clarity, these personalities served as leaders of different African countries at different ages, but the imposed culture of royal silence remained the same. As a result, Her Majesty never uttered a word when it mattered most.

16 For Oliver Lyttelton's statement, see HC Deb 4 May 1953, vol. 515 cc37–167, Central African Federation, 42, 83, 87
17 John C. Turner, "Explaining the Nature of Power: A Three-Process Theory," *European Journal of Social Psychology* 35 (2005): 1–22.
18 See Bernard M. Bass, *Bass and Stogdill's Handbook of Leadership: Theory, Research, and Managerial Applications Third Edition* (New York: Free Press, 1990), 225–73; Jeffrey Pfeffer, *Managing with Power: Politics and Influence in Organizations* (Boston: Harvard Business School Press, 1992), esp. chap. 4; and John C. Turner, *Social Influence* (Milton Keynes, UK: Open University Press, 1991).
19 Frantz Fanon, *The Wretched of the Earth* (New York: Grove, 1963), 36.
20 James S. Coleman, *Nigeria: Background to Nationalism* (Berkeley: University of California Press, 1958), 237.
21 Ann Laura Stoler and Frederick Cooper, "Between Metropole and Colony: Rethinking a Research Agenda," in *Tensions of Empire: Colonial Cultures in a Bourgeois World*, ed. Ann Laura Stoler and Frederick Cooper (Berkeley: University of California Press, 1997), 1; Michael Collins, "Nation, State and Agency: Evolving Historiographies of African Decolonization," in *Britain, France and the Decolonization of Africa: Future Imperfect?*, ed. Andrew W. M. Smith and Chris Jeppesen (London: University College London Press, 2017), 18–19. The Invention School in African studies emerged in the 1980s under the leadership of Leroy Vail as a framework for understanding the profusion of cultural innovation and practices—including educational, military, ecclesiastical, Republican, and monarchical ideologies—spurred by the Afro-European encounters. See Terence Ranger, "The Invention of Tradition in Colonial Africa," in *The Invention of Tradition*, ed. Eric Hobsbawm and Terence Ranger (Cambridge: Cambridge University Press, 1983), 211.
22 For insights into decolonization as a "balance sheet" historiography, see Erik Gartzke and Dominic Rohner, "The Political Economy of Imperialism, Decolonization and Development," *British Journal of Political Science* 41, no. 3 (2011): 525–56.
23 Wm. Roger Louis, *Imperialism at Bay, 1941–1945: The United States and the Decolonization of the British Empire* (Oxford: Oxford University Press, 1977); Wm. Roger Louis, *The British Empire in the Middle East, 1945–51* (Oxford: Oxford University Press, 1984). See also A. G. Hopkins, "Rethinking Decolonization," *Past and Present* 200 (2008): 211–47; Coleman, *Nigeria*, 236–37.
24 "Welcome to Our Queen and Duke," *Daily Mail* (Freetown), November 25, 1961.
25 For Maya Jasanoff's comment, see Edwin Rios, "Queen's Death Intensifies Criticism of British Empire's Violent Atrocities," *The Guardian* (London), September 10, 2022; Ben Domenech, "The Ignorance of Queen Elizabeth's 'Anti-colonialist' Critics," *The Spectator* (London), September 9, 2022.
26 See Mahmood Mamdani, *Citizens, and Subjects: Contemporary Africa and the Legacy of Late Colonialism* (Princeton, NJ: Princeton University Press, 1996), 62. Mamdani argues that apartheid was "the final step in a long and drawn-out deepening of indirect rule institution."

27 Rasheeduddin Khan, "Commonwealth and the Third World," *Indian Quarterly* 40, no. 1 (1984): 57–88.
28 Terry Evans and Viktor Jakupec, "From Modernization, Dependency and Soft Power Toward a Commonwealth of Learning," *Journal of Learning and Development* 8, no. 3 (2021): 473–86.
29 Marcus Power, "The Commonwealth, 'Development' and Postcolonial Responsibility," *Geoforum* 40, no. 1 (2009): 14–24.
30 A prospective exploration of these diverse and critical views of the Commonwealth has been provided in Khan, "Commonwealth and the Third World." A rejoinder to this is Power's "The Commonwealth, 'Development' and Postcolonial Responsibility," 14–24.
31 Collins, "Nation, State and Agency," 18–19.
32 Don Ross, "Game Theory," *The Stanford Encyclopedia of Philosophy* (Fall 2021 Edition), ed. Edward N. Zalta, https://plato.stanford.edu/archives/fall2021/entries/game-theory/. Emphasis in original.
33 The tendency for Britons and other commentators not to see something wrong with the history of colonialism has been a constant problem in Empire history. Shailja Patel, cited in Rael Ombuor, Rachel Chason, and Meena Venkataramanan, "In Former British Colonies, Ghosts of Past Haunt Mourning for Queen," *Washington Post*, September 12, 2022.
34 Sipho Hlongwane, cited in Ombuor, Chason, and Venkataramanan, "In Former British Colonies."
35 For Maya Jasanoff's comment, see Edwin Rios, "Queen's Death Intensifies Criticism of British Empire's Violent Atrocities," *The Guardian* (London), September 10, 2022; Domenech, "The Ignorance of Queen Elizabeth's 'Anti-colonialist' Critics."
36 Louis C. Jonker, "Why History Matters: The Place of Historical Consciousness in a Multidimensional Approach Towards a Biblical Interpretation in Original Research," *Verbum et Ecclesia* 34, no. 2 (2013): 1–7.
37 Natasha Robinson, "Developing Historical Consciousness for Social Cohesion: How South African Students Learn to Construct the Relationship between Past and Present," in *Historical Justice and History Education*, ed. Matilda Keynes, Henrick Astrom Elmerijo, Daniel Lindmark, and Bjorn Norlin (London: Palgrave Macmillan, 2021), 341–63.
38 Michel-Rolph Trouillot, *Silencing the Past: Power and the Production of History* (Boston: Beacon, 1995), 27. See also James Miles, "Historical Silences and the Enduring Power of Counter Storytelling," *Curriculum Inquiry* 49, no. 3 (2019); 253–59.
39 For instance, when the US basketball superstar Kyrie Irving posted antisemitic comments on social media in November 2022, his famous shoe brand, sponsored by Nike, was canceled.
40 Arthur Chapman and Caitriona Ni Cassaithe, "Sounding the Silences: History, Revision and Inclusion," *Public History Weekly* 10 (2022): 1–2.
41 Michael Freeman, *Concealing Silences and Inaudible Voices in Political Thinking* (Oxford: Oxford University Press, 2022). 153.

42 Derek Brown, "1956: Suez and the End of Empire," *The Guardian* (London), March 14, 2001. For a similar comment, see John M. Mackenzie, "The Persistence of Empire in Metropolitan Culture," in *British Culture and the End of Empire*, ed. Stuart Ward (Manchester, UK: Manchester University Press, 2001), 21–36; and David Cannadine, *Ornamentalism: How the British Saw Their Empire* (London: Allen Lane, 2001), 115–20.

43 For the reference to "old pig," see National Archives, KEW, PREM 11/5039, Visit of Ian Smith, Prime Minister of Southern Rhodesia, to UK, September 1964; records of meeting with Prime Minister. For the official policy of delay, see PREM 11/5048, Constitutional Development in Africa: Part 3, 1964.

44 Buchi Opene and Adamson Momoh, "Ibiam: Apostle of Morality," *Times International* (Lagos): December 8, 1986, 11; "Dick Tiger Joins Biafra Army," *Biafra Telegraph*, January 31, 1968; Dave Anderson, "Dick Tiger, 42, Nigerian Boxer Who Won World Titles, Dead," *New York Times*, December 16, 1971; and Gloria Emerson, "John Lennon Returns Award as a Protest," *New York Times*, November 26, 1969.

45 Frederick Forsyth, "Buried for 50 Years: Britain's Role in the Biafran War," *The Guardian* (London), January 21, 2020. For a study on Nigerian oil's role in Britain's policy, see Chibuike Uche, "Oil, British Interests and the Nigerian Civil War," *Journal of African History* 49 (2008): 111–35. It was revealed that the narrative accepted by the Commonwealth Relations Office and the BBC emanated from the British ambassador to Nigeria. Described as a racist egomaniac, Hunt enjoyed seeing Africans freeze "to attention when he entered the room—which Gowon did. At their single prewar meeting, Ojukwu did not. Hunt loathed him at once."

46 FCO 25/232, no 32, Nigeria: the secession of Eastern Nigeria: Despatch from Sir D. Hunt (Lagos) to Mr. Bowden reporting the declaration of independence by the new Republic of Biafra, June 9, 1967.

47 As a reminder, Elizabeth acted as a symbol of the British postwar identity that, by its nature, thrives on soft power. The Crown forewent a substantial portion of her royal authority and privileges at the Parliament's request in 1952. This compromise was made to foster a vision of a new British nation as a compassionate entity embodied in the postwar Commonwealth. The changes encroached on and often impeded her capacity to act, but Elizabeth's plans for her father's former colonial subjects persevered.

48 Buchi Emecheta, *The Joys of Motherhood* (London: Allison and Busby, 1979).

49 Prince William, the Duke of Wales, stated the obvious in Lord Hurd's *Elizabeth II: The Steadfast*: after more than ninety years, we see the incredible changes to the world since the Queen was born. Yet, the virtues of charity, family, duty, and compassion persevere." See Prince William cited in Simon Perry, "A Queen for All Times," in "Queen Elizabeth at 90," special edition, *Life*, April 1, 2016, 8. See Douglas Hurd, *Elizabeth II: The Steadfast* (London: Penguin, 2016).

BIBLIOGRAPHY

ARCHIVAL SOURCES

National Archives of Ghana, Accra
National Archives of Ireland, Dublin
National Archives of Kenya, Moi
National Archives of Nigeria, Benin
National Archives of Nigeria, Calabar
National Archives of Nigeria, Enugu
National Archives of Nigeria, Ibadan
National Archives of Nigeria, Kaduna
National Archives of Sierra Leone, Freetown
National Archives of The Gambia, Banjul
National Archives of the United Kingdom, Kew
National Archives Zimbabwe
UK Parliament – Parliamentary Archives, London

ORAL SOURCES

Anosike, Catherine. Owerri, Nigeria, December 21, 2008.
Kerubo, John. Mombasa, August 12, 2019.
Ochieng, Peter. Kampala, January 17, 2020.

NEWSPAPERS AND NEWS MAGAZINES

African Business Magazine	London
Africanews	Pointe-Noire/Lyon
Baltimore Sun	Baltimore
Bantu Mirror	Bulawayo

Belfast Telegraph	Belfast
Biafra Telegraph	Aba
Birmingham Daily Post	Birmingham
Bradford Observer	Yorkshire
Britannia and Eve	London
Chicago Daily Tribune	Chicago
Coventry Evening Telegraph	Coventry
Crown Chronicles	London
Daily Express	London
Daily Graphic	Accra
Daily Mail	London
Daily Mirror	London
Daily Monitor	Kampala
Daily Nation	Mombasa
Daily Telegraph	London
Das Reich	Berlin
Diamond Fields Advertiser	Kimberley
Dundee Courier	Dundee
East Africa	Kampala
East African Business Week	Kampala
East African Standard	Nairobi
Evening Express	London
Evening News	Accra
Express	London
Financial Post	Toronto
Financial Times	London
Forbes	New York
Global Times	Beijing
Gold Coast Leader	Accra
Gold Coast Times	Accra
Gold Coast Weekly Review	Accra
Imvo Zanbantsundu	King Williams Town
Independent	London
Indian Opinion	Durban
International Herald Tribune	Paris
Kenya Weekly News	Nairobi
Life	Tampa
Lisburn Herald, and Antrim and Down Advertiser	Antrim
Liverpool Echo,	Lancashire
Malaya Tribune	Singapore
Manchester Guardian	Manchester
Mombasa Times	Mombasa
Monitor	Kampala

Natal Mercury	Durban
New Frame	Braamfontein
New York Times	New York
Newsweek	New York
NEWZ PCST	Kampala
Nigerian Pioneer	Lagos
People	New York
People's Daily	Beijing
Premium Times	Abuja
Punch	Lagos
Reading Evening Post	Berkshire
Reuters	London
Shields Daily News	Northumberland
Standard	London
Sunday Independent	Dublin
Sunday Mirror	London
Sunday Observer	London
Sunday Times	London
Tell	Lagos
The Ashanti Sentinel	Kumasi
The Atlantic	Washington, DC
The Birmingham Post,	London
The Conversation	Melbourne
The Courier Mail	Brisbane
The Daily Mail	London
The Daily Squib	London
The Daily Telegraph	London
The Derby Journal	London
The Diplomat	Washington, DC
The East African	Nairobi
The Economic Times	London
The Economist	London
The Evening Telegraph	London
The Express	London
The Fortnightly Review	London
The Gazette	London
The Ghanaian Times	Accra
The Guardian	London
The Guardian Business News	Lagos
The Herald	London
The Illustrated London News	London
The Independent	Kampala
The London Gazette	London

The New Times	Kigali
The New York Times	New York
The News	Karachi
The Nigerian Daily Times	Lagos
The Observer	Kampala
The Observer	London
The Passive Resister,	Johannesburg
The Scotsman	Edinburgh
The Sidney Morning Herald	Sidney
The Spectator	London
The Sphere	London
The Stage	London
The Standard	Nairobi
The Straits Times	Kuala Lumpur
The Sun	London
The Sun	Port Harcourt
The Sunday Post	Dundee
The Sunderland Daily Echo and Shipping Gazette	Sunderland
The Telegraph	London
The Times	London
The Washington Post	Washington, DC
The Week	Lagos
The Yorkshire Observer	Yorkshire
Time Magazine	New York
Time	London
Time	New York
Times International	Lagos
Times Machine	New York
Ugandan Herald	Kampala
Umteteli	KwaZulu-Natal
United Nations Peacemaker	Nairobi
Vanguard	Lagos
Vogue	New York
Washington Post	Washington, DC
West Africa	London
West African Pilot	Lagos
Yorkshire	Leeds

DOCUMENTARY FILMS

Barbet Schroeder, *Général Idi Amin Dada: Autoportrait [General Idi Amin Dada, A Self Portrait]*. Documentary History, DVD 90 minutes, 1974. Produced by Jean-Francois Chauvel, Charles-Henri Favrod, and Jean-Pierre Rassam.
British Broadcasting Corporation. "Royal Tour of South Africa." Original Broadcast June 2, 1947. Available at https://www.bbc.co.uk/archive/royal-tour-of-south-africa-1947/zbyrpg8.
British Broadcasting Corporation. News Program. London, November 26, 1969. Available at https://genome.ch.bbc.co.uk/schedules/service_bbc_one_london/1969-11-26.
British Film Institute (BFI). "Sierra Leone Greets the Queen." 1961. Available at https://www.youtube.com/watch?v=9x_56-r8w0w.
British Film Institute (BFI). "General Idi Amin Dada: A Self Portrait." People and Politics, S. Hall (Director), Thames Television, June 20, 1974. Available at: https://www.youtube.com/watch?v=MicociKnptI.
British Film Institute (BFI). "Queen Greets Haile Selassie." Portsmouth, Hampshire, and London, 1954 www.youtube.com/watch?v=46l17LlB6-M.
British Film Institute (BFI). "Queen in Nigeria." FILM ID#: 2532.14 1956. Available at https://www.youtube.com/watch?v=cNAP9noiyD8.
British Film Institute (BFI). Record C, Reel 2, 1961. Available at www.youtube.com/watch?v=hqaSoBjD-N4.
British Film Institute (BFI). *Drums for a Queen*, Record C, Reel 2, 1961. Available at https://www.britishpathe.com/asset/75236/.
British Film Institute (BFI). "Tour of Triumph." London, 1965. www.youtube.com/watch?v=J-2l0xzGSIU.
King Bruce and the Black Beats. "The Queen's Visit." In Golden Highlife Classics, Retro3CD. Available at https://www.last.fm/music/King+Bruce+&+The+Black+Beats/_/the+queen's+visit.
King Edward VIII. Radio Address, December 11, 1936. Available at https://www.youtube.com/watch?v=XIaFLax4pL4.

ARTICLES, BOOKS AND MISCELLANEOUS

Alldridge, Thomas Joshua. *The Sherbro and Its Hinterland*. London: Macmillan, 1901.
Anderson, David. *Histories of the Hanged: The Dirty War in Kenya and the End of Empire*. New York: W.W. Norton and Company, 2005.
Anderson, David and Richard Grove. "Introduction: The Scramble for Eden: Past, Present and Future in African Conservation." In *Conservation in Africa: People, Policy and Practices*. Edited by David Anderson and Richard Grove, 1-12 Cambridge: Cambridge University Press, 1987.

Arnstein, Walter L. "The Warrior Queen: Reflections on Victoria and Her World." Presidential Address delivered at the North American Conference on British Studies at Asilomar, California, on November 1, 1997.

Aronson, Theo. *Crown in Conflict: The Triumph and Tragedy of European Monarchy, 1910-1918*. Manchester, NH: Salem House Press, 1986.

Article 22 of the League of Nations Covenant. "The Status of Mandated Areas in Africa." Signed on June 28, 1919.

Austen, Jane. *Pride and Prejudice with Illustrations by Hugh Thomson*. London: Printed for T. Egerton by Military Library Whitehall, 1813.

Awolowo, Obafemi. *Path to Nigerian Freedom*. London: Faber and Faber, 1947.

Ayandele, E.A. *The Educated Elite in Nigerian Society*. Ibadan: Ibadan University Press, 1974.

Bagehot, Walter. *The English Constitution Second Edition*. London: Chapman and Hall, 1867.

Baker, Aaron. "Sports Films, History, and Identity." *Journal of Sport History* 25, no. 2 (1998): 217-233.

Baker, Colin. *Sir Glyn Jones: A Proconsul in Africa*. London: Bloomsbury Academic Press, 2000.

Balala, Najib. "Tourism Sector Performance Report." Nairobi: Ministry of Tourism and Wildlife, 2019.

Balewa, Abubakar Tafawa. *Mr. Prime Minister: A Selection of Speeches Made by Alhaji, the Right Honorable Sir Abubakar Tafawa Balewa, K.B.E., M.P., Prime Minister of the Federal Republic of Nigeria*. Apapa: Nigerian National Press, 1964.

Balmer, John M.T. "A Resource-Based View of the British Monarch as a Corporate Brand." *International Studies of Management and Organization* 37, no. 4 (2007): 20-44.

———. "Scrutinising the British Monarchy: The Corporate Brand that was Shaken, Stirred and Survived." *Management Decision* 47, no. 4 (2009): 639-675.

———. "How the British Monarchy Became a Global Brand." *Highbrow Magazine*, May 30, 2023.

Bangura, Joseph J. *The Temne of Sierra Leone: African Agency in the Making of a British Colony*. Cambridge: Cambridge University Press, 2017.

Barnum, P.T. *The Humbugs of the World: An Account of the Humbugs, Delusions, Impositions, Quackeries, Deceits and Deceivers Generally, in All Ages*. New York: Carleton Publishers, 1866.

Bass, Bernard M. *Bass and Stogdill's Handbook of Leadership: Theory, Research, and Managerial Applications Third Edition*. New York: The Free Press, 1990.

Bentley, D.J. "John Rawls: A Theory of Justice." *University of Pennsylvania Law Review* 121, no. 5 (1973): 1070-1078.

Berlin, Isaiah. *Four Essays on Liberty*. Oxford: Oxford University Press, 1969.

Black, David R. and Janis van der Westhuizen. "Editorial: The Neglected Allure of Global Games?" *Third World Quarterly* 25, no. 7 (2004): 1191-1194.

Blommaert Jan and Chris Bulcaen. "Critical Discourse Analysis." *Annual Review of Anthropology* 29 (2000): 447-466.

Bogdanor, Vernon. *The Monarchy and the Constitution*. Oxford, Oxford University Press, 1995.

Booth, Douglas. "Hitting Apartheid for Six? The Politics of the South African Sports Boycott." *Journal of Contemporary History* 38, no. 3 (2003): 477-493.

Booth, Margaret Zoller. *Culture and Education: The Social Consequences of Western Schooling in Contemporary Swaziland*. Dallas: University Press of America, 2004.

Brendon, Piers. *The Decline and Fall of the British Empire, 1781-1997*. New York: Vintage Books, 2010.

Brett, E.A. "Rebuilding War-Damaged Communities in Uganda in the late 1980s." In *In Search of Cool Grounds: War, Flight, and Homecoming in Northeast Africa*. Edited by Tim Allen, 203-219. Trenton, NJ: African World Press, 1996.

British Documents on the End of Empire, Series B, Volume 1 Ghana. Edited by Richard Rathbone. London: Her Majesty's Stationery Office, 1992.

British Documents on the End of Empire Project Volume 4, The Conservative Government and the End of Empire 1957-1964 (in two parts). Edited by Ronald Hyam and Wm Roger Louis. London: The Stationery Office, 2000.

British Documents on the End of Empire Project. Volume 9, Central Africa, Part I: Closer Association, 1945-1958. Edited by Philip Murphy. London: The Stationery Office, 2005.

Broad, C.D. "Lord Hugh Cecil's 'Conservatism.'" *International Journal of Ethics* 23, no. 4 (1913): 396-419.

Burke, Edmund. *Reflections on the Revolution in France*. Edited by J.G.A. Pocock. Cambridge, MA: Hackert, 1987.

Canessa, Andrew, Ed., *Bordering on Britishness: National Identity in Gibraltar from the Spanish Civil War to Brexit*. New York: Palgrave Macmillan, 2019.

Cannadine, David. "The Context, Performance, and Meaning of Ritual: The British Monarchy and the 'Invention of Tradition,' c. 1820–1977." In *The Invention of Tradition*. Edited by Eric Hobsbawm and Terence Ranger, 157-163. Cambridge: Cambridge University Press, 1983.

———. "The Last Hanoverian Sovereign? The Victorian Monarchy in Historical Perspective, 1688–1988." In *The First Modern Society: Essays in English History in Honour of Lawrence Stone*. Edited by A.L. Beier, David Cannadine, and James M. Rosenheim, 127-166. Cambridge: Cambridge University Press, 1989.

———. *Ornamentalism: How the British Saw Their Empire*. London: Allen Lane, 2001.

———. "Churchill and the British Monarchy." *Transactions of the Royal Historical Society* 11 (2001): 249-272.

Central Intelligence Agency. Office of National Estimates, Staff Memorandum No.85-63, December 19, 1963.

Chapman, Arthur and Caitriona Ni Cassaithe. "Sounding the Silences: History, Revision and Inclusion." *Public History Weekly* 10 (2022): 1-2.

Charmley, John. *Splendid Isolation? Britain, the Balance of Power, and the Origins of the First World War*. London: Faber and Faber, 1999.

Charter of the Commonwealth. Signed by Her Majesty Queen Elizabeth II (CC-HMQE), Head of the Commonwealth, Commonwealth Day 2013.

Chernock, Arianne. "The Persistent Monarchy." September 5, 2012. Accessed December 3, 2019. www.publicbooks.org/the-persistence-of-monarchy/.

Chiudza, Paul Banda and Gift Wasambo Kayira. "The 1959 State of Emergency in Nyasaland: Process and Political Implications." *The Society of Malawi Journal* 65, no. 2 (2012): 1-19.

CHOGM. "Lusaka Declaration on Racism and Racial Prejudice." Lusaka, Zambia, August 1-7, 1979.
———. "Melbourne Declaration." Melbourne, Australia, September 30 – October 7, 1981.
———. "Goa Declaration of International Security." Goa, India, November 23-29, 1983.
———. "Nassau Declaration on World Order." Nassau, The Bahamas, October 16-22, 1985.
———. "Vancouver Declaration on World Order." Vancouver, Canada, October 13-17, 1987.
———. "Langkawi Declaration on the Environment." Kuala Lumpur, Malaysia, October 18-24, 1989.
———. "Ottawa Declaration on Women and Structural Adjustment Program." Ottawa, Canada, October 9-12, 1990.
———. "Aso Rock Declaration on Development and Democracy: Partnership for Peace and Prosperity." Abuja, Nigeria, December 3-8, 2003.
———. "The Millbrook Commonwealth Action Program on the Harare Declaration." Auckland, New Zealand, November 10-15, 1995.
———. "Harare Declaration." Lusaka, Zimbabwe, October 16-21, 1991.
———. "Kampala Declaration on Transforming Societies to Achieve Political, Economic, and Human Development, Kampala." Uganda, November 23-25, 2007.
———. Communique After Retreat. London, April 20, 2018.
Chouli, Lila. "The Popular Uprising in Burkina Faso and the Transition." *Review of African Political Economy* 42, no. 144 (2015): 325-333.
Churchill, Winston S. "Sinews of Peace," or "An Iron Curtain Has Descended." A Speech at Westminster College, Fulton, Missouri, March 5, 1946. At Churchill Press Photographs, Churchill Archive Center, Cambridge, CHPH 1A/FA/4A, Associated Press, 343-353.
———. "The Coronation of Elizabeth II: An Introduction to the Royal Broadcast." June 2, 1953. Published in Winston S. Churchill, *The Unwritten Alliance, Speeches 1953-1959*. New York: Rosetta Books, 1961.
———. *Never Give In! The Best of Winston Churchill's Speeches*. Edited by Winston S. Churchill. New York: Hyperion, 2003.
Clarke, Peter B. *West Africans at War, 1914-18, 1939-45. Colonial Propaganda and its Cultural Aftermath*. London: Ethnographica, 1986.
Clayton, Anthony and Donald Cockfield Savage. *Government and Labour in Kenya 1895-1963*. London: Routledge, 2012.
Coleman, James S. *Nigeria: Background to Nationalism*. Berkeley: University of California Press, 1958.
Collins, Michael. "Nation, State and Agency: Evolving Historiographies of African Decolonization." In *Britain, France and the Decolonization of Africa: Future Imperfect?* Edited by Andrew W.M. Smith and Chris Jeppesen, 17-42. London: University College London Press, 2017.
Commonwealth Business Council. *Globalization: Policies, Strategies, and Partnerships Edited Papers of the Commonwealth Business Forum 2000*. London: Commonwealth Business Forum, 2000.
Commonwealth Secretariat. *Commonwealth Information News Release* (London), 78/51, June 18, 1973.

———. *Strategic Plan, 2013/14 – 2016-17*. Approved by the Commonwealth Secretariat Board of Governors, May 23, 2013.

Connelly, Mark. *We can Take! Britain and the Memory of the Second World War*. London: Routledge, 2004.

Constantine, Stephen. "Monarchy and Constructing Identity in 'British' Gibraltar, c.1800 to the Present." *Journal of Imperial and Commonwealth History* 34, no. 1 (2006): 23-44.

Cook, Albert. "The Ordering Effect of Dramatized History: Shakespeare and Henry VIII." *The Centennial* 42, no. 1 (1998): 5-28.

Crawford, Marion and Jennie Bond. *The Little Princesses: The Story of the Queen's Childhood by Her Nanny, Marion Crawford*. New York: St. Martin's Griffin, 2020.

Dada, Idi Amin. "Economic Honeymoon Letter to Queen Elizabeth II." Kampala, January 1975.

Darwin, John. *Britain and Decolonization. The Retreat from Empire in the Post-War World*. London: St. Martin's Press, 1988.

Davies, Nicholas. *Elizabeth: Behind Palace Doors*. Edinburgh: Mainstream Publishing Projects, 2000.

Datta, Arunima. *Fleeting Agencies: A Social History of Indian Coolie Women in British Malaya*. Cambridge: Cambridge University Press, 2021.

Deakin, Ralph. *Southward Ho! The Tour of the Prince of Wales to Africa and South America*. Philadelphia: Lippincott, 1926.

Delafosse, Karina. "The Death of Queen Elizabeth II is a Reminder of the Pain of British Colonialism." *Local Today*, September 12, 2022.

Department of State. Central Files, 033.45J11/7–2458. A Memorandum of a Conversation with Under Secretary of State Herter concerning Ghana's Economic Aims, Conference Files: Lot 63 D 123, Nkrumah Visit.

Diamond, Jon, Peter Denis. *Archibald Wavell: Leadership, Strategy, Conflict*. London: Bloomsbury Publishing, 2012.

Dimbleby, Jonathan. *The Prince of Wales: A Biography*. London: Little, Brown and Co. 1994.

Dijn, A. de. "A Pragmatic Conservatism. Montesquieu and the Framing of the Belgian Constitution (1830–1831)." *History of European Ideas* 28 (2002): 227-245.

DK. *Queen Elizabeth and the Royal Family: A Glorious Illustrated History*. Edited by Constance Novis. London: Penguin Random House, 2015.

Dodds, Klaus, David Lambert, and Bridget Robinson. "Loyalty and Royalty: Gibraltar, the 1953–54 Royal Tour and the Geopolitics of the Iberian Peninsula." *Twentieth Century British History* 18, no. 3 (2007): 365–390.

Duncan, Alan. Foreign and Commonwealth Office, London to Senator Rick Scott. United States Senate, Washington, DC. February 19, 2019. Accessed August 3, 2020. www.rickscott.senate.gov/sen-rick-scott-prince-charles-trip-cuba-sends-wrong-message.

Earle, Jonathan L. *Colonial Buganda and the End of Empire: Political Thought and Historical Imagination in Africa*. Cambridge: Cambridge University Press, 2017.

Echeruo, Michael J.C. *In Victorian Lagos: Aspects of Nineteenth Century Lagos Life*. London: Macmillan, 1977.

Edward, H.R.H. Duke of Windsor. *A King's Story: The Memoirs of H.R.H. the Duke of Windsor K.G.* London: Cassell, 1951.

Eisenhower, Dwight D. "Inaugural Address." Washington, DC, January 20, 1953.

———. Public Papers of the President of the United States Dwight D. Eisenhower, 1957. Washington. DC: U.S. Government Printing Office, 1958.

———. Address Before the 15th General Assembly of the United Nations. New York, September 22, 1960.

El-Khawas, Mohamed A. "South Africa: A Challenge to OAU." *Africa Today* 24, no. 3 (1974): 25-41.

Elkins, Caroline M. *Legacy of Violence: A History of British Empire*. New York: Alfred A. Knopf, 2022.

Elvin, H. Lionel. "First Commonwealth Education Conference Oxford, July 1959." *International Review of Education* 6, no. 1 (1960): 79-82.

Emperor of Ethiopia. *1955 Revised Constitution of Ethiopia*. Chapter 1, Article II: "The Ethiopian Empire and the Succession to the Throne." Addis Ababa, Ethiopia, November 4, 1955.

Ethiopian News and Views. "Ethiopia: Golden Tray, Emperor Haile Selassie's Gift to Queen Elizabeth." Addis Ababa, September 7, 2017.

EuroStat Archives. EU-Commonwealth of Independent States CIS Statistics on GDP. March 10, 2017. Accessed June 1, 2020. https://ec.europa.eu/eurostat/statistics-explained/index.php?title=Archive:EU-Commonwealth_of_Independent_States_(CIS)_-_statistics_on_GDP&oldid=330099.

Evans, Peter William. "Astaire and Rogers: Carefree in Roberta." In *Hollywood and the Great Depression: American Film, Politics and Society in the 1930s*. Edited by Iwan Morgan and Philip John Davies, 124-138. Edinburgh: Edinburgh University Press, 2016.

Expenditure Survey Report 2001. Uganda Final Report. Kampala: Uganda Bureau of Statistics, 2001.

Fairclough, Norman. *Discourse and Social Change*. Cambridge: Cambridge University Press, 1992.

Falola, Toyin and Raphael Chijioke Njoku. *United States African Relations, 1400s to the Present*. New Haven, CT: Yale University Press, 2020.

Fanon, Frantz. *The Wretched of the Earth*. New York: Grove Press, 1963.

Feuerlicht, Ignace. "A New Look at the Iron Curtain." *American Speech* 30, no. 3 (1955): 186–189.

Finnegan, Ruth and David Murray. "Limba Chiefs." In *West African Chiefs: Their Changing Status Under Colonial Rule*. Edited by Michael Crowder and Obaro Ikime, 416-419. Ile-Ife, Nigeria: Africana Publishing Company, 1970.

Flint, John. "Planned Decolonization and Its Failures in British Africa." *African Affairs* 82, no. 328 (1983): 389-411.

FOCAC. The Chinese Ministry of Foreign Affairs. Accessed January 17, 2020. www.focac.org/eng/.

Forman, F.N. *Constitutional Change in the United Kingdom*. London: Routledge, 2002.

Fournier, Susan and Lara Lee. "Getting Brand Communities Right." *Harvard Business Review* (2008): 1-8.
Freedman, Michael. *Concealing Silences and Inaudible Voices in Political Thinking*. Oxford: Oxford University Press, 2022.
Fyfe, Christopher. *A History of Sierra Leone*. Oxford: Oxford University Press, 1962.
———. *A Short History of Sierra Leone*. London: Longmans, 1962.
Gaines, Kevin K. *African Americans in Ghana: Black Expatriates and the Civil Rights Era*. Chapel Hills: The University of North Carolina Press, 2006.
Gannon, Margaret. "The Basle Mission Trading Company and British Colonial Policy in the Gold Coast, 1918-1928." *The Journal of African History* 24, no.4 (1983): 503-515.
Garzke, Erik, and Dominic Rohner. "The Political Economy of Imperialism, Decolonization and Development." *British Journal of Political Science* 41, no. 3 (2011): 525-556.
Gautam, Urvashi. "Image of the Enemy: German and British propaganda in the Second World War." *Proceedings of the Indian History Congress* 73 (2012): 1099-1106.
Gershoni, Yekutiel. *Africans on African Americans: The Creation and Uses of an African-American Myth*. London: Macmillan, 1997.
Getachew, Adom. *Worldmaking after Empire: The Rise and Fall of Self-Determination*. Princeton: Princeton University Press, 2019.
Gibler, Douglas M. *International Conflicts, 1816-2010: Militarized Interstate Dispute Narratives, Volume I*. Lanham, MD: Rowan and Little, 2018.
Gilbert, Martin. *Never Despair: Winston S. Churchill, 1945-1965*. London: Heinemann, 1988.
Gilley, Bruce. "The Case of Colonialism." *Third World Quarterly* (2017): DOI: 10.1080/01436597.2017.1369037.
Goldsworthy, David. *The Conservative Party and the End of Empire, 1951-1957*. London: The University of London Institute of Commonwealth Studies, 1994.
Government of the Bahamas. 19th Conference of Commonwealth Education Ministers (19CCEM), Nassau, The Bahamas, June 22-26, 2015.
Gray, John. *Liberalism*. Milton Keynes: Open University Press, 1995.
Grundy, Kenneth W. "Nkrumah's Theory of Underdevelopment: An Analysis of Recurrent Themes." *World Politics* 15, no. 3 (1963): 438-454.
Gukiina, Peter. *Uganda: A Case Study in African Political Development*. Notre Dame, ID: University of Notre Dame Press, 1972.
Habermas, Jürgen. *Knowledge and Human Interests*, translated by J. J. Shapiro. Boston: Beacon, 1971.
———. *Theory and Practice*. Translated by J. Viertel. Boston: Beacon, 1973.
———. *The Theory of Communicative Action*, *Vol. I: Reason and Rationalization of Society*. Translated by T. McCarthy. Boston: Beacon, 1984.
Hailey, William Malcolm. *African Survey: A Study of Problems Arising in Africa South of the Sahara*. London: Oxford University Press, 1938.
Hardie, Frank. *The Political Influence of Queen Victoria, 1861-1901, 2nd Edition*. 1935 Reprint. London: Frank Cass, 1938.
Hargreaves, John D. *Decolonization in Africa*. London: Longmans, 1988.
Harris, Wilson. "The Education of the Queen." *The Atlantic*, Boston, MA, December 1943.

Hart-Davis, Duff. Ed. *King's Counsellor: Abdication and War: The Diaries of Alan Lascelles*. London: Weidenfeld and Nicholson, 2006.
Hart, H.L.A. *The Concept of Law*. Oxford: Oxford University Press, 1961.
Hathaway, Robert M. *Great Britain and the United States: Special Relations Since WWII*. Boston: Twayne Publishers, 1990.
Haugevik, Kristin M. and Atle L. Wold. "Churchill the Quotable." In John Callaghan, Martin Gilbert, Richard Overy, Robert McNamara, Richard Toye, Gill Bennett, Kristin M. Haugevik, and Atle L. Wold, "Churchill (1874-1965) Man and Mystery." *British Political Review* 4, no. 4 (2009): 1-12.
Hennessy, Peter. *The Prime Minister: The Office and Its Holder Since 1945*, First Edition. London: St. Martin's Press, 2000.
Henry, Pelling. *Winston Churchill*. London: Macmillan, 1974.
Hensbroek, Pieter Boele van. *Political Discourses in African Thought, 1960 to the Present*. Westport, Connecticut, London: Praeger, 1999.
Hills, Denis Cecil. *The White Pumpkin First Edition*. London: Allen and Unwin, 1975.
HM Queen Elizabeth II. "The Queen's Coronation Oath." June 2, 1953, on BBC TV. Accessed April 17, 2020. www.youtube.com/watch?v=52NTjasbmgw.
———. Address to the United Nations General Assembly. New York, October 21, 1957.
———. Speech Recording, BFI National Archives: "Sierra Leone Greets the Queen." Freetown, November 30, 1961. Accessed February 26, 2020. www.youtube.com/watch?v=9x_56-r8w0w.
———. "A Speech by The Queen at the Commonwealth Heads of Government Meeting in Malta." Valletta, Malta, November 27, 2015.
———. Welcome Address to the Commonwealth of Heads of Government Meeting (CHOGM). London, April 19-20, 2018.
———. "A Message from The Queen to the People of Ethiopia, Bottom of Form, December 21, 2018." Accessed June 12, 2020. www.royal.uk/message-queen-people-ethiopia.
HM Queen Victoria. *The Letters of Queen Victoria. 3rd. 1886-1901, 3rd. Series; a Selection from Her Majesty's Correspondence and Journal Between the Years 1886 and 1901, in 3 Volumes*. Edited by George Earle Buckle. London: John Murray, 1930.
———. Royal Archives (RA) VIC/ADDA27: Speech read by Queen Victoria in Council on the day of her accession, June 20, 1837.
Hodges, Geoffrey. *Kariokor: The Carrier Corps: The Story of the Military Labor Forces in the Conquest of German East Africa, 1914-1918*. Nairobi: Nairobi University Press, 1999.
Hoffer, Carol P. "Mende and Sherbro Women in High Office." *Canadian Journal of African Studies* (1972): 151-164.
Holms, John. "The Impact on the Commonwealth of the Emergence of Africa." *International Organization* 16, no. 2, Special Issue: Africa and International Organization (1962): 291-302.
Hongwu Liu and Geta Gebrhinot Berhe. *China-Africa Relations 2013: Annual Report*. Stellenbosch, South Africa: Center for Chinese Studies, 2013.
Hopkins, A.G. "Rethinking Decolonization." *Past and Present* (2008): 211-247.

Howarth, Caroline. "Representations, Identity, and Resistance in Communication." In *The Social Psychology of Communication*. Edited by Derek Hook, Bradley Franks, and Martin W. Bauer, 153-168. Houndmills, Basingstoke: Palgrave Macmillan, 2011.

Hughes, Kathryn. "Gender Roles in the 19th Century." May 15, 2014. British Library. *Discovering Literature: Romantics & Victorians*. Accessed May 30, 2024. https://www.britishlibrary.cn/en/articles/gender-roles-in-the-19th-century/.

Human Rights Watch. *Burundi: World Report* 2018: Events of 2017. New York: 2018.

———. Report: "Burundi: President Nkurunziza Dead Days After Vote." Nairobi, June 11, 2020.

———. Report: "South Africa: Attacks on Foreign Nationals." April 25, 2019.

Hunter, Ian. "The Commonwealth Arts Festival." *Journal of the Royal Society of Arts* 113, no. 5108 (1965): 605-611.

———. "The Commonwealth Arts Festival." A Speech at a Joint Meeting of the Society's Commonwealth Section with the Royal Commonwealth Society, Northumberland Avenue, London, March 25, 1965.

Hurd, Douglas. *Elizabeth II: The Steadfast*. London: Penguin, 2016.

Hyam, Ronald. *Understanding the British Empire*. Cambridge: Cambridge University Press, 2010.

Ibiam, Francis Akanu. "What About Africa?" An Address delivered by His Excellency, the Governor of Eastern Nigeria Sir Francis Akanu Ibiam, at the Third Assembly of the World Council of Churches. New Delhi, November 18 – December 6, 1961.

Instrument of Abdication. Signed by King Edward VIII and His Three Brothers, Albert (later George VI), Henry, and George, December 10, 1936.

International Bank for Reconstruction and Development (IBRD). No. E.135b 67058, *The Colombo Plan*. Prepared by Antonin Basch, January 23, 1950.

Jackson, Ashley. *Botswana 1939-1945: An African Country at War*. Oxford: Oxford University Press, 1999.

———. *The British Empire and the Second World War*. London: Hambledon Continuum, 2006.

James, Robert Rhodes. Ed. *Winston S. Churchill: His Complete Speeches, 1897–1963* 8 Volumes. London: Chelsea, 1974.

Jefferis, Keith, Sethunya Sejoe, and Kitso Mokhurutshe. *Economic Review, First Quarter*. Gaborone. Botswana, January-March 2019.

Jenkin, Thomas P. "The British General Election of 1951." *The Western Political Quarterly* 5, no. 1 (1952): 51-65.

"John Lennon Returns His MBE." Accessed July 18, 2020. www.youtube.com/watch?v=6m0glhvwhdI on July 18, 2020.

Johnson, David. *World War II, and the Scramble for Labour in Colonial Zimbabwe, 1939-1948*. Harare: University of Zimbabwe Publications, 2000.

Jonker, Louis, C. "Why History Matters: The Place of Historical Consciousness in a Multidimensional Approach Towards a Biblical Interpretation in Original research." *Verbum et Ecclesia* 34, no. 2 (2013): 1-7.

Judd, Denis. *Empire: The British Imperial Experience from 1765 to the Present*. New York: Basic Books, 1998.

Kabaka Yekka. Communiqué: "What News in Buganda." August 28, 1961.
Kabwegyere, Tarsis B. "The Dynamics of Colonial Violence: The Inductive System in Uganda." *Journal of Peace Research* 9, no.4, (1972): 303-314.
Kalu, Agwu. *Dr. Ibiam: The Challenge of his Life*. Aba, Nigeria: The Presbyterian Church of Nigeria, 1986.
Kamau, Peter Ngugi. "Elephants, Local Livelihoods, Landscape Change in Tsavo Kenya." PhD Dissertation, Louisiana State University, 2017.
Kasozi, A.B.K. *The Bitter Bread of Exile: The Financial Problems of Sir Edward Muteesa II During His Exile, 1966-1968*. Kasozi, Kampala: Progressive Publishing House, 2013.
Kavalski, Emilian. Review: *China's Struggle for Status: The Realignment of International Relations by Yong Deng*. *Europe-Asia Studies* 61, no. 8 (2009): 1499-1500.
Keith, Berriedale. "The Imperial Conference of 1930." *Journal of Comparative Legislation and International Law* 13, no. 1 (1931): 26-42.
Kenner, John. *A Forgotten Legacy: Canadian Leadership in the Commonwealth*. Bloomington: Trafford Publishing, 2011.
Kent, John. *British Imperial Strategy the Origins of the Cold War, 1944-49*. Leicester: Leicester University Press, 1993.
Kenyatta, Jomo. *Facing Mouth Kenya: The Tribal Life of the Gikuyu with an Introduction by B. Malinowski*. London: Mercury Books, 1938.
Khan, Rasheeduddin. "Commonwealth and the Third World." *India Quarterly* 40, no. 1 (1984): 57-103.
Khrushchev, Nikita S. "We Will Bury You." Speech for Poland's Mr. Wladyslaw Gomulka Send-Off Reception. Polish Embassy, Moscow, November 18, 1956. CIA declassified File No. CIA-RDP73B00296R00020004, February 7, 1962.
Kilson, Martin L. Jr. "Nationalism and Social Classes in British West Africa." *Journal of Politics* 20, no.2 (1958): 368-387.
Kingsley, Henrietta Mary. *Travels in West Africa*. London: Macmillan, 1897.
Kirk-Green, H. M. "His Eternity, His Eccentricity, or His Exemplarity? A Further Contribution to the Study of H. E. the African Head of State." *African Affairs* 90, no. 359 (1991): 163-187.
Kiste, John Van der. *George V's Children*. 1991. Reprint Stroud. Gloucestershire, 2003.
Korieh, Chima J. *Nigeria and World War II: Colonialism, Empire, and Global Conflict*. Cambridge: Cambridge University Press, 2020.
Korschun, Daniel. "Boundary-Spanning Employees and Relationships with External Stakeholders: A Social Identity Approach." *The Academy of Management Review* 40, no. 4 (2015): 611-629.
Kuhn, William M. "Ceremony and Politics: The British Monarchy, 1871-1872." *Journal of British Studies* 26, no. 2 (1987): 133-162.
Lacey, Robert Lacey. *The Crown: The Official Companion, Volume 1: Elizabeth II, Winston Churchill, and the Making of a Young Queen (1947-1955)*. London: Crown Archetype, 2017.
Lamb, David. *The Africans*. New York: Vintage Books, 1987.

Larcher, Oswald Wilkinson. "The Politics of Canadian Aid to the Commonwealth Caribbean." PhD Dissertation, The University of Waterloo, 1973.

Large, Daniel. "Beyond 'Dragon in the Bush': The Study of China–Africa Relations." *African Affairs* 107, no. 426 (2008): 45-61.

Lasse Heerten and A. Dirk Moses. "The Nigeria-Biafra War: Postcolonial Conflict and the Question of Genocide." *Journal of Genocide Research* 16, no. 2-3 (2014): 169-203.

Leakey, Louis S.B. *The Southern Kikuyu before 1903*. London, Academic Press, 1977.

Leopold, Mark. "'Print the Legend': Myth and Reality in the Last King of Scotland. In *Framing Africa: Portrayals of a Continent in Contemporary Mainstream Cinema*. Edited by Nigel Eltringham, 21-38. Oxford: Berghahn Publishers, 2013.

Levine, Donald. "Haile Selassie's Ethiopia: Myth or Reality." *Africa Today* 8, no. 5 (1961): 11-14.

Lewis, Vaughan A. "Commonwealth Caribbean Relations with Hemispheric Middle Powers." In *Dependency under Challenge: The Political Economy of the Commonwealth Caribbean*. Edited by Anthony Payne and Paul K. Sutton, 238-258. Manchester: Manchester University Press, 1984.

Library of Commonwealth. Document on "The Declaration of Commonwealth Principles, Issued at the Heads of Commonwealth Meeting in Singapore." January 14-22, 1971.

Linden, Ian and Jane Linden. "John Chilembwe and the New Jerusalem." *Journal of African History* 12 (1971): 629-651.

Lipset, Seymour Martin. "Some Social Requisites for Democracy, Economic Development and Political Legitimacy." *American Political Science Review* 53, no.1 (1959): 69-105.

———. *Political Man: The Social Basis of Politics*. London: Heinemann, 1960.

———. "The Social Requisites of Democracy Revisited." *American Sociological Review* 59 (1994): 1–22.

Little, K.L. "The Significance of the West African Creole for Africanist and Afro-American Studies." *African Affairs* 49, no. 197 (1950): 308-319.

Livingstone, David. *Livingstone's African Journal 1853-1863*. Berkeley: University of California Press, 1963.

Louis, William Roger. *Imperialism at Bay, 1941-1945: The United States and the Decolonization of the British Empire*. Oxford: Oxford University Press, 1977.

———. *The British Empire in the Middle East, 1945-51*. Oxford: Oxford University Press, 1984.

Low, D. A. *Buganda in Modern History*. Berkeley: University of California Press, 1971.

Lynch, Hollis R. *K.O. Mbadiwe: A Nigerian Political Biography, 1915-1990*. New York: Palgrave Macmillan, 2012.

Mackenzie, John M. *The Empire of Nature: Hunting, Conservatism and British Imperialism*. Manchester: Manchester University Press, 1988.

———. "The Persistence of Empire in Metropolitan Culture." In *British Culture and the End of Empire*. Edited by Stuart Ward, 21-36. Manchester: Manchester University Press, 2001.

Macmillan, Harold. "Wind of Change in Africa." Cape Town, February 3, 1960.

Mallet, Marie. *Life with Queen Victoria: Marie Mallet's Letters from Court, 1887-1901*. Boston: Houghton Mifflin, 1968.

Mamdani, Mahmood. *Citizens and Subjects: Contemporary Africa and the Legacy of* Late *Colonialism*. Princeton: Princeton University Press, 1996.

Mandela, Nelson. A Speech at the Banquet in Honor of Queen Elizabeth II. London, July 11, 1996.

Marcus, Harold G. "Ethio-British Negotiations Concerning the Western Border with Sudan, 1896-1902." *Journal of African History* 4, no. 1 (1963): 81-94.

———. *The Politics of Empire: Ethiopia, Great Britain and the United States 1941-1974*. Lawrenceville, NJ: Red Sea Press, 1995.

Marcus, Power. "The Commonwealth, 'Development' and Post-Colonial Responsibility.'" *Geoforum* 40, no. 1 (2009): 14-24.

Marr, Andrew. *The Real Elizabeth: An Intimate Portrait of Queen Elizabeth II*. New York: St. Martin's Griffin, 2013.

Marsh, Steve. "Personal Diplomacy at the Summit." In *Churchill and the Anglo-American Special Relations*. Edited by Alan P. Dodson and Steve Marsh, 116-141. New York: Routledge, 2017.

Martin, Michael L. "The Ugandan Military Coup of 1971: A Study of Protest." *Ufahamu: Journal of African Studies* (1972): 81-121.

Mason, Christopher. "Review of Moses Zikusooka's Book Documenting the Queen's Last visit to Uganda." Posted November 15, 2007. Accessed June 10, 2020. https://christophermason.wordpress.com/2007/11/15/review-of-a-book-documenting-the-queens-last-visit-to-uganda/.

Matusevich, Maxim. *No Easy Row for a Russian Hoe: Ideology and Pragmatism in Nigerian-Soviet Relations, 1960–1991*. Trenton, NJ: Africa World Press, 2003.

———. "Ideology and Pragmatism: The Biafra War and Nigeria's Response to the Soviet Union, 1966–1970." *Nigerian Journal of International Affairs* 28, nos. 1-2 (2002): 97–138.

Mbadiwe, Kingsley Ozuomba. *British and Axis Aims in Africa*. New York: Wendell Mallet and Company, 1942.

———. "Thank You Great Britain." Being Text of an Address, published in *West African Pilot*, Lagos, July 15, 1955, 1.

Mbiti, John S. *The Concept of God in Africa*. London: SPCK, 1970.

McBride, James. "The Commonwealth of Nations: Britain and the Future of Global Britain." *Council on Foreign Relations*, March 2, 2020.

McBrown, Gertrude Parthenia. "Prime Minister Kwame Nkrumah." *Negro History Bulletin* 16, no. 5 (1953), 98, 115-116.

McConnachie, James, Shafik Meghji, and David Read. *A Rough Guide to Nepal*. Bermondsey, London: Rough Guide, 2012.

McLaughlin, Peter. "Victims as Defenders: African Troops in the Rhodesian Defence System 1890-1980." *Small Wars and Insurgencies* 2, no. 2 (1991): 240-275.

Meidan, Michal. "China's Africa Policy: Business Now, Politics Later." *Asian Perspective* 30, no. 4 (2006): 69-93.

Melady, Thomas Patrick and Margaret Badum Melady. *Idi Amin Dada: Hitler in Africa*. Kansas City, MO: Sheed Andrews and McNeil, 1977.

Memorandum of Conversation. No. 294 Prime Minister Nkrumah's Talk with the President, July 23, 1958. Eisenhower Library, Whitman File, International File. Secret. Drafted by Deputy Assistant Secretary of State for African Affairs Joseph Palmer 2d.

Meyer, Jean, Jean Tarrade, Anne Rey-Goldzeiger, and Jacques Thobie. *Histoire de la France Coloniale. Volume 2 1914-1990*. Paris: Armand Colin, 1990.

Miles, James. "Historical Silences and the Enduring Power of Counter Storytelling." *Curriculum Inquiry* 49, no. 3 (2019); 253-259.

Mill, J.S. *Utilitarianism, Liberty, and Representative Government*. With Introduction by A.D. Lindsay. New York: Dutton, 1951.

Mitchell, Angus. Review: *Legacy of Violence: A History of British Empire* by Caroline Elkins. London: The Bodley Head, 2022." *Journal of Colonialism and Colonial History* 24, no. 1 (2023): doi: https://doi.org/10.1353/cch.2023.0002.

Mo Ibrahim Foundation. 2015 Ibrahim Index of African Governance – Index Report, 2015.

———. 2017 Ibrahim Index of African Governance – Index Report, 2017.

Mohamud, Naima. "Ben Enwonwu: The Nigerian Painter behind 'Africa's Mona Lisa." *BBC NEWS*, October 17, 2019. Accessed July 19, 2020. www.bbc.com/news/world-africa-50071212.

Montesquieu, Charles-Louis de Secondat. *De l'Esprit des lois* [*The Spirit of the Laws*]. Geneva: Chez Barrillot and Fils, 1748.

Monges, Miriam Ma'at-Ka-Re. "Candace Rites of Passage Program: The Cultural Context as an Empowerment Tool." *Journal of Black Studies* 29, no. 6 (1999): 827-840.

Moore, Jonathan. "The Transformation of the British Imperial Administration, 1919-1939." PhD Dissertation, Tulane University, New Orleans, 2016.

Morgan, Kenneth O. *Labour in Power 1945-1951*. Oxford: Oxford University Press, 1984.

Morrah, Dermot. *Princess Elizabeth, Duchess of Edinburgh: The Illustrated Story of the Life of the Heir Presumptuous*. London: Oldenus, 1950.

Muda, Muhammad. "The Significance of Commonwealth Games in Malaysia's Foreign Policy." *The Round Table* 87, no. 346 (1998): 211-226.

Mukasa, Ham. *Uganda's Katikiro in England*. London: Hutchinson, 1904.

Mulira, Eridadi M.K. EMKM/GEN/1/1. Unpublished Autobiography. University of Cambridge, undated.

Murphy, Philip. "The African Queen? Republicanism and Defensive Decolonization in British Tropical Africa, 1958-64." *Twentieth Century British History* 14, no. 3 (2003): 243-263.

———. "A Police State? The Nyasaland Emergency and Colonial Intelligence." *Journal of Southern African Studies* 36, no. 1 (2010): 765-780.

———. "Britain and the Commonwealth: Confronting the Past, Imagining the Future." *The Round Table: The Commonwealth Journal of International Studies* 100, no. 414 (2011): 267-283.

———. *Monarchy and the End of Empire: The House of Windsor, the British Government and the Postwar Commonwealth*. Oxford: Oxford University Press, 2013.

———. *The Empire's New Cloth: The Myth of the Commonwealth*. London: C. Hurst and Company, 2018.

Murphy, Philip and Ashton, S.R. *Central Africa: Crisis and Dissolution 1945-1958.* London: HMSO, 2005.
Murphy, Philip and Daisey Cooper. *Queen Elizabeth II should be the final Head of the Commonwealth.* London: Commonwealth Advisory Bureau /Institute of Commonwealth Studies, 2012.
Murray, Henry A. "Introduction to the Issue 'Myth and Mythmaking.'" *Daedalus* 88, no. 2 (1959): 211-222.
Mutesa II, Kabaka. *The Desecration of My Kingdom.* London: Constable and Company, 1967.
Mwakikagile, Godfrey. *Africa at the End of the Twentieth Century: What Lies Ahead.* Dar es Salaam, Tanzania: New Africa Press, 2013.
———. *Nyerere and Africa: End of an Era.* Pretoria: New African Press, 2010.
Mwalubunju, Ollen and Otitodun Elizabeth. *State Reconstruction in Zimbabwe.* Accessed July 30, 2020. Centre for Conflict Resolution, 2011, www.jstor.org/stable/resrep05175.
Nasson, Bill. "War Opinion in South Africa, 1914." *Journal of Imperial and Commonwealth History* 23, no. 2 (1995): 248-276.
Natarajan, Radhika. "The Commonwealth Arts Festival of 1965." *Journal of British Studies* 53, no. 3 (2014): 705-733.
NEWZ PCST. "When Idi Amin Wrote to Queen Elizabeth II over Honeymoon." Republished Kampala, October 27, 2016. Accessed June 4, 2020. http://newz.ug/when-idi-amin-wrote-to-queen-elizabeth-ii-over-honeymoon/.
Nixon, Rob. "Apartheid on the Run: The South African Sports Boycott." *Transition* 58 (1992): 68-88.
Njoku, Raphael Chijioke. "Deconstructing Abacha: Demilitarization and Democratic Consolidation in Nigeria After the Abacha Era." *Government and Opposition* 36, no. 1 (2001): 71-96.
———. "Nationalism, Separatism and the Neoliberal Globalism: A Review of Africa and the Quest for Self-Determination since the 1950s." In *Secession as an International Phenomenon.* Edited by Don Doyle, 338-380. Athens: University of Georgia Press, 2010.
Nkama, Okapni Jr. *Akanu Ibiam 1906–1995: A Compendium of the Humble* Hero. Enugu, Nigeria: Nkamedia Communications, 1995.
Nkoli, Mercy Nnyigide. "Migration and Development in Africa: Lessons from *Omenụkọ* and *Ije Odumodu Jere.*" *Journal of Popular Education in Africa.* 3, no. 2 (2018): 15–26.
Nkrumah, Kwame. *Ghana: The Autobiography of Kwame Nkrumah.* London: Nelson, 1957.
———. "Some Aspects of Socialism in Africa" (1966). In *African Socialism.* Edited by William H. Friedland and Carl G. Rosberg, 340-341. Stanford: Stanford University Press, 1964.
Norton, Philip. *The British Polity.* London: Longman, 2010.
Nwafo, David C. *Born to Serve: The Biography of Dr. Akanu Ibiam.* Ibadan: Macmillan, 1988.
Nyasaland Delegation of Chiefs and Citizens. *A Petition to Her Majesty Queen Elizabeth II Against Federation, Issue 99.* Accra: African Bureau, 1953.
Nyerere, Julius. "Ujamaa: The Basis of African Socialism" (1963). In *Africa's Freedom.* Edited by Julius Nyerere, 67-77. Dar es Salaam: Oxford University Press, 1968.
Obeng, Samuel Gyasi. *Conversational Strategies: Towards a Phonological Description of Projection in Akyem-Twi.* PhD Dissertation. York: The University of York (UK), 1987.

———. "Conversational Strategies: Towards a Phonological Description of Turn-Taking in Akan." *Journal of West African Languages,* 19, no. 1 (1989): 104-120.
———. "Pitch, Loudness and Turn Regulation in Akan Conversation." *York Papers in Linguistics* 15 (1991): 221-235.
———. "A Phonetic Description of Repair Sequences in Akan Conversation." *Text* 12, no. 1 (1992): 59-80.
———. *Conversational Strategies in Akan: Prosodic Features and Discourse Categories*. Köln, Germany: Rüdiger Köppe Verlag, 1999.
———. "Language and Liberty in Ghanaian Political Communication: A Critical Discourse Perspective." *Ghana Journal of Linguistics* 7 no. 2 (2018): 199-224.
———. "Grammatical Pragmatics: Language, Power and Liberty in African (Ghanaian) Political Discourse." *Discourse and Society* 31, no. 1 (2019/2020): 85-105.
Obeng, Cecilia Sem and Samuel Gyasi Obeng. *Invisible Faces; Hidden Stories: Narratives of Vulnerable Populations and Their Caregivers*. Oxford, UK: Berghahn Books, 2020.
Oberle, Philippe. *On Safari: 40 Circuits in Kenya: Rift Valley, Highlands, Mountains with 54 Pictures and 60 Sketches*. Unknown: P. Oberle, 1991.
Office of National Statistics. "GDP Monthly Estimate, U.K." London, June 9, 2020. Accessed June 13, 2020. www.ons.gov.uk/economy/grossdomesticproductgdp/bulletins/gdpmonthlyestimateuk/april2020.
Omaka, Arua Oko. *The Nigerian Humanitarian Crisis, 1967-1970: International Human Rights and Joint Church Aid*. Madison: Fairleigh Dickson University Press, 2016.
Omu, Fred I.A. "The Dilemma of Press Freedom in Colonial Africa: The West African Example." *Journal of African History* 9, no. 2 (1968): 279-298.
———. "The Nigerian Press and the Great War." *Nigeria Magazine* 96 (1968): 44-49.
Orizu, Nwafor. *Africa Speaks*! Enugu: Horizontal Publishers, 1990.
Orr, Clarissa Campbell. Introduction to *Queenship in Britain, 1660–1837: Royal Patronage, Court Culture, and Dynastic Politics*. Edited by Clarissa Campbell Orr. Manchester: Manchester University Press, 2002.
Osadolor, Osarhieme Benson. "The Benin Royalist Movement and Its Political Opponents: Controversy over Restoration of the Monarchy, 1897—1914." *The International Journal of African Historical Studies* 44, no. 1 (2011): 45-59.
Osuntokun, Akinjide. *Nigeria in the First World War*. Atlantic Highlands, NJ: Brill Academic Publication, 1979.
Ovenda, Ritchie, Ed. *The Foreign Policy of the British Labour* Governments. Leicester: Leicester University Press, 1988.
Ovendale Ritchie. "MacMillan and the Wind of Change in Africa, 1957-1960." *The Historical Journal* 38, no. 2 (1995): 455-477.
Owens, Edward. *The Family Firm: Monarchy, Mass Media and the British Public, 1932-53*. London: The University of London Press, 2019.
Owino, Meshak. "Tales from the Crypt: Medical Care of Kenya African Soldiers during and after the Second World War." In *War and Peace in Africa*. Edited by Toyin Falola and Raphael Chijioke Njoku, 241-264. Durham, NC: Carolina Academic Press, 2010.

Parshotam, Asmita. Interviews with Benita van Eyssen. "The Commonwealth Still Relevant for Africa?" April 20, 2018. Accessed May 30, 2020. www.dw.com/en/the-commonwealth-still-relevant-for-africa-today/a-43474891.

Paul, Kathleen. "'British Subjects' and 'British Stock': Labour's Postwar Imperialism." *Journal of British Studies* 34, no. 2 (1995): 233-276.

Pearce, Robert D. *The Turning Point in Africa: British Colonial Policy 1938-1948*. London: Frank Cass, 1982.

Perham, Margery. *Lugard, The Years of Adventure*. London: Collins, 1956.

Perry, Simon. "Ruling Great Britain." In "Queen Elizabeth II Special Issue." *Life Magazine*, December 1, 2022.

Prince Charles. "Respect for the Earth – A Royal View." The BBC Reith Lectures, May 16, 2000.

———. "Prince Warns of 'Playing God.'" *BBC News*, London, May 17, 2000.

———. Address to the Commonwealth of Heads of Government Meeting (CHOGM). London, April 19, 2018.

Princess Elizabeth. A Speech on her 21st Birthday, Cape Town, South Africa. April 21, 1947.

Pfeffer, Jeffrey. *Managing with Power: Politics and Influence in Organizations*. Boston, Mass.: Harvard Business School Press, 1992.

Pimlott, Ben. *The Queen: A Biography of Elizabeth II*. London, HarperCollins, 1996.

———. "Some Thoughts on the Queen and Commonwealth." *The Round Table* 87, no. 347 (1998): 303-305.

———. *The Queen: Elizabeth II and the Monarchy*. London: Harper Press, 2012.

Poetry, Tacu. *Symphony of Selected Poetry Volume 3*. Morrisville, NC.: Lulu Publishing, 2008.

Public Papers of the Presidents of the United States: Dwight D. Eisenhower, 1958. Washington, DC: GPO, 1959.

Rappaport, Helen. *Queen Victoria, A Biographical Companion*. Santa Barbara: ABC-CLIO, 2003.

Rasor, Eugene L. *Winston S. Churchill, 1874–1965: A Comprehensive Historiography and Annotated Bibliography*. Westport, CT: Greenwood Press, 2000.

Raugh, Harold E. Jr. "General Wavell and the Italian East African Campaign." *Military Review* 63, no. 7-12 (1983): 54-66.

Reade, Winwood W. *Savage Africa*. New York: Harper & Brothers, 1864.

Report of the Commission of Rapporteurs. League of Nations (LN) Council DOC.

Republic of Kenya Ministry of Education, Policy Framework for Nomadic Education in Kenya, in collaboration with UNICEF, March 2, 2011.

Rich, Timothy S. and Sterling Recker. "Understanding Sino-African Relations: Neocolonialism or a New Era?" *Journal of International and Area Studies* 20, no. 1 (2013): 61-76.

Richards, Dona. "The Implications of African America Spirituality." In *African Culture: The Rhythms of Unity*. Edited by Molefi Keke Asante and Kariamu Welsh Asante, 207-231. Trenton, NJ: Africa World Press, 1990.

Robinson, Natasha. "Developing Historical Consciousness for Social Cohesion: How South African Students Learn to Construct the Relationship between Past and Present." In *Historical Justice and History Education*, Edited by Matilda Keynes, Henrick Astrom

Elmerijo, Daniel Lindmark, and Bjorn Norlin, 341-363. London: Palgrave Macmillan, 2021.
Rosenzweig, Linda W. "The Abdication of Edward VIII: A Psycho-Historical Explanation." *Journal of British Studies* 14, no. 2 (1975): 102-119.
Ross, Don. "Game Theory." *The Stanford Encyclopedia of Philosophy* (Fall 2021 Edition). Edited by Edward N. Zalta. Accessed August 13, 2022. https://plato.stanford.edu/archives/fall2021/entries/game-theory/.
Ross, Gilbert. "The Prince of Darkness." *The American Council on Science and Health*. New York, May 26, 2000.
Rotberg, Robert I. "Africa's Mess, Mugabe's Mayhem." *Foreign Affairs* 79, no. 5 (2000): 47-61.
Rouvez, Alain. *Disconsolate Empires: French, British, and Belgian Military Involvement in Postcolonial Sub-Saharan Africa*. Lanham: University Press of America, 1994.
Royle, Trevor. *Orde Wingate: A Man of Genius 1903-1944. With Introduction by Andrew Roberts*. Barnsley, Yorkshire: Frontline Books, 2010.
Ryan, Catherine. *The Queen: The Life and Times of Elizabeth II*. London: Chartwell Books, 2018.
Sabiti, Bernard. *UgLish: Dictionary of Ugandan English, First Edition*. Kampala: Jean-Claude Mugunga, 2014.
Salm, Steven J. and Toyin Falola. *Culture and Customs of Ghana*. Westport, CT: Greenwood, 2002.
Sanger, Clyde. *Malcolm MacDonald: Bringing an End to Empire*. Montreal and Kingston: McGill-Queen's University Press, 1995.
Sapire, Hilary. "African Loyalism and its Discontents: The Royal Tour of South Africa, 1947." *The Historical Journal* 54, no. 1 (2011): 215-40.
Sato, Jin, Hiroaki Shiga, Takaaki Kobayashi, and Hisahiro Kondoh. "How Do 'Emerging' Donors differ from 'Traditional' Donors? An Institutional Analysis of Foreign Aid in Cambodia." *JICA Research Institute* No. 2 (2010): 1-47.
Saville, J. *The Politics of Continuity: British Foreign Policy and the Labour Government 1945-46*. London: Verso, 1993.
Scammon, Richard M. "British By-Elections, 1951-1955." *The Journal of Politics* 18, no. 1 (1956): 83-94.
Schatzberg, Michael G. *Political Legitimacy in Middle Africa: Father, Family, Food*. Bloomington: Indiana University Press, 2001.
Schlesinger, Arthur Jr. "Origins of the Cold War." *Foreign Affairs* 46, no. 1 (1967): 22-52.
Scott, Rick. Open Letter to His Royal Highness, the Prince of Wales. Washington, DC. February 8, 2019.
Sears, David O. "Whither Political Socialization Research? The Question of Persistence." In *Political Socialization, Citizenship Education, and Democracy*. Edited by O. Ichilov, 69-97. New York: Teacher College Press, 1990.
Sedgwick, Peter. "The Appalling Silence and Inactivity of the British Left as Biafrans face Death and Starvation from Socialist Workers." Translated by Ted Crawford, Marxist Internal Archive, July 10, 1969. Accessed August 19, 2020. www.marxists.org/archive/sedgwick/1969/07/biafra.htm.

Seely, Bob and James Rogers. *Global Britain: A Twenty-First Century Vision*. London: Henry Jackson Society and the Global Britain Program, 2019.

Shakespeare, William. *Henry VI Part 2, with Annotations and Introduction by Sidney Lee*. Ashuelot, NH: The Renaissance Press, 1591.

Shaloff, Stanley. "Press Controls and Sedition Proceedings in the Gold Coast, 1933-39." *African Affairs* 71, no. 284 (1972): 241-263.

Shawcross, William. *Queen and Country: The Fifty-Year Reign of Elizabeth II*. New York: Simeon Schuster, 2002.

Shelley, Mary Wollstonecraft. *Frankenstein: Or the Modern Prometheus – The 1818 Text*. Reprint; Oxford: Oxford University Press, 2009.

Shinn, David H. "An Opportunistic Ally: China's Increasing Involvement in Africa." *Harvard International Review* 29, no. 2 (2007): 52-56.

Simmons, Michael M. *Queen of People's Hearts: The Time and Mission of Diana, Princess of Wales*. Scotts Valley, CA: Create Space, 2017.

Sinnreich, Richard Hart. "An Army Apart: The Influence of Culture on the Victorian British Army." In *The Culture of Military Organizations*. Edited by Peter R. Mansoor and Williamson Murray, 155-184. Cambridge: Cambridge University Press, 2019.

SLGA. *Records of Paramount Chiefs*, Freetown, Typescript, 1899.

Smith, Sally Bedell. *Elizabeth the Queen: Inside the Life of a Modern Monarch*. New York: Random House, 2012.

Soames, Mary. Ed. *Speaking for Themselves: The Personal Letters of Winston and Clementine Churchill*. Toronto: Doubleday, 1998.

Spear, Thomas. "Neo-Traditionalism and the Limits of Invention in British Colonial Africa." *Journal of African History* 44, no. 1 (2003): 3-27.

Srinivasan, Krishnan. "What Are Commonwealth Values? Traditional Ones: Against Aggression and Authoritarianism." *International Journal* 53, no. 4 (1998): 622-633.

Stafford, Robert, A. "Review: *The Empire of Nature: Hunting, Conservatism and British Imperialism*." Edited by John M. Mackenzie. *The British Journal for the History of Science* 23, no. 1 (1990): 122-124.

Stahl, Anna Katharina. "Fostering African Development, Governance and Security through Multilateral Cooperation between China and Western Donors: The Case of China-DAC Study Group." In *China-Africa Relations: Governance, Peace and Security*. Edited by Mulugeta Gebrehiwot Berhe and Liu Hongwu, 74-96. Addis Ababa: Institute of Peace and Security – Addis Ababa University, 2013.

———. *EU-China-Africa Trilateral Relations in a Multipolar World: Hic Sunt Dracones*. New York: Palgrave MacMillan, 2017.

Stapleton, Tim. "Letters from Burma: Views of Black Zimbabwean Soldiers during the Second World War. In *War and Peace in Africa*. Edited by Toyin Falola and Raphael Chijioke Njoku, 265-283. Durham, NC: Carolina Academic Press, 2010.

Statistics South Africa. Statistical Release, *P0352.2 Domestic Tourism Survey Bi-Annual Report*, December 12, 2019.

Statute of Westminster. 1931, 22 and 23 GEO.5, c.2 (3) CH. 4. England. Printed by Swift Printing & Duplicating, for Percy Faulkner, C.B. Controller of Her Majesty's Stationery Office and Queen's Printer of Acts of Parliament, 1931.

Steele, David. "Salisbury and Soldiers." In *The Boer War: Direction, Experience and Image*. Edited by John Gooch, 3-20. London: Frank Cass, 2000.

Steinmetz, Jüergen T. Kenya Tourism Performance Report. January 10, 2020.

Stockwell, Sarah. *The British End of the British Empire*. Cambridge: Cambridge University Press, 2018.

Stoler, Ann Laura and Frederick Cooper. "Between Metropole and Colony: rethinking a Research Agenda." In *Tensions of Empire: Colonial Cultures in a Bourgeoise World*. Edited by Ann Laura Stoler and Frederick Cooper, 1-68. Berkeley: University of California Press, 1997.

Subramony, Mahesh. "Service Organizations and their Communities: Perspective and New Directions for Management Research." *Academy of Management Perspectives* 31, no. 1 (2017): 28-43.

Summers, Carol. "Local Critiques of Global Development: Patriotism in Late Colonial Uganda." *International Journal of African Historical Studies* 47, no. 1 (2014): 21-35.

Sun, Yun. "Africa in Focus: China and the East African Railways: Beyond Full Industry Chain Export." *Brookings*, Washington DC., July 16, 2017.

The Belfour Declaration, 1926. Inter-Imperial Relations Committee Report. Proceedings and Memoranda E (I.R./26) Series, Secret E. 129, No.129, November 1926. Printed for Her Majesty's Britannica Government, 1926.

"The Commonwealth. 'Our History.'" Accessed July 9, 2020. www.thecommonwealth.org.

"The Role of the Monarchy." Accessed January 16, 2023. https://www.royal.uk/role-monarchy#:~:text=The%20Sovereign%20acts%20as%20a,members%20of%20their%20 immediate%20family.

The State House of Uganda. "President Museveni Toasts to Queen Elizabeth's Life." The British High Commission, Nakasero, Kampala, June 17, 2017.

Thompson, T. Jack. "Prester John, John Chilembwe and the European Fear of Ethiopianism." *The Society of Malawi Journal* 68, no. 2 (2015): 18-30.

Thornton, Martin. *Churchill, Borden, and Anglo-Canadian Naval Relations, 1911–14*. New York: Palgrave Macmillan, 2013.

Thurston, Anne. *Records of the Colonial Office, Dominions Office, Commonwealth Relations Office, and Commonwealth Office – British Document on the End of Empire*. London: HMSO, 1995.

Tignor, Robert I. "Kamba Political Protest: The Destocking Controversy of 1938." *African Historical Studies* 4, no. 2 (1971): 237-251.

———. *Colonial Transformation of Kenya: The Kamba, Kikuyu, and Massai from 1900-1939*. Princeton: Princeton University Press, 1976.

Tiruneh, Gizachew. "The Kebra Nagast." *International Journal of Ethiopian Studies* 8, no. 1-2 (2014): 51-72.

Toor, Joanne and H.G. Picknell. "The Proper Place of Propaganda." *Columbia Journal of International Affairs* 5, no. 2 (1951): 77-80.

Torrent, Melanie. "A Commonwealth Approach to Decolonization." *Études anglaises* 65, no. 3 (2012): 347-362.

Tracey, Joseph. *An Historical Examination of Western Africa as Formed by Paganism and Muhammedanism, Slavery, the Slave Trade and Piracy*. Boston: Press of T.R. Marvin, 1845.

Traugh, Geoffrey. "Apartheid by Another Nature." *London Review of Books*, London, September 2, 2022.

Trevor-Roper, Hugh. "The Rise of Christian Europe." *The Listener* 70 (1963): 871-875.

Trouillot, Michel-Rolph. *Silencing the Past: Power and the Production of History*. Boston: Beacon Press, 1995.

Turner, John C. *Social Influence. Milton Keynes*. Maidenhead, Berkshire: Open University Press, 1991.

———. "Explaining the Nature of Power: A Three-Process Theory." *European Journal of Social Psychology* 35 (2005): 1-22.

Uche, Chibuike. "Oil, British Interests and the Nigerian Civil War." *Journal of African History* 49 (2008): 111-135.

Uganda Bureau of Statistics. A Report on the Uganda Business Register, 2001/2002. Uganda Bureau of Statistics, External Trade Statistics Bulletin Volume 1-2002. November 2002.

UK Parliament's House of Commons Library. Research Briefing – The Commonwealth in 2020, Friday, March 6, 2020. Accessed October 2, 2020. https://commonslibrary.parliament.uk/research-briefings/cdp-2020-0052/#:~:text=There%20are%20now%2054%20countries,reach%20%2413%20trillion%20in%202020.

US Department of State. *Foreign Relations of the United States, 1961-1963, Volume 21*. Washington, DC.: United States Government Printing Office, 1995.

Vail, Leroy. "Introduction: Ethnicity in Southern African History." In *The Creation of Tribalism in Southern Africa*. Edited by Leroy Vail, 1-20. Berkeley and Los Angeles: University of California Press, 1991.

Varga, John. "The Heartwarming Way Prince William Proposed to Kate Middleton Revealed." *Express*, London, October 23, 2019.

Veit, Richard and Christopher Gould. *Writing, Reading, and Research, 8th edition*. Boston: Wadsworth, 2010.

Verwoerd, Hendrik. Response to the "Winds of Change" Speech to the South Africa Parliament. Cape Town, South Africa, February 3, 1960.

Vestal, Theodore M. "Emperor Haile Selassie's First State Visit to the United States in 1954: The Oklahoma Interlude." *International Journal of Ethiopian Studies* 1, no. 1 (2003): 133-152.

Vivekanandan, B. "Commonwealth of Nations Today." *The Indian Journal of Political Science* 35, no. 1 (1974): 13-36.

Walker, Jonathan. *Operation Unthinkable: The Third World War: British Plans to Attack the Soviet Empire*. Cheltenham, Gloucestershire: The History Press, 2013.

Waller, Maureen. *Sovereign Ladies: Sex, Sacrifice, and Power – The Six Reigning Queens of England*. London: Macmillan, 2006.

Wallerstein, Immanuel. *The Modern World System I: Capitalist Agriculture and the Origins of the European World Economy in the Sixteenth Century*. New York: Academic Press, 1974.

———. *The Modern World System II: Mercantilism and the Consolidation of the European World-Economy, 1600—1750*. New York: Academic Press, 1980.

War, E.E. "The Colombo Plan." *Australian Outlook* 5, no. 4 (2008): 191-202.

Waswa, Sam. "Archives: Letter Reveals Amin's Friendship with Queen Elizabeth." *Chimp Reports*, Kampala, December 28, 2014.

Watkins, Daphne C. Chavella T. Pittman, and Marissa J. Walsh. "The Effects of Psychological Distress, Work, and Family Stressors on Child Behavior Problems." *Journal of Comparative Family Studies* 44, no. 1 (2013): 1-16.

Weiler, Peter. *British Labour, and the Cold War*. Stanford: Stanford University Press, 1988.

Wesley, Michael. "Interpreting the Cold War." In *Power and International Relations*. Edited by Desmond Ball and Sharyn Lee, 79-91. Canberra: Australian National University Press, 2014.

West, Michael Oliver. *The Rise of an African Middle Class: Colonial Zimbabwe, 1898-1965*. Bloomington: Indiana University Press, 2002.

Whelpton, John. *A History of Nepal Cambridge*. Cambridge University Press, 2016.

White, Luise. *The Comforts of Home: Prostitution in Colonial Nairobi*. Chicago and London: University of Chicago Press, 1990.

William, Shawcross. *The Queen Mother: The Official Biography*. London: Alfred A. Knopf, 2009.

World Bank. Group Report: Economic and Statistical Analysis of Tourism in Uganda. Washington, DC.: 2013.

———. National Accounts Data, and OECD National Accounts Data Files. Accessed June 6, 2020. https://data.worldbank.org/indicator/NY.GDP.MKTP.CD.

Wylie, Diana. "Confrontation over Kenya: The Colonial Office and Its Critics, 1918-1940." *Journal of African History* 18 no. 3 (1977): 427-447.

Yoda, Lalbila. "The Influence of the USA on the Political Ideas of Kwame Nkrumah." *The Round Table: The Commonwealth Journal of International Affairs* 326 (1993): 187-198.

Young, Crawford. *The Politics of Cultural Pluralism*. Madison: The University of Wisconsin Press, 1976.

Yu, George T. "Africa in Chinese Foreign Policy." *Asian Survey* 28, no. 8 (1988): 849-862.

Ziegler, Philip. "Churchill and the Monarchy." In *Churchill: A Major Assessment of His Life in Peace and War*. Edited by Robert Blake and William Roger Louis, 187-198. New York: W.W. Norton, 1994.

———. *King Edward VIII*. New York: Knopf, 1991.

Zimmerman, Carle C. "Family Influence upon Religion." *Journal of Comparative Family Studies* 5, no. 2 (1974): 1-16.

Zweig, David and Bi Jianhai. "China's Global Hunt for Energy." *Foreign Affairs* 84, no. 5 (2005): 25-38.

INDEX

Abacha, Gen. Sani, 153, 155
Aberdare National Park, 140
Addis Ababa, 109
Africa Tour-De-Force, 30, 97, 105
Africa, the Caribbean, and the Pacific (ACP), 138
African Academy of Arts and Research (AAAR), 58
African decolonization, 15, 20, 31, 59, 163, 166, 168
African historical memory, 170-171
African loyalism, 46
African Union (AU), 138. *See also* Organization of African Union (OAU).
Afro-British relations, 100
Ahiara Declaration, 127
Akufo-Addo, Nana Dankwa, 152
Aksum cathedral, 110
Albert, prince, 40, 43. *See also* George VI, king.
Alexander, Victoria, queen, 22, 35-40, 44-45, 49, 66, 84, 110, 115, 120, 164; coronation, 84; cultural ideals, 22, 39, 49; exchanges with Emperor Menelik, 38, 115; gender ideals, 38, legacies, 40, 44; political interventions, 37; popularity among Brits, 36; push for military confrontations, 38; support for the army, 45; warrior queen, 66
Alexandra, princess, 95, 145
Algeria, 97, 142, 166
Altrincham, John Grigg, lord, 78

American-British alliance, 30. *See also* Anglo-American friendship.
Anglo-American friendship, 30, 90
Anglophiles, 99
Ankole, 82
Anne, princess, 49
Ark of the Covenant, 110. *See also* Tabot.
Astaire, Fred, 97
Attlee, Clement Richard, 59, 61-62, 76, 122; Churchill description of him, 62; loss of power to Churchill, 76; preparations for decolonization, 59, 61; privy to the Cape Town discourse, 61-62
Australia, 52-53, 123-124, 142; competition in the festival of Empire, 142; disappointment with the Suez Canal crisis, 124; relationship with the British Empire in Southeast Asia, 123
Awolowo, Obafemi, 58, 105
Ayer, A. J., 125
Azikiwe, Nnamdi, 48, 98, 105-106
Balewa, Abubakar Tafawa, 95, 105
Balmer, John M.T., 25, 34-35, 165
Banda, Kamuzu Hastings, 52, 55, 58, 70; complaint to Creech Jones, 52, 58; London visit, 70, meeting with Kenyatta, 55
Bantu United Society, 47
Basutoland, 51, 105. *See also* Lesotho.
Bath, Somerset, 107
Bechuanaland, 50-51, 105. *See also* Botswana
Belgium, 119, 129-130

Bell-Gam, Leopold, 165
Berlin, Isaiah, 64
Bevin, Ernest, 122
Biafra, 24-25, 67, 123, 127-131, 153, 173-174; bloodiest Africa civil conflict, 123; British policy towards, 130-131; causes, 24, 174; consequences, 127-128; 130, 153, 173; ideological crisis, 129-130; international dimensions, 127-128, 130; Queen Elizabeth silence, 24, 67, 127-129-131, 173
Biya, Paul, 155
Blair, Cmdr. Chandos, 118
Blair, Tony, 152
Bo Durbar, 102
Botha, Gen. Louis, 23
Botha, Peter Willem, 155, 166
Botswana, 51, 105, 140-141. *See also* Bechuanaland.
Bourguiba, Gen. Habib, 86
Bowden, MP Herbert, 18
Bowes-Lyon, David, 43, 49
Bowes-Lyon, Elizabeth, duchess, 40-41
Brexit, 21, 31, 137, 143, 152, 155, 157-159, 162
British Borneo Territories, 123
British Conservatives, 35, 169
British Establishment, 16, 21-22, 59, 65, 67, 72, 163, 170. *See also* Whitehall.
Brockway, MP. Fenner A., 80-81
Buckingham Palace, 25, 35, 44, 61, 84, 104, 108, 111, 114-115, 117, 133
Buckmaster, Viscount, lord, 112
Buganda, 24, 37-39, 50, 80-84, 111; monarch, 38-39, 50, 67, 80-84, rumors of romantic overtures, 84. *See also* Uganda.
Bunyoro, 81-82
Burke, Edmond, 34
Burma, 47, 59
Cameroon, 138, 155
Campbell, Evan, 173

Canada, 52-53, 122, 124-126, 134, 139, 142-143
Cape Town, 10, 16, 26, 29, 46, 48, 50-51, 53, 58-59, 61-69, 72, 74, 77, 88, 121, 142, 163; episode, 58
Caribbean Aid Program (CAP), 123
Central Africa Republic (CAR), 138
Central African Federation (CAF), 25, 58, 69, 78. *See also* Nyasaland Emergency.
Ceylon, 59
Chad, 138
Charles III, king, 30, 149-153, 155-156, 160, 162; new commonwealth head, 30, 149-158, 160, 162. *See also* Charles, prince.
Charles, prince, 42, 49, 91, 149-151, 156-157; birth, 49; commonwealth manifesto, 151; Hong Kong journal, 151; image setback, 150; marriage, 149; prince of Wales, 42, 149, 157; Reith Lecture, 156-157; separation from Diana, 151
China, 31, 78-79, 118, 138, 147, 152-154, 160-161, 170; African-Sino collaboration, 160 assistance to African nationalists, 79; East African project agreement, 161; economic grip on Africa, 154; rediscovery of Africa, 31, 147, 152, 161, 170
Church of England, 25, 34, 40-42, 50, 157
Churchill, Winston, 21, 23, 37, 51, 58-59, 62, 68-70, 75-77, 91, 97, 109, 122, 173; bond with Elizabeth, 75-77; electoral defeat by Atlee, 58, 62, 69; host of Selassie, 107; imperial preservationist, 75; Iron Curtain speech, 74; opposition to Nyasaland delegation, 70; rejection of the Atlantic Charter, 68; Suez Canal crisis, 75; support for Elizabeth Africa tours, 51, 91, 97; wartime popularity, 58
Cohen, Gov. Andrew, 24, 29, 80-81, 166, 174; Kabaka II deportation, 24, 80-81

Index 263

Cold War, 16, 28, 30, 50, 54, 63, 70, 72, 74-75, 77-80, 85, 87, 91, 97-98, 102, 108, 119-120, 123-124, 133, 135, 160, 169-170, 174; alliances, 120, 124; effect on African decolonization, 16, 28, 30, 50, 54, 72-75, 77, 173; effect on Elizabeth, 16, 28, 30, 135, 169, 174; intersection with Commonwealth, 16, 28, 30, 80; politics, 63, 133, 163; problems, 54, 98, 102, 119, 123, 173; thaw, 28, 133, 160, 197

Colombo Plan for South and Southeast Asia (CPSSA), 123, 137,

Colonial Office (CO), 16, 24-25, 54, 56, 60, 74, 82, 95, 100, 105, 116, 150, 164; rescind of Kabaka II's deportation, 82; misuse of the royal brand, 16, 24, 37, 74, 84, 173

Commonwealth, 10, 15-16, 18-25, 24, 28-31, 36, 50-54, 59-60, 62-65, 72, 74-80, 82, 87-95, 97-99, 104-105, 110-114, 116, 118-128, 130-140, 142-143, 145, 147, 149-164, 167-170, 172, 174; challenges, 80, 88, 123-124, 152-153, 156, 160; Elizabeth's visions of, 10, 24, 63, 82, 132, 134, 151, 169; empire placeholder, 122, 168; victories, 135, 137; sanctions, 65, 132, 147, 154-155, 160; reassessment and repurposing, 132; setbacks, 123-124, 137

Commonwealth African Assistance Program (SCAAP), 123

Commonwealth Business Forum (CBF), 159

Commonwealth Enterprise and Investment Council (CEIC), 159

Commonwealth Festival of Arts, 132

Commonwealth Fund for Technical Cooperation (CFTC), 133

Commonwealth Games, 142-143

Commonwealth Parliamentary Association (CPA), 76

Commonwealth Relations Office (CRO), 25, 60, 74, 89, 96, 131-132, 150

Commonwealth Scholarship Commission (CSC), 139

Commonwealth Secretary's Office (CSO), 79

Conservative Party, 58. *See also* Tory Party.

Corbett, Jim Edward, 28

Cotts, Mitchell, 110

COVID-19 pandemic, 21, 137, 151-152, 155, 158, 161

Crossman, MP, H.R.S., 124,

Crown, 9-10, 16, 18-22, 25-27, 29, 30, 33-35, 36, 38, 40-44, 46, 52-53, 60, 68, 74, 76-77, 79, 82, 84, 89, 91, 97, 115, 124, 132, 136, 150, 152, 157, 164-168, 171, 173-174; African loyalism, 19, 22, 25-27, 36, 60; branding credentials, 25, 29, 34-35, 38; character, 34, 168; corporate institutions, 25, 29, 31, 33-34, 41, 43, 61, 115, 155, 165; expectations, 35, 44, 46, 124, 165; hypnotic role, 18; indulgence in global recognition, 164; misrepresentations, 16, 20; 37, 74, 84, 173; mysteries of, 34, 36; partnership with British Establishment, 21, 36, 52; portrayal of, 124; symbol, 33-34, 136, 166, 171; stakeholders, 25, 29, 31, 33-35, 40-44, 50, 72, 76-77, 147, 165, 167-168, 173; tool, 22, 33-34, 82, 84, 89, 91, 167; under Churchill, 34, 168; Whitehall management of, 25, 33-34

Cumming-Bruce, Francis E., 98

Dawe, G-G. Arthur James, 56

Diana, princess, 149, 150-151

Discourse analysis and the Cape Town speech, 62

Dorman, Maurice, 100

Douglas-Home, Alec, 112, 114, 116

Duke of Edinburgh, 9, 51, 85, 102, 104, 107-108, 115. *See also* Mountbatten Philip, prince.

Economic and Monetary Community of Central Africa (EMCCA), 138

Eden, Anthony, 124, 173

Edward II, king, 39
Edward VIII, king, 40-44, 49
Efik, 49
Eisenhower, Dwight David, 73, 75, 77-78, 86, 88
Embu, 56
Emecheta, Buchi, 175
Empire brand, 163-164,
Equatorial Guinea, 138, 154
Eritrea, 57, 111
Esau and Jacob, 170
Ethiopian Coptic Church, 110
European Commission (EC), 138
European Convention of Human Rights, 125
European Union (EU), 137, 158, 170
Evans, Harold, 89
Exalted Order of the Queen of Sheba, 108
Exon, Robert, 125
Fanon, Frantz, 166
Fascism, 48, 53, 63
Fidel, Castro, 73
Field, Winston, 173
First World War, 41-42, 46, 65
Flood, J.E.W., 24
Foreign Direct Investment (FDI), 86, 138
Forsyth, Frederick, 173-174
Forum on China-Africa Cooperation (FOCAC), 160
Fourah Bay College, 102-104
Foxtrot ballroom dance, 85, 92
France, 48, 54, 119, 124, 128-130, 166
Frankenstein story, 164
Freetown, 99-104, 145, 168
Gabon, 138
Gaitskell, Hugh, 125
Gallinas Perri chiefdom, 104
Game Theory, 170
Garner, Saville, 125
Gbo chiefdom, 104
George VI, king, 21-22, 24, 26, 29, 40, 43, 51, 57, 61, 63-65, 68-69, 77, 149, 152; ascension, 43; death, 26, 29, 77; intention to decorate African veterans, 24; portrayed by QE as a 'symbol of steadfastness,' 65; reinvention of the Commonwealth, 149; speech in the House of Lords after the South African tour, 57, 64, 69; visit to South Africa, 51, 61, 63-64. *See also* Albert, prince.
Ghana, 10-11, 18, 30, 58, 79, 85, 87-88, 89, 91-93, 95, 97, 99, 103, 119, 124, 136-137, 139, 140, 144-146, 167-168; independence, 85, 87, 144-146, 167-168; commonwealth membership, 88; US relations, 86, 90, 94; Queen Elizabeth visit, 91-93, 95. *See also* Gold Coast.
Gibbs, Humphrey, 80
Gibraltar peninsular, 18
Global Britain, 110, 152, 171
Goa Declaration, 134
Gold Coast, 48, 79, 98, 145. *See also* Ghana.
Gondor, 110
Gorbachev, Mikhail Sergeyevich, 156
Gowon, Gen. Yakubu, 166, 174
Grahame, Maj. Ian, 118
Griffiths, MP. James, 35, 81, 125
Gulama, Ella Koblo, 104
Guma Valley Water and Electric project, 102
H.M. Queen Elizabeth II (b. Alexander Mary Windsor), 9-10, 15-26, 28-31, 33-41, 43-46, 48-54, 58-59, 61-82, 84-85, 87-90, 92-95, 97-100, 102-111, 114-124, 126-129, 131-133, 135-135, 138-147, 149-154, 158, 162-175; abdication trauma, 40-41; African affairs/policies, 20, 24-25, 68, 163; African mission, 18, 22, 26, 37, 122, 164-165, 168, 172; African relations, 85, 97, 164; African tours, 17-18, 30, 49, 59, 95, 97, 99, 119-120; British Establishment proxy, 67, Cape Town speech, 29, 48, 51, 53, 58, 61-63, 65-68, 72; childhood, 40, 144; coronation, 70, 76-78, 174; dance of

destiny, 165; dance with Nkrumah, 85, 92-94, 145; death, 9, 25, 122, 171, 175; decolonization mission, 26, 51, 62-68, 71; devotion to the Commonwealth mission, 31, 97, 121, 147, 163, 174, doing hide-and-seek with Amin, 111; experimental learning in Africa, 46, formative years, 43, 65; Her imperial family and the Africans, 35; inspired tropes of culture, 30, 139; Malta conversation, 122; mission announcement, 16, oath/pledge of office, 77, 88, 165, 174, princess, 16, 18, 40, 43-45, 49, 51, 58, 61, 68; queen of independence, 66; queenship preparation, 40; she elephant, 28; silences, 15, 19, 25, 33, 36, 60, 68, 115, 172; wedding, 26, 49, 51, 144

Haile Selassie I, emperor, 50, 106-111, 196-197; British royal honors, 106; descent, 196-197; exile, 106, 108; London visit, 108; hosting British royals, 109-111

Hailey, Malcolm, 56

Hall, Viscount, lord, 23

Harare, 134-135, 138, 154; conference, 134; declaration, 135, 138, 154, 160

Harrington, Lt. Col. J.L., 38

Hart, H.L.A., 16

Hayek, Friedrich, 15

Healey, MP. Denis, 130

Her Majesty's Government, 72, 81, 92, 124, 131, 133, 164, 170, 173; as a colonial brand, 164, 170; as decolonization tool, 164; negative perception of in Africa, 173

Hills, Denis Cecil, 117

HMS *Kenya*, 29

HMS *Vanguard*, 63

Holy Ghost Fathers, 129

Hopkinson, Henry, 102-103

House of Windsor, 21, 25, 29, 33, 39

Hunt, David, 24, 173-174

Hutu, 155

Ibiam, Akanu Francis, 129, 173

Ibibio, 49

Igbo, 11, 35, 49, 61, 129, 131

Ihetu, Richard (aka Dick Tiger), 129, 173

India, 41, 46, 52-53, 59-60, 69, 122, 124-125, 134, 137, 159; against nuclear proliferation, 134; independence, 46, 53, 59

Indian National Congress (INC), 60

Information and Communication Technology (ICT), 157

Italian Somaliland, 57

Jemmeh, Yahya, 153

Jones, Creech Arthur, 23, 52, 58, 125

Jubilee Palace, 109

Kabaka Mutesa II, 2, 25, 38, 50, 67, 80, 111-113, 166, 173; at Queen Elizabeth II's investiture, 50; first deportation, 25, 38, 67, 173; second exile, 111

Kabaka Yekka (KY), 83

Kagame, Paul, 155

Kaiyamba chiefdom, 104

Kamba rebellion, 55-56, 70

Kampala, 29, 81-82, 112, 115, 117-118, 136

Kant, Immanuel, 15

Kavuma, P.N., 82

Kebra Nagast (KN), 106-107

Kennedy, John Fitzgerald, 73, 90

Kenya, 10, 16-17, 19, 24, 26-29, 33, 50, 54-56, 59, 68, 70-72, 82, 91, 105, 111, 136-137, 139-142, 146, 161, 163, 167, 173

Kenya's Intelligence Service, 112

Kenyan Land and Freedom Army, 70. *See also* Mau Mau.

Kere Nyang, 27. *See also* Mt. Kenya.

Khrushchev, Nikita S., 73, 75, 89

Kikuyu, 26-27, 56, 70; mythology, 27

Kimanthi, Dedan, 71

Kimbo, Theuri Njugi, 72

King David, 106

King Solomon, 106-108

King, Martin Luther Jr., 63, 86
Kiwanuka, Benedicto, 83
Knighthood of Grand Cross of the Royal Victorian Order, 80
Korean War, 109
Krio, 100, 106
Labour Party, 35, 122
Lagos, 24, 38, 40, 137, 145, 174
Lagos Plan, 137
Laithwaite, Gilbert, 98
Lang, William, C.G., 41, 44-45
Lari murders, 70
Lascelles, Alan (aka Tommy), 63, 65
League of Nations, 56, 109
Lee, MP. John, 131
Lennon, John, 123, 129, 173
Lennox-Boyd, Alan, 83
Lesotho, 50-51, 105, 142. *See also* Basutoland.
Lewis, Samuel, 99
Libya, 29, 57, 116, 118. *See also* Tripolitania and Cyrenaica.
Livingstone, David, 45
Lusaka Declaration on Racism and Racial Prejudice (LDRRP), 133-134
Lyttleton, Oliver, 37, 81
MacDonald, Malcolm John, 19, 56
Mackenzie, Bruce, 112
Macleod, Iain, 100-106; admiration for Balewa, 106; on future of democracy in the Sierra Leone colony, 101; on Margai's leadership, 100, views about Nigerian radicals, 105-106; visit to Sierra Leone, 103
Macmillan, Harold, 73, 89, 94, 125
Makerere University, 82
Malan, Daniel Francois, 50, 124-125
Malawi, 19, 42, 55, 69-70, 79, 105, 136, 167. *See also* Nyasaland.
Malayan Peninsula, 123
Malta, 121-122
Manchester, William, 125
Mandela, Nelson, 121, 132, 136, 168

Margai, Albert, 131
Margai, Milton, 100, 145
Marlborough House, 132
Marquand, MP. Hilary, 105
Marten, Henry, 44
Mary of Teck, 43
Massaquoi, Woki, 104
Mau Mau, 24, 27, 67, 70-72, 82, 91, 111, 173. *See also* Kenyan Land and Freedom Army.
Mauritius, 138, 140
Maximilian, Ferdinand, 109
Mbadiwe, Kingsley Ozumba (aka K.O.), 56-58
McCarthy, Gov. Charles, 100
Melbourne Declaration, 134
Member of the British Empire (MBE), 104
Mende, 100, 104
Menelik I, 38, 106-107, 115
Meru, 56
Mills, John Stuart, 56
Ministry of Tourism, Wildlife, and Antiquities (MTWA), 141
Mitchell, Harry, 19
Mo Ibrahim Democracy Index Reports, 156
Mombasa, 26, 29, 161, 146
Monophysite Christians, 106
Montesquieu, Charles Louis, 34
Morocco, 97
Morrison, Herbert, 122
Moscow, 88, 156
Mossad, 112
Mountbatten, Philip, prince, 49, 51, 109, 119, 145, 150, 173. *See also* Duke of Edinburgh.
Mozambique, 138, 169
Mt. Kenya, 27. *See also* Kere Nyang.
Mugabe, Robert, 78, 153-154, 166
Museveni, Yoweri, 138-139
Mwang II Mukasa (kabaka), 37-38
Nairobi, 10-11, 26, 161
Namibia, 57, 60, 127, 133, 140, 142. *See also* South West Africa.

Nassau Declaration, 134
Nasser, Col. Gamal Abdel, 29, 124
Natal Province, 60
Nazism, 48, 53, 63
Nehru, Jawaharlal, 125
Neville Chamberlain, 38, 59
New Elizabethan Monarchy, 21, 74, 146-147
New York, 58, 87-88, 114
New Zealand, 52-53, 77, 125
Newfoundland, 52
Nigeria, 10, 17, 19, 21, 24-25, 30, 38, 42, 48, 50, 57, 61, 67, 85, 95, 98, 102-103, 105-106, 123, 126-131, 136-139, 144-146, 150, 153-156, 159-162, 168, 173-175
Nile River, 82
Njeri, 27, 140, 163
Nkamanya, 35, 122, 175
Nkrumah, Kwame, 73, 85-89, 91-94, 98, 119, 132, 135-136, 145; alliance communist ideologue, 87, 92, 98; connection with Queen, 91-94; coup d'état, 94, 89, 119; dance with Elizabeth, 85, 92-94, 145; decolonization agitation, 88; dictum, 135-136; hydroelectric project, 91; meeting US presidents, 86, 90; Moscow alliance, 88;
Northern People's Congress (NPC), 105
Northern Rhodesia, 69-70, 78-79. *See also* Zambia.
Nozick, Robert, 15
Nyasaland, 25, 33, 35, 37, 42, 50, 52, 54, 58, 67, 69-70, 78-79. *See also* Malawi.
Nyasaland Delegation, 35, 37
Obedient Boys of the Empire (OBE), 99. *See also* Order of the British Empire (OBE).
Obeng, Samuel, 62, 64
Obote, Milton, 83-84, 92, 111-113, 119
Ojike, Mbonu, 58
Ojukwu, Lt. Col. Chukwuemeka Odumegwu, 24, 127, 166, 174
One-Belt-One-Road (OBOR), 161

Order of the British Empire (OBE), 99, 101, 129. *See* Obedient Boys of the Empire (OBE).
Organization Internationale de la Francophonie (OIF), 138
Organization of African Unity (OAU), 109, 113, 127, 130. *See also* African Union (AU).
Oumee, Gen. Idi Amin Dada, 38, 84, 99, 111, 113-114, 118-119, 166; exchanges with Elizabeth, 84, 111, 119; expulsion of Asians, 116; preemptive coup, 111
Owen Falls Dam, 82, 139
Pakistan, 46, 59
Parker, Jim, 174
Perham, Margery, 130
Point of no return: Empire and the decolonization rhetoric, 53-54
Postwar Commonwealth, 168
Professional Standards Framework for Teachers and School Leaders (PSFTSL), 140
Qua Iboe Mission Institute, 48
Quality Education Provision to Nomadic Communities for Africa and Asia (QEPNCAA), 140
Queen of Sheba, 140
Queen's Coronation Medal (QCM), 129
Ramphal, Shridath, 134
Ramsey, Arthur Michall, 89
Ranaji, Jang Bahadur, 107
Rawls, John, 15
Republic of the Congo, 138, 168
Robertson, Gov. James, 85, 98
Rogers, Ginger, 92
Rosebery, lord, 37
Rotary Club, 34
Royal Branding Mix, 33, 49, 59, 116, 128, 151, 167
Royal Family, 25, 29, 33, 35, 43, 49, 51, 93-95, 152, 157-150
Royal Stakeholders, 29, 33-35, 41, 43-44, 72, 165, 167

Royal tours, 17, 30, 59, 95, 97, 119, 120
Royal West African Frontier Force (RWAFF), 85, 103
Ruskin College Oxford, 103
Russia, 31, 41, 75, 88-90, 92, 118, 130, 137, 151-152, 158
Saint Helena, 165
Salisbury, lord, 37, 49
Salter, Clive, 24, 70-71, 174
Sandys, Duncan, 88, 133
Sardauna of Sokoto, 105
Saro-Wiwa, Ken, 105
School Leaders Capability Framework (SLCF), 140
Scotland, 117, 119, 129, 143
Second World War, 22, 24, 40, 44, 46, 48, 51, 53-54, 56, 66, 106, 109-110, 122, 163-164
Seeiso, Mabereng, prince, 142
Sentebale, 142
Sharpeville massacre, 125
Sherbro, 100, 104
Sierra Leone, 10, 19, 30, 42, 91, 98-104, 110, 119, 131, 139, 144, 146, 167-168; conformity to colonial obedience, 100-102, 105; hydroelectric project, 102-103; royal regiment, 103; royal visit, 30, 42, 91, 98-104; women empowerment, 105-106.
Simpson, Wallis Warfield, 40, 41, 43,
Singapore, 112, 133
Smith, Ian, Douglas, 79-90, 166
Smuts, Gen. Jan, Christian, 23-24, 51, 59, 60-81, 64, 67, 69, 166
Snelling, A.W., 88-89, 92, 150
South Africa, 10, 19-24, 26-28, 37, 41-42, 46, 48-53, 56-57, 59, 60-63, 65, 69, 78, 94, 112-113, 117, 126, 125-127, 133, 137, 140-143, 155, 157, 159, 162-163, 167-168, 171; apartheid, 109, 112, 133, 136, 143, 153, 155, 168, 171; British relations, 60-61, 65, 113, 125, 127, 133; commonwealth relations, 124-126, 133, 140, 143, 159; communists, 42; developing market, 137, 140-141, 159; immigration issues, 162; Macmillan's speech, 94; minority rule, 63, 67, 70, 78-79, 124; nationalist party, 46; 69; royal visit, 16, 23-24, 26, 28, 42, 49, 60-61, 63; parliament, 50, 94; presence in South West Africa, 52, 57, 60; QE's birthday speech, 16, 62; QE experiential learning, 46, 54; race relations, 60-61, 63-64, 69, 117, 124, 125, 132, 142-143, 166; transition to democracy, 143; Union of South Africa, 50, 56-57, 60; veterans, 24, 51, 60, 64, 66; white supremacists, 78;
South Sudan, 161
Southern Rhodesia, 47, 51, 59, 69-70, 78-80, 109, 131-132, 167, 173. See also Zimbabwe.
South West Africa, 51, 57, 60. See also Namibia.
Spain, 19
Spiritans, 129
Sri Lanka, 123
Stonehouse, MP. John, 125
Strijdom, Johannes, Gerhardus, 124
Sudan, 97, 105, 124, 139, 161
Suez Canal crisis, 25, 67, 75, 124, 153, 173
Swaziland, 51, 140
Tabot, 110. See also Ark of the Covenant
Taitu, Itege, empress, 38
Takoradi Broadways Dance Band, 92
Tanganyika, 94, 105. See also Tanzania.
Tanzania, 105, 128, 136, 142, 167. See also Tanganyika.
Temne, 100
Temple, William, 56
Thatcher, Margaret, 133-134, 149
The dove and the hawks, 22
The Gambia, 42, 91, 99, 103, 105, 136, 139, 145, 153-154, 160, 167
The Netherlands, 129-130, 171
Thokoza (township), 162

Thornley, C.H., 26
Thorpe, Jeremy, 125
Tilney, MP. John, 102, 130-131
Tooro, 82
Tory Party, 122
Tour-de-triumph meets noble Selassie, 106
Treetops Hotel, 27, 72, 140, 173
Tripolitania and Cyrenaica, 57. *See also* Libya.
Trouillot, Michel-Rolph, 172
Tunisia, 86, 97
Tusk Trust, 142
Tutsi, 155-156
Uganda, 17, 24-25, 29-30, 37, 39, 50, 67, 80-84, 91, 95, 99, 104, 111-120, 133, 136, 138-141, 161, 166, 173; agreement, 39, 81; decolonization crisis, 82; London conference, 83, royal tour, 82, 84, 91, 95. *See also* Buganda.
Uganda People's Congress (UPC), 83
Uganda Tourism Board (UTB), 141
Uhuru, 146, 173. *See also* Mau Mau.
Ukraine, 31, 137, 151-152, 158
Unilateral Declaration of Independence (UDI), 25, 80, 173
Union of Soviet Socialist Republic (USSR), 73, 75, 127-128
United Nations (UN), 52, 57, 60, 64, 87-88, 109, 114; Assembly, 87
van Zyl, G-G. Brand, 51
Vancouver Declaration on World Trade, 134
Verwoerd, Hendrik, 127
Victorian ideals, 22
Von Lettow-Vorbeck, 42
Wade, Donald, 125

Wales, 117
Wall, MP. Major Patrick, 124
Washington, D.C., 75, 77, 86, 89-90, 156
Whitehall, 16, 18, 20, 25, 30, 33, 46, 50, 53, 59, 60, 67, 72, 79, 82, 95, 101, 119, 129, 147, 150, 164-167, 169-171, 173-174; appeasement of white minorities, 60, 67, 127; colloquialism, 165; commonwealth scheme, 16, 18, 21, 46, 147, 169, 171; decolonization plans, 53, 59, 79, 82, 101, 171; postcolonial republican constrictions, 150; royal mission, 16, 18, 20, 25, 30, 33, 46, 50, 72, 95. *See also* British Establishment.
Willem-Alexander, king, 171
William, prince, 141-142
Wilson, Harold, 79, 116-117, 122, 129, 131, 173
Wolde-Giorgis, Girma, 142
World Bank, 160-161
World Trade Organization (WTO), 138
Yamacouba of Sherbro, 104
Yew, Lee Kuan, 127
Yohannes IV, 108
Yoko, Soma (aka Mammy), 104
Yoruba, 49
Zambia, 46, 69-70, 127-128, 132-133, 162. *See also* Northern Rhodesia.
Zawditu, empress, 108
Zimbabwe, 10, 46-48, 69, 101, 127, 132, 134, 153-155, 160-162, 166. *See also* South Rhodesia.
Zimbabwean African National Union (ZANU), 154
Zulu, 28